谨以此书献给黄达和他钟爱的金融学科！

This book is dedicated to Huang Da and the financial discipline.

感谢中国人民大学财政金融学院对本书的出版给予的大力支持！
Thanks to the School of Finance of Renmin University of China for the great support for the publication of the book.

黄达

黄达传略

Brief Biography of Huang Da

宋科 编著

中国人民大学出版社
· 北京 ·

即将小学毕业并将面对『坎坷少年』的岁月

1925—1950年

Rough Life in Youth
in 1925—1950

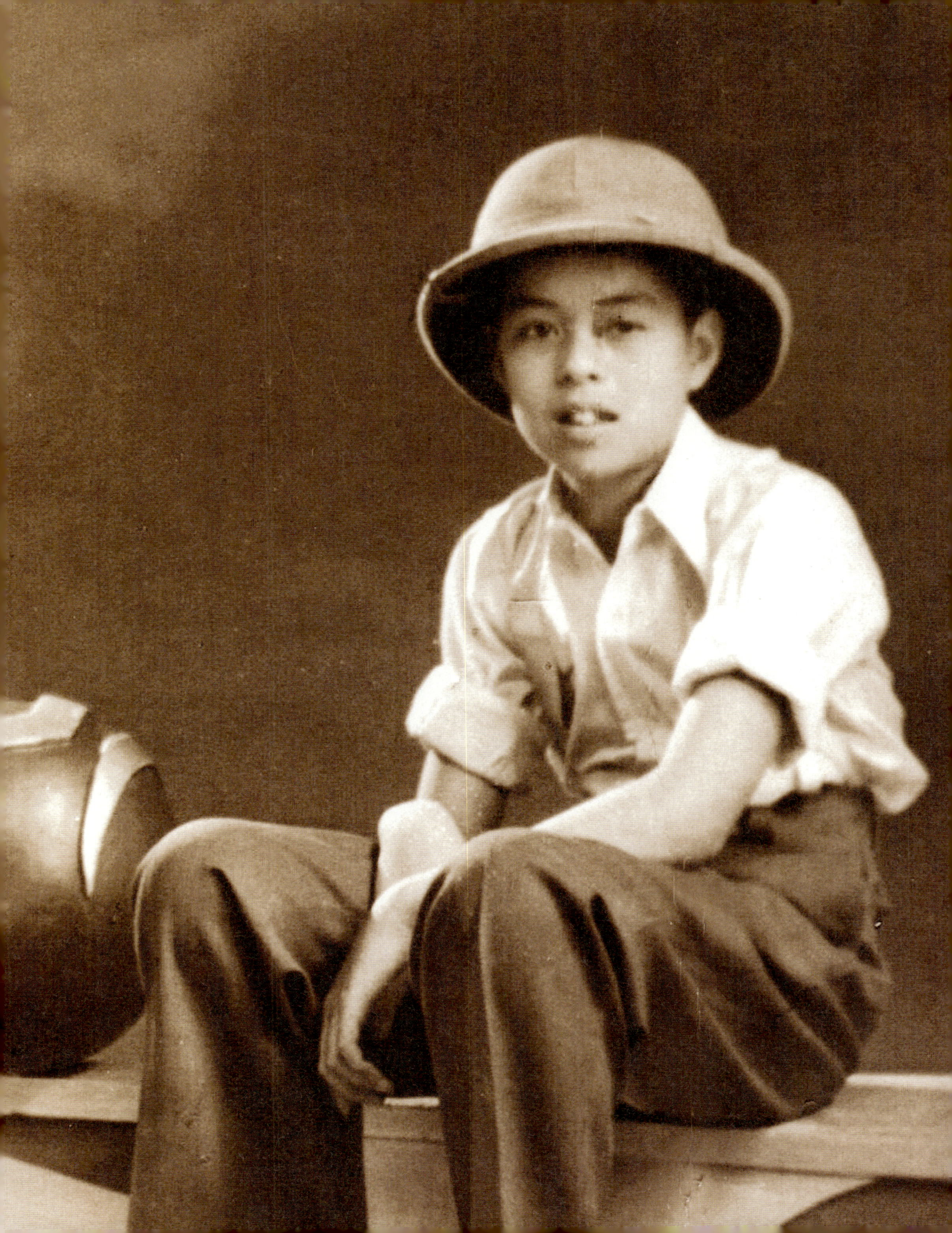

『初识金融』

听从组织分配但还不知即将

20 世纪 50 年代

Getting Acquainted with Finance
in the 1950s

在教研天地中逐渐积累『思想「萌芽」』

20 世纪 50 年代末——改革开放前后

"Budding" Thoughts
in the End of 1950s — around the Launch
of Reform and Opening Up

攀登巅峰

改革开放前后——20世纪80年代末

Reaching the Academic Peak
in around the Launch of Reform and Opening
Up — the End of 1980s

漫展风华

20世纪90年代

The Global Vision in View
in the 1990s

老骥伏枥

新世纪以来

Aiming for the Far-off Future
in the 21st Century

序
Preface

“一提起 1950 年秋季学期开始，我走上讲台，讲授货币银行学，人们都赞许我相伴这门课程走了很长很长的路程。到 2010 年，‘很长’有了一个极具标志性的度量单位：一个甲子。于是自己也觉得这的确是很长很长的了。好像我的一生就是作为一名导游，了解、欣赏、介绍并全身心地参与装点中国货币银行学景观的旅程。”黄达在《与货币银行学结缘六十年》（中国金融出版社，2010）一书中如是写道。

“金融天地，浩淼幽深；揽胜揭秘，乐何如之！”用一甲子的生命去演绎和享受“钟于斯，老于斯”的执着，以至我们根本无法彻底分辨黄达与金融。

教授、博士生导师、系主任、校长、金融学会会长、金融学家、经济学家、教育家等一串串响亮的名头之下，黄达归根结底认为自己是个不时自我欣慰，能够捕捉到幸福感的教书先生而已。

从金融学教材到课程体系，再到金融学科体系，黄达一路引领金融学科的建设与发展。直到耄耋之年，黄达依然在思索和参悟：何为金融？如何建设金融学科？如何培养金融学人才？如何归纳古往今来金融演变的脉络并把握其变幻多端的发展前景？

从货币流通、通货膨胀、财政信贷综合平衡，到宏观调控和货币供给、金融体制改革、资本市场，再到国际货币体系和人民币国际化，一个个金融名词的背后，是无数次伏案攻读、仔细推敲而不得其门的困惑，是无数次豁然开朗、“佳句偶得”后的快然自足，然后随之而来的又大多是自己难以为力的思绪：“这点点理论观点在指导实践和决策中能够起点作用吗？”他常会以一种阿 Q 式的自我解嘲来自我宽慰：“教书的能有多大能量，但只要是真理，总会有学生来实施、来发扬光大的……”

"At the mention of my first lecture on money and banking in the fall semester in 1950, I have always been praised for my long teaching life, as long as 60 years by 2010. That's indeed a long time for me. It seems that throughout my life, I have acted as a tour guide to learn, appreciate, introduce and fully engage in the journey of money and banking research in China. " This is what Huang Da wrote in his book *My Fate with Money and Banking for 60 Years* (published by China Financial Publishing House in 2010).

"The world of finance is vast and deep enough to explore its mysteries for fun." Spending all his life on finance, Huang Da is so obsessed with finance that it is hard for us to distinguish him from finance.

With a great number of titles including the professor, doctoral supervisor, dean, university president, chairman of Chinese Society for Finance and Banking, finance expert, economist and educator, Huang Da believes in the final conclusion that he is merely a teacher who can sometimes feel delighted about himself and derive happiness from being a teacher.

From finance textbooks to curriculum system and the financial theoretical system, he has led the construction and development of finance until now. Today, as an octogenarian, Huang Da still keeps asking about and comprehending: What is finance? How to construct the financial discipline? How to cultivate experts on finance? How to summarize the evolution of finance throughout the ages, and how to grasp its changing outlook?

Currency circulation, inflation, overall balance of financial credit, macro-control, money supply, financial system reform, capital market, international monetary system and RMB internationalization—all these financial terms are attributable to countless research and careful thinking about the unresolved confusion before countless enlightenments and satisfaction for getting results. Afterwards, he would

从中国人民大学财政信用借贷系、财政贸易系，到财政系、财政金融系，再到今天的财政金融学院，黄达作为这个“大家庭”的一分子，始终与大家一起探讨，一起钻研，一起为中国金融学科的发展鼓与呼。

无论何时何地，即使是在金融已经成为显学中的显学，各种荣誉与光环接踵而至的今天，黄达始终保持着略显书生气的真性情。

这就是黄达，一个视金融学术如生命的人！

《黄达传略》无意于“全景式”地展现先生的人生传奇——这个几近无法完成的任务。若能以平铺直叙、图文相互交映的方式，将先生在生活、学习、工作的若干画面娓娓道来，让读者在浏览一张张历史照片、一行行朴素文字的同时，捕获到原本“遥不可及”的先生最为真实的生活瞬间，如此足矣！

在中国金融学界，黄达的事迹或许会对我们有所启迪……

be immersed in the hard nuts to crack: "Will these theoretical perspectives play a role in guiding practice and decision-making? " He often found excuses to console himself like Ah Q: "How can a teacher play a big role? Anyway, there must be students who will implement and popularize them as long as they are the truths... "

No matter whether he worked in the Department of Public Finance and Credit Loan, the Department of Public Finance and Trade, the Department of Public Finance, the Department of Finance and Monetary Economics, or currently the School of Finance, as a member of the "big family", Huang Da has always discussed, argued with others as well as cheered for the development of China's finance.

No matter where and when, even though nowadays, finance has become a most notable subject with numerous honorable reputations, Huang Da is still true to himself, always maintaining his style of a scholar.

This is Huang Da, a scholar who regards his academic research on finance as his life!

Brief Biography of Huang Da doesn't mean to display his legendary life in a panoramic way, which is almost an impossible task. Illustrated narration on his life, study and work is enough for readers to get his life moments that are "far-fetched" but real by way of enjoying the historic pictures and simple words!

In the academic field of finance in China, Huang Da's story may give us some inspiration...

目录
Content

第一章
Chapter One

坎坷少年
1925—1950年

Rough Life in Youth
in 1925—1950

生于“20后”
Born in the 1920s

1925年2月22日，黄达出生在天津一个知识分子家庭。他排行老三，有两个姐姐。那时他的祖母尚健在，管理家务。母亲是家庭妇女，家庭生计全靠常年在外地做工程师的父亲的薪水维持，日子过得虽不算宽裕却也衣食无虞。

长辈的偏爱，姐姐的呵护，使得童年的黄达沉浸在家庭的温馨当中。

然而，初中二年级时的一场变故改变了黄达的生活轨迹。这一年，父亲的不幸病逝中断了黄达温馨而短暂的儿时记忆。失去顶梁柱的黄家日渐贫寒。而且，当时天津正处于日本侵略军的占领时期，城市满目疮痍，百姓苦不堪言。国与家的双重不幸让黄达过早地感悟到生活的艰难与坎坷。

迫于生计，黄达不得不辗转于富人区与贫民区之间，跟富贵人家打交道，与穷苦人民攀谈往来，与上中下阶层的各式人等频繁接触。残酷的生活情状、“病态”社会的众生相深深地镌刻在这位十几岁少年的脑海当中。

强烈的生活与地位的反差，也让黄达亲身感知了人情冷暖与世态炎凉，但是由此掌握的第一手社会资料却让他终身受益。此间，他似懂非懂地了解了一些金融概念，朦胧地意识到何为银行、股票、黄金、经纪人、当铺以及印子钱等等。这些零散的知识拼凑出少年黄达脑海中模糊的“金融”图景，成为他从事科学研究工作后理论联系实际的有用“素材”。

“温馨的童年，贫苦的少年，中学毕业后坎坷的谋生。”黄达曾在日后的《自述》中如是描述此时的生活。

Huang Da was born in a family of intellectuals in Tianjin on February 22, 1925. He was the third child with two elder sisters. At that time, it was his grandmother who kept house. His mother was a housewife. All the family expenses relied on his father's salary for perennial work outside as an engineer. Though not rich, he had no need to worry about his food or clothes.

With the care of the elders and his sisters, Huang Da enjoyed the warm family life in his childhood.

However, when he was in grade two in middle school, an accident changed Huang Da's life. Huang's father passed away, which ended his short but warm memory in childhood. Without the bread earner of the family, his family was reduced to poverty. Then Tianjin was occupied by the Japanese invaders, resulting in a devastated city and miserable people. Misery of both the country and his family made Huang Da experience a tough life prematurely.

To make a living, Huang Da had to have frequent contact with all walks of life, including both the rich and the poor. The harsh living conditions and "morbid "social look of the lower and medium class were deeply impressed in this teenager's mind.

Strong contrast in life and status made Huang Da understand the fickleness of human nature. But he benefited a lot from the first-hand social experience. In this period, he had contact with some financial concepts, and got a rough understanding of the concepts of the bank, stock, gold, broker, pawnshop and usury. These knowledge fragments were pieced together into a vague picture of "finance " in the teenager's mind, which became his useful "materials " to integrate theory with practice after he took up the scientific research work.

"I lived a happy childhood, but became poor as a teenager, and made a tough living after my graduation from middle school. " This is what Huang Da said in *Autobiography* about his life then.

年少志高

Ambitious Aspiration

“艰难困苦，玉汝于成”。古之成大器者，离不开艰难困苦的磨炼。

自小以来，家庭、熟悉的亲戚朋友，在黄达的心中深深地种下这样的观念：只有知识才是一辈子谁也夺不走的真依靠。同时，在大家的帮助与督促下，他也养成了勤于学习的好习惯。

日后来看，正是这一时期刻苦努力的学习，为他在若干年后误打误撞闯进金融学的宏伟殿堂打下了坚实的基础。确切地说，这是从孩童到步入社会的漫长时光。但其间最为关键的是他的高中时代。“一个人的思想品格基础是在青少年时期奠定的，其文化底子也是在中学时期打下的。比如，初中时数学学不好，高中时可能还能弥补，但若高中时再学不好，到大学就很难学了。”对黄达而言，能够享受到较好的高中教育，算是不幸中的万幸了。

在天津市立第一中学，黄达度过了三年高中生活。这所学校师资阵容强、教学质量高、校风校纪严，是当时天津最为著名的男生学校，也是天津第一所官办中学，有着可以追溯至光绪年间的悠久历史。

在这里，黄达受教于杨学涵、裴学海以及王荫浓等名师，使他获益终身。杨学涵是数学老师，学问扎实，风骨清介，治学严谨，令学生肃然起敬。在他的严格教育下，黄达学到了最基础的高中数学，培养了从数量方面思考问题的基本素养。裴学海和王荫浓都是语文老师，对黄达的影响同样很大。裴学海是著名的语言文学家，长于古汉语虚词研究及音韵、训诂等。他拆音析句，辨字正源，把黄达带入了汉语语言学的圣殿。王荫浓是毕业于北大的高材生，文学造诣深厚。在他的引领下，黄达游历于中国古往今来的文学园地，徜徉在博大精深的中国文化之间，王荫浓为黄达理解这个伟大的民族打开了一扇窗户。

在老师们的教导下，黄达打下了历史、文学与思辨的功底，形成了基本的人文素养。日后，他的著述逻辑严谨、文采飞扬、妙语连珠，读来如水银泻地、一气呵成，文字之间透露着自有韵味儿的“黄氏风格”，大都源自于此。

除了在课堂内努力汲取营养之外，这所中学的一个图书馆成为他的另一个“老师”。

"Enduring hardship helps one to succeed." Any success since the ancient times cannot do without hardship.

His family and close relatives and friends in his childhood left an impression on Huang Da that only knowledge could be relied on in a real sense and could never be taken away by anybody. Meanwhile, under their help and supervise, he formed a good habit of diligently study.

His hard study during this period laid a solid foundation for him to enter the magnificent hall of finance.To be specific, it was a long time from a childhood to entering the society. In the meantime, his high school days were the most critical.

"A man's characters are shaped in his teenage years, and his knowledge foundation is laid in middle school. For example, poor math in middle school can probably be made up for in high school. But if it fails again in high school, it is hard to catch it up in university. " As for Huang Da, he enjoyed good high school education, which could be seen as a silver lining for him.

Huang Da spent three years in No.1 Middle School of Tianjin for high school education. With qualified teachers, high teaching standards and strict disciplines, the school was regarded as the most famous boys' school at that time, as well as the first government-run school in Tianjin. This time-honored school could date back to the reign of Emperor Guangxu in the Qing Dynasty.

In this school, Huang Da learnt from many famous teachers such as Yang Xuehan, Pei Xuehai and Wang Yinnong, which benefited him for all his life.Yang Xuehan, a math teacher, was respectable for his solid knowledge, noble qualities and rigorous scholarly research. Owing to his strict teaching, Huang Da learnt the most fundamental math in high school and developed the basic way of thinking in terms of quantity. Pei Xuehai and Wang Yinnong, both Chinese teachers, also had great influence on Huang Da. Mr. Pei was a famous linguistic expert on the function words in ancient Chinese, phonology and gloss. His explanation on rhyme and words as well as distinguishing words and their origins led Huang Da into the sacred hall of the Chinese language. Mr. Wang, a graduate from Peking University, had profound knowledge on literature. With his teaching, Huang Da wandered in the world of literature throughout the ages, and marveled at the extensive and profound Chinese culture. This helped him open a window to understanding the soul of the Chinese nation.

With their education, Huang Da laid a foundation in the fields of history, literature and intellectual quests, and cultivated the basic humanities. This was the origin of his later "Huang-style " logic and literacy expression sparkling with witticism and flowing smoothly like quicksilver

当然与现在动辄上万平方米的现代化图书馆相比，这个图书馆小得有点可怜，但就是这样的小天地却将黄达带进知识的海洋，让他享受着无穷无尽的乐趣。

由于家离学校比较远，黄达每天中午都待在学校，先用不到半小时的时间把早上带的午饭迅速吃完，剩下的一个半小时便去泡图书馆。那时，他阅读的主要是中外文学作品，也杂七杂八地看一些科技知识性读物。

那时的黄达读书不求甚解，主要是浏览，看故事。这样的方法不仅使他书读得多，涉猎知识面宽阔，而且对于拓展他的思维和视野大有裨益。特别是在最能吸吮知识的年龄段得到这样连续两三年集中高强度的阅读机会。

事实上，年纪不大的黄达在阅读方面却是“老资历”。上小学时，他就大量阅读家中藏书，如《红楼梦》《水浒传》《二度梅》《孟丽君》等中国古典文学。本家亲戚中的几个大学生知道黄达的爱好后，也向他推荐一些中国 20 世纪 30 年代的新文学作品和西方文艺复兴后的文学名著。

更难能可贵的是，在学校图书馆之外，他还读到了艾思奇的《大众哲学》、苏联波格达诺夫的《经济学大纲》《社会学大纲》的中译本等马克思主义书籍。虽然并不甚了了，却能唤起他对于真理的无尽向往。

日本投降不久，他又读到毛泽东主席的《新民主主义论》《中国革命和中国共产党》等革命书籍。由于身处日本占领区，从“进步”学生那里借到这些“禁书”是要冒很大风险的。

大量的课外阅读，不仅对黄达在不久后从事社会科学研究大有裨益，而且受“进步”书籍的熏陶，黄达还看到了指引自己思想进步的理想之光。他在书里依稀看到了一个有别于旧社会的美好世界，这会成为自己一生为之不懈奋斗和追求的理想吗？黄达不止一次地思索。

不久后，他便找到了正确答案。

1946 年底，21 岁的黄达加入中国共产党。

spilling over the ground.

Besides learning in class, he also benefited a lot from a library in the high school. It was much smaller than today's modern libraries covering over 10,000 square meters. However, it brought Huang Da into the sea of knowledge to enjoy endless joy.

As Huang Da lived afar from school, he stayed at school every noon. After having lunch brought by him in the morning within half an hour, he spent the rest one and a half hours in the library. At that time, he read the Chinese and foreign literary works as well as some readings on science.

At that time, Huang Da was content with superficial understanding by dipping into the stories. In this way, he read a lot with a wide range of knowledge, which was greatly beneficial for him to broaden his thinking and perspective.It was unforgettable for Huang Da to have a plenty to read for about three consecutive years during the period when he was the most capable of absorbing knowledge.

As a matter of fact, Huang Da, though a young lad, was sophisticated in reading. When he was in primary school, he read a lot of his home collections, such as the Chinese classical literatures including *Dream of the Red Chamber, Heroes of the Marshes, Marriage for Peace* and *Meng Lijun*. Some relatives of his who were university students knew his hobby and recommended to him new literacy works of China in the 1930s and those after the Renaissance in the West.

Besides reading in the school library, he also read the books on Marxism, such as *Public Philosophy* by Ai Siqi, *Economics* by Bogdanov in the Soviet Union, and Chinese version of *Outline of Sociology*. Although he didn't quite understand them, the books aroused his endless yearning for truth.

Soon after the surrender of Japan, he read *On New Democracy* and *the Chinese Revolution and the Communist Party of China* by Chairman Mao Zedong. These books used to be banned in the areas occupied by Japan, so borrowing them from "progressive " students was risky.

Extensive reading laid a solid foundation for his future engagement in social science research. Especially those "progressive " books enlightened him to march ahead. In these books, he saw a beautiful world different from the old society. Would it be his ideal goal to pursue? Huang Da asked himself about it many times.

Yes! Before long, he got the right answer.

At the end of 1946, Huang Da joined the CPC at 21 years old.

“邂逅”金融
"Encountering" Finance

高中的时光转瞬即逝，升学摆在黄达的面前。这是他人生中面临的第一次最为重要同时又最为“简单”的选择，因为他一直以来追寻着的梦想就是——子承父业，当一名工程师！

在升学的志愿中首选工科，将来当工程师，退而求其次的是文学、历史，没有教师，没有经济学，更甭提金融。在他当时的脑海里，金融无疑属于外星球。

所谓造化弄人。一切都会变，而且一切变得又都很快。特别是在那样一个战火纷飞、国无宁日的年代。在经历两个“转角”之后，他不久将遇见相伴一生的“缘分”——不是工程，而是金融。

原来，金融离自己并不远。

报考失败是他经历的第一个“转角”。高中毕业报考之际，一场严重的伤寒让踌躇满志的黄达告别了梦想中的工程师。病愈后，他在政府当小职员、照相馆搭伙计、亲戚家打“秋风”。漂泊离自己越来越近，而梦想离自己却越来越远。直到1946年春，黄达经过国民党统治区的北平，徒步穿越太行山，进入中国共产党的解放区张家口，并考入华北联合大学。

这一年，黄达称之为“参加革命元年”。

不久，内战全面爆发，华北联合大学从张家口撤出，辗转于晋西北和冀中平原。在解放战争意想不到地即将迎来胜利大转折的1948年秋，华北联合大学与北方大学合并为华北大学。1950年，新中国成立之初，又以华北大学为班底组建中国人民大学。

在华北联大，黄达开始是法政学院财经系的学生，在此期间他参加了土地改革。后转为政治学院的研究生，研究“边政建设”，即抗日根据地（那时叫“边区”）的政权建设。不久后的1947年3月，他又被调到校部工作，并于当年年底第二次参加土地改革。两次土地改革，使一个从城市走出来的青年真正接触了农民、了解了农村。

1950年秋季学期，黄达被指定在一年制的专修科讲授“货币银行学”，从此以后，他的工作再没有变过。“在那个波澜壮阔、翻天覆地的年代里，个人的荣辱得失和

His years in high school passed in the blink of an eye. He was ready to enter the university. This was his first time to make the most important but "simplest " choice, as the dream that he had kept pursuing was to inherit his father's occupation as an engineer!

He placed engineering on top of his major application list, followed by literature and history. Teaching and economics were not included, not to mention finance. In his dream world, finance undoubtedly belonged to an alien planet.

Oddly enough, everything changed as quickly as possible, especially in the era of war. After passing two "turning points", he soon would encounter his lifelong "fate " — finance, instead of engineering.

Finance turned out to be close to him.

Failure in admittance to university was the first "turning point " for him. When he graduated from the high school, serious typhoid forced this ambitious young man to say farewell to his dream as an engineer. After his recovery, he worked in the governmental department, photo studio and his relative's business. His wandering life made him far away from his dream. In the spring of 1946, Huang Da walked through Beiping which was governed by the Kuomintang (KMT) and the Taihang Mountain to reach Zhangjiakou, a liberated area of the Communist Party of China (CPC), and entered the North China Union University.

This year meant the first year of his revolution in Huang Da's opinion.

Before long, the civil war broke out completely. The North China Union University moved from Zhangjiakou to Northwest Shanxi and Central Hebei Plain. In the fall of 1948, when the War of Liberation was about to witness the turning point of unexpected victory, the North China Union University and the North University were merged into the North China University. In 1950, not long after the founding of the People's Republic of China, the Renmin University of China was set up on the foundation of the North China University.

In the North China Union University, Huang Da studied in the department of finance in the School of Law and Politics at first, when he participated in the land reform. Later, he turned to be a postgraduate in the Institute of Politics to make research on the "construction of boundary administration ", which referred to the administration construction in the anti-Japanese area (or "border area "). In March 1947, he was transferred to the president office. At the year end, he participated in the land reform for the second time. Thanks to the two land

事业理想仿佛都非常渺小。”被动地接受“货币银行学”的教学任务成为他此时走过的第二个“转角”，也成为他找到自己一生不离不弃事业的开始。尽管这项事业离当初的梦想确实有点遥远。

然而，人生的乐趣就在于“你永远想不到明天的你会是什么样子”。此时黄达的体会应该最为深刻。

所谓“转角遇到爱”。黄达没有想到，这次被动的“转角”之后，竟然“邂逅”了自己的“真爱”——金融！这着实是一次美丽的“邂逅”！因为这份“邂逅”而来的“真爱”竟然有着很长很长的“保鲜期”：一辈子！

“虽然想着‘革命成功之后’还是学工，但当中国人民大学成立之际，分配我从事经济理论教学，也就欣然接受了这一关乎终身职业的人生安排。”以后的岁月，黄达与金融相伴一生。

黄达如是说，亦如是做。

是年，黄达年仅 25 岁。

reforms, this urban youth had real contact with farmers and rural areas.

In the fall semester in 1950, he was assigned the job to teach the Economics of Money and Banking to one-year junior college students, and never changed his job thereafter. "In the era of dramatic changes, personal gains and losses, career and pursuit seemed dwarfed. " Forced to teach the Economics of Money and Banking was the second "turning point " of Huang Da. He found his career that he never gave up for all his life, although it was far away from his original dream.

However, the pleasure of life lied in the fact that "you never know what you will be tomorrow". Huang Da had the most profound experience about that.

It had never anticipated that at this "turning point", he encountered his "true love"—"finance"! This was indeed a beautiful "encounter "! The "true love" that he "encountered" lasted as long as his lifetime!

"Although expecting to engage in engineering after the success of revolution, I was glad to accept the assignment that lasted for my lifetime to teach economic theory on the occasion of the founding of the Renmin University of China. "Thus, Huang Da spent the rest of his life on finance.

Huang Da did as what he said.

That year, Huang Da was only 25 years old.

1

图 1 为不满一周岁时的黄达，也是他目前留存下来最早的一张个人照。

This is Huang Da at less than one year old, and his first photo remained as well.

2

图 2 为 1917 年左右，黄达的母亲高淑贞年仅 21 岁时的个人照。

高淑贞是家庭妇女，不识字，性情温顺，从不打骂孩子；与婆婆、妯娌和谐相处。在 20 世纪 40 年代，曾与黄达和他的二姐度过极其贫困的岁月。黄达的父亲黄树人，天津北洋工学院毕业，工程师。在亲友里是有名的正派人士，不吸烟、不喝酒、不嫖赌。在黄达上小学之前，他已经教黄达学会了初小二年级的语文和算术，以及三项基本功：写字的笔顺，拼音符号和查字典。遗憾的是，黄达没有留存下父亲的照片。

This is a photo of Huang Da's mother at the age of 21 in around 1917.

Gao Shuzhen, Huang Da's mother, was a housewife who was illiterate. She was mild, never spanked or scolded her children, and got along very well with her mother-in-law and sisters-in-law. In the 1940s, she spent the extremely hard years together with Huang Da and his second elder sister. Huang Shuren, Huang Da's father, graduated from Tianjin Northern Warlords Institute of Technology as an engineer. In the eyes of his relatives, Huang Shuren was a man of integrity who did not smoke or drink or whore or gamble. Before Huang Da went to primary school, he had taught Huang Da Chinese and Math for students of grade two of primary school. Besides, he taught Huang Da three basic skills: the order of strokes of Chinese characters, Pinyin and how to look up a word in the dictionary. It is a pity that Huang Da did not have any of his father's photos.

图 3 为未满一周岁的黄达（右一）与祖母（右二）、大姐（左二）和二姐（左一）在一起。

在黄达刚出生时，他的祖母尚健在，负责管理家务。她不识字，但沉稳、精明、节俭、严谨，熟知治家和亲朋交往的礼数，一直井井有条地主持家务。在黄达的记忆里，祖母对他特别钟爱：那时家里吃饭，平时每顿饭只有一个菜，当吃白菜汤氽丸子的时候，旁人的"定额"都是一个丸子，黄达是两个。在黄达上初中二年级时，祖母不幸辞世。

Huang Da(first from the right), who was less than one year old, was with his grandmother (second from the right), eldest sister (second from the left) and second elder sister (first from the left).

When Huang Da was born, his grandmother was still alive and did housework. She was illiterate, too, but she was calm, smart, frugal, rigorous, and familiar with homemaking and etiquette with friends and relatives. She did housekeeping in an orderly way. In Huang Da's memory, his grandmother was particularly good to him: Normally, the family had one dish for each meal. When it was cabbage with quick-boiled meat balls, the others each had one ball, but Huang Da had two. Grandma passed away when Huang Da was in grade two in middle school.

3

| 右页图 |→

图 4 为四五岁间的黄达（左一），与大姐（左二）黄芸和二姐（右一）黄华在一起。

大姐黄芸，上过天津南开中学，1939 年进入共产党的晋察冀边区抗日民主根据地。新中国成立后一直在国家教育部幼教部门工作。二姐黄华，上过初中，抗日战争期间已是中共地下党员。日伪时期开始在天津公安局当小职员，新中国成立后一直在天津市公安局工作。两个姐姐现均已谢世。

Huang Da (first from the left) at the age of four or five, was with his eldest sister Huang Yun (second from the left) and second elder sister Huang Hua (first from the right).

Huang Yun is the eldest sister of Huang Da. She was once a student of Tianjin Nankai High School, and went to the anti-Japanese democratic base area in the Shanxi-Chahar-Hebei border area, which was established by the Communist Party of China, in 1939. After the founding of new China, she had been working in the childhood education department under the Chinese Ministry of Education. Huang Hua, his second elder sister, received middle school education and had become an underground member of the Communist Party of China during the Anti-Japanese War. When the Japanese invaders supported puppets to control China, she worked in Tianjin Public Security Bureau as a clerk and had been working in it after the founding of new China. Both his sisters have passed away.

4

5

图 5 为 11 岁左右时的黄达。

This is Huang Da at the age of around 11.

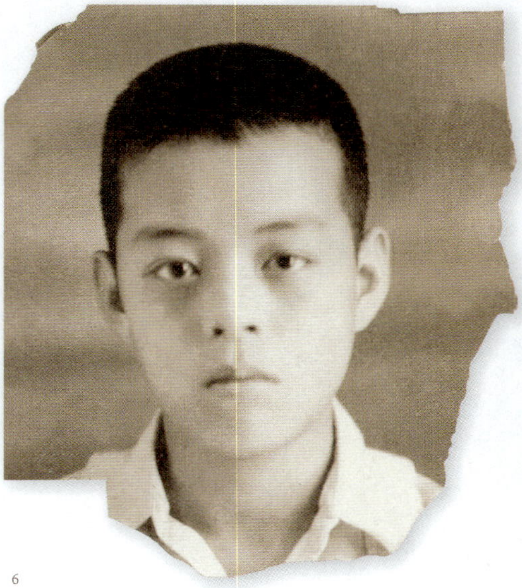

6

图 6 为小学毕业时的黄达。

This is a photo of Huang Da when he graduated from primary school.

7

图 7 为 1943 年中学毕业前夕，黄达（后排右六）在原“天津市立第一中学”校址的教学楼转角处与同期毕业班同学合影。

“天津市立第一中学”，天津人习惯称为“铃铛阁中学”，是天津最为有名的男生学校，由于学生入校一律剃光头，故又被称为“和尚学校”。从清光绪二十七年正月十九日（1901 年 3 月 9 日）正式创立（初名“官立中学堂”）算起，这所学校已经有百余年的历史。百年间，十易其名，新中国成立后，定为现名“天津市第三中学”。校歌歌词有“劫灰余地尚荆榛，是我校之生辰”之句。任仲夷、于方舟、魏寿昆等许多享誉中外的著名专家学者和知名人士曾就读于此。

1991 年 2 月 22 日，黄达曾专门为母校九十周年题词：“回忆母校，崇尚质朴；品学兼重，勤径苦舟；根深基固，毕生受益。”以表达他对于这所校风质朴、师资一流的母校的感激之情。

This is a group photo of Huang Da (sixth from the right in the back row) with his schoolmates of the same graduating class at the nook of the teaching building at the original site of "No. 1 Middle School of Tianjin" and on the eve of graduation from middle school in 1943.

"No. 1 Middle School of Tianjin," or "Tianjin Lingdangge Middle School," to quote from Tianjin locals was the most famous boys' middle school in Tianjin. Because new students were asked to shave their hairs, the school was also known as "school of monks." Since its formal establishment (under the name of "Government-aided Middle School") on March 9, 1901, the school has had a history of over 100 years. Over the years, it changed its names ten times. After the founding of new China, it was renamed "Tianjin No. 3 High School" and has been using it since. In the school song, there is the line of "the school was born in the wilderness after disasters." Ren Zhongyi, Yu Fangzhou, Wei Shoukun and many experts, scholars and well-known figures who are famous both at home and abroad were its students.

On February 22, 1991, Huang Da inscribed to the school for its ninetieth anniversary, in which he wrote, "My alma mater worships modesty, gives priority to both morals and scholarly attainments. There is no loyal road to learning. With solid deposits, I benefit from my education here for the whole life." With the inscription, he expressed his gratitude for his alma mater that features an excellent tone and first-class faculty.

8

图8为1943年中学毕业前夕的黄达。

This is Huang Da on the eve of graduation from middle school in 1943 .

9

图 9 为 20 岁左右的黄达。照片本为黑白照，后由黄达自己着色。

This is a photo of Huang Da at about 20 which was black and white and colored by Huang Da later.

右页图 ⟼

图 10 为 1944—1945 年间，黄达与朋友、同学在大众照相馆的合影。右一康俊山，在天津居民区经营一家个体小照相馆——大众照相馆。1943 年后，黄达这期高中毕业生与他建立了友情。解放战争期间，他由黄达的同学刘铁淳介绍加入中国共产党。天津解放前夕地下党曾送出国民党军的城防图，他是其间的成员之一。右三顾通，右四郑树仁，黄达高中三年的亲近同学，新中国成立后均为无党派人士。右五解崇熙，也是黄达高中时期的亲近同学，家境比较优裕。他聪明外露，在高中时对国民党、共产党以及时局都能侃侃而谈，但同学们好像并不认为他有什么政治背景。高中毕业后不久，英年早逝。

This is a group photo of Huang Da and his friends and classmates in Dazhong Studio during 1944 and 1945. The first one from the right is Kang Junshan who ran a small private studio—Dazhong Studio—in the residential area in Tianjin. After 1943, he developed friendship with Huang Da and the other graduates of his class. During China's war of liberation, he was introduced by Liu Tiechun, one of Huang Da's classmates, to become a member of the Communist Party of China, and was one of the underground CPC members to deliver the city's garrison chart of Kuomintang on the eve of liberating Tianjin. The third one from the right is Gu Tong and the fourth one from the right was Zheng Shuren, both of whom were close to Huang Da in high school. After the founding of new China, they become personages without party affiliation. The fifth one from the right was Xie Chongxi from a rich family. He was also one of the closest classmates to Huang Da in high school. He seemed to be very smart, and had unique opinions on Kuomintang, the Communist Party of China, as well as the current political situation, but his classmates seemed to think that he did not have any political background. Shortly after he graduated from high school, Xie Chongxi died young.

右页图 ⟼

图 11~14 为中国人民大学历史沿革图。

中国人民大学（Renmin University of China）直属于教育部，由教育部与北京市共建，是一所以人文社会科学为主的综合性研究型全国重点大学。它的前身是 1937 年诞生于抗日战争烽火中的陕北公学，以及后来的华北联合大学和华北大学。1950 年 10 月 3 日，以华北大学为基础合并组建的中国人民大学隆重举行开学典礼，成为新中国创办的第一所新型正规大学。

1946 年，黄达经过国民党统治区的北平，徒步穿越太行山，进入中国共产党解放区张家口，并考入华北联合大学（中国人民大学的前身）。在这里，黄达开启了一生的事业，虽然学校名称和办学地点几经变换，他却从未离开。

These photos show the historical development of Renmin University of China.

The Renmin University of China, directly under the Chinese Ministry of Education, and built by the Chinese Ministry of Education and Beijing government together, is a comprehensive, research-based national key university led by humanities and social science disciplines. Its predecessors were Shanbei Public School born during the Anti-Japanese War, and then North China Union University and North China University. On October 3, 1950, the Renmin University of China, which was established on the basis of North China University, held an opening ceremony, and became the first new-type formal university created by new China.

In 1946, Huang Da passed Beijing, which was under the control of Kuomintang then, walked through Taihang Mountains, arrived at Zhangjiakou, an area having been liberated by the Communist Party of China, and passed the entrance exam to the then North China Associated University (predecessor of Renmin University of China). There, he started his lifelong career, and has stayed despite the changes of school names or sites.

15

图 15 为 1949 年，时任华北大学正定分校第十一区队助理的黄达在正定教堂的宿舍兼工作室内办公。

Huang Da was working in his dorm, which was also his studio, in Zhengding Church in 1949. Huang Da was the assistant of the 11th section of North China University in Zhengding.

13

14

图 13 为 1948 年，成立之初的华北大学。

1948 年春，中共中央决定将华北联合大学和北方大学合并，成立华北大学，以便集中力量扩大办学规模，为迎接全国解放培养大批建设干部。北方大学 1945 年 11 月成立于晋冀鲁豫边区，是中共晋冀鲁豫中央局和边区人民政府创办的一所规模较大、学科专业比较齐全的高等学府。

This is the photo of North China University in its first year in 1948.

In the spring of 1948, the Central Committee of the Communist Party of China decided to merge North China Union University and North University into North China University so as to concentrate on expanding the school and train batches of cadres for the incoming national liberation. North University, established in the Shanxi-Hebei-Shandong-Henan border area in November 1945, was a big university with a complete set of subjects and majors and established by the Bureau of the Central Committee of the Communist Party of China in the Shanxi-Hebei-Shandong-Henan Border Area and local people's government.

图 14 为 1950 年 10 月 3 日，刘少奇在中国人民大学开学典礼上讲话。

新中国成立之初，为了培养具有马克思列宁主义素养和专业知识的新中国建设人才，中共中央决定以华北大学为基础，合并中国政法大学，调来华北人民革命大学部分干部组建中国人民大学。1949 年 12 月 16 日，中央人民政府政务院第十一次政务会议根据中共中央政治局的建议，通过《关于成立中国人民大学的决定》。

This photo records Liu Shaoqi at the opening ceremony of the Renmin University of China on October 3, 1950.

When new China was first founded, the Central Committee of the Communist Party of China, in order to train talented people with the deposits of Marxist-Leninist theories and professional knowledge for building new China, decided to merge China University of Political Science and Law on the basis of North China University, and assigned some cadres of North China People's Revolution University to establish the Renmin University of China. On December 16, 1949, the Government Administration Council of the Central Government of China passed Decision on the Establishment of the Renmin University of China at the 11th government administration meeting following the suggestion of the Political Bureau of the Central Committee of the Party.

11

12

图 11 为 1937 年 11 月 1 日，陕北公学隆重举行开学典礼。

“七七”事变以后，为培养成千上万的革命干部，满足抗日战争的需要，中共中央于 1937 年 7 月底决定创办陕北公学——中国共产党直接领导创办的一所革命大学。

This is the photo of the opening ceremony held in Shanbei Public School on November 1, 1937.

After the "Marco Polo Bridge Incident" in 1937, the Central Committee of the Communist Party of China made the decision at the end of July 1937 to create Shanbei Public School in order to train tens of thousands of revolutionary cadres and meet the demand of the Anti-Japanese War. It was a revolutionary university directly created by the leaders of the Central Committee of the Communist Party of China.

图 12 为 1946 年，华北联合大学全体教职工大会现场。

1939 年夏，抗日战争的形势发生了变化，日寇、国民党顽固派加紧进攻解放区。6 月，中共中央决定陕北公学、延安鲁迅艺术学院、延安工人学校、安吴堡战时青年训练班四校联合成立华北联合大学，开赴华北敌人后方办学。7 月 7 日，华北联合大学在延安宣告成立。

The photo records the scene of the staff and faculty meeting of North China Union University in 1946.

In the summer of 1939, the situation of the Anti-Japanese War changed, and the Japanese invaders and Kuomintang stroke hard enough to attack the liberated areas. In June of the same year, the Central Committee of the Communist Party of China decided to merge Shanbei Public School, Yan'an Luxun Arts College (now known as Yan'an University Luxun Arts School), Yan'an Workers School and Anwubao Wartime Youth Training Class into North China Union University, and run it at the enemy rear in northern China. On July 7 of the same year, North China Union University was announced establishment in Yan'an.

第二章
Chapter Two

初识金融

20 世纪 50 年代

Getting Acquainted with Finance in the 1950s

“土法上马”
"Finding His Own Way to Work"

“时代背景不同，每个人自己的条件不同，但科学之路总会被有志者走出来的。”这句话，用来形容初识金融的黄达再合适不过。

没有教材、没有提纲、没有受过教育学和经济学的正规训练，仅仅是听了苏联专家的讲课，凭借有限的文化底子，就直接走上经济学的讲坛，这无异于赶鸭子上架。学校宽慰大家：“苏联专家给你们讲，你们再给同学们转述，问题不大”，这除了给自己壮壮胆外，没啥实质作用。

靠天靠地不如靠自己，自学成才最可靠。

经过一段时间的摸爬滚打，黄达找到了“土法上马”的好法子。所谓“土法上马”，也就是不经过几年专业理论和高等教育的培养，不经过给教授当助教的实际历练，一下子就蹦到讲台上，硬要在讲授实践里自我造就一个大学教师。具体步骤有二：第一是“学”，从不懂到懂；第二是“教”，从“自己懂”到“使人懂”。在此过程当中，唯有坚持教学相长、师生共勉、持之以恒才能获得成功。

但是，“学”本身就很难！需要花费很大功夫。特别是对于金融学这个“舶来品”而言，单靠有限的中译本文献显然无法解决问题。除了细啃郭大力、王亚南译的《资本论》、列宁的《帝国主义论》译本以及李达的《货币学概论》等书籍之外，处于“借助字典阅读外文文献”层次的黄达还需要过翻译关。学习之苦可想而知。

“学然后知不足，教然后知困”，相比较“学”难，“教”亦难！

为人师者看似简单，实践起来却非常困难，其学问之大唯有真正登上讲台方能体会。“有时候往往是感觉到懂了却无法用学生听懂的语言表述出来。这就要求授课人，首先自己必须真懂，其次还要注重教学技巧。”

功夫不负有心人。不到一个学期，由于讲课效果好，黄达成了主要的授课者。一年后，他还被任命为货币流通与信用教研室（现在中国人民大学财政金融学院货币金融系的前身）主任。

"Despite different individual conditions against different backgrounds, the road to science would be built by ambitious people. " This is appropriate to describe Huang Da's first acquaintance with finance.

Without textbooks, outlines, formal training on education and economics, he started to teach economics merely depending on his limited academic basis after attending lectures by experts from the Soviet Union. For Huang Da, this was the same as putting him on the spot. He was comforted by the university leaders that "it is all right if you repeat everything as told by the Soviet experts ". These words in fact didn't work except an emboldening function.

Nothing is reliable than oneself. Thus, self-learning is the most reliable way.

Thanks to his hard work, Huang Da "found his own way to work", which meant that without years of professional training or practice of acting as a tutor, he directly came to the platform as a college teacher. To be specific, there were two steps to work in his way: to "learn " what he didn't understand and to "teach " "what he understood " to others "for them to understand ". He insisted that success could only be acquired by perseverance in interactive teaching and mutual encouragement between teachers and students.

However, to learn is a hard job! That takes great pains. Especially for finance, a western invention, merely relying on the Chinese version of documents was clearly incapable of solving problems. Besides reading the Chinese version of *On Capital* translated by Guo Dali and Wang Yanan, *Imperialism* written by Lenin and *Introduction of Economics of Money* by Li Da, Huang Da had to translate by himself although he could only read foreign documents with the help of a dictionary. It is easy to imagine the difficulty of learning.

To learn makes one realize his deficiency, and to teach makes one know the difficulties. In comparison, to "teach " was more difficult than to "learn ".

Teaching seems simple and is actually difficult in practice, which can only be understood by standing on the platform. "Sometimes, it is hard to express it clearly enough for students to understand even if the teacher understands it himself. This requires that the teacher must have a deep understanding first and above all, and also pay attention to the teaching skills. "

No pain no gain. In less than a semester, Huang Da became a major lecturer as his teaching was well received. One year later, Huang Da was appointed as the head of the Teaching and Research Group of Currency Circulation and Credit in the Department of Finance (currently the Department of Money and Finance in the School of Finance in the Renmin University of China).

从翻译教材到编写教材

From Translation to Composition of Textbooks

新中国成立初期，大政方针“一边倒”，大到国家的政策法规，小到行业的运行规则，各行各业都在学苏联“老大哥”。

金融学科的建设亦不例外。学科体系、课程设计都完全照搬苏联，当然还有教材编写。

在教材和专著间，黄达更看重的是教材。如果说金融学科是一座宏伟壮丽的宫殿，那么教材，特别是好的教材将是支撑其巍然屹立的基座。能够写出一部能够流传后世、影响几代人的好教材是每一个教育者的崇高理想。

从那时起，黄达好像只是抱着总要编出好教材给学生看的朴素想法，开始了超越一个甲子的历程。当然，严格来说，最开始还不是编写而是翻译。

当时，中国人民大学货币流通与信用教研室翻译了三本苏联教材——《苏联货币流通与信用》（北京三联书店，1954）、布列格里的《资本主义国家的货币流通与信用》（中国财政经济出版社，1955）以及《苏联信贷组织与计划》（中国财政经济出版社，1956）。这三本书的翻译出版虽能解教材短缺的燃眉之急，但是由于国情不同、语言表述有异等问题，直接“趸”过来的教材很难被学生完全理解。

教材不能仅仅靠翻译，不能唯“洋人”马首是瞻，一定要改变！要编写有“中国味道”的教材是那个时期金融学人共同的心声！而真正落实到行动，迈出第一步的是黄达以及他所在的教研室。

回过头来看，在“文化大革命”之前，黄达及其同事编写教材的尝试实际走了两步：“改编”与“合并”。借此先后编写的两部教材填补了当时国内缺少原汁原味中国教材的空白，而且作为高校财经类学生的通行教材，一直沿用到改革开放初期。

第一步“改编”，改编哪本教材？布列格里的《资本主义国家的货币流通与信用》凭借逻辑严谨、内容充实等优势迅速“拔得头筹”。事实上，这本教材包

At the beginning of the founding of the People's Republic of China, both national policies and industrial regulations "leaned to one side " so that all trades and professions learnt from Big Brother of the Soviet Union.

It was no exception with the construction of the financial discipline. Its subject system and course design as well as composition of textbooks completely copied those of the Soviet Union.

Huang Da attached more importance to textbooks than monographs.If the finance subject was a magnificent palace, the textbooks, especially the excellent ones, would be foundation as its support. It was a lofty ideal of an educator to compose an excellent textbook that could be handed down and exert influence on the future generations.

With the simple idea of composing textbooks for his students, Huang Da embarked on his composition that lasted for over 60 years. His "close contact" with them started in this period, and to be strict, with translation rather than composition.

In this period, the teaching and research group of currency circulation and credit of Renmin University translated three books from the Soviet Union—*Currency Circulation and Credit in the Soviet Union* (published by Beijing SDX Joint Publishing Company in 1954), *Currency Circulation and Credit in Capitalist Countries* written by З.Я.Брегель(published by China Financial and Economic Publishing House in 1955) and *Credit Organization and Plan* (published by China Financial & Economic Publishing House in 1956). Although these translated versions met the pressing need for textbooks, they could hardly be understood by students due to different national conditions and expressions.

Our textbooks could not merely rely on translation to follow the foreigners' lead. Instead, the situation must be changed! Composing Chinese-style textbooks was the common aspiration for financial scholars at that time! It was Huang Da and his teaching and research group who took the first step in this respect.

In retrospect, before the cultural revolution (1966—1976), Huang Da and his colleagues made two attempting steps in fact: adaptation and mergence. The handwritten manuscript by Huang Da, by and large, filled in the gaps of the authentic Chinese textbooks. They were universally used by students majoring in finance until the beginning of reform and opening up.

The first step is adaptation. Which book was chosen for adaptation? *Currency Circulation and Credit in Capitalist Countries* was chosen for its strict logics and

含着20世纪前二三十年西方货币银行学的精华。因此，“学苏联”变成了间接的“学西方”。

1951 年提出设想，1954 年开始动手，直到 3 年后的 1957 年，经过周作仁、杨承祚、黄达以及林与权四人对文字表述的大换血、充实和增补，改编后的《资本主义国家的货币流通与信用》由中国人民大学出版社正式出版发行。

这本书是黄达主持编写并公开发行的教材之中的“处女作”，也是新中国成立后由中国人自己编写的第一本金融学教材。西南财经大学的曾康霖教授在若干年后提起这本“蓝皮书”时，依然记忆犹新，把它称为自己学习金融的“启蒙书”。但是，由于当时没有复印技术，文稿需要反复抄录，加之期间政治运动的干预等原因，编写过程中的艰辛成为留给黄达的唯一感受。当正式出版后拿到这本书时，他不禁在扉页上写道：“……两年半的经营近日方始出版，方知编书之不易！”

第二步“合并”，合并什么？突破苏联的框架，将讲述资本主义的教材与讲述社会主义的教材合并——可行吗？！在今天看来稀松平常的事情，在那个时代可算得上“创举”，而真正能将《资本主义国家的货币流通与信用》和《苏联社会主义国家的货币流通与信用》两部教材送进“熔炉”，却又得益于那个“亢奋”的时代——“大跃进”。用黄达的话说，就是受“大跃进”的忽悠。

1959 年，合并后的教材《货币信用学（上册）》出版，为了显示与西方课程有所区别，并未采用《货币银行学》的名称。封面署名“黄达等集体编写”。下册由于“反右倾”运动的突然来袭，虽已编写完成，但未能出版。

“反右倾”运动之后，黄达决定重启《货币信用学（上册）》的修订和下册的修改出版，但是，就在即将成稿之际，黄达被下放至北京市北新桥人民公社挂职担任副主任，修订工作戛然而止。这本教材虽然命途多舛，但其影响却一直延续到改革开放的初期。比如《货币信用学》这个名称，一直延续许久。

与黄达一样，参与修订的周升业教授也得到了同样的“待遇”——被下放至

abundant contents. This book actually contained the essence of the western money and banking in the first twenty to thirty years of the 20th century. Therefore, "following the Soviet Union " became "following the West ".

The idea was put forward in 1951, and was put into operation in 1954. Three years later, in 1957, the adapted version of *Currency Circulation and Credit in Capitalist Countries* was at first published by China Renmin University Press after being rewritten, enriched and supplemented by Zhou Zuoren, Yang Chengzuo, Huang Da and Lin Yuquan.

This was the first openly published textbook written by Huang Da, and also the first finance textbook written by Chinese after the founding of New China. Professor Zeng Kanglin from Southwest University of Finance and Economics still remembered this "blue-covered book" when mentioning it several years later. He called it "enlightenment book" to his finance study. However, it needed repeated transcribing as there was no copy machine at that time. This, together with the intervention by the then political movements, left the only impression on Huang Da that it was a painstaking work. When receiving the publication, he couldn't help but writing on the flyleaf: "...It is finally published after two and a half years of efforts. Now I know that writing a book is not an easy job! "

The second step is mergence. Which books were chosen for mergence? Is it feasible to break through the framework of the Soviet Union and merge the textbooks on capitalism with those on socialism?! The common thing today was indeed an "innovation" at that time. The mergence of *Currency Circulation and Credit in Capitalist Countries* and *Currency Circulation and Credit in the Soviet Union* benefited from that exciting era —" The Great Leap Forward", and in Huang Da's word, flickered by "The Great Leap Forward".

In 1959, the emerged version of *Money and Credit* (Vol.1) made its debut. To show its difference from the western courses, it didn't take the name of *Economics of Money and Banking*. The book was under the signature "Huang Da and his team". Though the writing was completed, Vol.2 was not published because of the sudden occurrence of "Anti-rightist Movement".

After the Anti-rightist Movement, Huang Da decided to restart revising *Money and Credit* (Vol.1) and its Vol.2. Unfortunately, on the occasion of its completion, Huang Da was transferred to work as Associate Director in Beixinqiao People's Commune, so the revision stopped. Although the preparation of this textbook was

京郊农场。提及周升业，中国金融学界无人不知、无人不晓，是个响当当的人物。他小黄达三岁，1952 年北京大学毕业后考入中国人民大学读研究生，1955 年留校任教。自留校起，由于志趣相投，他与黄达随即成为并肩战斗的“战友”，共同推动中国金融学科发展，开始了 60 余年的友谊。

not smooth, its influence lasted till the earlier stage of reform and opening up. For example, the name *Money and Credit* was used for a very long time.

Professor Zhou Shengye who participated in the revision work had the similar experience with Huang Da—He was transferred to a farm in suburb Beijing. Zhou Shengye was a well-known person who was three years younger than Huang Da. In 1952, after his graduation from Peking University, he entered the Renmin University of China as a postgraduate, and retained to work in the university in 1955. From then on, with a common goal, he and Huang Da became comrades in arms, working hand in hand to promote the development of finance in China. Their friendship lasted for over 60 years.

囿于时代的困惑

Trapped in Confusion of the Era

一边编教材，一边写论文，是教师从事科研工作的两大抓手。20 世纪 50 年代，除了编写教材之外，黄达还逐渐找到了创作的灵感，不断通过写作来进行知识积累和自我充实。

这一时期，他沿着理解马克思主义经典著作、了解苏联的实践经验，并最终与中国实际相互照应的基本路径摸索着前进。所写文章大多以向中国学界介绍货币银行学理论为主。具体来看，一是理解马克思主义经典著作中有关货币、信用及银行论述的本意并力求用比较易于理解的形式写成文章；二是了解苏联关于货币、信用及银行的理论与实践，特别是了解其政策观点和理论观点形成的背景，并加以介绍；三是了解中国货币、信用与银行的实际，以求理论联系实际，把苏联经验与中国实践结合在一起。

然而，时代与知识的局限，难免使一个土生土长的金融学“初学者”有时候“搞反了方向”，得出日后看来“不成立的论断”。

对此，黄达从不避讳。

发表在 1953 年《教学与研究》第 5 期上的《关于苏联货币制度的几个问题》，是黄达公开发表的第一篇文章。为了弄懂“老大哥”的货币、银行、信贷问题，他着实花费了不少精力。在 1999 年，黄达将此文收入《黄达文集》（上、下卷）时所作的“解题”里举了这样一个例子：苏联人把诸如“借款人到期归还”的基本常识提到“信贷原则”的高度，曾经让他百思不得其解。很长一段时间以后，他才发现，这是因为在苏联，国有企业认为不归还从国家银行借的钱天经地义——都是国家的，何必还呢？“应该说，当时只是弄懂了一个近乎‘废话’的原则在它们30年代初的‘信用改革’中所以产生的原因，而还不能像今天这样体会到苏联模式的国有经济所先天带来的难以治疗的内伤。”

再来看 1958 年，这是个全民“拼胆”的年代。这一年，黄达也相信了货币不久就会消亡的论断，并写了一篇“全然是呓语”的文章《农村金融工作的大跃进丰富了马克思列宁主义的信用理论》（《金融研究》，1958 年第 4 期）。这篇文章

Compiling textbooks and writing papers are the two must-dos for a teacher engaged in scientific research, and must be paid sufficient attention to. In the 1950s, apart from compiling textbooks, Huang Da gradually found the inspiration and kept writing to accumulate knowledge and improve himself.

In this period, he followed the basic route to understand Marxist classics, learn the Soviet Union's practical experience and finally have them coordinated with the Chinese reality. Most of his papers focused on introducing the theory of money and banking to the Chinese academia. To be specific, firstly, interpreting the connotations on money, credit and banking in the Marxist classics, and including them into his papers in an easy-to-understand way. Secondly, introducing the theory and practice on money, credit and banking in the Soviet Union, especially in the context of how the views of policies and theories came into being. Thirdly, clarifying China's reality in money, credit and banking in order to link theory with practice, and combine the Soviet Union's practices with China's practice.

However, due to constraint of the era and knowledge, it is inevitable for a beginner of finance to go the opposite direction and conclude to an invalid theory.

Huang Da was never shy about it.

Some Questions on the Monetary System in the Soviet Union published in *Teaching and Research* (Vol. 5) in 1953 was the first paper published by Huang Da. He spent a lot of energy to understand the issues of currency, banking and credit of Big Brother. In 1999, in the note he made when he included this paper into the *Essays of Huang Da* (Vol. 1 and Vol. 2), he set such an example to make comments: "The borrower is due for return" is the basic knowledge, but the Soviets regarded it as a credit principle, which confused him for a long time. After a while, he found that it was because in the Soviet Union, SOEs believed that it was common to refuse to return the money borrowed from the national bank. Why to return it as it belongs to the country? "It should be said that at that time, he just found the reason why a common principle occurred in the 1930s' credit reform, yet not understood the incurable injury of the nation-owned economy in the Soviet model."

The year 1958 was a "bold " era for all people. That year, Huang Da believed the judgment that money would soon vanish, and wrote a paper "full of crazy talks " with the title of The Great Leap Forward in

同样被黄达收录进 1999 年版的《黄达文集》（上、下卷），并如此解题，“把这篇文章选入，可以自警，也可以使没有这类经历的人对于那种岁月的思想紊乱多少获得点形象的概念。”“如果要肯定点什么，恐怕在于真心真意想为确确实实存在的现实经济问题寻求理论答案的努力。”

事实上，学者坦荡、严谨、求实的学术风骨与人格魅力已远远掩盖了时代的尴尬。

Rural Finance Enriches the Credit Theory of Marxism-Leninism (published in Vol.4, *Financial Research*, 1958). It was also included in the *Essays of Huang Da* (Vol. 1 and Vol. 2) published in 1999. He made comments that "this paper is alerting and provides some concrete images of disorder in mind in that era for people with no similar experiences ", and that "if there must be something to get the nod, it is the whole-hearted efforts to seek the academic answers to the substantive economic issues that did exist ".

In fact, the scholar's academic characters and personal charisma with magnanimous, rigorous and realistic attitude have greatly concealed the awkwardness of the age.

2-1

建校之初的中国人民大学
Renmin University of China at the Beginning of Its Establishment

中国人民大学成立之初的校址是在城内，以铁狮子胡同一号（北洋军阀时期曾是段祺瑞的执政府）为中心，散居在或近或远的数十处。

现在的西郊校址为1951年左右开始兴建。最初的布局是，正对校门是灰砖的教学楼（现在的求是楼，1951年建成）；右手是由南向北并列三座，而后一度被当作单身教工宿舍的红楼楼群（现在的红一、二、三楼，1951年建成）；教学楼以西是由许多间灰砖平房教室组成的大院；其西北是红砖的图书馆（现在的学生活动中心，1952年建成）；沿校址北边和西边是许多一层、二层没有厨房、卫生间的筒子宿舍：一部分住学生，一部分住职工，后来逐渐建造了三层楼的单元宿舍。

建校伊始，教师大多住在城内，有课乘班车去西郊校区。1956年，黄达在西郊校区分得一间红楼宿舍，全家搬到西郊校区则是在“文化大革命”的前两三年。

The Renmin University of China was first established in town—made up of dozens of places, far off or near, with No. 1 Tieshizi Hutong (used to be the site of the consulate of Duan Qirui under the regime of the Northern warlord clique) being the center.

Construction of the university in the western suburbs today was initiated in about 1951. At the very beginning, it was a teaching building of gray bricks directly facing the school gate (Qiushi Building now, built in 1951); on the right hand side, there were three red buildings in a row from south to north, which were later used as dormitories for single men and women teachers (No. 1 Red Building, No. 2 Red Building and No. 3 Red Building, built in 1951); that west of the teaching building was a big yard with many bungalow classrooms of gray bricks; that northwest of the teaching building was the library (now Students' Center, built in 1952); along the north and west sides of the original site were many bungalow or two-floor dormitories without kitchens or bathrooms, some for the students and some for the staff. Later, some three-floor dormitory buildings were built.

At the beginning, most teachers lived in town, and took the regular bus to the campus in the western suburbs to give classes. In 1956, Huang Da was given a dorm room in the Red Building on the campus in the western suburbs. It was not until two or three years before the Cultural Revolution that his family moved to the campus of the Renmin University of China in the western suburbs.

图 16~20 为 20 世纪 50 年代初期，位于铁狮子胡同一号的中国人民大学主校区，以及散居在或近或远的本科校区、专修科校区、预科校区以及工农速成中学校区等。

1952 年底，中国人民大学已经初具规模，设有 9 个系、38 个教研室、1 个编译室，此外还有专修科、预科、马列主义研究班、研究生班、马列主义夜大学、夜校、函授专修班和附设工农速成中学。

These pictures record the main campus of the Renmin University of China in No. 1 Tieshizi Hutong, and the campuses far off or nearby like the undergraduates' campus, the special training courses campus, the preparatory courses campus, and the campus of the short-term middle school for workers and farmers in the early 1950s.

Till the end of 1952, the Renmin University of China had begun to take shape, having nine departments, 38 teaching and research groups, one compilation and translation center, as well as special training courses, preparatory courses, a Marxism workshop, a graduates' class, a night school of Marxism, night schools, correspondence specialized courses and a short-term middle school for workers and farmers.

16

图 16 为 20 世纪 50 年代初期的铁狮子胡同一号。
This is the photo of No. 1 Tieshizi Hutong in the early 1950s.

17

图 17 为本科校区。

This is the undergraduates' campus.

18

图 18 为专修科校区。

This is the special training courses campus.

19

图 19 为预科校区。

This is the preparatory courses campus.

20

图 20 为工农速成中学校区。

This is the campus of the short-term middle school for workers and farmers.

21

图 21 为 20 世纪 50 年代，中国人民大学西郊校区求是楼（原名灰楼、教学一楼）。

建成于 1951 年的这幢楼，庄重朴实，两株高大挺拔的古松巍立在左侧，是中国人民大学西郊校区在 20 世纪五六十年代的主要标志性景观。尽管当时它只有三层，但在 50 年代初期，在北京郊外尚属罕见，人们称之为“西郊大厦”。据称，当年从西直门到颐和园的大路两侧，除了农科院有一座黄砖旧楼，唯有中国人民大学的灰楼是新建的高大建筑。

This is Qiushi Building (formerly known as the Gray Building, No. 1 Teaching Building) on the campus of the Renmin University of China in the western suburbs.

Built in 1951, the building was simple and elegant, two tall and straight pines standing on its left side. It was the main scenic spot on the campus of the Renmin University of China in the western suburbs in the 1950s and 1960s. Although it had only three stories, it was rare in downtown Beijing and the suburbs in the early 1950s. People all called it "Xijiao Mansion." It is said that, at both sides of the road from Xizhimen to the Summer Palace, except an old building of yellow bricks owned by the Academy of Agriculture, only the Gray Building of the Renmin University of China was a newly-built big building.

22

23

24

图 22 为 1951 年建成的中国人民大学西郊校区红楼楼群。

红楼楼群由红一、二、三楼自南向北并列而成。开始作为学生宿舍，后长期作为单身教工宿舍。2002 年，为了满足学校扩大招生的需要，红楼被调整为学生宿舍并沿用至今。

This picture records the red building group on the campus of the Renmin University of China in the western suburbs which were built in 1951.

The red building group was made up of No. 1, No. 2 and No. 3 Red Buildings standing in a row from south to north, at first as the student dormitory, then as the staff dormitory for a long time. In 2002, as the Renmin University of China needed to expand its student size, the red buildings were rebuilt into students' dormitories and have been used for the purpose until now.

图 23 为 1952 年建成的中国人民大学西郊校区第一代图书馆。

1992 年，学校第三代图书馆投入使用后，该图书馆改作“学生活动中心”，一直延续至今。

This is the first-generation library on the campus of the Renmin University of China in the western suburbs that was built in 1952. In 1992, when the third-generation library of the university was put into use, it was used as "Students' Center" and has been used for the purpose until now.

图 24 为 20 世纪 50 年代初期中国人民大学西郊校区校门。

This is the school gate of the campus of the Renmin University of China in the western suburbs in the early 1950s.

2-2

担任中国人民大学货币流通与信用教研室主任

Serve as the Head of Teaching and Research Group of Currency Circulation and Credit

1950年秋，中国人民大学财政信用借贷系货币流通与信用教研室，开始在苏联专家的带领下讲授“货币流通与信用”课程。当时教研室的中国教师，包括崔希默、孔生、肖清、郭丁、林与权、李振江、车孤萍、栾重威和黄达等人。崔希默是财政信用借贷系主任。

然而，该教研室的中国教师不仅没有学过“货币银行学”，而且没有相关的中文教材，苏联专家推荐的俄文教材也迟迟没有寄到。在当时，中国人民大学其他专业的状况也与此类似。

学校采取的“应急措施”是由苏联专家制订课程计划，在讲授某一章的前一周（甚至是当周）由苏联专家向中国教师传授本章内容（专家用俄文讲，翻译口译为中文），而后再采取“车轮战法”—— 一位教师讲一章，轮流上讲台。

在上述措施实行了将近一学年后，1951年临近暑假，教研室将为学生“系统辅导”和出考题、配考签、写答案的任务交给了已经担任货币流通与信用教研室主任的黄达。

直到今天，黄达还保存着当年撰写的《“货币流通与信用”考试题——1950/1951学年，专修科财政银行班》手稿。这份由黄达在16开的白纸上手写的稿件大体可以说明当时初次讲授这门课程一年所达到的水平，也可以说是第一份由教研室教师自己编写出来的“教材”，更是今天上百万字《金融学（第三版）》的雏形。

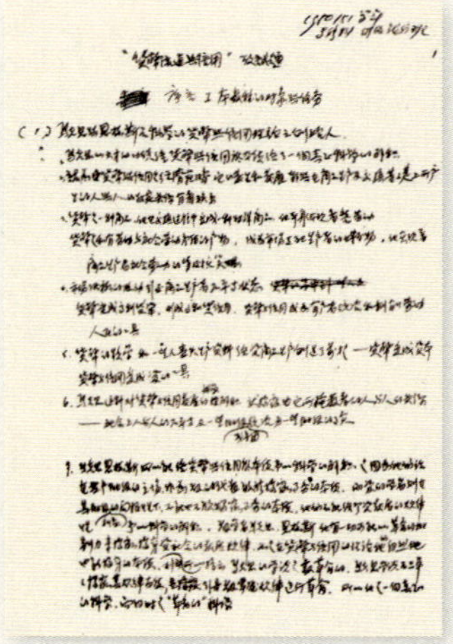

25

图25为1951年黄达撰写的“货币流通与信用”考试题手稿。

This is the script of the Exam Paper on Currency Circulation and Credit by Huang Da in 1951.

In the fall of 1950, the Teaching and Research Group of Currency Circulation and Credit of the Department of Public Finance and Credit Loan of Renmin University of China began to teach Currency Circulation and Credit under the leadership of the Soviet experts. The Chinese teachers of the group include Cui Ximo, Kong Sheng, Xiao Qing, Guo Ding, Lin Yuquan, Li Zhenjiang, Che Guping, Luan Chongwei and Huang Da, etc. Cui Ximo was the head of the Department of Public Finance and Credit Loan.

However, its Chinese teachers had never learned the Economics of Money and Banking, nor did they have relevant Chinese textbooks. It was even worse that the Russian textbooks recommended by the Soviet experts were not yet received. Other departments of the Renmin University of China had the same situation.

The school took an emergency measure, that is, it asked the Soviet experts to develop the curriculum, and then to teach the Chinese teachers a specific chapter one week before (even in that very week) it was to be taught (the experts spoke Russian which were then interpreted into Chinese). Then "wheel tactics " were adopted—one teacher teaching one chapter, and all the Chinese teachers giving classes in turn.

After the above measure was taken for nearly a whole school year, the teaching and research group assigned Huang Da to give the students "systematic assistance," set the examination paper, distribute the examinees' name labels, and give the answers when the summer vocation was coming in 1951.

The scripts of the Exam Paper on Currency Circulation and Credit 1950 / 1951 was the review and summary of monetary credit taught by the teaching and research group in the first academic year (1950 / 1951) since the establishment of Renmin University. This document demonstrated the general teaching level of the course. It is not only the first "textbook " compiled by the teachers of the teaching and research group themselves, but also the origin of today's textbook *Economics of Money and Finance*, a book of nearly a million Chinese characters.

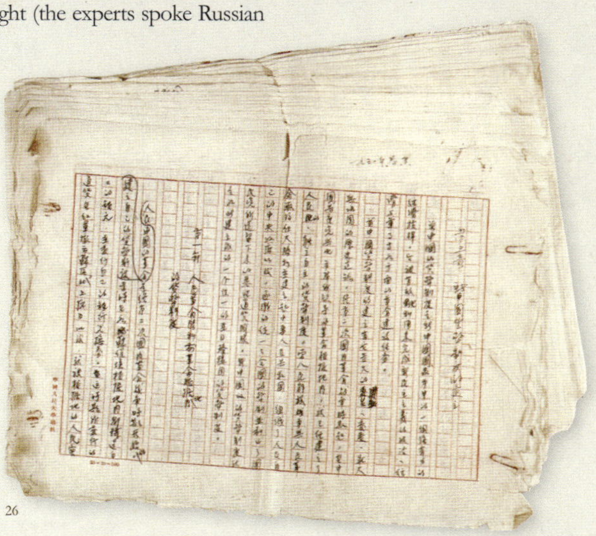

26

图 26 为 1951 年黄达撰写的题为《新中国货币制度的建立》的讲义手稿。

为了贯彻学校的“理论联系实际，苏联经验与中国实际相结合”的方针，建校伊始，中国教师即着手编写有关中国货币与信用问题的讲义，在当时构成货币流通与信用课程的“中国部分”。

This is the lecture script of *On the Establishment of the Currency System in New China* written by Huang Da in 1951.

In order to thoroughly implement the university's philosophy of "putting theories into practice, combining Soviet experience with China's reality," the Chinese faculty had started preparing lectures on the currency and credit problems in China since the establishment of the university, and the lectures they compiled became the "China Part" of the course of Currency Circulation and Credit.

下页图

图 27 为 20 世纪 50 年代初期，中国人民大学部分教师与苏联专家合影。前排左十一（小孩儿除外）为时任中国人民大学校长的吴玉章，第二排左二为黄达。

Some teachers of the Renmin University of China had a group photo with the Soviet experts in the early 1950s. The 11th from the left in the first row (except children) was Wu Yuzhang, the then president of the Renmin University of China, and the second from the left in the second row was Huang Da.

27

28

图 28 为 1951 年，中国人民大学货币流通与信用教研室部分教师、研究生和中南财经学院、西南财经学院、上海财经学院等校的进修教师，在中国人民大学老校区铁狮子胡同一号的合影。第二排左一为黄达。

Some teachers and postgraduates of the Teaching and Research Group of Currency Circulation and Credit of the Renmin University of China had a group photo with teachers from Zhongnan College of Economics and Law, Southwestern College of Economics and Law and Shanghai College of Economics and Law who were pursuing further education. They were in No.1 Tieshizi Hutong on the old campus of the Renmin University of China. The first from the left in the second row was Huang Da.

29

图 29 为 1951 年，中国人民大学货币流通与信用教研室部分教师在集体备课，墙上贴的是教师自己绘制的教学图表。自左至右分别为：郭丁、傅美文（俄文翻译）、孔生、李振江、黄达和栾重威。

Some teachers of the Teaching and Research Group of Currency Circulation and Credit of the Renmin University of China were preparing for the class in 1951. On the wall were the teaching charts drawn by the teachers themselves. People from the left to the right in the picture are Guo Ding, Fu Meiwen (Russian translator), Kong Sheng, Li Zhenjiang, Huang Da and Luan Chongwei.

右页图

图 30 为 1959 年 3 月 30 日，时任中国人民大学财政信用借贷系副主任的黄达在中国人民大学第五届党代会上发言。

On March 30, 1959, Huang Da, the then deputy head of the Department of Public Finance and Credit Loan of the Renmin University of China, addressed the 5th Party Congress of the Renmin University of China.

30

右页图 ⟼

图 31 和图 32 为黄达主持编写的《资本主义国家的货币流通与信用》（中国人民大学出版社，1957），以及黄达等集体编写的《货币信用学（上册）》（中国人民大学出版社，1959）。

在整个 50 年代，黄达以及他所在的教研室主要编写了两部教材：一是根据苏联有关教材由黄达主持改编的《资本主义国家的货币流通与信用》，分别于 1957 年 1 月、4 月由中国人民大学出版社分上、下两册出版；当年 5 月，中国人民大学出版社出版了该教材的合订本。这部教材是新中国成立后由中国人自己编写的第一本金融学教材，当时被形象地称为“蓝皮书”。二是 1959 年 9 月由中国人民大学出版社出版的《货币信用学（上册）》。而后，由于 1959 年秋的“反右倾”运动，下册未能出版。该教材革命性地将“社会主义的货币流通与信用”和“资本主义国家的货币流通与信用”合而为一，论点不再完全照搬苏联，而是有了自己学习马克思主义经典著述的体会和根据中国情况概括出来的看法。

These are *Currency Circulation and Credit in the Capitalist Countries* (China Renmin University Press, 1957) and *Money and Credit* (Vol.1)compiled under the direction of Huang Da.

During the entire 1950s, Huang Da and the teaching and research group mainly compiled two textbooks, namely *Currency Circulation and Credit in the Capitalist Countries* and *Money and Credit*. The former was adapted from related Soviet textbooks and under the direction of Huang Da, and published by China Renmin University Press in two volumes in January and April, 1957, respectively; in May of the same year, China Renmin University Press published the bound volume of it. It is the first textbook on finance that was compiled by the Chinese after the founding of new China, and was vividly reputed as the "Blue Paper." The latter was published by China Renmin University Press in September 1959. Due to the "Anti-rightists" Movement in the autumn of 1959, the second volume of the book was not published. The book revolutionarily combined "socialist currency circulation and credit" with "currency circulation and credit in the capitalist countries" and instead of entirely copying the views in the Soviet Union, had its own experience of learning Marxist classics and views generalized on the basis of China's situation.

資本主义国家的貨币
流通与信用
中国人民大学出版社

31

貨币信用学
HUOBI XINYONG XUE
上册
黄达等集体編写
中国人民大学出版社

32

2-3

与家人在一起
Be with Families

1952年夏，黄达与罗淑珍完婚。罗淑珍曾在北京大学先修班学习。1948年进入位于解放区的华北大学。留校后一直在中国人民大学出版社工作，直至离休。2005年，于北京逝世。

黄达与罗淑珍育有二子。大儿子黄小坚生于1953年，20世纪80年代后期出国进修，曾在美国微软公司担任软件工程师，目前入籍加拿大，定居美国。二儿子黄恒生于1957年，是副高级工程师，目前在中央人民广播电台工作。

In the summer of 1952, Huang Da and Luo Shuzhen got married. Luo Shuzhen studied preparatory courses in Peking University, and went to study in North China University in the liberated area in 1948. Later, she had been working in China Renmin University Press till she retired. She passed away in Beijing in 2005.

Huang Da has two sons, Huang Xiaojian and Huang Heng. Huang Xiaojian was born in 1953, received his further education abroad in the late 1980s, and worked as the software engineer at Microsoft. He has become a Canadian citizen and settled in the United States. Huang Heng was born in 1957, and is working for the Central People' s Broadcasting Station. He is an associate senior engineer.

33

34

图33为1952年7月6日，黄达（右一）与罗淑珍（左一）的结婚照。

This is the wedding picture of Huang Da (first from the right) and Luo Shuzhen (first from the left) on July 6, 1952.

图34为1955年，黄达（左二）与罗淑珍（左一）等人游览北京香山。

In 1955, Huang Da (second from the left) and his wife Luo Shuzhen (first from the left) visited Beijing Fragrance Hill with their friends.

右页图

图35为1955年春，黄达（右一）与罗淑珍（左一）在天安门广场。

This records Huang Da (first from the right) and his wife Luo Shuzhen (first from the left) at Tian'anmen Square in the spring of 1955.

36

图 36 为黄小坚（左一）和黄恒（右一）在院子里玩耍。

Huang Xiaojian(first from the left) and Huang Heng (first from the right)were playing in the yard.

37

图 37 为黄小坚（右一）和黄恒（左一）的合影。当时已经戴上红领巾的大儿子黄小坚正读小学。

This is a group photo of Huang Xiaojian (first from the right) and Huang Heng(first from the left). Huang Xiaojian with a red scarf was a primary school student.

第三章

Chapter Three

思想“萌芽”

20 世纪 50 年代末—改革开放前后

"Budding" Thoughts

in the End of 1950s — around the

Launch of Reform and Opening Up

走进宏观分析的新天地

Entering the New World of Macro-analysis

1960 年开始，自然灾害、政治运动一波紧似一波地席卷了神州大地。黄达和他所钟爱的金融学科受到了很大的冲击，而对于他的冲击似乎来得更快。

一切还是源自被“大跃进”“忽悠”而编写的《货币信用学（上册）》。尽管是理论上的尝试，但是所谓的“混淆社会主义与资本主义两种社会制度本质区别”岂不是典型的“修正主义”！在 1960 年秋，黄达遭到持续一个学期、百余次会议的严厉批判。幸运的是，第二年初夏，黄达便被告知：自己对两种制度的区分是明确的，不存在混淆的错误——警报解除！即使如此，每每谈及此事，黄达总难免感慨良多。

而后的几年，是新中国历史上最为艰难和不幸的岁月——“三年经济困难期”，人口首次也是唯一一次出现了负增长。经济困难给老百姓带来了深重的灾难，严重阻碍了经济的发展。而不幸当中的万幸是，政治气氛却相对比较宽松。

此时，金融学界在经历了十年政治生活与教学研究的锤炼后，得到了难得的反思机会。黄达也由最初对于金融朦朦胧胧的“臆断”，经过消化吸收再创造，开始逐步形成自己的学术观点。一些重要的文章开始见诸报端。

《银行信贷原则和货币流通》（《经济研究》，1962 年第 9 期）一文，是这一时期黄达的代表作品之一。在这篇文章中，他提出了两个全新的见解：一是关于货币流通范围问题，在当时只把现金视为货币的背景下，他认为，现金量与存款量之和构成整个国民经济中的货币量，现金与存款的运动构成与商品流通相对应的统一的货币流通；二是关于银行信贷与货币流通的关系问题，他认为，货币流通是以银行信用为基础的，银行贷款的扩大与收缩直接调节着流通中的货币量。这本来是一个并不难理解的真命题，在当时，由于与主流观点不一致而引起广泛争议。

一直到 1981 年，在广州召开的首次全国货币理论研讨会上，金融理论界才对这一问题取得了基本共识。

此外，从 1956 年开始，计划经济当中的术语“三平”，即财政收支平衡、物资供求平衡和信贷收支平衡，进入理论研究的视野。专业的直觉让黄达意识到：“三平”应该纳入货币银行学的框架！黄达没有想到，此时的“顿悟”将成为他日后攀越货

Since1960, China began suffering natural disasters and political movements. Huang Da and his favorite finance subject were hit hard. The hit on him seemingly came faster.

It was the Great Leap Forward that induced him to write *Money and Credit* (Vol. 1). Although it was a theoretical trial, wouldn't it be a typical "revisionism" to blur the essential difference between socialism and capitalism! In the fall of 1960, Huang Da was severely criticized in more than 100 conferences that lasted for a semester. Fortunately, however, in the early summer next year, Huang Da was informed that he had clearly distinguished the two systems, and thus he hadn't made any mistakes on confusion. The alert was lifted! Despite that, whenever Huang Da talked about it, he was always emotional.

In the coming few years, the People's Republic of China experienced the hardest and most unfortunate years in history—"three-year economic difficulty", when the first and the only negative population growth occurred. Economic difficulty brought serious disasters to common people and held back the economic development. One of the fortunate parts out of all the misfortunes was that the political climate was relaxed.

At this time, the financial academia had a rare opportunity for reflection after a decade of political life and teaching research. After the initial understanding of finance, and recreation through digestion and absorption, Huang Da gradually developed his own academic viewpoints. Some important papers began to appear in the newspaper.

One of Huang Da's representative works in the period was Principles of Bank Credit and Currency Circulation (published in Vol. 9, *Economic Research,* 1962). In this paper, he proposed two fresh views: One was about the scope of currency circulation. Against the background in which cash is regarded as the only currency, he believed that the total amount of cash and deposit made up currency in the whole national economy, and the movement of cash and deposit made up the unified currency circulation in response to the circulation of commodities. The other was about the relationship between bank credit and currency circulation. In his opinion, currency circulation was based on bank credit. The expansion and contraction of bank loans directly adjusted the amount of currency in circulation. This was originally a true proposition that was not difficult to understand, however, it aroused extensive controversy at that time as it was different from mainstream viewpoints.

It was not until 1981 that basic consensus was reached

币银行学巅峰的“云梯”。

这一时期，黄达形成的思想日后被收录进《我国社会主义经济中的货币和货币流通》（中国财政经济出版社，1964）——黄达的第一本个人专著。尽管在他看来“这本小书的内容，今天看来，没有多少可以称道的地方”，但是，这毕竟是那个时期黄达独立研究财政金融问题的思想结晶。而且，从那时起，由于对“三平”等总量问题的关注，他已经开始跳出货币银行学的专业局限，从宏观的角度去考虑问题，走进了更为宽广的宏观经济学天地。

此时，宏观经济分析的框架已经在黄达的脑海中生根发芽……

in the financial academia in the First National Currency Theory Symposium held in Guangzhou.

In addition, since 1956, the "three balances " in planned economy, i.e. balance between financial revenue and expenditure, balance between goods demand and supply, and balance between credit revenue and expenditure, came into the attention of theoretical research. Thanks to his professional intuition, Huang Da was aware that the "three balances " should be included into the framework of money and banking. He didn't realize that the then "insight " would become a "ladder " for him to climb up to the summit of the subject in the future.

In that period, Huang Da's thoughts were later included into his first personal monograph—*Currency and Currency Circulation in Socialist Economy in China* (published by China Financial and Economic Publishing House in 1964). In Huang's opinion, "there is little deserving praise in the contents of this book today ". After all, this was the crystallization of Huang's independent research on fiscal and financial issues at that time. Moreover, from then on, owing to his concerns on the "three balances ", he began to jump out of the limitation of money and banking, to think from the macroscopic perspective, and to enter a broader world of political economy.

At that time, the framework of macroeconomic analysis had taken root in Huang Da's mind...

“土八路”的“洋问题”

" Modern Problems" Faced by the "Indigenous" Scholar

在金本位的时代，马克思说：“货币天然是金银。”

在布雷顿森林体系，1 美元 =0.888 671 克黄金，其他货币与美元挂钩。

而 1948 年新华社的社论明确指出，解放区的货币，从它产生的第一天开始，即与金银完全脱离关系。

相同问题却有不同解释，孰是孰非？货币与黄金之惑困扰着当时的理论界。

特别是对于一名教师来讲，这是个非常严肃的问题，因为课堂上一双双渴求的眼睛告诉黄达，他必须要自己先搞清楚，才能让别人明白。

为此，一向不怎么与人争执的黄达，开始了他人生中第一次也是最后一次直接的论战。严格地说，这并不算什么真正的论战，因为黄达的策略很“友好”——不是“针锋相对、非此即彼”，而是“摆陈利害、点到为止”。

事情的缘起是一篇以石武为笔名的文章《试论人民币在马克思主义货币理论上的根据》，这篇文章发表在 1957 年《经济研究》第 2 期上。作者在文章中提出了一个鲜明的观点——“人民币已根本和金或银隔断关系”，然而他的论证依据却是马克思主义货币理论。这显然有失偏颇！黄达随即写就辩驳之作《人民币是具有内在价值的货币商品的符号》，并发表在同年《经济研究》的第 4 期上。他据理力争的论点有两个：其一，如果真正尊重马克思价值论的原意，就只能论证出人民币是具有内在价值的货币商品的符号，反之亦然；其二，在社会主义经济的现实生活中，人们在调节货币流通时完全可以无须考虑贵金属而只需考虑市场供求平衡的要求。

他的反驳非常之艺术！一来他批判了当时学术界流行的、以石武为代表的“非黄金”思想；二来他用隐晦的说法表述了“在纸币流通的条件下，当把马克思的流通货币量模型和纸币流通模型连在一起时，就可以转化成有名的‘交易方程式’”这一论断，但又没有在行文中明确地把马克思和费雪联系在一起。因为后者在当时意味着政治问题。

论战在一个回合之后便告结束。这次论战没有为黄达赢得“全胜”，却使他

In the golden-standard era, Marx said: "Currency is gold and silver in nature."

In the Bretton Woods System, one US dollar equals to 0.888671 gram of gold, and other currencies are pegged with the US dollar.

In an editorial from the Xinhua News Agency in 1948, the currency in the liberated areas was totally separated from gold and silver from the very first day of its creation.

The same question bore different explanations. Then which one was right? The relationship between currency and gold confused the then academia.

Especially as for a teacher, this was a very serious problem. That's because the desiring eyes in the class told Huang Da that he must make it clear first and convey it to others.

For this reason, Huang Da, who used to hide his light instead of quarreling with others, had his direct debate for the first and also the last time. Strictly speaking, it was not a debate in a real sense, as Huang Da's strategy was "friendly"—"Conveying meaning by displaying advantages and disadvantages", rather than "giving tit for tat".

It stemmed from an article titled Discussion on the Foundation of Renminbi on the Marxist Currency Theory with the pen name of Shi Wu, which was published in the Vol. 2, *Economic Research* in 1957. The author proposed a distinctive point of view that "Renminbi had thoroughly cut off the relationship with gold or silver". However, his argument was based on the Marxist currency theory. This was obviously biased. In response, Huang Da wrote Renminbi Is the Sign of Money Commodities with Intrinsic Value as his dispute, which was published in the Vol. 4, *Economic Research* in the same year. He had two arguments. Firstly, if the original meaning of the Marxist theory of value was respected in a real sense, it could only demonstrate that Renminbi was the sign of currency commodities with intrinsic value, and vice versa. Secondly, in the real life of socialist economy, when adjusting currency circulation, people only needed to take into consideration the requirements on the balance of market supply and demand, regardless of the precious metal.

His retort was very skillful! On one hand, he criticized the "non-gold" concept represented by Shi Wu, which was prevalent in the academia then. On the other hand, he metaphorically expressed his statement that "under the condition of socialist economy, the well-known 'equation of exchange' could be generated by linking the Marxist model of amount of currency in circulation

尴尬地赢得一个不大不小的名号——"黄金派"。

事实上，即使经过深入的思考乃至论战，在当今的货币制度中黄金到底有什么作用这个问题，却始终如阴霾一般笼罩着黄达。

20世纪60年代初，他找到了一本苏联学者弗·伊·米哈列夫斯基的著作《第二次世界大战后资本主义体系中的黄金》。从中他似乎看到了一丝厘清这一问题的曙光，于是凭着自学的俄语开始着手翻译，并组织同样自学俄语的同事一起干。恰巧这时，同样研究货币银行学，并在日后成为中国金融改革领军人物的刘鸿儒，留苏归国。他非常赞同翻译这本书并主动承担几章的翻译。

于是，两位日后长期深刻影响着中国金融的青年学者，正式开始了携手为中国金融改革与发展而奋斗的历程。该书后于1965年由中国财政经济出版社出版发行。

即使如此，这本书的翻译并没有完全解决黄达本来想解决的疑问。反而是在翻译过程中，让黄达这个"土八路"遇到了新的"洋问题"——"没想到翻译这门学问是如此的甘苦与深邃"。

"幸亏人大贸经系的陈今淼、经济系的项冲以及本系的王传纶，在翻译过程中给予了无私的帮助。"正是得益于同事们的帮助，黄达才能顺利解决这个"洋问题"。对此，黄达感念至今。

在他看来，也许应该特别提出的是1922年出生的王传纶。他长黄达三岁。1938年，他以优异的成绩考入国立西南联合大学，师从陈岱孙先生，"江湖"人称江南才子。随后，他又辗转于清华大学、英国格拉斯哥大学学习，并于1953年开始在中国人民大学任教，此后再未离开。

在中国人民大学近六十年"跌跌撞撞在前行"的途中，王传纶与黄达相互帮扶，共事一生。2009年，中国人民大学作为试点率先在人文社科领域设立一级教授（这是现行教师评价体系中，文科教师所能获得的最高荣誉）。凭借他们为财政金融学科所做出的开拓性贡献，黄达与王传纶分别被授予首批一级教授和荣誉一级教授的称号。而后于2011年6月和12月，两人又先后获得"中国金融学科终身成就奖"。

with that of note circulation ". But in his paper, he didn't connect Marx with Fisher in a clear way, as the latter meant political issue at that time.

The debate ended in one round. Huang Da didn't win a "complete victory ". Instead, he got an embarrassing title of "gold-oriented ".

Despite deep thinking and debate, Huang Da was still troubled by the role of gold on earth in the present currency system.

In the early 1960s, he seemed to see a silver lining in *Gold in the Capitalist System after the World War* **II**, a book written by Mikhalevski, a Soviet Union scholar. With his knowledge of Russian learnt by himself, he embarked on translating the book together with his counterparts who had also learnt Russian by themselves. At this time, Liu Hongru, a researcher on money and banking, returned to China after his study in the Soviet Union, who later became a leader in Chinese financial reform. He couldn't agree more with the translation task and took initiative to translate several chapters.

Hence, the two young men, who exerted deep-going and long-lasting influences on finance in China, officially embarked on their joint efforts for the reform and development of financial system in China. In 1965, the book was published by China Financial and Economic Publishing House.

It is proved afterwards that the translation failed to completely solve Huang Da's problem. But in the process of translation, this "indigenous" scholar was confronted with "modern" problems—"I never thought that translating is such an arduous and profound job."

"I would like to extend my appreciation to Chen Jinmiao in the Department of Trade, Xiang Chong in the Department of Economy and Wang Chuanlun of our department in the Renmin University of China for their selfless help in translation." Thanks to the help from his colleagues, Huang Da had been able to solve the "modern" problem. Huang Da has always remembered this with gratitude.

Maybe, the one that deserved special mention was Wang Chuanlun, who was born in 1922, three years older than Huang Da. In 1938, Wang Chuanlun was enrolled into National Southwestern Associated University with distinction to learn from Mr. Chen Daisun, a gifted scholar in the public eyes. Afterwards, Wang Chuanlun went to Tsinghua University and University of Glasgow in UK. He began to teach in the Renmin University of China in 1953 and never left.

For nearly 60 years, Wang Chuanlun and Huang Da stumbled along to work hand in hand throughout their

让我们永远记住这些场景！这不仅属于两位老人，更是所有为中国财政金融学科发展做出贡献的老前辈们应共同享有的荣光！

遗憾的是，2012年9月13日，王传纶教授怀揣着中国知识分子的坚守、信仰与敬畏永远地离开了他所钟爱的财政金融学事业。两年后，在《王传纶经济文论》《学术泰斗王传纶》出版座谈会上，黄达用八个字来评价他这位知心老友——“真有学问，有真学问！”

王传纶教授的弟子李扬在《王传纶经济文论》代序中曾写下这样一段文字——“王传纶教授凭借深厚的学养和睿智的视野，创造性地贯通中西文化，徜徉于金融与财政两大研究领域，成为我国经济理论界公认的宗师之一”，大抵代表了学界对于王传纶教授的普遍赞誉。

life. In 2009, the Renmin University of China carried out the pilot work to award the first grade professor in the fields of humanity and social science. This was the top reputation that professors of liberal arts would acquire in the current professional evaluation system. Owing to their pioneering contributions made in the fiscal and financial subject, Huang Da and Wang Chuanlun were awarded as one of the first grade professors and honorary first grade professors respectively. In June and December 2011, they both received the "China's Annual Financial Discipline Lifetime Achievement Award " respectively.

Let us always remember the honor! It not only belongs to the two old scholars, but also is shared by all the predecessors who have made contributions to the development of the fiscal and financial subject in China!

Unfortunately, on September 13, 2012, Professor Wang Chuanlun left his favorite career forever with his perseverance, belief and respect shared by all Chinese scholars. Two years later, on the seminar of the publication of *Selected Works of Wang Chuanlun on Economics* and *Magnate Scholar Wang Chuanlun, an Academic Star*, Huang Da made comments on his bosom friend that "he is really knowledgeable with real knowledge! "

Li Yang, a student of Professor Wang Chuanlun, said in the preface of *Selected Works of Wang Chuanlun on Economics*: "Professor Wang Chuanlun, with his profound knowledge and intelligent vision, merged culture in the West and East in an innovative way. Engaged in both of the financial and fiscal fields, he was regarded as one of the acknowledged master in the economic theory circle in China. " This represented universal praise given by the academia to Professor Wang Chuanlun.

“藕断丝连”
"Unseverable Links"

1960 年以后的几年，尽管属于中国知识界的天空偶有“晴日”，但整体上来讲，一直是在“风雨不断”的大环境中勉强度日。

此时，一场让所有人意想不到的更为猛烈的暴风雨正向他们袭来！

1966 年，记载着无数人的辛酸与苦痛的运动——“文化大革命”，不期而至。幸福与欢乐在刹那间凝固，青春年华被永远封存于那个黑白颠倒的时代。

“文化大革命”期间，中国人民大学的遭遇可谓“惨痛”——停办！大批干部、教师遭到批斗，各级党政组织陷于瘫痪。1970 年 10 月，北京市革命委员会正式通知中国人民大学停办，全部教学、科研工作随之停止。幸运的是，时任党委书记兼副校长郭影秋高瞻远瞩地提出了按建制把人大的师资集中整编到几所大学去的办法，为日后迅速恢复中国人民大学奠定了坚实基础。

按照当时的安排，哲学系被安排到北大，政治经济学系被安排到北师大，财经各专业人员被安排到北京经济学院。在经济学院，以原中国人民大学财政金融两个专业的教员为骨干成立了一个经济研究所，担任该所所长兼党支部书记的是陈共——与黄达同一时代的又一位学界大家。

陈共，与黄达同年开始在财政金融系任教，同样淡泊名利、专心治学，日后同样为新中国经济学科的发展做出开拓性贡献。唯一不同之处在于，陈共精于财政，是新中国财政学科的主要奠基人之一。

黄达、陈共加上王传纶、周升业，日后被大家亲切地称为“财金四老”。伴随着新中国成长的步伐，“四老”携手并肩，“叱咤风云”半个多世纪，开创了中国财政金融学科的大局面！

但是，与那个时代的国家、学校一样，此时“四老”的遭遇同样“惨痛”。即使如此，日后，黄达却用一种更为辩证的态度去审视自己当年的得与失。

“失，好像还可以量化；得，却是无影无形而又无时不在。”

十年间，黄达经历了作为“走资派”被批斗、蜗居斗室审查历史、长期被排除在“革命群众”的队伍之外的痛苦经历，吃了不少苦头。失去自由和尊严的他却得到了一

During the several years after 1960, broadly speaking, the Chinese academia struggled in turbulence despite the occasional peace.

A more violent storm burst towards them!

In 1966, the Cultural Revolution came unexpectedly, bearing countless people's bitterness and pain. All of a sudden, happiness and joy suspended. The youth time was sealed forever in the era of confusion.

During the Cultural Revolution (1966—1976), the suffering of the Renmin University of China was "terrible ", as it was closed down! Many officials and teachers were criticized and denounced. The Party and administrative organizations at all levels were paralyzed. In October 1970, the Revolutionary Committee of Beijing made an official announcement on the closing of the Renmin University of China, which was followed by the suspension of all teaching and scientific research. Fortunately, Guo Yingqiu, secretary of the Party Committee and vice president, with a broad and long view, proposed the method of integrating the faculties into other universities according to the organizational system, which laid a solid foundation for the future recovery of the Renmin University of China in a rapid way.

According to the arrangement, the Department of Philosophy, the Department of Political Economy and faculties in finance and economics were transferred to Peking University, Beijing Normal University and Beijing School of Economics respectively. In Beijing School of Economics, the institute of economy was set up mainly by faculties in the fiscal and financial majors from the original Renmin University of China. Chen Gong served as the director and secretary of the Party branch. He was another important figure in the same era with Huang Da.

Chen Gong embarked on teaching in the Department of Finance in the same year with Huang Da. He is also indifferent to fame and wealth, but concentrates his attention on his scholarly research. He is another innovative contributor to the development of China's economy. The only difference is that Chen Gong excels in fiscal affairs and is one of the major founders of fiscal subject in China.

Huang Da, Chen Gong, Wang Chuanlun and Zhou Shengye were regarded as the "four founding fathers of fiscal and financial subjects " afterwards. Along with the pace of development in China, the four founding fathers worked hand in hand to ride the whirlwind for more than half a century and opened up new prospects of the fiscal and financial subject in China!

But even so, the four founding fathers suffered as miserably as the country and universities in that era. But, later, Huang Da reviewed his gains and losses in a dialectic way.

"The losses could be measured, but the gains are always inherent. "

In the decade, Huang Da was criticized and denounced as a "capitalist-roader ", and was forced to review his history in captivity. For a long time, he was

样珍贵的东西——内心的宁静。

“夫君子之行，静以修身，俭以养德，非淡泊无以明志，非宁静无以致远。夫学须静也，才须学也。非学无以广才，非志无以成学。”诸葛亮诠释的是“静”之于治学、之于修身的理论内涵，而黄达践行的是“静”之于治学、之于修身的现实意义。

抓住一片宁静，继续前进！不能放弃继续研读金融的机会！这段时间，黄达始终保持着与货币银行学“藕断丝连”的联系，这让黄达在不知不觉间“厚积”了专业知识，为他后半生学术研究上的“薄发”又扩展了立足的基础。

先把时间定格在“文化大革命”初年。此时的黄达已经失去行动的自由。他把成稿于 1964 年的《如何看待价格》一文带在身上，终日推敲打磨。该文表述了一个非常简单的思想：“价格是生产关系的体现。进一步的推论是：价格合理与否的尺度并不在于它是否符合价值，而在于它是否能满足生产关系对价值通过价格再分配的客观要求。”这段时间成为黄达思考价格问题的起点，为他日后研究通货膨胀，并将价格研究纳入货币银行学的框架埋下伏笔。

1969 年，为响应党中央上山下乡、接受贫下中农再教育的号召，中国人民大学师生先后分 8 批共 2 600 人来到江西的“五七干校”。黄达也随队而去，一去就是三年。

1972 年初，随着“干校”的撤销，黄达终于回到北京。所谓“吃一堑长一智”，为了继续进行学术研究而又不再犯政治禁忌，此时黄达非常“讨巧”地找到了一个研究题目——工农产品价格剪刀差。之后的一年多时间里，他跑图书馆、收集资料、查阅文献，先后编了 24 个表，画了 18 张比价图。以这些图表的总说明为基础，黄达整理的《旧中国工农产品价格剪刀差》一文，被收录进《农产品成本与价格论文集》（中国社会科学出版社，1983）。随后，根据原稿补充修订而成的《工农产品比价剪刀差》一书，于 1990 年由中国社会科学出版社出版发行。至此，黄达在“文化大革命”期间少有的学术成果终于面世。

转眼间到了 1974 年。这是个“文化大革命”期间非常特别的年份——“四人帮”

excluded from the revolutionary masses and suffered a lot. But at the expense of losing freedom and dignity, he gained something precious. It was peace, the inner peace from the bottom of his heart.

"As a man of moral integrity, he keeps meditating to improve himself, and lives a frugal life to cultivate his moral characters. Without simplicity, he couldn't reveal aspirations, and without tranquility, he couldn't attain farness. Learning needs a tranquil environment and talents must be accumulated through learning. Without hardworking, it is incapable to develop the competence. Without a steadfast will, the academic success will not be achieved. " This is what Zhuge Liang interpreted on the theoretical connotation of "tranquility " in respect of making scholarly research and cultivating moral character. What Huang Da practiced was the practical meaning of "tranquility" as to do scholarly research and cultivate moral character.

Grasp the tranquility to move on! Don't give up any chance to do more research on finance! In that period, Huang Da maintained the unseverable ties with money and banking. This made him accumulate a lot of professional knowledge unconsciously, and extended the foundation for him to advance his academic research in the rest of his life.

It was in the early stage of the Cultural Revolution that Huang Da lost his freedom. He took with him the How to Treat the Price, which was completed in 1964, to make further revision all day long. The paper expounded a simple idea: "Price is the reflection of relation of production. The further corollary is: The rationality of price depends on whether it is able to meet the objective requirements of value redistribution via price by the relation of production, rather than whether it accords with the value." This became the starting point for Huang Da to think about the price and set the stage for his research on inflation and incorporating price into the framework of money and banking in the future.

In 1969, to answer the call to settle in rural areas to be re-educated by the poor and lower-middle farmers, 2,600 faculties and students in the Renmin University of China went to the "May 7th Cadre School " successively in eight batches. Huang Da was one of them, and stayed there for three years.

In early 1972, after the "Cadre School " was cancelled, Huang Da finally returned to Beijing. In order to make further academic research without offending the political taboo, he learnt from his experience and tactically chose a research topic, namely the price scissors of industry and agriculture. For more than one year afterwards, he hanged around the library to collect materials and documents, and worked out 24 tables and 18 price charts. Based on the general specification of these tables and charts, Huang Da wrote the Scissors Difference between Prices of Industrial and Agricultural Products in Old China, which was included in *Collected Papers on the Costs and Prices of Farm Produces* (published by China Social Sciences Press

的倒行逆施到了白热化的程度。年初，一场由“四人帮”推动的政治闹剧“批林批孔、评法批儒”席卷全国。尚处于被审查状态的黄达被指派到“评法批儒”小组工作。尽管时间不长这场运动便烟消云散，但由此带来的读古书风潮并没有随之结束。

绵延五千年的中国文化源远流长，不仅有指南针、火药、造纸、印刷、丝绸、瓷器等享誉世界的先进技术和工艺，还有璀璨夺目的诗词歌赋、戏曲文艺，以及震烁古今的治国方略与经济哲学。然而，很长一段时间以来，中国知识界却言必称西方。“评法批儒”阴差阳错地给大家提供了一个了解自己老祖宗的机会。

借此阅读中国古文典籍，参悟中国传统文化——黄达牢牢抓住了这个难得的机会！

运动伊始，黄达便一头扎进纷繁浩瀚的古文典籍当中，反复欣赏、鉴读，充分汲取先辈们留下来的精神养分，直到“文化大革命”结束。《商君书》《管子》《盐铁论》《史记》等等，思维严密、文字华美、结构清晰、内涵丰富，特别是有关财经问题的经典论述，让他乐在其中，如痴如醉。

古文典籍，加上马克思主义的经典原著，加上虽然困难但也总能接触到的西方经济思想，再加上中国实际，多味酿制知识之“美酒”所不可或缺的原料，经过1950—1976年近三十年的积淀，黄达终于揽之于怀。剩下的工作就是把它们同时装进“发酵缸”，经过若干道工序，最终酿出历久弥香的“美酒”。

不久后，黄达品尝到了自己用土法酿制的“美酒”。当然，有此口福的远不止黄达本人。

这种独特的“酿造”工艺就是黄达从事经济金融基础理论研究所秉承的思维框架和研究方法。三十一年后，《黄达书集》出版之际，黄达对此进行了一个更为精准的概括——“古今中外、含英咀华”。

in 1983). Subsequently, *Scissors Difference between Prices of Industrial and Agricultural Products,* which was revised and supplemented on the basis of the original version, was published by China Social Sciences Press in 1990. Thus far, the few academic achievements made by Huang Da during the cultural revolution finally made their debut.

In the twinkling of an eye, the perverse acts of the "Gang of Four " reached a fever pitch in 1974, a special year in the cultural revolution.At the beginning of the year, the country was wept over by "Criticizing Lin Biao and Confucius, Legalists and Confucianists " driven by the "Gang of Four ". Huang Da, still being examined, was assigned to work in the "Criticizing Legalists and Confucianists " group. Although the movement didn't last long, its influence on reading ancient books didn't end with it.

The time-honored Chinese culture lasted for 5,000 years. It brought world-renowned advanced techniques including compass, gunpowder, papermaking, printing, silk, porcelain, brilliant poetry and opera, and unprecedented statecraft and economic philosophy. However, for a long time, China's intelligentsia put the only eye to the West.

The movement of "Criticizing Legalists and Confucianists ", by accident, provided a chance for people to know more about the Chinese ancestors.

Reading ancient classics and appreciating traditional culture—Huang Da grasped this rare opportunity for him!

At the beginning of the movement, Huang Da concentrated his attention on the countless ancient classics. He kept repeatedly reading them to fully absorb the spiritual nutrients handed down by ancestors until the end of the Cultural Revolution. Huang Da found pleasure and was absorbed in the Book of *Lord Shang, Guan Zi, Discourses on Salt and Iron, Historical Records,* etc., especially those classics on finance, owing to their rigorous thinking, beautiful expression, clear structure and abundant connotation.

The Chinese classics, classics on Marxism, the western economic thoughts that were hard but able to acquire, and the reality in China were combined to become the indispensable raw materials for making the "wine " of knowledge. Over nearly 30 years of accumulation from 1950 to 1976, Huang Da finally held them all in mind. The rest of his job was to add them in the "fermenter" simultaneously, and brewed the "fine wine" that got better with age.

Before long, Huang Da tasted the "wine " made in his native way. Of course, he was not the only man to enjoy it.

This unique way of "brewing " referred to the thinking frame and methodology that Huang Da followed in the research on the basic economic and financial theories. Thirty-one years later, when the *Selected Books of Huang Da* made its debut, he gave a more precise conclusion that "it was to relish the joys of literature at home and abroad at all times. "

3-1

红楼里的青年教师们
Young Teachers in the Red Buildings

20世纪60年代初，中国人民大学财政贸易系包括财政教研室、金融教研室（那时的正式名称是货币流通与信用教研室，习惯简称货币教研室）和会计教研室，分别对应三个专业。

当时，西郊校区的红楼是严格意义的单身教师宿舍，学校大部分教师住在这里。副教授以上，一人一间；其他教师，两人一间。由于交通条件极为不便，除了单身教师争取住进红楼，成家的（或在城内有学校分配的房舍，或在城内有自己的住处）也多力争在红楼有一个床位，到星期六再回家与家人团聚，叫“过礼拜六”。红楼的环境非常安静，吃饭有食堂，又可避开家事拖累，教师们从上午到晚上都能安心读书、备课。上午十时有课间操，教师们会出来做操、散步，同时还可以彼此交换学术见解。晚饭前有段时间到操场运动或自由交流。值得一提的是，在中国人民大学财政贸易系学术发展历程中具有“经典”意义的论文《信贷收支差额问题》，就是同住一间宿舍的周升业和侯梦蟾在此期间写出的。当时国务院第五办公室的研究人员在《光明日报》看到这篇文章，极为赞赏，并主动与财政系建立了经常性的联系。

从1956年到“文化大革命”前两年的这段时间，黄达的日常生活就是如此度过的。

In the early 1960s, the Department of Public Finance and Trade of the Renmin University of China was made up of the Finance Teaching and Research Group, the Banking Teaching and Research Group (officially known as Teaching and Research Group of Currency Circulation and Credit , and habitually shortened as Currency Teaching and Research Group then) and the Accounting Teaching and Research Group, each for a major.

At the time, the red buildings on the campus in the western suburbs were dormitories for single teachers in a strict sense, and accommodated most teachers of the university. Associate professors and above each had a dorm room; every two of the rest teachers had to share a dorm room. Due to the extremely inconvenient traffic, not only single teachers each strove for a dorm room in the red buildings, but married teachers (either having rooms allocated by the university or having residences in the town) also did so, and went back to the town to get together with their families on Saturdays. Life in the red buildings was quiet. There was the dining hall, and no household chores, so teachers could sit down to read and prepare for classes from the morning to the evening. At 10 o'clock in the morning every day, there were setting-up exercises, and teachers would go out and do the exercises or go for a walk while exchanging scholarly opinions. Before dinner, they had some time to go to the playground, exercising or exchanging ideas freely. It is worth mentioning that On the Balance of Receipts and Payments of Credit Funds, a paper that was "classic" in the academic development of the Department of Public Finance and Trade of the Renmin University of China, was written by Zhou Shengye and Hou Mengchan who shared a dorm room in this period. Researchers in the fifth office of the National State Council of China spoke highly of the paper when reading it on *Guangming Daily,* and willingly maintained constant contacts with the Department of Public Finance since then.

Huang Da lived such a life in the period from 1956 to two years before the Cultural Revolution.

38

上页图

图38为1958年，黄达（右二）与财政、金融、会计专业的几位教师一起观察他们的收获——苤蓝。

当年的“大跃进”时期，异想天开的事儿极多，其中有一项是号召教师在校园内种菜，以实现自给自足。财政信用借贷系教师在红二楼与红三楼之间也“开垦”了一小片地，黄达因曾经种过蔬菜而被指定为“技术指导”。

In 1958, Huang Da (second from the right) and several teachers from the majors of Finance, Banking and Accounting were observing their vegetable—turnip cabbage.

During the Great Leap Forward movement, there were speculations, one of which was calling the teachers to plant vegetables on the campus for self sufficiency. Teachers of the Department of Public Finance and Credit Loan "reclaimed" some land between No. 2 Red Building and No. 3 Red Building. Huang Da was appointed as the "technical advisor" for his experience of planting vegetables.

39

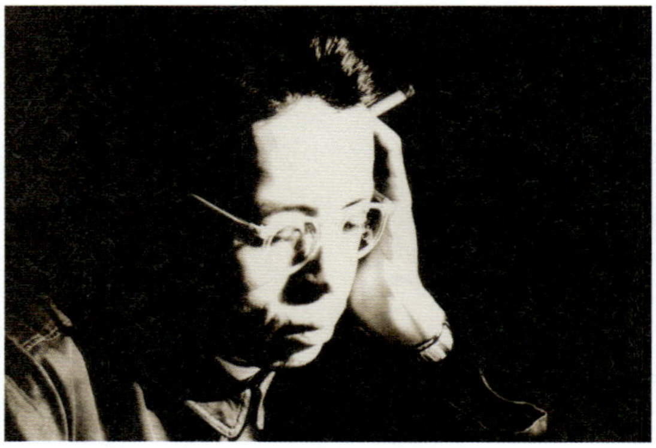

40

图39为1957年，黄达在红二楼宿舍读书。

Huang Da was reading in his dorm room in No. 2 Red Building in 1957.

图40为20世纪60年代初，黄达在红二楼宿舍写作。

Huang Da was writing in his dorm room in No. 2 Red Building in the early 1960s.

41

图 41 为 1961 年夏，黄达（后排左一）与中国人民大学财政教研室、货币教研室的同事在一起。

当时，尽管正处于国家经济“三年困难”时期，政治氛围却相对比较宽松，大家的心情也颇为舒畅。正是在这样的环境下，财政教研室与货币教研室聚在一起，难得地组织了这次郊游。

In the summer of 1961, Huang Da (the first from the left in the last row) was with his colleagues in the Public Finance Teaching and Research Group and the Currency Teaching and Research Group of the Renmin University of China.

Although it was during the three years of economic difficulty for China, China's political atmosphere was relaxing and people were cheerful. It is against such a background that teachers of the Public Finance Teaching and Research Group and the Currency Teaching and Research Group got together for the picnic.

图42和图43为1962年4月1日，黄达写在《现代名目论货币学说及其先驱者》一书扉页上的即兴打油诗。

新中国成立初期，公开发行的各类著作很少，真正有学术价值的金融专业著作则更少。20世纪50年代中期，黄达难得买到一本由苏联老一代（跨沙俄和苏联两个时期）学者爱杰利南特（А.Б.Эйдельнант）所著的《现代名目论货币学说及其先驱者》。该书的外文原版于1948年在莫斯科出版，中译本由生活·读书·新知三联书店于1954年出版（申谷译、孙亚明校）。

好书来之不易，黄达对此倍加珍爱。然而书不久后被人借走，一直未还。他也想不起被何人借走，原本想再补购一本，却由于书店早已售罄而作罢。直到1962年，刚刚经过1958年“大跃进”和1959年“反右倾”运动，当时社会的政治气氛难得宽松。不少出版社清理库存，有些书籍又在新华书店销售，有些则流入旧书摊。在偶然的一个周末，黄达在逛旧书摊的时候发现了这本书。这令他欣喜万分。

在回家的路上，黄达回忆起与这本书的因缘，不禁“诌出”一首打油诗，并写在该书的扉页上。“此书本来有，何时来借走？黄鹤渺无踪，用时空抖手。遍寻旧书肆，处处皆言否；希望已绝矣，不必再强求。那想今日中，老天降福佑；土埋尘封下，饿狗见骨头。雀跃回家转，来它三杯酒！所好不一样，没笑书痴丑。”

在黄达看来，这首诗本身确属“打油”级别，难登大雅之堂，但能够真实记录一个教书先生在那样岁月里的心境，也还是有点意思的。

This is the nonsense verse Huang Da wrote on April 1, 1962 on the fly-leaf of the book *Modern Nominal Money Theories and Their Precursors*.

At the beginning of new China, books of various types that were publicly published were rare, let alone finance books truly having a scholarly value. In the mid 1950s, Huang Da luckily bought a book *Modern Nominal Money Theories and Their Precursors* by А.Б.Эйдельнант, one of the old-generation Soviet scholars, who survived the Tsarist Russia period and the Soviet Union period. The original of the book was published in Moscow in 1948, and its Chinese translation (translated by Shen Gu and proofread by Sun Yaming) was published by SDX Joint Publishing Company in 1954.

Since it was hard to buy the book, Huang Da cherished it very much. However, someone borrowed the book shortly after Huang Da bought it, and did not return it. Huang Da could not remember who borrowed the book, so he planned to buy another one, only to give up the idea because the store had sold it out. It was not until 1962 when the political atmosphere became relaxing again after the Great Leap Forward Movement in 1958 and the Anti-rightists Movement in 1959, and many publishing houses began to clear up their inventory and some books were sold in Xinhua Bookstore and some were sold at secondhand book stalls that Huang Da occasionally discovered the book when patronizing secondhand book stalls in a weekend. He was thrilled.

Recalling his story with the book on his way back, Huang Da wrote a nonsense verse on the fly-leaf of the book. "I had this book, but forgot who borrowed it away. When I needed it, I could not find it. I visited all the secondhand bookstores, only to be told that they did not have the book. I was desperate, and stopped pushing myself. It is so surprising that the book suddenly appears today. It to me is like a bone to a hungry dog. I jump with excitement, and drink for my good luck! Ah, do not laugh at me for my loving book."

To Huang Da, it is a nonsense verse, and too rude to be printed, but it truthfully records his mind as a teacher in those years, and is interesting.

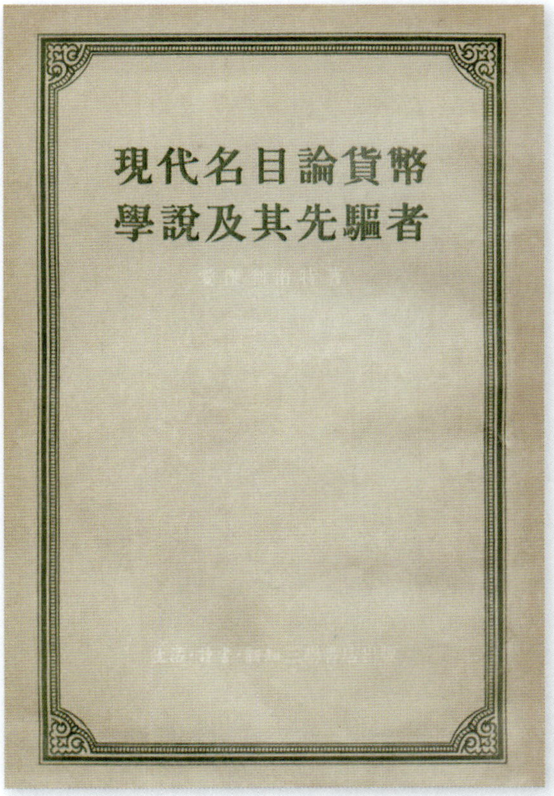

42

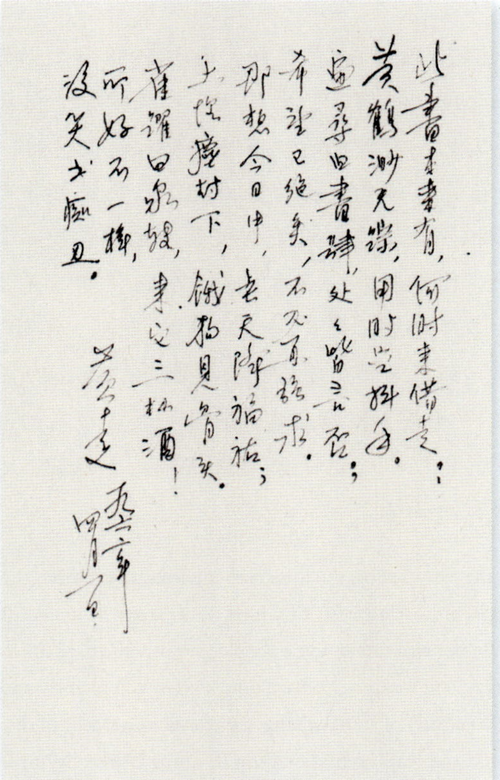

此书本来有，何时来借走：
黄鹤渺无踪，用时只搔首。
遍寻旧书肆，处处皆言否；
希望已绝矣，不必再强求。
那想今日中，老天降福祐；
大槐树下，饿狗见骨头。
蒐罗旧纸堆，专定三杯酒！
所好不一样，设笑太痴丑。

黄达 五六年四月 日

43

3-2

60年代的中国人民大学
Renmin University of China in the 1960s

在20世纪60年代初，由于1958年之后不止一次的政治运动，中国人民大学校领导之间，校领导、中层领导和教学骨干相互之间处于极不协调的状态。在运动里，有整人的，有被整的，有既曾整人也被整的，心存怨气，难以坐在一起讨论工作。

在吴玉章老校长的努力之下，上级领导部门调整了学校的领导班子，调来了郭影秋担任校党委书记兼副校长，主持学校工作。郭影秋到任之后，一是贯彻上级领导的“团结起来向前看”的方针，使学校走上可以正常工作的轨道；二是针对校园建设多年举棋不定、停步不前的状态，明确以西郊校区为主，并在教学一楼之后陆续建起新教学楼（现在的公共教学二楼，1964年建成）、新图书馆（现在的藏书馆，1966年建成）和后来建成的资料楼（现在的人文楼，1986年建成），形成了中心教学区的框架——这是今天依然矗立的框架，也是我们今天能够形象地触摸到的郭影秋校长的业绩。

In the early 1960s, the leaders themselves, the leaders, the middle-level leadership and the backbone teachers of the Renmin University of China were extremely uncoordinated due to the repeated political movement after 1958. In the movement, some people gave others a hard time, some were given a hard time, also some gave others a hard time and were given a hard time, so they complained, and couldn't sit down to discuss about work.

With efforts of Wu Yuzhang, the former president of the Renmin University of China, the higher leadership adjusted the leading body of the Renmin University of China, and assigned Guo Yingqiu to serve as the secretary of the Party Committee and vice president of the university to preside over school work. After Guo Yingqiu took office, he thoroughly implemented the guiding principle of "uniting as one and looking to the future " to bring the university back to normal operation; and given the situation of hesitating school building which ceased to move forward, clarified that the campus of the Renmin University of China in the western suburbs would be the focus, and built a new teaching building (No. 2 Public Teaching Building now, built in 1964), a new library (the book collection library now, built in 1966) and a reference building (Humanities Building now, built in 1986), establishing the framework of the central teaching area. It is still the framework, and the achievements of President Guo Yingqiu that people can vividly touch today as well.

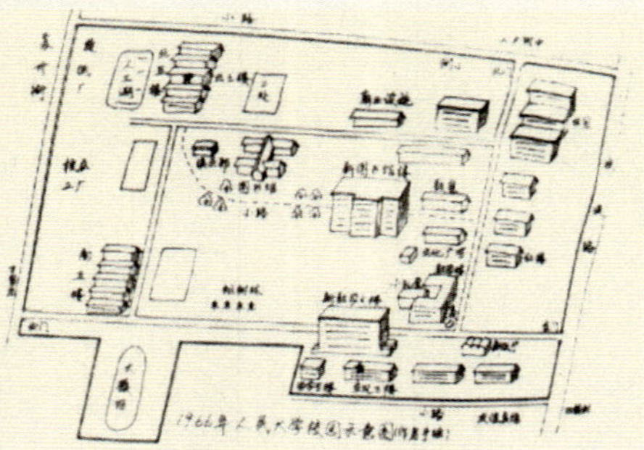

44

图44为1966年中国人民大学校园某手绘地图。

This is a hand-depicted map of the campus of the Renmin University of China in 1966.

45

46

图 45 为今天位于中国人民大学品园五楼北侧的吴玉章老校长塑像。

This is a sculpture of former President Wu Yuzhang, which is standing on the campus of the Renmin University of China.

图 46 为今天位于中国人民大学国学馆前的郭影秋老校长塑像。

This is a sculpture of former President Guo Yingqiu, which is standing on the campus of the Renmin University of China.

47

图47为1965年，黄达参加中国人民大学第十六届学校运动会，最终获得男子教工组一千六百米比赛第一名。

从20世纪50年代中期开始，黄达就开始跑步锻炼，一直坚持到1985年。

In 1965, Huang Da took part in the 16th sports meeting of the Renmin University of China, and won the first place in men teachers' 1,600m.

Since the mid 1950s, Huang Da had been doing body exercises by running. He was doing so till 1985.

| 右页图 ⟼

图48为1965年，吴玉章校长到场为参加中国人民大学第十六届学校运动会的运动员颁奖。前排左一为黄达，后排左二为吴玉章。

本次活动由郭影秋校长推动召开，属当年活跃校园生活的重要举措之一。

In 1965, President Wu Yuzhang appeared to present awards to the athletes of the 16th sports meeting of the Renmin University of China. The first from the left in the front row is Huang Da, and the second from the left in the back row is Wu Yuzhang.

It was held thanks to the efforts of President Guo Yingqiu, and was one of the most important events to activate the then campus life.

48

3-3

第一部专著——《我国社会主义经济中的货币和货币流通》
The First Monograph: *Money and Currency Circulation in China's Socialist Economy*

1960年底之后的两三年，中国经济学界曾获得可以对经济理论进行冷静反思的机会。期间，黄达和他的同事没有急于重新开始编写教材，而是想在这样的氛围中从理论上进行反思，以期为下一步教材建设打下基础。

经过几年的努力，黄达于1964年出版了自己的第一部个人专著——《我国社会主义经济中的货币和货币流通》。本书的核心内容有四部分：一是关于社会主义经济中货币为什么不能取消的论述；二是关于货币职能，也就是对《货币信用学(上册)》有关货币职能讲述的再整理；三是对1957年撰写的《人民币是具有内在价值的货币商品的符号》一文的整理；四是对1962年撰写的曾引起同行争议的《银行信贷原则和货币流通》一文的整理。

在黄达看来，尽管以今天的眼光，该书并没有多少可以称道的地方，不过就当时而言，一方面，1958年的"大跃进"以其反面教训促使他大大加深了对经济规律的理解。在当时社会、政治大背景的约束还是限制着思想认识进展的大背景下，他已经多少有了自己观察、剖析经济金融问题的独立视角。另一方面，该书记录了当时中国金融学界的现实状况，为我们今天了解历史提供了一些有用信息。

In the two or three years after the end of 1960, China's economists had a chance to calmly reflect on economic theories. During the period, Huang Da and his colleagues, instead of rewriting textbooks, intended to reflect on economic theories in the hope of building a foundation for the editing of teaching materials later.

With years of efforts, Huang Da published his first monograph—*Money and Currency Circulation in China's Socialist Economy*—in 1964. The core contents of the book are made up of four parts: opinions on why currency can't be cancelled in the socialist economy; re-collation of money functions, that is, re-collation of the narration on money functions in *Money and Credit* (vol.1); collation of paper Renminbi is the Sign of Money Commodities with Intrinsic Value that Huang Da wrote in 1957; and collation of paper Principles of Bank Credit and Currency Circulation, which caused disputes and was written by Huang Da in 1962.

To Huang Da, the book is nothing special today, but it shows that the Great Leap Forward movement in 1958 and its lessons had rendered Huang Da to deepen his understanding of the economic rules, and Huang Da had developed unique angles to observe and analyze economic and financial problems against the background that the then social and political backdrop still held back the development of ideology; and it records the real situation of China' s finance section back then and provides some useful information for people to understand history.

49

图 49 为 1964 年，黄达的第一部个人专著——《我国社会主义经济中的货币和货币流通》（中国财政经济出版社，1964 年）。

This is *Money and Currency Circulation in China's Socialist Economy,* the first monograph of Huang Da (China Financial and Economic Publishing House, 1964)

3-4

第一部译著——《第二次世界大战后资本主义体系中的黄金》

The First Translation: *Gold in the Capitalist System after WWII*

20世纪60年代初期，黄达与留苏归国的刘鸿儒等共同翻译了苏联学者弗·伊·米哈列夫斯基的著作《第二次世界大战后资本主义体系中的黄金》（中国财政经济出版社，1965年），而后又在王传纶等同事的帮助下，陆续翻译了英格兰银行的《资金流量核算入门（1952—1970年）》（中国人民大学财政系1981年油印；黄达译，王传纶校）、莱威·钱得勒（L. V. Chandler）和斯姆·哥尔特菲尔特（S. M. Goldfeld）的《货币银行学》（中国财政经济出版社，1981年；中国人民大学财政教研室与金融教研室译，黄达译第16、17章，王传纶总校订）、弗兰科·莫迪利亚尼（Franco Modigliani）和托马索·帕多阿-斯基奥帕（Tommaso Padoa-Schioppa）的《对于工资"加100%"指数化的开放经济的管理》（中国人民大学财政教研室与金融教研室1982年油印；黄达译，王传纶校）以及"三十国集团"的《欧洲市场的信用创造：可供选择的理论和控制的含义》（中国人民大学财政金融系1982/1983学年或稍晚一些油印；黄达译，王翔飞校）等教材或著作。

《第二次世界大战后资本主义体系中的黄金》是黄达的第一部译著。当年，中国人民大学的图书馆里有这本书的俄文版，但具体是如何发现的，黄达自己也回想不起来了。大概在1961年，黄达发现此书后开始翻译第二章——价值尺度的职能与黄金表示的价格。最初，他只想翻译个别章节，但翻译中觉得内容颇有见地，遂有翻译全书的打算。后来财政贸易系资料室资料员彭再勤和货币教研室教师林与权也加入翻译队伍。但他们三个人都是在20世纪50年代初期的某个暑假，通过"俄文速成"打下的俄文功底，能否完成全书翻译，并无把握。就在这个时候，刘鸿儒留苏归国。据他介绍，该书作者是苏联老一辈学者，很有学问，很受人敬仰。他非常赞同把全书翻译出来并愿意参与翻译——他与他的夫人翻译了近40%的篇幅。

译文由黄达负责统校和定稿。一方面要统一译文风格，解决各位译者留下来的难题，并为中国读者补充一些注释。另一方面，黄达还给自己加了一个任务——把原书里截至1950年、1951年的数字补充到1962年、1963年。这涉及几十种外文期刊，有的要到当时对外贸易部资料室查阅。其中有一份南非的统计期刊，是最后在中国银行研究所书库里找到的。研究所的同志交给黄达一把钥匙，告知书库的位置，以及在书库的哪一个角落有可能找到。非常幸运的是，在书架上、桌子上、地板上堆满着的尘封已久的和刚刚堆进来的书刊之中，黄达找到了要找的刊物……

In the early 1960s, Huang Da and Liu Hongru et al. (Liu returned from the Soviet Union after furthering his education there) translated *Gold in the Capitalist System after WWII* (China Financial and Economic Publishing House, 1965) by Soviet scholar V. I. Mikhalevski. Later with the help of Wang Chuanlun and his other colleagues, they translated *Introduction to Flow of Funds Accounts* (*1952—1970*)of the Bank of England (mimeographed by the Department of Public Finance of the Renmin University of China in 1981, translated by Huang Da, proofread by Wang Chuanlun), *The Economics of Money and Banking* by L. V. Chandler and S. M. Goldfeld (published by China Financial and Economic Publishing House in 1981, translated by the Finance Teaching and Research Group and the Banking Teaching and Research Group of the Renmin University of China; translation of chapters 16 and 17 by Huang Da, proofread by Wang Chuanlun, *The Management of An Open Economy With "100% Plus" Wage Indexation* by Franco Modigliani and Tommaso Padoa-Schioppa (mimeographed by the Finance Teaching and Research Group and the Banking Teaching and Research Group of the Renmin University of China in 1982, translated by Huang Da, proofread by Wang Chuanlun), and *Credit Creation in the European Market: Theories to Be Chosen and Meaning of Control* of Group 30(mimeographed by the Department of Finance of the Renmin University of China in 1982 or 1983 or slightly later, translated by Huang Da, proofread by Wang Xiangfei), among other textbooks or books.

Gold in the Capitalist System after WWII is the first translation of Huang Da. In those years, the Renmin University of China had the Russian version of the book, but Huang Da can't recall how he discovered it. It probably happened in 1961 when Huang Da began to translate the second chapter of the book Functions of the Measure of Value and Prices Shown in Gold. He planned to translate only several chapters, but found the book to be full of insights during translation, so he changed his mind and planned to translate the whole book. Later, Peng Zaiqin, a reference clerk in the reference room of the Department of Public Finance and Trade, and Lin Yuquan, a teacher of the Currency teaching and research group, joined him. However, their Russian was "quickly learned " in some summer vacation in the early 1950s, so they were not sure if they could truly complete the translation of the whole book. Then Liu Hongru returned from the Soviet Union after furthering his studies there. According to him, the author of the book was a senior scholar in the Soviet Union, very learned and much respected, so Liu agreed to translate the whole book and join the translation team. Liu and his wife translated nearly 40% of the book.

Huang Da was responsible for proofreading and finalizing the translation. On the one hand, he had to unify the translation style, solve the problems left behind by the translators, and add some annotations for the Chinese readers. On the other hand, he gave himself another task—to add figures of 1962 and 1963 after those that ended up in 1950 and 1951. It would involve dozens of foreign journals, some of which had to be checked in the reference room of the Foreign Trade Ministry (now known as the Ministry of Foreign Economic Relations and Trade).Some South Africa statistical journal was finally found in the library of the Institute of the Bank of China. Staff of the institute gave Huang Da a key, and told the location of the library and possible corners to find the journal. Luckily, amidst the books and journals on the shelves, the tables or the floor, either covered with dusts or just put in, he found the one he wanted...

图 50 为黄达、刘鸿儒等翻译的苏联学者弗·伊·米哈列夫斯基的著作《第二次世界大战后资本主义体系中的黄金》（中国财政经济出版社，1965）。

This is *Gold in the Capitalist System after WWII* by Soviet scholar V. I. Mikhalevski and translated by Huang Da, Liu Hongru, et al. (China Financial and Economic Publishing House, 1965).

50

3-5

“五七干校”的非“革命群众”

The Non-revolutionary Masses of "May 7th Cadre School "

1969 年 11 月，中国人民大学的大部分教职工以及部分家属奔赴江西余江县，建立“五七干校”。黄达那时还没有取得“革命群众”的身份（这种非“革命群众”的身份直到“文化大革命”结束为止），而且没有资格进入第一批下干校的队伍。直到次年，黄达才被“批准”下干校。

“五七干校”分几个连，第四连由原部门经济学各系组成。其中第一班是种菜的，负责全连的蔬菜供给，简称“菜班”。黄达被分配在这个班，一直到 1972 年底“五七干校”结束回到北京。在这个班里，黄达属壮劳力，常常挑粪桶，给蔬菜施肥。

在干校期间，黄达曾两上井冈山。第一次是在 1971 年初农历春节的假期。当时，四连有几位同志自己组织上井冈山，领头的是连长，但不属于连里的活动。黄达有幸被允许同去。他们先到南昌参观了当年新建的“万岁馆”（现在好像变成了一个大商场）。令大家惊诧的是，最主要的大幅油画，竟然把人所共知的朱德、毛泽东井冈山会师改成毛泽东、林彪会师。第二天早上，他们从南昌乘长途汽车赴井冈山，傍晚到茨坪，在招待所吃的是红米饭南瓜汤。第二天上午在茨坪参观了几个主要革命景点。回去的路上，由于长途汽车不知什么原因没有来，除了几位坚持要等车的，黄达等几人决定步行从茨坪经黄洋界下山。启程不久，开始下雪，越下越大，走了一下午才到黄洋界。一路上没有碰到什么人。黄达因腹泻，体力受影响，被其他人落下很远，但也在傍晚坚持到了黄洋界哨所。那时的哨所还是一座孤零零的小木屋，周围没有什么建筑。由于当天是除夕，哨所只有一个人值班。值班员是大军南下的老兵，在东北老家已没有什么亲人了，就在这里成了家，生儿育女，落地生根了。他说，第二天也要下山回家。哨所里只有点白面，他给黄达他们煮了一大锅面糊糊，里面撕了几根小葱，热乎乎的大家喝得很香。“风雪黄洋界”的场景，黄达至今仍记忆犹新。第二天，雪停了，他们早早起身下山。走到中午，碰见先前等车的几位。他们是这天早上等上了车，赶上了步行的。于是一起乘车，当晚赶到湘潭。次日参观了毛主席故居和展览馆，然后回干校。

在茨坪参观后，连长曾召集座谈会，有几位发言泛泛地讲收获很大，但大多建议回干校再好好座谈。据黄达回忆，回干校后没有人再提座谈的事。但是在那次短短的座谈会上，令他记忆深刻的是，有一个人说革命景点的介绍突出林副统帅不够，而会下好几个人嘟囔：历史都篡改了，还不够！

第二次上井冈山是四连组织的全连“政治学习”活动。第一站是参观学习“三湾改编”，然后沿秋收起义队伍上山的路线逐次参观上山过程的重要革命史迹；到

In November 1969, most of the faculty and some of their families went to Yujiang County, Jiangxi to establish a "May 7th Cadre School". Huang Da was not yet identified as one of "the revolutionary masses" then (and it continued till the end of the Cultural Revolution) and was not qualified to be a member of the team to build the "May 7th Cadre School". It was not until the following year that he "was approved" to go to "May 7th Cadre School".

The "May 7th Cadre School " had several companies. Company Four was made up of the departments of economics. Class One was designated to plant vegetables and supply vegetables to the whole company, so it was shortened as "the Vegetable Class". Huang Da was in the class and did not return to Beijing till "May 7th Cadre School " ended at the end of 1972. In this class, Huang Da was a physically strong labor, who often carried buckets of slops to fertilize the vegetables.

In "May 7th Cadre School ", Huang Da went to Jinggangshan twice. In the Spring Festival vacation in early 1971, some people from Company Four organized a trip to Jinggangshan. Although the company commander led the team, it was not an official activity. Huang Da was allowed to go with them. They first went to Nanchang and visited the newly-built "Long Live Hall " (which seems to have become a big shopping mall today). There they were surprised that the main big oil painting changed Zhu De and Mao Zedong who joined their forces at Jinggangshan into Mao Zedong and Lin Biao. In the next morning, they took a long-distance bus to Jinggangshan, got to Ciping in the evening, and had red rice and pumpkin soup. In the next morning, they visited some major revolutionary spots in Ciping. On their way back, the long-distance bus did not show up for one reason or another. Except some who insisted on waiting for the bus, Huang Da and the others decided to go down the mountains on foot. It snowed shortly after they embarked on road, and the snow became heavier and heavier. It took them a whole afternoon to reach Huangyangjie, and they did not meet an actual person on the way. Huang Da lagged behind for having diarrhea, but got to Huangyangjie outlier in the evening. It was no more than a small isolate log cabin, without any buildings around. It was New Year's Eve, and there was only one man on duty in the outlier. Being a veteran, the one on duty did not have any family in his hometown in northeastern China, and got married and raised children and settled down in Huangyangjie. He would also go down the mountain and back home the following day. There was some wheat flour, and he made a pot of porridge with shallots for Huang Da and the others. The hot porridge was good. It is unforgettable, and still fresh in the mind of Huang Da. The snow stopped the following day, and Huang Da and the others got up early to go down the mountain. Till noon, they met those who insisted on waiting for the bus. Together, they took the bus and arrived at Xiangtan, visited the former residence of Chairman Mao and the exhibition hall the following day, and went back to the "May 7th Cadre School " the next day.

After the visit to Ciping, the company commander held a meeting, at which some vaguely said that they learned a lot, but most suggested to have another seminar back in the "May 7th Cadre School". Huang Da recalled that no one mentioned the seminar anymore back in the "May 7th Cadre School", but at the short meeting, as Huang Da remembered it clearly, when someone said that the introduction to Lin Biao was not enough, several people murmured, "How could it be not enough! Even history has been falsified."

The second time Huang Da went to Jinggangshan was to attend the company's activity of "political study". It took a week or longer. Their first stop was where "Sanwan Reorganization" was carried out, and then they visited major spots of revolution along the route the Autumn Harvest Uprising team went up the mountain. In Ciping, they learned the revolutionary history of the Communist Party of China of insisting on the struggle in the Jinggangshan Mountains. Now Huang Da remembers two things clearly. The first is the beautiful sceneries around Jinggangshan—the verdant peaks and mountains, the greenery, the green bamboos, the bamboo fences, the farmhouses with white walls and black roofs, as well as the terraces with mirror-like water surface. There was not any tourist. In the quietness, people just forgot the complications and annoyances before they realized it. It is indeed a missing wonderland. The second is the memorial of revolution history in each village which was in great harmony with the surrounding farmhouses, and the guides. Each day, they listened to one or two or three guides telling the stories of battles vividly and specifically. They

茨坪后，则逐次参观坚持井冈山斗争的革命史迹。前后约有一周时间或更长一些。黄达现在还有两点颇深的回忆：一是湘赣边界井冈山周围的秀丽风光。环绕坪坝的是浓荫满山的峰峦，草木葱茏，翠竹挺拔，依山傍溪的竹篱和白墙黑屋顶的农舍，错落的梯田水面平整如镜。没有游人，沐浴于清幽宁静之中，人们不知不觉地忘却尘世的喧嚣和种种烦恼，真的是再也无福回到的仙境。二是几乎每一个小村落都有与周围农舍风格协调的革命史迹纪念馆，都有讲解员。每天要听一两次、两三次的讲解，讲解战斗的过程十分具体生动，令人感叹。星星之火创造了燎原的历史，但看不到前景的“文化大革命”却好像是创造历史者自己陷入了困扰之中。这不能不引起难以摆脱的迷茫、怅惘……

难得碰到有人带着相机，黄达他们在井冈山留下两张照片。如今，照片中人大多已作古。

51

图 51 为 1972 年，黄达（右三）在井冈山与四连一班部分成员在一起。左一至左三分别为：王文生、江昭、田新，左五为侯大乾，右一为严瑞珍。

Huang Da (third from the right) was with members of Class One, Company Four in Jinggangshan in 1972. From first to third from the left: Wang Wensheng, Jiang Zhao, Tian Xin,fifth from the left and first from the left were Hou Daqian and Yan Ruizhen respectively.

couldn't help but lament. A single spark started a fire, but the Cultural Revolution which took hope away from people seemed to be a puzzle for the history creators. Huang Da and the others felt lost and perplexed.

It was lucky that someone took a camera. Huang Da and the others were able to take two pictures in Jinggangshan. Today, most of the people in the picture have passed away.

52

图 52 为 1972 年，黄达（左三）在井冈山与四连一班部分成员在一起。左一为严瑞珍，右一和右二分别为祝卓、田新。

Huang Da (third from the left) was with members of Class One, Company Four in Jinggangshan in 1972. First from the left was Yan Ruizhen, first and second from the right were Zhu Zhuo and Tian Xin respectively.

下页图

图 53 为 1970 年左右，江西余江刘家站农场欢迎中国人民大学在该农场创办“五七干校”。

Liujiazhan Farm in Yujiang, Jiangxi welcomed the Renmin University of China to establish "May 7th Cadre School" on the farm around 1970.

热烈欢迎中国人民大学来
团结起来·争取更大的
走五七

坊创办五七干校大会

3-6

“文化大革命”期间的“力作”——《工农产品比价剪刀差》

The "Masterpiece " during the Cultural Revolution: *Scissors Difference Between Prices of Industrial and Agricultural Products*

1972年底，黄达从“五七干校”回到北京。那时，本来什么事也不干，只是天天在家买点菜，做点饭，做点木工活，或躺在床上看屋顶，倒也受不到什么批判。然而知识分子的“劣根性”对于如此悠闲却并不感到舒服。似乎不读点书，不思考点什么问题——不管是三皇五帝、南极北斗，还是分子原子等等，就如同不吃饭、不睡觉一样的难受。于是一度成为“五七战士”的教师们又都重操旧业，找个题目，做点研究。

当时，黄达既非“革命对象”，又没有资格同“革命群众”共同活动，所以只好自己找个题目研究。而这个题目似乎又需要满足若干条件：一是别犯当时“文化大革命”的忌讳；二是同自己的专业有点关系；三是有资料可找；四是单枪匹马也能搞出点结果；等等。经过筛选，黄达找到了大体符合如上条件而且自己也感兴趣的题目——剪刀差。

1958年以后，出现了一个很流行的论断：由于农副产品收购价格不断提高和农村工业品销售价格上升幅度极小，使得工农产品价格的对比迅速向有利于农民的方向转化，到1958年，从统计资料看，这种价格对比的水平已经与战前1930—1936年间的平均水平相当，所以工农产品比价剪刀差已不复存在。这个论断很显然是以1930—1936年间不存在工农产品比价剪刀差为前提的。然而，那时是否真的不存在剪刀差，这本身就需要证明。奇怪的是，提出和赞同这个论断的人似乎都没有考虑到还有做出这种证明的必要。虽然漏洞如此明显，但辗转引用，一时之间俨然成为定论。此前，人们论证半殖民地半封建的旧中国时也有一个公认的定论——帝国主义列强通过剪刀差残酷地掠夺中国。

在黄达看来，仅仅是空泛的推论似乎没有太大的说服力，所以他很想考察考察实际资料，看一看1930—1936年间到底是否存在着剪刀差。如的确不存在，这个1958年已无剪刀差的论断当然成立；如存在，这一论断就不攻自破了。通过1973年整整一年的查对，已有资料表明，1930—1936年间，中国不仅存在着工农产品价格的剪刀差，而且是剪刀差的高峰期。这不仅达到了黄达最初为这个课题所确定的目标，而且他开始意识到工农产品比价问题之中包含着非常丰富的内容，我们所涉猎的部分也许只不过是其皮毛。遗憾的是，由于黄达懂点古文，不久后被分派去评注“法家”，这份稿子便被搁置起来。直到1990年此书才由中国社会科学出版社出版发行。

At the end of 1972, Huang Da returned to Beijing from "May 7th Cadre School". He did nothing but go to the market to buy vegetables and cook, or doing some woodworking or watching the roof in bed, so he was not criticized. However, his "character " as an intellectual made him very uneasy in such leisure. Not reading or thinking—about either the three sage kings or five virtuous emperors of China, the South Pole, the Big Dipper or the molecular—seemed to make him unhappy as not having meals or sleeping. Therefore, teachers who were "May 7th soldiers " got back into their old job, finding a topic and doing some researches.

Huang Da was not a "target", and was not entitled to attend activities together with "the revolutionary masses", either, so he had to find a topic to study. It seemed that the topic had to meet several requirements like not violating taboos of the then Cultural Revolution; being somewhat related to his major; having reference materials; leading him to some findings even if he did it alone. After screening, Huang Da found a topic that roughly met the above requirements and was to his interest—scissors difference.

A judgment became popular after 1958, that is, due to the growing purchase prices of agricultural by-products and the small rise in the sales prices of industrial products in the rural area, the price comparison between industrial and agricultural products soon turned to the direction favoring the farmers. Till 1958, seen from statistics, such price comparison had been equivalent to that during 1930 and 1936. Therefore, the scissors difference between industrial and agricultural products did not exist at all. Obviously, the judgment was preconditioned by the nonexistence of the scissors difference between industrial and agricultural products during 1930 and 1936. However, it needed to first prove whether it was true that scissors difference did not exist then. Strangely, those who put forward and agreed about the judgment seemed to have never considered the necessity to prove it. Despite the loophole, the judgment was just like a final conclusion. Before that, there had been an accepted conclusion when people expounded and proved the semi-colonial and semi-feudal old China, that is, the imperialist powers cruelly plundered China through the scissors difference.

To Huang Da, simple illative conclusion seemed to be less convincing, so he wanted to observe some real data to see if scissors difference existed during 1930 and 1936. If it did not, the judgment that there had not been any scissors difference in 1958 was of course tenable; but if it did, the judgment collapsed of itself. Through a whole year of check and verification in 1973, established materials showed that, during 1930 and 1936, scissors difference between industrial and agricultural products did exist in China, and was on the peak. It achieved the goal set by Huang Da when he first chose the topic, but helped him realize that the price relations between industrial and agricultural products embodied rich contents, and the part people had delved in might be nothing more than superficial knowledge. Unfortunately, Huang Da knew some ancient Chinese, so was soon designated to annotate "Legalism". The above script was put aside, and was not published by China Social Sciences Press till 1990.

图 54 为黄达在“文化大革命”期间的“力作”——《工农产品比价剪刀差》（中国社会科学出版社，1990）。

This is the "masterpiece" of Huang Da during the Cultural Revolution—*Scissors Difference between Prices of Industrial and Agricultural Products* (China Social Sciences Press, 1990).

54

第四章

Chapter Four

攀登巅峰

改革开放前后—20 世纪 80 年代末

Reaching the Academic Peak in around the Launch of Reform and Opening Up — the End of 1980s

“财政”+“金融”=?

"Fiscal Science" + "Financial Science" = ?

1976 年，“文化大革命”——这场新中国史无前例的浩劫，终于结束!

1977 年，中国人民大学迎来了复校的喜讯。财政金融学科的原班人马大多数回到学校，原来的财政与金融两个教研室合并组建财政金融教研室。

时过境迁，除了大家对于财政金融专业的那份挚爱，一切都仿佛跟十年前不再一样。被剥夺教书育人权利的教师们，终于能够将压抑多年的专业情感尽情释放。此刻，大家的脑海中不约而同地闪现出同一个念头：尽快编出一本教材，完成十年前未竟的事业!

可是，编一本好教材谈何容易，更何况还是一本囊括财政学与金融学的教材。

这本教科书所要论证的对象是什么？如何描述？这些看似简单的问题难倒了黄达、陈共、侯梦蟾、周升业和韩英杰这几个“积极分子”。尽管财政、金融以及财务等范畴之间存在内在的质的统一，这一论断作为“综合平衡”思想的核心，早在 20 世纪 50 年代末、60 年代初就已经得到大家的一致认可，但是，在编写教材时，如何准确地界定和描述这个统一客体，似乎又很难。

经过反复的讨论，教研室制定了打好这场硬战的“路线图”——先分工推进，然后在编写过程中就“对象”的界定进一步沟通交流，最后再将主体与客体“一锅端”。事实证明，这绝对是“攻城拔寨”的好方法。

经过两年多的时间，这部定名为《社会主义财政金融问题》的教材，由中国人民大学出版社于 1981 年出版发行。

尽管对于“对象”的界定到最后也没有达到预期的效果，但是这部教材对于推动中国金融学科发展的历史功绩值得肯定。可以说，这部教材已经完全摆脱了新中国建立后苏联教科书对中国金融教材的影响，首次建立了一个把货币、价格、资金、财政、金融连接为一体的学科体系，并从经济生活中货币层面的宏观均衡论证了对这些范畴进行综合研究和教学的必要性。

毫无疑问，这是大大的突破!

1987 年，该书获北京市哲学社会科学和政策研究优秀成果一等奖；1988 年，获

The year 1976 marked the end of the Cultural Revolution, the unprecedented disaster in the history of the People's Republic of China!

In 1977, with the resumption of the Renmin University of China, its original faculties on fiscal science and financial science returned, and the Teaching and Research Group of Fiscal Science and the Teaching and Research Group of Financial Science were merged into one.

Over time, everything seemed changed except everyone's emotion on fiscal science and financial science. The teachers, deprived of their rights to teach, finally released their emotions that had been suppressed for years. At this moment, an idea flashed into everyone's mind spontaneously:to compile a textbook as soon as possible to accomplish the cause unfinished ten years ago!

Yet, it was not an easy job, not to mention compiling a textbook incorporating both the fiscal science and financial science.

What's the topic of the textbook? And how to describe the topic? These seemingly simple problems confused the active members, such as Huang Da, Chen Gong, Hou Mengchan, Zhou Shengye and Han Yingjie. Although the theme that internal unification of quality between fiscal science and financial science, as the core of "comprehensive balance", was unanimously recognized in the early 1950s and late 1960s, it seemed difficult to accurately define and describe the unified object in the textbook.

After repeated discussions, the teaching and research group worked out the "roadmap" to overcome the difficulty—cooperating through division of labor first and above all, further communicating on the definition of the "subject", and finally combining the subject and object. It was proved that it was a good way to crack the hard nut.

After their efforts of more than two years, *Socialist Fiscal and Financial Problems* was published by China Renmin University Press in 1981.

Although the definition of "subject" failed to achieve the effect as expected, this textbook deserved recognition for its role in promoting the development of China's finance. It could be said that this textbook had thoroughly got rid of the influence of those in the Soviet Union after the founding of People's Republic of China. It was the first time to establish a disciplinary system combining currency, price, capital, fiscal issues

全国高等学校优秀教材奖；1989 年，获中国财政学会全国优秀理论研究成果荣誉奖。应该说，更大的褒奖是：20 世纪 80 年代的财经类学生，对于金融学、财政学的了解大都从这部教材开始。

多年后，黄达把《社会主义财政金融问题》与 80 年代中期的《财政信贷综合平衡导论》、90 年代的《货币银行学》、新世纪的《金融学》一起，并称为自己留且仅留的“四部教材”。可见，这部教材对于黄达而言意义非凡。如果有机会仔细品读这四部教材，你会发现它们竟有如此多的相同之处——著作的生命周期与经济的改革周期遥相呼应，淡雅的文墨与鲜活的理论相得益彰，先前的实践探索与后期的思想升华一脉相承！

这一阶段，与教材的成功编写同步，黄达的个人成就也获得了肯定。1978 年，担任财政金融系主任；1979 年，被评为教授；1981 年成为国务院批准的第一批博士生导师。

一条宽广、平坦的事业之路开始在黄达的脚下延伸。

对黄达而言，这本书还有一个更为特殊的意义。由于得到谷书堂、曾启贤、徐禾等政治经济学知名教授的首肯，这本书遂成为将黄达送进政治经济学圈子的“第二块敲门砖”。在当时，经济学分为政治经济学与部门经济学两大块，在政治经济学是龙头，高居部门经济学之上的情况下，这意味着，黄达攀上了经济学家的“高枝”。

而“第一块敲门砖”，则要从三年前谈起。

and finance together, and prove the necessity of comprehensive research and teaching in this regard through macroscopic equilibrium on the currency issue in economic life.

Undoubtedly, this was a great breakthrough!

In 1987, the book got the first prize of excellent research results in the fields of philosophy, social science and policy research. In 1988, it was accredited as an excellent textbook for colleges and universities nationwide. In 1989, it won the prize of honor as an excellent national theoretical research result in the China Society of Public Finance. It should be said that a bigger prize was that it helped the university students of finance open the door to their major in the 1980s.

Many years later, Huang Da took *Issues on Socialism Finance*, *Introduction of General Equilibrium on Public Finance and Credit* in mid-1980s, *Economics of Money and Banking* in the 1990s, and *Economics of Money and Finance* in the 21st century as the only four preserved textbooks for him. It was obvious that this textbook was of great significance to him. If you have a chance to carefully read the four textbooks, you will find that they have many in common—their life cycle echoes with the reform cycle of economy, elegant expressions and fresh theories perfectly match each other, and thought sublimation follows the practical exploration!

During the period, Huang Da's personal achievements were recognized along with the success of the textbooks. In 1978, he served as Director of Department of Finance. In 1979, he was appointed as a professor. In 1981, he was granted as one of the first doctoral supervisors with the approval of the State Council.

A broad and smooth road of career extended beneath Huang Da's feet.

For Huang Da, this book had a more special meaning. With the consent of renowned professors on political economics including Gu Shutang, Zeng Qixian and Xu He, this book became the "second stepping stone" for Huang Da to enter the circle of political economics. At that time, economics was divided into political economics and sector economics, with the former playing the leading role. It meant that Huang Da put himself under the "patronage" of economists.

And the "first stepping stone" started from three years ago.

学术生涯的路标

Landmark in His Academic Career

1978年，是中国改革开放元年。这一年，以邓小平为核心的党中央开辟了一条建设中国特色社会主义道路，三十多年来，中国人民沿着这条道路取得了举世瞩目的成就。

1979年，是中国物价体制改革元年。这一年，从提高粮、油料、生猪等18种主要农产品收购价开始，国家开始有计划地调整价格。从此，伴随着计划与市场的此消彼长，价格改革成为贯穿中国改革开放进程的一条主线，延续至今。

同样在这一年，“通货膨胀”成为中国理论界热议的话题。当年，黄达的一篇“应景”之作《谈谈我们的物价方针兼及通货膨胀问题》，由于在理论界首次正面明确提出“通货膨胀”这个与官方口径不一致的说法，可谓一石激起千层浪。经济学界，或赞扬之，或批判之，而且好像踩了政治上的“红线”。

理顺不合理的价格关系、改革不合理的价格管理体制，让价格杠杆成为优化资源配置的基础工具，这个在今天看来本不是问题的问题，在当时人们普遍把物价保持基本稳定当作社会主义优越性的环境下，却是一个大大的问题。本来《中国社会科学》要在它的1979年试刊号上发表，但由于话题敏感，未敢刊登。后来，在经过改题目、取消小标题文字以及删除“通货膨胀”字样等“技术处理”后，才以《试论物价的若干问题》发表在1980年底的《中国社会科学》第6期上。1998年，该文获得首届“薛暮桥价格研究奖”。1988年《黄达选集》（山西人民出版社）出版时，黄达将两篇文章同时刊出，以作对比。

文章中，黄达认为：不合理的比价必须调整，而调整比价将会使物价水平有所提高，所以物价水平会在时而平稳、时而有所提高的交替过程中呈现上升的趋势；但是只要把物价水平的变动控制在调整比价所必需的限度内，就不会成为发展经济的障碍。反之，比价不合理的矛盾越积越多，对经济发展不利。基于这一认识，他进一步提出，对于基本稳定的物价方针，应区分为短期和长期来理解。作为短期的物价方针，要尽可能控制物价水平上升的幅度，不使相邻年度之间有跳跃性的波动；而作为长期的物价方针，则应允许物价水平平稳地、小幅度地慢慢提高，采取这样

The year 1978 witnessed the starting of the reform and opening up in China. The Central Committee of the Communist Party of China with Deng Xiaoping as its core blazed a way towards socialism with Chinese characteristics. Over the past 30-odd years, the Chinese people achieved tremendous achievements by following this way.

In 1979, China embarked on its reform on price. It started its planned adjustment of prices with increasing the purchase price of 18 major farm products, such as grains, oilseeds and hogs. Henceforth, with the eliminating planned economy and growing market economy, the price reform has become a mainstream throughout the process of reform and opening up and has continued up to this day.

It is in that year that "inflation " became a hot spot in the theory circle in China. *Discussions on* Our Guidelines on Price and Inflation, which was written by Huang Da for the occasion, made a big splash as he was the first to propose "inflation" which was inconsistent with the official line. It attracted a mixed response in the economic circle, and seemed stepping on the political "red line ".

Straightening out irrational price relations, reforming the irrational system on price management, and making the price leverage the basic tool to optimize resource allocation is no longer a problem today, but used to be a big problem under the circumstance that people universally regarded the maintenance of stable price as a socialist superiority. The paper was planned to be published in the prototype edition of *Social Sciences in China* in 1979, but failed due to its sensitive topic. After the "technical approaches " such as changing the title, canceling the subtitle and deleting the word of "inflation ", the paper was finally published in Vol.6, *Social Sciences in China* at the end of 1980 with the title of Discussion on the Issues Concerning Price. In 1998, the paper won the first "Xue Muqiao Price Research Award ". In 1988, the two versions were simultaneously published for comparison in the *Collected Works of Huang Da* (Shanxi People's Publishing House) in 1988.

According to Huang Da's viewpoint in the paper, irrational price parity must be adjusted so as to increase the price level. Therefore, the price level would go on an upward trend in the process of alternative price stability and rise. But it would not become an obstacle for economic development as long as the change of price level was controlled within limits necessary for the price adjustment. On the contrary, the increasing contradictions resulted from irrational price parity would hamper the economic development. On this basis, he further proposed that the basically stable price guideline should be interpreted in the short term and in the long term respectively. As for the short-term price guideline, the rising of price level should be put under control as much

的方针绝不等于实行通货膨胀政策。

这场争论为黄达赢得又一个颇具形象性的绰号——“徐徐上涨”，以至于每逢开会，总难免有人指指点点，“看，徐徐上涨来了……”即便如此，由于对真理的坚持，这篇文章成为黄达日后走进政治经济学圈子的“第一块敲门砖”。

随后的几年，黄达依旧在不同的场合坚持着同样的观点——社会主义与通货膨胀不能相容的论断不能成立，通货膨胀事实上长期存在。

同时，沿着这样的思路，黄达一直在科研和教学中继续进行拓展、摸索，希望找到一个能够彻底阐明这个问题的理论框架。

1981年，黄达取得了阶段性的胜利。当年，他与周升业共同署名的《什么是信用膨胀，它是怎样引起的》一文在第11期的《经济研究》上发表。“在这篇文章中，我自己认为，更主要的是这一次形成了分析信贷资金供求数量对比问题的系统思路。剖析信贷问题，在经济学中往往使人有走入迷宫的感觉；多年用来分析这一问题的传统思路似乎又很难把人领出迷宫。正是由反复理不清的困境所推动，我把我们教研室集体形成的剖析信贷资金供求问题也即货币供求问题的思路加以推演，并建立了基本模型。对我自己来说，这是‘飞跃’，是获得了可以解开有关难题的钥匙”。1999年，黄达将该文收入《黄达文集》时，如此解题。

如果说这篇文章是黄达攀登学术高峰的里程碑，那么三年后出版的《财政信贷综合平衡导论》（下称《导论》）才真正标志着黄达达到了个人学术生涯的巅峰。

“万山磅礴必有主峰，龙衮九章但挈一领。”这一年，黄达59岁，已近花甲之年。

“这本书是自己倾注心血的成果，敝帚自珍，特别钟爱。记得看到过徐悲鸿的一幅群马图，他的自题词是：‘一得从千虑，狂愚辄自夸，以为真不恶，古人莫之加。’好像这最能点透自己对这本书的情感。”虽然无法体会此时黄达内心复杂的情感，但是从他日后回忆的这段文字当中，我们能隐约感受到作者在经历了三十多年矢志不渝的艰苦攀登之后，终达“泰山之巅”的喜悦和宽慰。

《导论》将诸如通货膨胀、信用膨胀、财政收支等问题纳入财政信贷综合平衡

as possible to avoid jumping fluctuation between adjacent years. As for the long-term price guideline, the price level should be allowed to rise in a steady and modest way, which didn't mean to implement the policy of inflation.

The dispute brought Huang Da another iconic nickname, "slow rise", so that there was always someone pointing at him in the meeting: "Look, that 'slow rise' man comes... " Despite that, owing to his persistence in truth, Huang Da entered the circle of political economics with this paper as his first "stepping stone".

In the following years, Huang Da still upheld the viewpoint on different occasions that the argument of incompatibility of socialism and inflation couldn't hold and inflation existed for a long time in fact.

Meanwhile, with such an idea, Huang Da kept his exploration in scientific research and teaching, in the hope of setting up a theoretical framework to fully clarify this issue.

In 1981, He gained a phased victory when What's Credit Inflation and How it Happened? (with Zhou Shengye as co-authors) was published in Vol. 11, *Economic Research*." In this paper, in my opinion, the most important thing is to develop a theoretical idea on analyzing the comparison of supply and demand on credit fund. Analysis on credit could be likened to a labyrinth in economics. Traditional ideas for analyzing this issue for years didn't seem a way out of the labyrinth. Driven by the confusion, I made a deduction of the ideas of analyzing the supply and demand on credit fund, i.e. that on currency, which was collectively developed by our teaching office, and set up a fundamental model. For me, it meant a leap forward, and also the key to solve related problems. "This was what Huang Da said when he included the paper into *Essays of Huang Da* in 1999.

If this paper was regarded as a milestone for Huang Da to climb up to the academic summit, *Introduction of General Equilibrium on Public Finance and Credit* (hereinafter referred to as the *"Introduction"*) published three years later marked the summit of Huang Da's personal academic career in a real sense.

"There must be a peak standing in majestic rolling mountains, and there must be a collar to pick up the complicated imperial robe. " That year, Huang Da was 59, almost an old man.

"This book is greatly cherished as it bears my painstaking efforts. I remember that Xu Beihong wrote an inscription on his painting of horses to express his confidence and ambition to resist foreign aggression, which seems to express my own emotions on this book. "Although it was hard to understand his complicated emotions at the bottom of his

的框架当中，并为这些问题的分析和论证构建了一个统一的分析系统。这本书从国民经济发展的全局出发，透过纷繁复杂的现象，“提炼”出货币信用的一般规律，抽象出简单的理论模型，并将这些具有普适性的理论观点一步步推向经济实际。即使是从当前“次贷危机”爆发以来世界各国的宏观应对策略及其效果来看，该理论不仅对中国经济增长中的诸多财政金融问题以及经济平稳增长具有深刻的解释力与政策指导意义，而且对于世界各国如何进一步把握经济均衡亦具有重要借鉴价值。

当时，武汉大学知名经济学家曾启贤教授对这本书特别欣赏并为之专门写了一篇长长的书评：“《导论》虽然没有包含宏观经济理论的全部内容，但为建立宏观经济控制理论进行了有益的探索。”也有人说：“《导论》是对计划经济中财政信贷综合平衡问题的最后总结。”《导论》虽然是以计划经济作为推导的背景，是立足于中国现实国情的一本颇为中国式的财政金融理论著作，对任何分析和推导所做出的论断，均以在中国曾经发生或者现存事实为支撑，但是它却得出了放之计划经济与市场经济而皆准的一般真理，在中国货币金融思想史上占据了重要的地位，也由此为奠定中国宏观经济均衡理论基础做出了一份贡献。以至一名香港学者看到此书后，竟断定作者曾留学欧美。

《导论》因其突出的理论贡献，先后于 1986 年、1995 年和 2013 年分别获得“孙冶方经济科学著作奖”、“全国高等学校人文社会科学研究优秀成果一等奖”以及“中国经济理论创新奖”三项代表中国经济学科最高荣誉的奖项。

“天行有常，不为尧存，不为桀亡。”事实上，真理存在于具有普适性的自然规律当中，与制度和环境并无必然联系。

在黄达看来，正是置身于计划经济制度这样一个大“实验室”当中，他才能通过对简明的商品货币关系的分析，较为轻松地得出西方经济学需花大力气才能得出的理论论断。

具体而言，长期以来，土生土长的“黄达们”只能通过有限的渠道接触和了解西方经济学。在改革开放前，一是中国几千年来本民族积淀的经济理论。这在当时

heart, judging from his words of memory, we had a glimpse of his joy and relief after reaching the summit after over 30 years of unswerving efforts.

The *Introduction* included inflation, credit inflation, fiscal revenue and expenditure, etc. into the framework of overall balance of public finance and credit, and established a unified analysis system to analyze and argue these issues. From the perspective of overall situation of national economic development, he made efforts to break through the complicated phenomena to extract the general rules on currency credit, abstract the simple theoretical model, and put these general theories into practice step by step. Even in respect of the coping strategies and effects of the international community after the present "subprime crisis " broke out, his theories not only had far-reaching explanatory power and policy implication on numerous final problems and the stability in China's economic growth, but also served as a valuable reference for the international community to further grasp the economic equilibrium.

At that time, Zeng Qixian, a renowned economist in Wuhan University, extended his appreciation to this book and wrote a long book review: "The *Introduction,* despite its failure to contain all contents of macroeconomic theory, carried out beneficial exploration on the theory of macroeconomic control. " It is also said that "The *Introduction* was the final conclusion on overall balance of public finance and credit in the planned economy. " The *Introduction*, in the context of planned economy, was a Chinese-style theoretical work on finance based on realistic national situations. All the arguments resulting from any analysis and induction were based on the past or extant facts, but they led to the truth universally applicable for both of the planned and market economy. For this reason, it occupied an important position in the history of thoughts on currency and finance in China, and made contributions to laying the foundation of macro-economic equilibrium theory. A Hong Kong scholar who read the book even asserted that the author must have studied overseas.

Owing to its outstanding theoretical contributions, the *Introduction* won three China's highest honors in economics, including the Sun Yefang Award for Economic Science Works, first prize of National Award on Outstanding Humanities and Social Sciences Research Outcome of Universities and Colleges, and China's Economic Theory Innovation Award in 1986, 1995 and 2013, respectively.

"Nature is the true law, which will not be changed by a wise emperor like Yao or a tyrant like Jie. " In fact, the truth exists in the universal law of nature with no necessary connections with the system and environment.

已经是许许多多年不被看重的理论，但不被看重实际上却不可能在中国人的头脑中全然清空。二是第二次世界大战前从西方引进的现代经济学，其中马克思主义经济学影响迅猛，占据了当时年轻一代的头脑。三是新中国成立后统治并实施了多年的计划经济理论。而改革开放后，中国经济学界才再次全力引进在第二次世界大战后迅速发展的西方现代经济学。

“那时的中国经济学人，就好像装备着从大刀长矛、汉阳造，到卡宾枪这些杂牌武器的一队士兵，但凭借着振兴中华的热情，凭借着贴近、熟悉自己生存的土壤，凭借着从实际出发、科学求实的指导思想，奉献了一系列有关改革的路径和对策的建议。”而黄达本人作为其中的一分子，也是这样长年累月地积累自己经济学的基础知识，并努力用来耕耘中国的经济学园地。

之后的很多年，黄达依然沿着《导论》提出的基本思路，在教学当中不断观察现实问题，提炼基本理论。经过十多年的积累，他又写就与《导论》在思想上一脉相承而在内容上不尽相同的《宏观调控与货币供给》（中国人民大学出版社，1997 年出版，1999 年修订版）一书。这本书在很大程度上适应了改革开放后，西方现代经济学逐步走进课堂、走进经济决策的现实情状，但就其理论研究价值来看，并没有超越《导论》。

“从 1984 年出书之后的二十多年间，虽然笔耕未辍，但自己总感到没有能够再次达到这段研究所曾经达到过的水平。”在 2005 年的《足迹——〈黄达书集〉说明》一文中，黄达这样写道。

——欣慰与遗憾同时跃然纸面。

In Huang Da's eyes, it was in the "lab" of systems on planned economy that he easily came to the theoretical conclusion through analysis on the brief relationship between goods and currency, which could not be obtained by western economics without great efforts.

For a long time, Huang Da and his native counterparts could only contact and learn the western economics through a limited number of channels. Before the reform and opening up, one channel was the economic theories accumulated by the Chinese nation for thousands of years. This had been valued for many years. The second one was the modern economics introduced from the West before World War II. The Marxist economics exerted so great influences that it occupied the mind of the youth. The third one was the theory on planned economy that held a prominent position in implementation after the founding of the People's Republic of China. It was after the reform and opening up that the economic circle of China once again fully introduced the western modern economics, which had witnessed rapid development after World War II.

In Huang Da's eyes, "the Chinese economists then could be likened to soldiers armed with motley weapons ranging from swords, spears and home-made guns to carbines. With enthusiasm in revitalizing the Chinese nation, however, they took root in their familiar environment of existence and offered a series of proposals on the path and countermeasures of reform, with the guiding principle of seeking the truth in a scientific way from reality." As one of them, Huang Da followed the similar way to accumulate his fundamental knowledge on economics and worked hard on economics in China.

For many years afterwards, Huang Da continued to follow the basic ideas proposed in the *Introduction* to observe the reality in teaching so as to abstract fundamental theories. Through a decade of accumulation, he completed *Macroeconomic Regulation and Money Supply* (published by China Renmin University Press in 1997, with the revised edition published in 1999) with the same thoughts but different contents from the *Introduction*. This book, to a great extent, adapted to the reality that western modern economics had been gradually accepted as a subject and a basis for economic decision-making since the reform and opening up. But it didn't exceed the *Introduction* with respect to its values to research on theories.

"Over the 20-odd years after the publication in 1984, although I kept writing, I never reached the level again that I had once reached during that period of my research." This was what Huang Da said in *My Footprint—Preface on Selected Books of Huang Da* in 2005.

Gratification and regret could both be found in this article.

得天下英才而教育之

Being a Good Judge of Talents and Teaching Them

“君子有三乐，而王天下不与存焉。父母俱存，兄弟无故，一乐也。仰不愧于天，俯不怍于人，二乐也。得天下英才而教育之，三乐也。”

孟子的“君子三乐”中，前两乐，属于亲情与个人之乐，很多人都能做到，而第三乐有所不同，并不是所有人都能“得天下英才而教育之”。因为“得天下英才”不易，能够有机会、有能力“教育之”则更不易。

尽管不易，但是黄达做到了，而且做得很出色！

迄今为止，我们无法统计有多少人读着黄达的书走进金融学的神圣殿堂，喜欢上金融学；有多少人在课堂上领略过黄达的精彩讲演，在书房里聆听过黄达的耐心启发；有多少人追随着黄达的思想，在金融学这个广阔的天空尽情翱翔；有多少人为黄达坦荡、率真、宽容、大度的做人准则所折服，把黄达视为思与行的精神导师。但是，有一个数字是可以统计的，那就是黄达门下的亲传弟子——16 位博士。

作为国务院批准的第一批博士生导师，与多数“桃李满天下”的先生相比，这个数字不是少，而是非常非常的少。究其原因，这主要还是源于黄达对教书育人始终坚持的严谨求实的态度。

一直以来，黄达都是中国金融界最为耀眼的“明星”之一，想成为黄达门下弟子的人并不在少数，其中不乏已经事业有成的官员和商界名人。“我知道这些人是没有时间认真做研究的，能不能写出论文来还要打个问号，他们需要的是一个头衔，但这与我的想法并不一致。”当然，他知道自己可能也把一些确实想提高专业水平的官员和成功商人拒之门外，但黄达并不想违背原则。

黄达成为博士生导师是在 1981 年，而直到 1985 年他才招收了第一批博士。“成为博导的最初几年更多的时间用于对这一教育制度的观望从而没有急于招生，后来由于事务性工作繁忙，招人而不育人与一个老师的责任不符。”黄达解释说。

周慕冰（中国农业银行董事长）、王松奇（中国社会科学院金融所原党委书记、副所长）、邓乐平（西南财经大学中国金融研究中心教授）有幸成为黄达的第一批博士，组成了他的第一个博士生团队。本着为人师者的高度责任心，为了集中精力带好这三人，黄达在随后的三年内再没有招收博士生，直至他们顺利毕业。1988—1992 年，

"There are three delights for a man, which have no relationship with governing the world. The first is having parents both in good health and brothers living a sound life; the second is not to disgrace others and the God; and the third is to be a good judge of talents and teach them."

Among the "three delights of a man" proposed by Mencius, the first two delights are about kinship and personal delight, which can be obtained by most people, while the third one is different as it is hard to reach by all. That's because it's not an easy job to be a good judge of talents, and even harder to have the chance and ability to "teach " them.

But Huang Da did it, and even did it very well!

To this day, it is unable to count out how many people have approached the sacred hall of finance and take a fancy by reading Huang Da's books; how many people have listened to Huang Da's excellent lectures in class and his patient enlightenment in the study; how many people have followed Huang Da's thoughts to enjoy flying in the vast sky of finance; and how many people have been impressed by Huang Da's life criteria on candor, forthrightness and generosity, and deemed him as their spiritual mentor on thoughts and practice. However, a number is countable, that is the number of Huang Da's disciples – 16 doctors.

As one of the first doctoral tutor approved by the State Council, he has rather fewer disciples than most his counterparts who have students all over the country. That's mainly because Huang Da always holds the rigorous and realistic attitude towards teaching.

Huang Da has always been one of the shining "stars " in finance in China. Many people hoped to follow Huang Da to study, some of whom were successful officials and businessmen. "I know they have no time to do research seriously. Whether their paper can be written out is questionable. What they need is just a title, which is inconsistent with what I desire." Of course, he was clear that he probably declined those who really wanted to upgrade their professional level, but Huang Da refused to go against his principles.

It was in 1981 that Huang Da became a doctoral tutor, but he didn't mentor his first doctors until 1985. "During the first years as a doctoral tutor, I spent more time on looking on the educational system so that I was not rushing to recruit doctors. Afterwards, considering my busy routine work, recruiting without mentoring them doesn't conform to the responsibility of a teacher. " explained by Huang Da.

Zhou Mubing (director of Agricultural Bank of China), Wang Songqi (former secretary of the Party Committee and deputy director of the Institute of Finance and Banking of the Chinese Academy of Social Sciences) and Deng Leping (professor of the Institute of Chinese Finance Studies of Southwestern University of Finance and Economics) were lucky enough to be Huang Da's first doctors, and formed his first doctoral team. With high sense of responsibility, Huang Da didn't recruit more doctoral candidates during

黄达每年招收一名博士生，组成了他的第二个博士生团队，这四人中便包括中央财经大学原校长王广谦、中国人民银行副行长陈雨露以及中国人民大学李焰教授、刘振亚教授。以后的若干年，黄达基本保持着平均 1~2 年招一名博士生的节奏，李鹰、刘成、郭浩、林琳、左毓秀、李向科、孔燕以及向东先后成为他的学生。2006 年，他收下的最后一名弟子韩文秀，如今是国务院研究室副主任。

1952 年，中国人民大学曾招收一批当年应届本科毕业生为研究生。黄达作为其中三位的导师，指导地们的论文写作。周升业毕业留校，成为知名教授；龚浩成回上海，曾任上海财经学院院长，后任中国人民银行上海分行行长；梁文森分配到中国社会科学院，曾作过刘国光先生的助手，后到深圳发展。

能够成为黄达的亲传弟子，得到先生无论是做人还是做学问的全方位指导，无疑是幸福的！2005 年，黄达 80 寿辰之际，陈雨露写下的这段文字，大抵能代表弟子对于先生的感激与敬仰之情："回味黄达先生的人生，点点滴滴，给我们既有温暖的感动，又有严肃的鼓励。作为黄达先生的学生，有幸得到先生的耳提面命，循循善诱的指导，自由平等的切磋，感受他严谨求实的学风，学习他精雕细琢的精神。他给予我们的是传世之作，更是传世之行。先生的传世之作自不必赘言，他将半个多世纪的精力献给了我国的金融教育事业，直到如今他也从没离开过三尺讲台，著作等身，桃李天下，自然是他应得的回报。阅读先生的文字，文才风流，倾听先生的演讲，醍醐灌顶，而先生达观的人生境界和包容的态度，又时刻打动和影响着我们。"

较之亲传弟子，黄达的另一个弟子群体——"私淑弟子"的数量就无法给出一个确切的数字。

私淑弟子——私：私下；淑：善。这是不能从自己所敬仰的前辈直接受业者的自我称谓。

洪琦、李扬、李晓西、李健、刘曼红、瞿强、宋逢明、涂永红、夏斌、王国刚、汪昌云、吴晓灵、吴晓球、谢平、于学军、张杰、赵锡军、庄毓敏……

一个个在中国金融界响亮的名字，我们无法尽数，但闪耀在他们身上的共同的品质我们却能清楚地看到——对于老师的敬爱、对于先生的仰慕以及对于事业的执著。

the following three years until their graduation in order to concentrate his attention on instructing them well. From 1988 to 1992, Huang Da recruited one doctor each year, who combined to form his second doctoral team. They included Professor Wang Guangqian, former President of the Central University of Finance and Economics, Professor Chen Yulu, Deputy Governor of the People's Bank of China, Professor Li Yan, and Professor Liu Zhenya from the Renmin University of China. In the following years, Huang Da maintained recruiting one doctor candidate in one year or two on average. The lucky men included Li Ying, Liu Cheng, Guo Hao, Lin Lin, Zuo Yuxiu, Li Xiangke, Kong Yan and Xiang Dong. In 2006, he recruited his last doctoral candidate, Han Wenxiu, who is now Deputy Director of Research Office of the State Council.

In 1952, Renmin University of China has enrolled some fresh Bachelor's graduates to proceed with master's degree. Huang Da was the supervisor of three of them and guided their thesis writing. Zhou Shengye stayed at Renmin University of China and became a famous professor. Gong Haocheng went back to Shanghai, held the post of president of Shanghai College of Finance and Economics and then president of PBoC Shanghai Branch. Liang Wensen went into CASS, once to be an assistant to Mr. Liu Guoguang, and then went to Shenzhen to develop his career.

It is undoubtedly happy to be Huang Da's disciples to get his instruction in an all round way on both how to be a man and how to learn! In 2005, to celebrate his 80th birthday, Chen Yulu wrote the following words, which probably could represent his appreciation and respect as a disciple. "In retrospect to every bit of Huang Da's life, we are warmly moved and seriously encouraged. As one of his disciples, I'm lucky enough to enjoy his earnest and systematic instruction, free and equal discussion, rigorous and practical style of study, and spirit of seeking for perfection. He has presented us with works and practices that can be handed down throughout the ages. Apart from his renowned works, he has been committed to financial education for more than half a century until today. A large number of works and students are naturally rewards that he deserves. I'm enlightened by his works and lectures. His philosophical realm of life and inclusive attitude always touch and influence us."

In contrast with his disciples, those who respect Huang Da but have had no chance to be his formal students are countless.

They include Hong Qi, Li Yang, Li Xiaoxi, Li Jian, Liu Manhong, Qu Qiang, Song Fengming, Tu Yonghong, Xia Bin, Wang Guogang, Wang Changyun, Wu Xiaoling, Wu Xiaoqiu, Xie Ping, Yu Xuejun, Zhang Jie, Zhao Xijun, and Zhuang Yumin etc.

These resounding names in the Chinese financial world are hardly counted out. But their quality in common is clear—their respect and admiration to their teacher, and their persistence in their cause.

4-1

复校初期的中国人民大学财政系
Department of Public Finance in the Early Days after the Renmin University of China Resumed Operation

1950 年，中国人民大学成立时设立的财政信用借贷系（1950—1960）是最早的八大院系之一。后于 1960 年，财政信用借贷系与贸易经济系合并成立财政贸易系（1960—1973），直至“文化大革命”期间中国人民大学停办。

1978 年，中国人民大学复校伊始，财政贸易系重新分设，黄达被任命为分设之后的财政系（1978—1988）系主任，成为该系自 1950 年以来的第 5 任系主任。而后又几经变换，1988 年成立财政金融系（1988—1997），1997 年建院，成立中国人民大学财政金融学院（1997— ）并延续至今。

在复校后第一次全系教工会上，黄达以系主任的身份分析了财政系面临的形势、问题和任务等，要求全体教职员工“要订个人规划，实事求是，不要‘共产风’那种吹牛皮，不要苏联‘副博士书目’那种形式主义”；要“充分发扬民主，充分发扬每个教师的积极性”以此来推动财政系的发展。随后，在财政系第一次迎新会上，黄达对新生的学习以及相关专业情况进行了说明，并要求学生应该正确认识自己所肩负的严肃学习任务，努力做到“红专统一，德智体全面发展”。

In 1950, when the Renmin University of China was founded, the Department of Public Finance and Credit Loan (1950—1960) was one of the earliest eight departments. In 1960, the Department of Public Finance and Credit Loan and the Department of Trade and Economics were merged into the Department of Public Finance and Trade (1960—1973) and lasted until Renmin University stopped running during the Cultural Revolution.

When the Renmin University of China started running again in 1978, the Department of Public Finance and Trade was divided anew. Huang Da was appointed head of the Department of Public Finance (1978—1988) and became the fifth head of the department since its establishment in 1950. Several transformations thereafter, the Department of Finance was established in 1988 which became the School of Finance in 1997 and continues today.

At the first faculty meeting of the department after the resumption of the Renmin University of China, Huang Da analyzed the situation, problems and tasks faced by the department; and requested the faculty to each develop a plan and have their feet on the ground, to abandon the behavior of boasting and formalism, and to "give full play to democracy and the activeness of each and every teacher " so as to advance the development of the Department of Public Finance. Later, at an evening party to welcome the newcomers held by the department, Huang Da explained the setting of majors and newcomers' studies, and asked the students to correctly understand their task of getting knowledge and to "be politically sound and professionally competent, get all-around development of moral, intellectual, physical, and labor education".

55

图 55 为 1978 年，中国人民大学举行复校会师大会。

所谓“会师大会”，是因为 1970 年 10 月中央决定中国人民大学停办后，原有各系所被成建制地划归到北京大学、北京师范大学、北京经济学院等几所院校，复校后原有系所则成建制地回归、会师。

In 1978, the Renmin University of China held a reunion meeting for its resumption.

It was a reunion meeting because the departments of the Renmin University of China were allocated to Peking University, Peking Normal University, Beijing School of Economics when the Central Government of China decided to stop running the Renmin University of China in October 1970. They "returned" and "reunited" upon the resumption of the Renmin University of China.

闫达五
Yan Dawu

1987 年 1 月—
1988 年 1 月
任财政系主任

January 198—January 1988, head of the Department of Public Finance

韩英杰
Han Yingjie

1988 年 1 月—
1992 年 6 月
任财政金融系主任

January 1988—June 1992, head of the Department of Finance

安体富
An Tifu

1992 年 6 月—1997 年 5 月
任财政金融系主任，
1997 年 5 月—2002 年 1 月
任财政金融学院院长

June 1992—May 1997, head of the Department of Finance

May 1997—January 2002, dean of the School of Finance

陈雨露
Chen Yulu

2002 年 1 月—
2007 年 9 月
任财政金融学院院长

January 2002—September 2007, dean of the School of Finance

郭庆旺
Guo Qingwang

2007 年 9 月—
2017 年 8 月
任财政金融学院院长

September 2007—August 2017, dean of the School of Finance

庄毓敏
Zhuang Yumin

2017 年 8 月—至今
任财政金融学院院长

August 2017—so far, dean of the School of Finance

崔希默
Cui Ximo

1950 年 3 月—
1953 年 7 月
任财政信用借贷系主任

March 1950—July 1953, head of Department of Public Finance and Credit Loan

高岚
Gao Lan

1953 年 7 月—
1957 年 12 月
任财政信用借贷系主任

July 1953—December 1957, head of Department of Public Finance and Credit Loan

赵锡禹
Zhao Xiyu

1957 年 12 月 —1960 年 6 月任财政信用借贷系主任，1960 年 6 月—1961 年 5 月任财政贸易系主任
新中国成立前，在会计学界有“南潘北赵”的说法。“南潘”是指在上海开创立信会计教育事业的潘序伦教授，“北赵”则是指时任辅仁大学会计系主任的赵锡禹教授。

December 1957—June 1960, head of the Department of Public Finance and Credit Loan; June 1960 —May 1961, head of the Department of Public Finance and Trade.

Before the founding of new China, there was the saying that "in southern China, it is Master Pan; in northern China, it is Master Zhao" in the accounting world. "Master Pan" here refers to Prof. Pan Xulun, founder of Lixin Accounting education in Shanghai; "Master Zhao" refers to Prof. Zhao Xiyu, the then head of the Accounting Department of Furen Catholic University of Beijing.

曾洪业
Zeng Hongye

1961 年 6 月—
1969 年 9 月
任财政贸易系主任

June 1961—September 1969, head of the Department of Public Finance and Trade

黄达
Huang Da

1978 年 3 月—
1983 年 8 月
任财政系主任

March 1978—August 1983, head of the Department of Public Finance

陈共
Chen Gong

1983 年 9 月—
1987 年 1 月
任财政系主任

September 1983—January 1987, head of the Department of Public Finance

图 57 为中国人民大学财金学院历任院长（系主任）。

These are the pictures of the deans (heads) of the School of Finance.

图 56 为中国人民大学自 20 世纪 50 年代初直至复校初期的东门。

This is the east gate of the Renmin University of China from the early 1950s to the early days after the university resumed operation.

56

58

图 58 为 2010 年 4 月 25 日，中国人民大学财政金融学院历任院长（系主任）在“韩英杰教授学术思想暨八十寿辰座谈会”上的合影。从左至右分别为：郭庆旺、安体富、陈共、黄达、韩英杰、陈雨露。

On April 25, 2010, deans (department heads) of the School of Finance of the Renmin University of China took a group photo at "Han Yingjie Scholarly Ideas and Han's 80th Birthday Symposium". From the left to the right are Guo Qingwang, An Tifu, Chen Gong, Huang Da, Han Yingjie and Chen Yulu.

59

图 59 为 1982 年夏，中国人民大学 78 级财政金融专业学生毕业合影。第二排左五至左八分别为：周升业、黄达、张尚武、韩英杰。

In the summer of 1982, the finance majors of Class 1978 of the Renmin University of China took a group graduation photo. From the fifth to the eighth from the left in the second row are Zhou Shengye, Huang Da, Zhang Shangwu and Han Yingjie.

60

图 60 为 1982 年 10 月，黄达（右一）与周升业（左一）应深圳特区邀请论证应否发行特区货币，期间两人同游肇庆七星岩。

In October 1982, Huang Da (first from the right) and Zhou Shengye (first from the left) discussed the necessity to issue a separate currency in the special economic zones at the invitation of Shenzhen Special Economic Zone. There they visited the Seven Star Crags in Zhaoqing.

61

图 61 为 20 世纪 80 年代初，黄达在家中读书。

In the early 1980s, Huang Da was reading at home.

62

图 62 为 1984 年夏，中国人民大学财政系部分老师送丁玮出国。第二排左四为黄达。

In the summer of 1984, some teachers of the Department of Public Finance of the Renmin University of China saw Ding Wei off. The fourth one from the left in the second row is Huang Da.

63

图 63 为 1985 年夏，中国人民大学财政系金融教研室全体教师在校门前合影。这是一张当时极为难得的合影。从左至右依次为：孔军、黄传玺、李春、朱毅峰、沈瑞年、黄达、张瑛、肖清、李炽、周升业、沈伟基、杜兴满、蒋永军、陶湘。

In the summer of 1985, teachers of the Finance Teaching and Research Group of the Department of Public Finance, the Renmin University of China took a group photo in front of the school gate. It is a precious group photo. From the left to the right are Kong Jun, Huang Chuanxi, Li Chun, Zhu Yifeng, Shen Ruinian, Huang Da, Zhang Ying, Xiao Qing, Li Zhi, Zhou Shengye, Shen Weiji, Du Xingman, Jiang Yongjun and Tao Xiang.

64

图 64 为 1987 年 4 月，中国人民大学财政系组织集体春游，部分教师在京郊戒台寺“莲界香林”（乾隆手书）雕龙横匾前合影。从左至右分别为：陈志华、蒋永军、朱毅峰、黄达、周平、廖红。

In April 1987, the Department of Public Finance of the Renmin University of China organized a spring outing, and some teachers took a group photo in front of the horizontal board with dragon designs of Jietai Temple in the suburbs of Beijing. From the left to the right are Chen Zhihua, Jiang Yongjun, Zhu Yifeng, Huang Da, Zhou Ping and Liao Hong.

65

图 65 为 1987 年 11 月 1 日，黄达与财政系校友一起参加中国人民大学建校五十周年纪念活动。前排左四为黄达，右一为韩英杰，后排右一为时任系党总支书记张尚武。

On November 1, 1987, Huang Da and the alumni and alumnae of the Department of Public Finance attended the activities to commemorate the 50th anniversary of the Renmin University of China. The fourth one from the left in the front row was Huang Da, the first one from the right was Han Yingjie, and the first one from the right in the back row was Zhang Shangwu, the then secretary-general of the Party branch.

66

图 66 为 1988 年 6 月 11 日，中国人民大学财政金融系部分教师宴请来访的著名财政学家 Oldman 教授。从左至右分别为：Oldman、王传纶、安体富、黄达、袁振宇、时任外事处长金戈。

On June 11, 1988, some teachers of the Department of Finance of the Renmin University of China entertained visiting Prof. Oldman, a very famous finance expert. From the left to the right are Oldman, Wang Chuanlun, An Tifu, Huang Da, Yuan Zhenyu and Jin Ge, the then director of the department of foreign affairs.

67

图 67 为 1989 年 2 月，黄达（右四）、韩英杰（左四）与中国人民大学财政金融专业研究生在一起。

In February 1989, Huang Da (fourth from the right) and Han Yingjie (fourth from the left) were with the postgraduates of the Finance major of the Renmin University of China.

68

图 68 为 1989 年 4 月 20 日，中国人民大学金融专业干部专修班全体师生合影留念。前排左六至左八分别为：李云、黄达、朱毅峰。

On April 20, 1989, the teachers and students of the Finance Class for Cadres of the Renmin University of China took a group photo. From the sixth to the eighth from the left in the front row are Li Yun, Huang Da and Zhu Yifeng.

4-2

为改革开放提供第一本财政金融教材
——《社会主义财政金融问题》
The First Financial Textbook—*Issues on Socialism Finance*

《社会主义财政金融问题》是中国人民大学财政系在改革开放后提供的第一本财政金融教材。该书第一至五篇分别由黄达、陈共、侯梦蟾、周升业和韩英杰编写。全书的统编定稿由黄达负责，侯梦蟾也参加了部分统编工作。

从20世纪60年代初的“三年困难时期”开始打算撰写此书，到1981年最终出版面世，历时约二十年。该书重点解决了五个问题：一是社会主义财政金融问题所要研究的对象；二是研究财政金融问题所应体现的社会主义特征；三是正确处理理论论述同现行政策、现行规章制度之间的关系；四是有关资金、财政、货币流通等概念的界定；五是将货币、价格、资金、财政和金融连接为一体。

事实证明，《社会主义财政金融问题》取得了不小的突破，获得了各方的赞誉，同时更成为20世纪80年代高等院校财经类学生认识金融学、财政学的开始。

Issues on Socialism Finance is the first textbook on finance after the reform and opening up written by Finance Department of Renmin University. Section I-V are written by Huang Da, Chen Gong, Hou Mengchan, Zhou Shengye and Han Yingjie respectively. The compilation was presided over by Huang Da and participated by Hou Mengchan.

It has been about 20 years from the beginning of the writing during the three-year difficulty in the early 1960s to the publication of the book in 1981. The book focused on five key issues: research object of socialism finance, socialism features in financial research, relationship between theory and current policy and regulations, concept of capital, public finance, currency circulation, etc., and connection between money, price, capital, public finance and finance.

In fact, *Issues on Socialism Finance* has made a breakthrough along with praises from all sectors. It marked the beginning of the recognition of finance and public finance among the students in finance and economics colleges in 1980s.

| 右页图 ⟼

图69为《社会主义财政金融问题》（上、下册，中国人民大学出版社，1981）。

This is a picture of *Issues on Socialism Finance* (Vol. 1 and Vol. 2, China Renmin University Press, 1981).

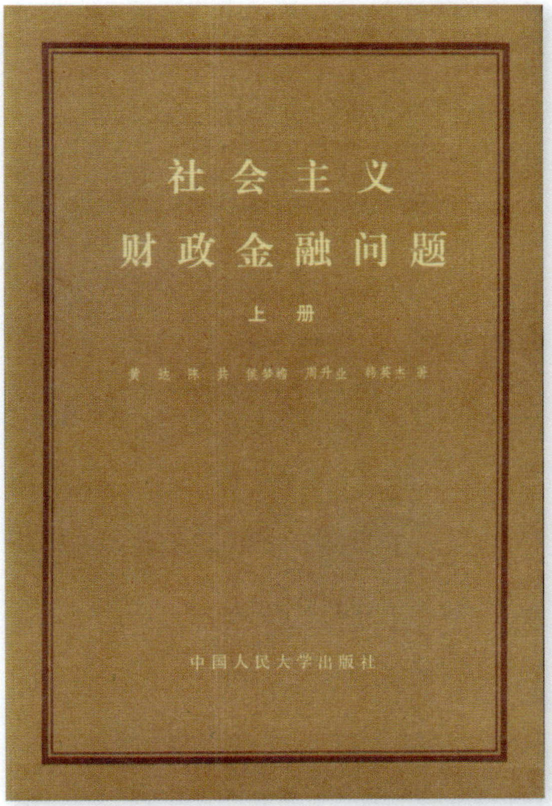
社会主义
财政金融问题
上册
黄达 陈共 侯梦蟾 周升业 韩英杰 著
中国人民大学出版社

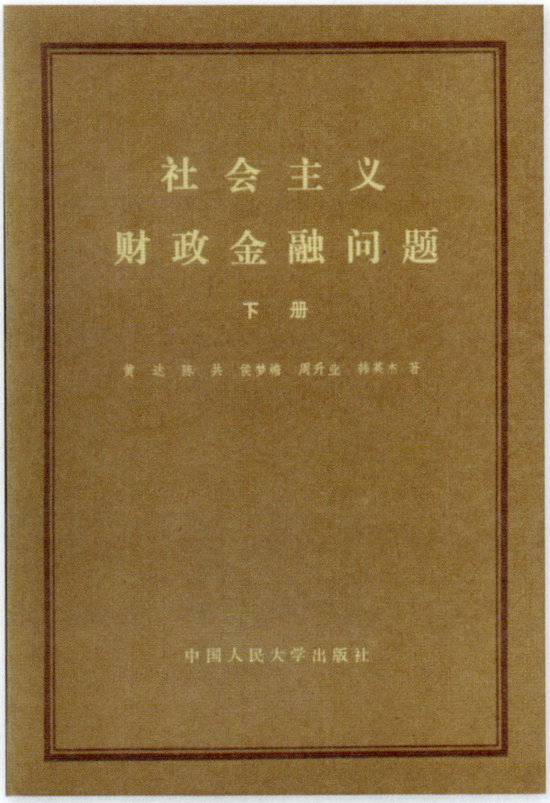
社会主义
财政金融问题
下册
黄达 陈共 侯梦蟾 周升业 韩英杰 著
中国人民大学出版社

69

4-3

巅峰之作——《财政信贷综合平衡导论》

The Peak Work—*Introduction of General Equilibrium on Public Finance and Credit*

20 世纪 70 年代和 80 年代之交的这几年，在改革开放的冲击下，经济生活相继提出了一系列问题：日益加重的物价波动和通货膨胀威胁、银行信贷规模的急速扩张和信用膨胀、变得难以把握的货币供给、财政收支从结余迅速转为赤字、利用外资的从无到有以及是否可以同人民币脱钩……

大量接踵而至的新问题，推动着黄达不断地思考、写作，他日益意识到必须建立起能够把这些问题放在一个系统中加以分析的框架。事实上，中国理论界在 20 世纪 50 年代就已经提出了一个被称为“财政信贷综合平衡”的框架，问题是如何按照“系统”的要求使这个框架得到逻辑的论证——凡纳入这个框架的问题均能用协调一致的思路进行剖析并得出相互呼应、补充、兼容的论断。沿着这个问题指明的方向，黄达在 1983 年系统思考并写出《财政信贷综合平衡的再探索》，并于次年由中国金融出版社以《财政信贷综合平衡导论》（以下简称《导论》）为名出版。

《导论》提出的分析框架建立在商品货币关系极大简明化的计划经济体制之上。正是由于它本质上并未脱离商品货币关系，因而据以得出的论断便具有适用于一般市场经济的意义。在黄达看来，假如没有十月革命和 20 世纪的社会主义运动，谁也建立不起十几亿人口的计划经济社会制度的“实验室”。而当人们反复论证出这个实验并不成功时，却不怎么重视这个难得的实验室使得人们能够得出在西方市场经济条件下要费极大力气才能得出的理论论断。当他在后来大量接触西方宏观经济学的时候，才真正感受到正是对计划经济综合平衡的研究帮助自己尽快达到他们的境界。

遗憾的是，在完成这本书的写作之后，黄达虽然笔耕未辍，但是随着时间的推移，他的关注点也日益转移到对改革和建设思路的剖析、发展趋势的评估和主要症结的把握等方面。尽管 1997 年由中国人民大学出版社出版的《宏观调控与货币供给》一书就基本思路来说，与《导论》一脉相承，但与《导论》所曾经达到过的水平还有一段距离。

In the transitional years from the 1970s to 1980s, China's economy saw a series of problems under the shock of the reform and opening-up policy—growing price fluctuations, threat of inflation, rapid expansion of bank loans, expansion of credits, monetary supply hard to control, the rapid change from financial surplus to deficits, development of the use of foreign capital and whether to delink with renminbi···

A lot of new problems that came one after another kept Huang Da thinking and writing. He came to realize the necessity to build a framework to enable the analysis of the problems in one system. As a matter of fact, China's theorists had put forward a framework named" General Equilibrium of Public Finance and Credit" in the 1950s. The point was how to logically demonstrate the framework according to the requirements of the "system," that is, all problems that were brought into the framework could be analyzed in a consistent way and lead to relevant, supplementary and compatible conclusions. In such direction, Huang Da thought systematically and wrote *Re-exploration of the General Equilibrium on Public Finance and Credit,* and published it in the name of *Introduction of General Equilibrium on Public Finance and Credit* (hereinafter referred to as *"Introduction"*) through China Financial Publishing House.

The analytical framework put forward in *Introduction* was built on the planned economic system where the commodity-money relationship was very simple. Because it was not divorced from the commodity-money relationship, the conclusions thus obtained were of significance to general market economy. To Huang Da, without the October Revolution and the socialist movement in the 20th century, it was impossible to build a "lab" of the planned economic system in a society of more than a billion people. When people repeatedly demonstrated it to be unsuccessful, they failed to pay due attention to the fact that the lab enabled them to get theoretical judgments which could be achieved only with great efforts under the Western market economic conditions. When he himself began to read Western macro economics a lot, Huang Da truly realized that his studies on the overall balance of the planned economy helped him quickly get to where they were.

Unfortunately, after finishing the book, though he kept writing, Huang Da shifted his focus of attention to analyzing the ideas of reform and construction, and evaluating the development trend and the central issues therein as time went by. Although *Macroeconomic Regulation and Money Supply* published by China Renmin University Press in 1997 was a continuation of *Introduction* in terms of the fundamental idea, there was a distance from it to the level once reached by *Introduction*.

70

图 70 为 1984 年，中国金融出版社出版发行的《财政信贷综合平衡导论》的精装本和简装本。

该书因其突出的理论贡献，先后于 1986 年、1995 年和 2013 年，分别获得“孙冶方经济科学著作奖”“全国高等学校人文社会科学研究优秀成果一等奖”以及“中国经济理论创新奖”三项代表中国经济学科最高荣誉的奖项。

In 1984, China Financial Publishing House published the hardback and paperback of *Introduction of General Equilibrium on Public Finance and Credit.*

For its prominent theoretical contribution the books won "Sun Yefang Award for Economic Science Works," first prize of "National Award on Outstanding Humanities and Social Sciences Research Outcome of Universities and Colleges" and "China's Economic Theory Innovation Award," the three highest honors for economic subjects in China, in 1986, 1995 and 2013, respectively.

图 71 为 1987 年 3 月 31 日，孙冶方经济科学奖励基金委员会邀请黄达参加 1986 年度“孙冶方经济科学著作奖”颁奖仪式的会议通知。

This is the notice issued by Sun Yefang Economic Science Foundation on March 31, 1987 to invite Huang Da to attend the award-presenting ceremony of 1986 "Sun Yefang Award for Economic Science Works".

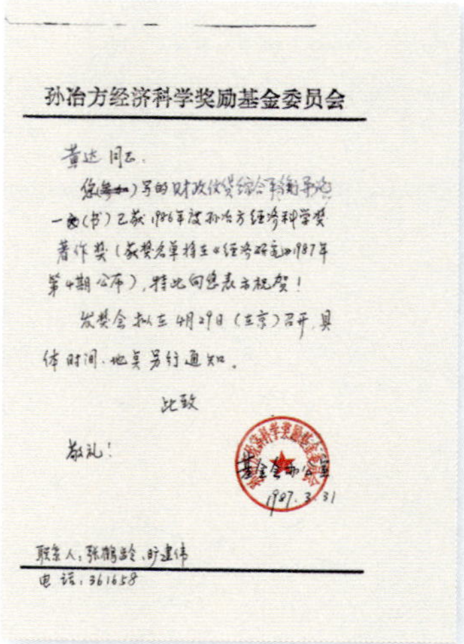

孙冶方经济科学奖励基金委员会

黄达同志：

您写的财政信贷综合平衡导论一书（书）已获1986年度孙冶方经济科学奖著作奖（获奖名单将在《经济研究》1987年第4期公布），特此向您表示祝贺！

发奖会拟在4月29日（北京）召开，具体时间、地点另行通知。

此致

敬礼！

基金会办公室
1987.3.31

联系人：张鹤龄、叶建伟
电话：361658

71

72

73

图 72 为 1997 年 2 月，由中国人民大学出版社出版发行的《宏观调控与货币供给》。

This is *Macroeconomic Regulation and Money Supply*, published by China Renmin University Press in February 1997.

图 73 为 1999 年 7 月，由中国人民大学出版社出版发行的《宏观调控与货币供给》(修订版)。

This is *Macroeconomic Regulation and Money Supply* (Revised Edition) published by China Renmin University Press in July 1999.

4-4

第一次主持课题——“货币供求量问题研究”

The First Time to Preside over a Research Topic—"Study on the Quantitative Issue of Currency Supply and Demand "

1986年春夏之交，全国哲学社会科学“七五”规划会议拟定了包括“货币供求量问题研究”在内的一批国家重点课题。黄达因故未能与会，但由于之前相关研究得到广泛认可，与会专家一致推荐他担任经济学重点课题“货币供求量问题研究”的主持人。这是黄达第一次独立主持重大课题研究。

为了能够较好地完成课题研究任务，他在与课题组成员反复论证后，将研究目标确定为，结合中国实际进行理论探索，而非计量模型研究。之所以如此选择，主要的考虑在于，关于货币供求的理论问题，在当时似乎已是一个早为人们所熟悉的问题，也是一个早已解决了的问题。但事实并非如此，无论从过去熟悉的计划经济理论来说，还是从当时努力引进的西方经济理论来说，往往满足于表面理解和似是而非的观念极多，急需正本清源，求得理论上的提升。否则，在现代化的建设过程中有效地利用货币这个杠杆就无从谈起。

经过几年的认真研究，课题组最终形成了“货币供求问题研究系列专著”（5卷本），由中国人民大学出版社在1990—1993年间先后出版。具体包括：《中国的货币需求——理论与实证的考察》（邓乐平，1990）、《经济运行中的货币供给机制》（周慕冰，1991）、《货币政策与经济成长》（王松奇，1991）、《银行信用管理与货币供应》（尚明、吴晓灵、罗兰波，1992）以及《中国货币流通的回顾与展望》（王庆彬、周升业，1993）。

| 右页图 |⟶

图74为“货币供求量问题研究”课题最终成果——1990—1993年间由中国人民大学出版社出版的“货币供求问题研究系列专著”。

The final achievement of the research topic "Study on the Quantitative Issue of Currency Supply and Demand"—Monograph Series of Study on the Quantitative Issue of Currency Supply and Demand that were published by China Renmin University Press during 1990 and 1993.

At the turn of spring and summer in 1986, a group of key national research topics including "Study on the Quantitative Issue of Currency Supply and Demand " were studied out at the Planning Meeting on National Philosophy and Social Sciences during the "7th Five-year Plan" Period. Huang Da did not attend the meeting for some reason but, since his previous related studies were widely recognized, all the attending experts recommended him to preside over the key economic research topic of "Study on the Quantitative Issue of Currency Supply and Demand. " It was also the first time Huang Da presided over a major research topic independently.

After studying it repeatedly with the other team members, Huang Da set the goal as doing theoretical explorations based on China's reality instead of studying the econometric model, mainly out of the following consideration: the theoretical problem of monetary supply and demand seemed to have been very familiar to people, and a problem that had far been solved. It was not true actually. Either the planned economic theories in the past or Western economic theories which were introduced to China with great efforts had many concepts that seemed to have been understood, but were actually not. They had to be corrected for theoretical improvement, or it would be impossible to effectively utilize the leverage of currency in the process of modernization.

After years of devoted studies, the team finally finished Monograph Series of Study on the Quantitative Issue of Currency Supply and Demand (5 volumes), and had them published by China Renmin University Press during 1990 and 1993. Specifically, the five books are *Demand for Money in China Theoretical and Empirical Observation* (Deng Leping, 1990), *Money Supply Mechanism in Economic Operation* (Zhou Mubing, 1991), *Monetary Policy and Economic Growth* (Wang Songqi, 1991), *Bank Credit Management and Money Supply* (Shang Ming, Wu Xiaoling and Luo Lanbo, 1992) and *Retrospect and Prospect-Chinese Currency Circulation* (Wang Qingbin and Zhou Shengye, 1993).

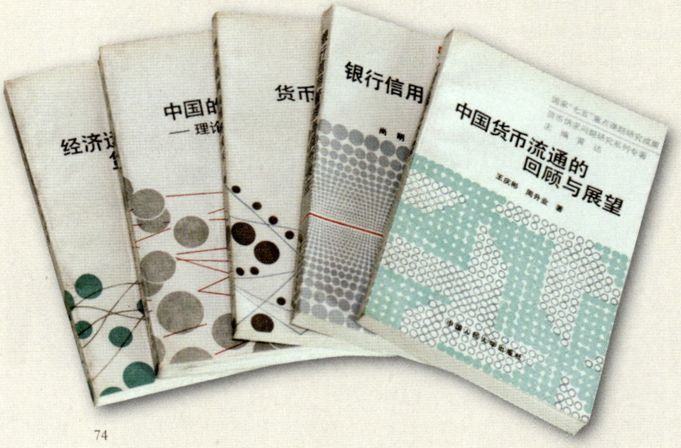

74

75

图 75 为 1987 年 5 月 20—23 日，“货币供求量问题研究”课题组在北戴河召开第一次课题研讨会，全体与会专家合影。前排左一、左二分别是袁振宇与安体富，右一、右二分别是周慕冰与吴晓灵；后排从左至右分别是：贝多广、王松奇、王传纶、黄达、周升业与王庆彬。

During May 20 to 23, 1987, the team of "Study on the Quantitative Issue of Currency Supply and Demand" held its first seminar in Beidaihe. All attendees took a group photo. The first and second one from the left in the front row is Yuan Zhenyu and An Tifu respectively; the first and second one from the right is Zhou Mubing and Wu Xiaoling respectively; from the left to the right in the back row are Bei Duoguang, Wang Songqi, Wang Chuanlun, Huang Da, Zhou Shengye and Wang Qingbin.

图 76 为 1987 年 5 月 20—23 日，“货币供求量问题研究”课题组在北戴河召开第一次课题研讨会，部分与会专家在会议期间交流。从左至右分别是袁振宇、安体富、王庆彬、王传纶、黄达与周升业。

During May 20 to 23, 1987, the team of "Study on the Quantitative Issue of Currency Supply and Demand" held its first seminar in Beidaihe. Some attendees were exchanging ideas. From the left to the right are Yuan Zhenyu, An Tifu, Wang Qingbin, Wang Chuanlun, Huang Da and Zhou Shengye.

76

77

78

图 77 为 1988 年 5 月 5 日，“货币供求量问题研究”课题组在“中国人民大学黄山学术交流中心”召开第二次课题研讨会，全体与会专家合影。后排左九为黄达。

On May 5, 1988, the team of "Study on the Quantitative Issue of Currency Supply and Demand" held its second seminar in "Huangshan Academic Communication Center of the Renmin University of China ." All attendees took a group photo. The ninth one from the left in the back row is Huang Da.

图 78 为 1990 年 7 月 14—16 日，“货币供求量问题研究”课题组在大连召开第三次课题研讨会，全体与会专家合影。第一排左二为中国人民银行原副行长尚明，第二排右一为黄达。

During July 14 to 16, 1990, the team of "Study on the Quantitative Issue of Currency Supply and Demand" held the third seminar in Dalian. All attendees took a group photo. The second from the left in the first row is Shang Ming, former deputy governor of PBoC.The first one from the right in the second row is Huang Da.

4-5

走上中国人民大学领导岗位

Take up the Leading Position of the Renmin University of China

1983 年，黄达被任命为中国人民大学副校长。两年后，袁宝华兼职担任中国人民大学校长，黄达实际上成为主持常务工作的副校长，给袁宝华校长当助手。当时，学校面临两个比较突出的问题：一是中国人民大学应办成什么样的大学；二是领导班子有无“文化大革命”遗留的“一派掌权”问题。

由于年龄较大，不太想从事学校行政工作，想专心从事教学等原因，黄达从 1985 年之后的三四年间，每年都向袁宝华校长递交辞职报告，可袁校长回复说：“再过一段时间，我也不干了，咱俩共进退。”于是，“无奈”的黄达只好继续干下去，而且在 1991 年袁宝华卸任校长之后，他还被袁校长推荐担任中国人民大学校长。直到 1994 年卸任校长，黄达前后有 11 年时间担任学校主要领导职务。

In 1983, Huang Da was appointed vice president of the Renmin University of China. In 1985, Yuan Baohua began to take charge of the Renmin University of China， and Huang Da worked as his assistant and was in charge of routine work. The university was faced with two big problems then: What kind of university should the Renmin University of China be? Was there the "one-party control " phenomenon left behind by the Cultural Revolution in its leadership?

Not wanting to be involved in school administration, but to engage in teaching, because of age, Huang Da submitted a resignation letter to Yuan Baohua each year in three or four years after 1985, only to be replied with "I will quit after a period of time, so wait for me and then let's do it together." Having no choice, Huang Da had to continue. In 1991 when Yuan Baohua left off his post, he recommended Huang Da to be the president of the Renmin University of China. Till he left office as the president in 1994, Huang Da had taken important leading positions of the university for 11 years.

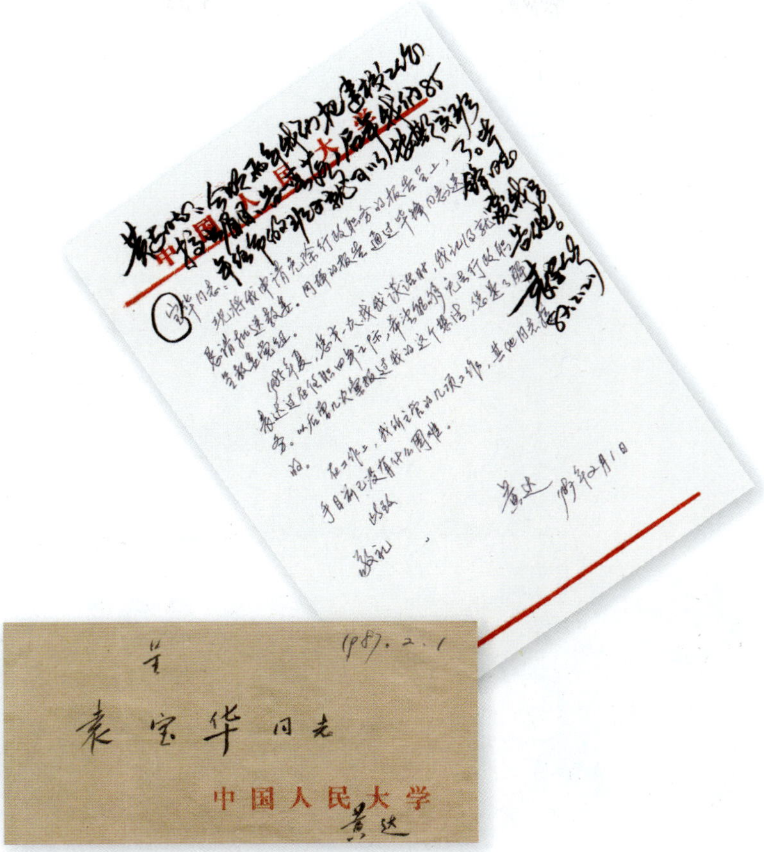

79

图 79 为 1987 年 2 月 1 日黄达写给时任中国人民大学校长袁宝华的辞职报告和信封。

辞职报告原文为："宝华同志：现将我申请免除行政职务的报告呈上，恳请批送教委。同样的报告通过毕锋同志送呈教委党组。1985 年夏，您第一次找我谈话时，我记得就表达过在任职四年之际，希望能够免去行政职务。以后曾几次禀报过我的这个想法，您是了解的。在工作上，我所主管的几项工作，其他同志接手目前已没有什么困难。此致，敬礼。黄达，1987 年 2 月 1 日。" 随后，袁宝华校长批示："黄达同志：今明两年我们把建校工作搞出眉目，告一段落。后年我们 1985 年任命的班子就可以按期交班了。毕锋同志处我另告他。袁宝华，1987 年 2 月 2 日。"

These are the resignation letter and its envelop that Huang Da wrote to Yuan Baohua, the then president of the Renmin University of China.

The resignation letter read, "Comrade Baohua, I now submit to you my resignation letter, please sign it and submit it to the State Education Commission. The same letter has been submitted to the leading party group of the State Education Commission by Bi Feng. In the summer of 1985, you and I had the first talk and, as far as I remember, I expressed the wish to resign my administrative post at the fourth year. I have expressed such idea many times, and you know that. The work in the charge of me can be easily taken over by the others. Best regards. Huang Da on February 1, 1987." President Yuan Baohua replied, "Comrade Huang Da, we will do something for school construction this year and next year, and then call it a day. The year after next, we will be relieved on schedule. I will talk with Bi Feng about this. Yuan Baohua on February 2, 1987."

4-5-1 >

作为校领导参与的种种活动

Various activities as school leaders

80

图 80 为 1979 年，中国人民大学召开纪念五四运动六十周年科学讨论会。主席台中间作报告者为成仿吾老校长。

In 1979, the Renmin University of China held a symposium to commemorate the 60th anniversary of the May 4th Movement. The one delivering a speech on the podium was Cheng Fangwu, former president of the Renmin University of China.

| 右页图 ⟼

图 81 为 1980 年，中国人民大学在首都体育馆隆重举行建校三十周年纪念大会。

In 1980, the Renmin University of China held a meeting in the Capital Gymnasium to celebrate its 30th anniversary.

81

82

图 82 为 1983 年 12 月 29 日，黄达在中国人民大学第八次党代会上发言。

On December 29, 1983, Huang Da was delivering a speech at the 8th Party Congress of the Renmin University of China.

83

图 83 为 1987 年 5 月 3 日，国家教委在西三旗举行经济学位硕士点评估会议，全体与会专家合影留念。第一排左二至左十分别为：曾康霖、厉以宁、刘鸿儒、黄达、许毅、滕文藻、朱开轩、钱荣堃、邓子基。

On May 3, 1987, the State Education Commission held a meeting in Xisanqi to evaluate the program of master's degree in economics. All the attendees took a group photo. From the second to the tenth from the left in the first row are Zeng Kanglin, Li Yining, Liu Hongru, Huang Da, Xu Yi, Teng Wenzao, Zhu Kaixuan, Qian Rongkun, Deng Ziji.

84

图 84 为 1987 年 5 月 15 日，钱学森（左二）应袁宝华（左一）老校长的邀请在北京科学会堂作题为“社会主义建设的总体设计——党和国家的咨询服务单位”的学术报告，首都学术界人士和中国人民大学师生共 500 余人听取了报告。右一为黄达。

“同志们要我来讲‘吴玉章学术讲座’的第一讲，我感到很光荣，但又感到自己能力有限，困难不少；可是我也想借这个机会来表示我对吴玉章同志的敬意。”在报告中，钱学森先生不仅有力地阐明了他设立社会主义建设总体设计部对国家可持续发展的伟大构想，并且充分地表达了他对中国人民大学培养党和国家栋梁之才的殷切希望。

On May 15, 1987, at the invitation of Yuan Baohua (first from the left), Qian Xuesen (second from the left) gave a scholarly report entitled "Master Design of the Socialist Construction—Advisory Service for the Party and the Country." More than 500 scholars in the capital, and the students and teachers of the Renmin University of China listened to the report. The first one from the right was Huang Da.

"I am much honored to be asked to give the first lecture of ' Wu Yuzhang Scholarly Lectures'. Despite my limited capabilities and many difficulties, I still intend to take the chance to express my respect for Wu Yuzhang." In the report, Qian Xuesen effectively demonstrated his great idea to set up the ministry of grand design of socialist construction and its contribution to sustainable national development, and fully expressed his hope that the Renmin University of China could train more talented people for the Party and the country.

85

图 85 为 1987 年 7 月 29 日，时任中国人民大学校长袁宝华和副校长黄达与南疆新闻班学员在一起。前排左三为黄达，左四为袁宝华。

On July 29, 1987, Yuan Baohua, the then president of the Renmin University of China, was with Huang Da, the then vice president of the Renmin University of China, and students of the South Xinjiang journalism class. The third one from the left in the front row was Huang Da, and the fourth one from the left in the first row was Yuan Baohua.

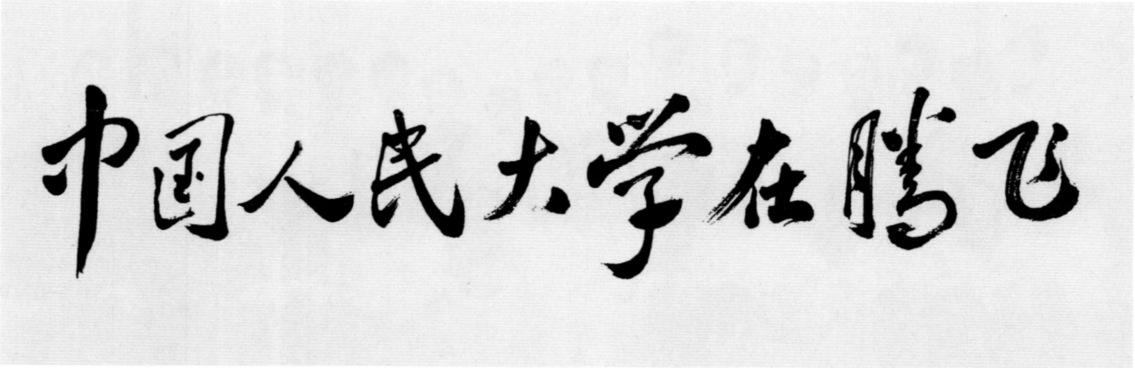

86

图 86 为 1987 年 10 月，中国人民大学建校五十周年之际，黄达为学校纪念画册题写“中国人民大学在腾飞”。

In October 1987, at the 50th anniversary of the Renmin University of China, Huang Da inscribed "The Renmin University of China is taking off" on the school album.

87

图87为1987年夏，黄达（第一排右二）出席中国人民大学大型企业厂长（经理）岗位职务培训班结业典礼。

In the summer of 1987, Huang Da (second from the right in the first row) attended the closing ceremony of the professional training class of heads (managers) of large enterprises given by the Renmin University of China.

88

图 88 为 1987 年 10 月 13 日，黄达（左二）在山西临汾检阅中国人民大学学生军训队伍。这是中国人民大学历史上第一次举行学生军训。

On October 13, 1987, Huang Da (second from the left) was inspecting the students of the Renmin University of China who were receiving military trainings in Linfen, Shanxi. It was the first military training organized by the Renmin University of China for its students.

89

图 89 为 1988 年底，黄达出席北京市职称评定委员会会议。左三为黄达，右三为委员会主任、著名水利专家张光斗教授。

At the end of 1988, Huang Da attended a meeting of Beijing Professional Appraisal Committee. The third one from the left was Huang Da, and the third one from the right was Prof. Zhang Guangdou, director of the committee and a famous irrigation expert.

90

图 90 为 1987 年 11 月 1 日，黄达与华北大学校友一起参加中国人民大学建校五十周年纪念活动。第一排左六为中国人民大学建校初期的校领导班子成员李新，第二排左四为黄达。

On November 1, 1987, Huang Da and the alumni and alumnae of North China University attended the activities to commemorate the 50th anniversary of the Renmin University of China. The sixth one from the left in the first row was Li Xin, a member of the leadership of the Renmin University of China when it was first established; and the fourth one from the left in the second row was Huang Da.

91

图 91 为 1989 年 9 月 9 日，时任中国人民大学校长袁宝华、副校长黄达、党委书记李文海，在庆祝教师节五周年表彰大会现场为获奖教师颁奖。从左至右分别为：黄达、袁宝华和李文海。

On September 9, 1989, Yuan Baohua, the then president of the Renmin University of China, Huang Da, the then vice president of the Renmin University of China, and Li Wenhai, the then secretary of the Party Committee of the Renmin University of China, presented awards to the teachers at the commending conference at the 5th anniversary of the Teachers' Day. From the left to the right are Huang Da, Yuan Baohua and Li Wenhai.

图 92 为 1989 年 9 月 9 日，时任中国人民大学校长袁宝华（右一）与副校长黄达（左一）出席庆祝教师节五周年表彰大会。

On September 9, 1989, Yuan Baohua (first from the right), the then president of the Renmin University of China, and Huang Da (first from the left), the then vice president of the Renmin University of China, attended the commending conference at the 5th anniversary of the Teachers' Day.

92

93

图 93 为 1990 年 3 月 8 日，中国人民大学在西山宾馆进行职称评定。部分与会专家合影留念。前排左一为李法坤，左五至左八分别为：彭明、甘惜分、戴逸、高铭暄；后排从左至右分别为：李文海、张向舒、胡乃武、郑杭生、黄达、周新城。

On March 8, 1990, the Renmin University of China carried out evaluation of academic titles in Xishan Hotel. Some of the attendees took a group photo. The first from the left in the front row is Li Fakun, the fifth to the eighth from the left are Peng Ming, Gan Xifen, Dai Yi and Gao Mingxuan; from the left to the right in the back row are Li Wenhai, Zhang Xiangshu, Hu Naiwu, Zheng Hangsheng, Huang Da and Zhou Xincheng.

94

图 94 为 1990 年 3 月 8 日，中国人民大学在西山宾馆进行职称评定。部分与会专家合影留念。前排从左至右分别为：杜厚文、人事处干部、余学本、钟契夫、陈共、孙健；后排左一和左二分别为胡乃武、黄达，右一为韩嘉骏。

On March 8, 1990, the Renmin University of China carried out evaluation of academic titles in Xishan Hotel. Some of the attendees took a group photo. From the left to the right in the front row are Du Houwen, a cadre of the personnel department,Yu Xueben, Zhong Qifu, Chen Gong, Sun Jian; the first and the second from the left in the back row are Hu Naiwu and Huang Da, the first from the right is Han Jiajun.

4-5-2>

新中国成立初期，为了能够把正规办学和向社会办学、校内办学和校外办学、脱产学习和不脱产学习结合起来，真正解决大规模经济建设需求与专业人才短缺的矛盾，中国人民大学开始尝试进行函授教育。1951 年 11 月 5 日，刘少奇副主席在中国人民大学创办函授教育的报告上批示："可根据此办法在平津及其他城市的若干机关先行试办，待有经验后，再发指示。函授部组织亦从缓办，先指定二三人试办。"同年 11 月 17 日，中国人民大学成立了以成仿吾副校长为主任的函授教育委员会。1953 年 2 月 7 日，第一批中国人民大学函授生在北京、太原和天津三地同时举行开学典礼，标志着新中国函授教育事业正式起步。

1952 年 1 月，作为组织实施函授教育的教学管理部门的中国人民大学函授部成立，1959 年 10 月，更名为函授学院。1984 年 7 月，创办于 1950 年 9 月的中国人民大学夜大学划归函授学院。1994 年 2 月函授学院再次更名为成人高等教育学院。后又于 2004 年 10 月，与中国人民大学网络教育学院合并组建中国人民大学继续教育学院。

黄达初进校领导班子，函授是其分工的一项。

In the early years of New China, the Renmin University of China began to try to offer correspondence education in order to combine regular school-running with school running by different social sectors, off-job education with on-the-job education; and to truly solve the contradiction between the demand for large-scale economic development and the shortage of professionals. On November 5, 1951, Liu Shaoqi, the then vice chairman of China, replied to the report, submitted by the Renmin University of China and on offering correspondence education, "It can be tried in some organs in Peking and Tianjin and other cities. With experience obtained, an instruction may be issued. The setting of the Correspondence Education Department should slow down and two to three members of the staff may be designated to pilot it. " On November 17 of the same year, the Renmin University of China set up a Correspondence Education Commission with its Vice President Cheng Fangwu being the director. On February 7, 1953, an opening ceremony was held concurrently in Beijing, Taiyuan and Tianjin for the first students of correspondence courses, marking the first step officially taken by China in correspondence education.

In January 1952, the Correspondence Education Department of the Renmin University of China was established as the management department responsible for organizing the implementation of correspondence education. In October 1959, it was renamed College of Correspondence Education. In July 1984, the Night College of the Renmin University of China, created in September 1950, was incorporated into the College of Correspondence Education. In February 1994, the College of Correspondence Education was renamed again into College of Adult Higher Education. Later in October 2004, it was merged with the College of Online Education of the Renmin University of China into the School of Continuing Education, the Renmin University of China.

As a new leader, teaching was one of Huang Da's responsibilities.

95

图 95 为 1983 年冬，黄达在中国人民大学函授学院毕业生会上讲话。

In the winter of 1983, Huang Da was delivering a speech at the meeting of graduates of the College of Correspondence Education, the Renmin University of China.

96

图 96 为 1984 年 9 月 9 日，黄达在沈阳故宫。此次沈阳之行是他代表中国人民大学专门考察该地区函授的办学情况。

On September 9, 1984, Huang Da was in the Shenyang Imperial Palace. He went to Shenyang to inspect the running of correspondence education there on behalf of the Renmin University of China.

97

98

图97为1987年7月28日，黄达（右二）代表中国人民大学专门赴新疆喀什看望函授学生。

On July 28, 1987, Huang Da (second from the right), on behalf of the Renmin University of China, went to Kashi of Xinjiang to visit students of correspondence course.

图98为1987年7月30日，黄达（左一）与新疆喀什当地领导交谈。

On July 30, 1987, Huang Da (first from the left) was talking with the local leaders of Kashi, Xinjiang.

99

图 99 为 1987 年 7 月 30 日，黄达（后排左三）与喀什大清真寺的大阿訇在一起。

On July 30, 1987, Huang Da (third from the left in the second row) was with the grand imam of the great mosque in Kashi.

4-5-3>

改革开放以来，高校学术交流方面“闭关锁国”的政策也同时结束了。但对于中国人民大学来讲，由于是在抗日战争环境下创建并在“闭关锁国”政策下发展起来的，海外的学术联系非常缺乏。所以开展对外学术交流，较北大、清华、北师大等兄弟院校要困难许多。中国人民大学就是在这样的起点上一直坚持并创造条件努力推进对外学术交流方针。

Since China adopted the reform and opening-up policy, it ended the "isolation " policy on academic exchanges among universities. However, the Renmin University of China did not have many academic contacts with foreign universities, because it was created during the Anti-Japanese War period and right under the "isolation " policy. Therefore, to have academic exchanges with foreign universities was much more difficult for it than for Peking University, Tsinghua University, Beijing Normal University, etc. From such a starting point, the Renmin University of China has been creating conditions to strive to push forward the principle of foreign academic exchanges.

100

图 100 为 1981 年 3 月底，黄达（第二排左四）与同事在中国人民大学图书馆（现藏书馆）接待来访的外国专家。

At the close of March 1981, Huang Da (fourth from the left in the second row) and his colleagues received the visiting foreign experts in the then school library.

101

图 101 为 1987 年 1 月 27 日，时任中国人民大学副校长黄达（左一）在春节期间代表学校宴请森新一教授（左二）。

1917 年，森新一出生在中国沈阳，1945 年在中国东北参加中国革命工作，1957 年到中国人民大学任日语专家，为建立学校的日语专业做出了巨大贡献。他在承担培养中青年日语教师任务的同时，还为中国人民大学和北京市高校文科公共日语编写教材，参加了《毛泽东选集》一至四卷日文版的翻译定稿工作。"文化大革命"期间，他与夫人回到日本。1980 年 8 月，他们再次受聘为中国人民大学日语专家，并长期定居中国至今。同年，他们被国家外国专家局授予"外国老专家"称号，享受相应的政治和生活待遇并获得在中国的永久居留权。

On January 27, 1987, the then vice president of the Renmin University of China Huang Da (first from the left) invited Prof. Shinichi Mori (second from the left) to dinner on behalf of the university.

Prof. Shinichi Mori was born in Shenyang in 1917, became a revolutionary member in northeastern China in 1945, and then a Japanese language expert in the Renmin University of China in 1957, before making great contribution to establishing the Japanese major. While cultivating young and mid-aged Japanese language teachers, he wrote public Japanese language textbooks for the Renmin University of China and for the universities of liberal arts in Beijing; and took part in the translation and proofreading of volumes 1-4 of *Selected Works of Mao Zedong*. During the Cultural Revolution, he and his wife returned to Japan. In August 1980, they were invited once again to be the Japanese language experts of the Renmin University of China, and have been settled here. The same year, they were presented the title of "Senior Foreign Experts" by China's State Administration for Foreign Experts Affairs, and enjoyed corresponding political and life treatment and obtained the right to live in China permanently.

102

图 102 为 1987 年 10 月，时任中国人民大学副校长黄达（左二）会见波兰籍华裔留学生校友胡佩芳（右一）。左一为郑杭生。

胡佩芳（1931—2014）是波兰籍华裔女作家、翻译家、中国作协和波兰作协会员，曾于 20 世纪 50 年代就读于中国人民大学，后与波兰留学生结婚并定居波兰。在旅居波兰近 60 年的时间里，她始终积极致力于向波兰民众传播中国传统文化、民间艺术以及文学作品，为宣传中国、促进中波文化交流以及加深两国人民的了解做出了突出贡献。2014 年，胡佩芳被追授为代表国家至高荣誉的"荣耀艺术"文化勋章，以表彰她为中波两国文化交流做出的贡献。

In October 1987, the then vice president of the Renmin University of China Huang Da (second from the left) received Hu Peifang (first from the right), a Chinese-Polish student and an alumnus of the university. First from the left is Zheng Hangsheng.

Hu Peifang (1931—2014), a Chinese-Polish woman writer and translator, and a member of China Writers Association and Polish Writers Association, was a student of the Renmin University of China during the 1950s. Later, she married a Polish student in China and settled in Poland. She lived in Poland for nearly 60 years, during which she was active to spread traditional Chinese culture, folk arts and literary works to the Polish people, contributing a lot to publicizing China, promoting cultural exchanges between China and Poland, and deepening mutual understanding. In 2014, Hu Peifang was posthumously given the cultural medal of "Honor Art," the highest honor of China in the field to praise her for her contribution to the cultural communication between China and Poland.

4-6

国家政策咨询、学术活动和校外讲学

Participate in Policy Consulting, Academic Activities and Off-campus Lectures

4-6-1>

按照苏联理论，社会主义国家根本不存在通货膨胀，中国当然不能例外。即使是在改革开放初期，不能对通货膨胀有丝毫妥协，或者说目标只能是“零”通货膨胀率，仍然是当时官方的、正统的看法。

1980年初，国家计划委员会综合局宫著铭却在给中央领导的一封信中明确指出我国摆脱不了通货膨胀，并提出应把2%定为最优通货膨胀率的建议。为此，当年2月上旬，国务院财贸小组就此问题专门召集了包括黄达在内的三十多位知名专家就通货膨胀问题进行论证。

通货膨胀是黄达长期重点关注的问题。事实上，1979年初，在他那篇引起争议的论文《谈谈我们的物价方针兼及通货膨胀问题》中已经明确指出通货膨胀的实际存在。同年底，在中国金融学会第二次代表大会组织的学术交流中，他又以《关于目前“货币过多”的几个问题》为题阐述了自己的想法。在此次座谈会上，黄达再次表达了自己一以贯之的观点。他认为“社会主义与通货膨胀不能相容”的论断不能成立，通货膨胀在我国长期存在。他指出，我国通货膨胀的实质是在生产发展迟缓、劳动生产率没有什么提高甚至有所下降的情况下，强制压低消费份额（实际消费水平）来保证过大比例积累的手段。而且，之所以存在长期的通货膨胀，其直接原因就是财政赤字和信用膨胀。

右页图 ⟼

图103为1980年2月上旬，黄达在国务院财贸小组组织的座谈会上的发言手稿。后经黄达本人删改整理，以《社会主义也有通货膨胀》为题收入《黄达自选集》《黄达文集（再续）》与《黄达经济文选》。

This is the manuscript of Huang Da's speech at the symposium held by the Public Finance and Economics Team of the State Council in early February 1980. Later, it was revised by Huang Da before being collected in *Self Collected Works of Huang Da*, *Essays of Huang Da (Extention 2)* and *Selected Economic Essays of Huang Da* under the title of Socialism Has Inflation, too.

According to the Soviet theory , inflation did not exist in the socialist countries at all, of which China was no exception. Despite the fact that China had just adopted the reform and opening-up policy, it remained the official and orthodox view at the time to not compromise a little on inflation, or to realize the goal of "zero " inflation.

Early in 1980, Gong Zhuming from the State Planning Commission wrote a letter to the central leadership of China, in which he clearly pointed out that there was no way for China to get away from inflation, and suggested to set the optimal inflation rate at 2%. To that end, in early February that year, the Public Finance and Economics Team of the State Council invited more than 30 famous experts including Huang Da to hold a discussion on inflation.

Inflation is an issue to which Huang Da has been paying attention. As a matter of fact, early in 1979, in his much controversial article On China's Policy of Commodity Prices and Inflation, Huang Da had explicitly pointed out the existence of inflation. At the end of that year, in an academic exchange organized by the 2nd Congress of China Society for Finance and Banking, he expounded his ideas with On Some Problems with the Present "Too Much Currency". At the seminar, Huang Da expressed his consistent views once again, thinking that the judgment— " socialism is incompatible with inflation "—was untenable, and that inflation would exist in China for a long time. He pointed out that inflation was essentially a means of ensuring an excessively high proportion of accumulation by forcefully reducing the shares of consumption (net consumption level) under the circumstance where production developed slowly and productivity was not improved, even fell. Besides, the immediate causes for lasting inflation were fiscal deficits and credit inflation.

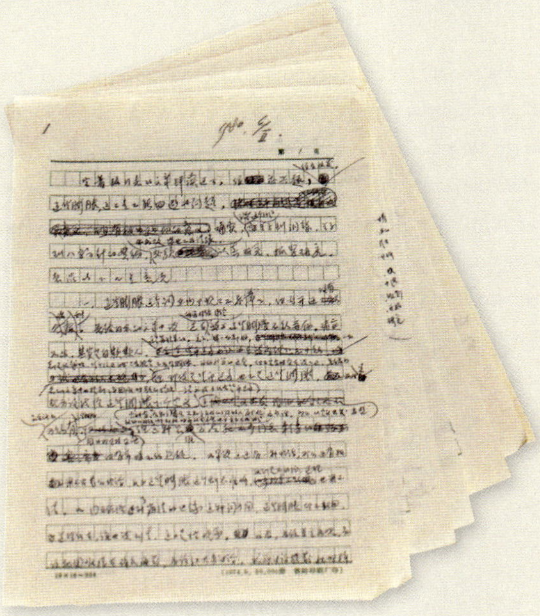

103

4-6-2>

改革开放之前，“信用膨胀”很少被提及。

1979 年，黄达在写那篇有争议的通货膨胀文章时，曾使用过这个词，但也只是行文中用以表示信用扩大并非基于流通客观需求的经济现象，而并没有明确把它作为一个确定的经济范畴来看待。

直到 1980 年初，“信用膨胀”才逐渐被人关注。一方面，1979 年银行存贷款都以前所未有的幅度增长，现金增发数量也大大高于往年。另一方面，1980 年银行开始发放在计划经济中被严格禁止的用于形成固定资产的“中短期贷款”。

1980 年 11 月底，中国金融学会和中国社会科学院财贸经济研究所在苏州召开小型“银行作用理论座谈会”，三四十位金融学界和业界的知名专家悉数出席。由于在会前不久，政府文件中出现了“信用膨胀”字样，于是会议自然聚焦于“信用膨胀”问题。黄达在会上详细阐述了信用膨胀的概念、成因和衡量方法。他强调财政大量透支、大量发放没有物资保证的短期贷款（物资保证不实的也应包括在内）、大量发放没有相应长期性信用资金来源的长期贷款等是引起信用膨胀的主要原因。此外，他还提出了多层次的信用膨胀统计方法。

Before China adopted the reform and opening-up policy, "credit inflation " was rarely mentioned.

In 1979, Huang Da used the word in his much controversial article on inflation, but only to help express the economic phenomenon that credit inflation was not based on the objective demand for circulation, instead of using the word as a specific economic category.

It was not until early 1980 that "credit inflation " began to draw people's attention. On the one hand, bank deposits and loans grew by unprecedented margins and ever more notes were issued in 1979, while on the other, banks began to issue "medium- and short-term loans " in 1980 which were used to form fixed assets and were strictly prohibited in the planned economy.

In late November 1980, China Society for Finance and Banking and the Institute of Finance and Trade Economics, Chinese Academy of Social Sciences held a small "Forum on the Theories of the Banks' Role " in Suzhou. Thirty or forty renowned experts in the financial sector and enterprises attended the forum. Because the government used "credit inflation " not long before the convening of the forum, the attendees naturally focused on the quantitative issue of "credit inflation. " On the forum, Huang Da expounded the concept, causes and measurement of credit inflation. According to him, the excessive fiscal overdraw, the issuance of short-term loans without material guarantee for long (which shall also involve loans with untruthful material guarantee), the issuance of long-term loans without any source of long-term credit capital were also main reasons for credit inflation. Besides, he put forward the multi-level statistical method of credit inflation.

104

105

图 104 为 1980 年 11 月底，黄达与在苏州出席“银行作用理论座谈会”的专家在一起。后排右一为黄达，前排右二为时任中国金融学会秘书长孙及民。

In late November 1980, Huang Da was with some experts attending the "Forum on the Theories of the Banks' Role" in Suzhou. The first one from the right in the back row is Huang Da, and the second one from the right in the front row is Sun Jimin, the then secretary-general of China Society for Finance and Banking.

图 105 为 1980 年 11 月底，黄达在苏州出席“银行作用理论座谈会”期间的个人留影。

This is a picture of Huang Da in late November 1980 when he attended "Forum on the Theories of the Banks' Role" in Suzhou.

4-6-3>

一直以来，黄达始终认为，研究金融必须同时以同等的关注度研究财政。特别是在改革开放后，担任中国财政学会常务理事、副会长等职又为他深入研究财政问题提供了便利。

1981年10月底至11月初，中国财政学会在南京召开年会和理论讨论会，就“生财、聚财、用财之道”等热点问题展开讨论。黄达出席会议并发表了自己的看法。他认为，第一，1980年底确定的调整中必须保持一定速度的大方针是正确的。第二，要保持一定的速度就需要一定数量的资金，而资金供给有其客观限度，不能满足需求；并着重指出，当时上下忽悠的“只要聚财有道，资金问题不难解决”的观点是有问题的。第三，既然保持速度与可供资金之间存在一定矛盾，对此，难免要少许搞点膨胀。他特别强调:“如果要搞点膨胀，必须正视它，承认它。……如果搞了膨胀而不承认，特别是一边搞，一边还认为走着阳光大道，那么危险就大多了，而我们目前似乎有点这种危险。”

Since the reform and opening up, Huang Da served as the executive member and vice chairman of China Society of Public Finance for years. He believes that equal attention should be paid to public finance while studying finance.

At the turn of October and November 1981, China Society of Public Finance held its annual meeting and a theoretical symposium in Nanjing, and the attendees had a discussion on hot topics including "making money, gathering money and using money. " Huang Da attended the meeting and expressed his views. According to him, the policy of keeping a certain speed of adjustments set at the end of 1980 was correct; it needed a certain amount of capital in order to keep a certain speed, while capital supply was objectively limited, and could not meet the need. He stressed that the then view that "with good ways of gathering money, it is easy to solve the problem of capital " was not right. He also believed that inflation would be inevitable for the contradiction between speed and capital available. He especially highlighted, "There will be inflation, and we must face it and admit it...If inflation is there and we refuse to acknowledge it while thinking that we are on a bright road, it would be dangerous, and we seem to be more or less in such a danger now. "

106

图106为1980年初，中国财政学会成立大会在佛山召开。黄达（右一）出席会议并与部分专家合影留念。

Early in 1980, Huang Da attended the inauguration meeting of China Society of Public Finance held in Foshan. He was with some experts during the meeting. The first one from the right is Huang Da.

107

图 107 为 1981 年 10 月底至 11 月初，黄达在出席中国财政学会于南京召开的年会期间，游览莫愁湖。

At the turn of October and November 1981, Huang Da attended the annual meeting of China Society of Public Finance in Nanjing. This was his photo taken by the Mochou Lake.

4-6-4>

1980 年底到 1995 年，黄达曾担任中国价格学会常务理事、副会长等职务，长期对中国的价格理论与实践问题保持高度关注。

1982 年 2 月，中国价格学会在昆明召开以“稳定物价方针”为主题的研讨会。黄达出席会议，并以“复杂的物价问题不能简单看待”为核心表达了自己对于物价方针的看法。他认为稳定物价方针不应从“稳定”两个字的字面含义去理解，而应根据我国多年来的实践进行概括。“保持基本稳定，进行必要的合理调整与在非常情况下采取暂时的冻结相结合”应当是当时我国稳定物价的方针。同时，他还从马克思主义货币理论的角度对稳定物价进行了理论分析，强调在判断物价稳定与否时，应当结合工资的状况。

Huang Da was the executive director and vice chairman of China Society of Price from the end of 1980 to 1995, and was paying close attention to price theories and practice in China.

In February 1982, China Society of Price held a symposium themed with "policy on stabilizing prices". Huang Da attended the symposium, and expressed his views on the commodity price policy around "complicated commodity price issue can't be treated simply. " He believed that the policy on stabilizing prices should not be understood by the literal meaning of "stabilizing, " but generalized by China's practices over the years. It should be China's policy of stabilizing commodity prices to "maintain stable commodity prices on the whole, take necessary and reasonable adjustments, and combine it with the adoption of temporary freezing under exceptional circumstances. " Meanwhile, he made a theoretical analysis of stabilizing commodity prices from the angle of Marxist currency theories; and highlighted the necessity to take into consideration the concurrent wage situation when judging commodity price stability.

| 右页图 |→

图 108 为 1982 年 2 月，黄达（右二）与在昆明出席中国价格学会理论研讨会的专家在一起。

In February 1982, Huang Da was with some experts presenting theoretical symposium held in Kunming by China Society of Price. The second one from the right is Huang Da.

108

4-6-5>

1983年5月，应山西金融学会的邀请，黄达在太原做了题为《关于货币流通范围的问题》的学术讲演。

关于货币流通范围，20世纪60年代初，黄达在《银行信贷原则和货币流通》一文中首次专门论及。文章明确提出把非现金流转也看作是货币流通的观点。由于不符合从苏联引进的主流观点——“只有现金的运动才构成货币流通”，遂引起当时学术界的广泛讨论，赞同与批判兼而有之。改革开放之后，黄达在一系列文章和讲演中均提及这一问题，但没有以此作为中心主题。本次太原演讲，黄达以货币流通范围为主题，全面地剖析问题讨论的过程、错误理论观念的由来、为什么对错误观念产生了怀疑、克服这样的观念必须排除的理论责难以及这一争论的实践意义。

事实上，在两年前的广州全国货币理论讨论会上，关于货币流通范围的问题已经在金融理论界取得基本共识。随后，金融系统内部的广大从业人员也逐渐接受了“大”货币流通的观念。但要把这样的观念贯彻到实际操作之中，则面临着很多难以想象的困难。以至随后的一些年份黄达依然为之费了不少笔墨。

直到1994年，中国人民银行才正式公布了国际通用的货币量统计口径。

In May 1983, at the invitation of Shanxi Society for Finance and Banking, Huang Da gave a scholarly speech titled On the Sphere of Currency Circulation.

As for the sphere of currency circulation, Huang Da had a special discussion of it in his article Principles of Bank Credit and Currency Circulation in the early 1960s. In that article, he expressly put forward the view that non-cash flow of money shall also be regarded as part of currency circulation. Since it went against the mainstream idea—"only the flow of cash constitutes currency circulation "—introduced from the Soviet Union at the time, it caused extensive discussions in the scholars including both the approvers and the criticizers. Huang Da mentioned the issue in a series of articles and speeches since China adopted the reform and opening-up policy, but did not make it the central topic. In the above speech in Taiyuan, he took the sphere of currency circulation as the topic to analyze the process of discussion on the issue, the reasons why there were erroneous concepts, the reasons why he began to doubt the erroneous concepts, the theoretical blame to be gotten rid of in order to overcome such concepts, and the significance of such debate in practice.

In fact, at the National Seminar on Currency Theories held in Guangzhou two years before that, the world of finance and economics had got a consensus on the sphere of currency circulation. Later the vast jobholders inside the financial system gradually accepted the concept of "big " currency circulation. However, there were many unimaginable difficulties to put the concept into practice. That's why Huang Da wrote a lot on it in the following years.

In 1994, the People's Bank of China officially released the international standard on the statistical coverage of the amount of currency.

右页图 ⟼

图109为1983年5月，黄达（后排右三）在太原讲学期间，与中国人民银行山西省分行的人大校友合影留念。

Huang Da was with some of Alumni of the Renmin University of China who were working in the People's Bank of China Shanxi Branch in May 1983 when he was giving lectures in Taiyuan. The third one from the right in the back row is Huang Da.

109

4-6-6>

1985 年 11 月，黄达应谭崇台和曾启贤两位教授之邀，专赴武汉大学为师生讲授“财政信贷综合平衡”。谭崇台教授是最早把西方发展经济学系统引入中国的经济学家之一，为发展经济学在中国的传播与发展做出了重大贡献。曾启贤教授是 20 世纪 80 年代活跃在我国经济学界的一位知名学者。他曾为黄达的《财政信贷综合平衡导论》写了长篇书评。

In November 1985, at the invitation of two professors, namely Tan Chongtai and Zeng Qixian, Huang Da made a special trip to Wuhan University to teach its teachers and students "General Equilibrium of Public Finance and Credit." Prof. Tan Chongtai, as one of the first Chinese economists to introduce the development economics system in the West into China, makes great contribution to the spread and development of development economics in China. Prof. Zeng Qixian was a well-known economist in China in the 1980s. He wrote a long book review on Huang Da's book *Introduction of General Equilibrium on Public Finance and Credit.*

110

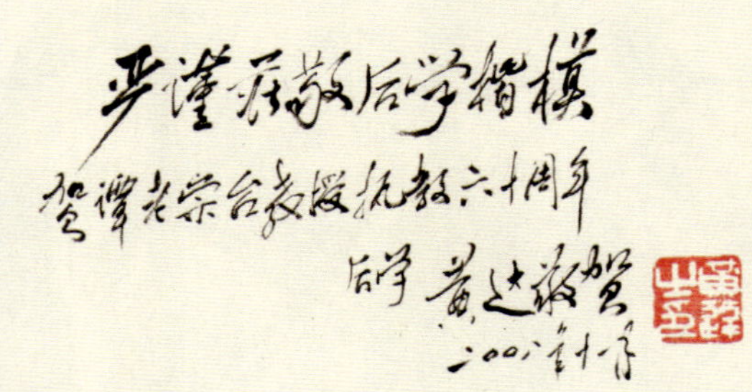

111

图 110 为 1998 年 3 月 20 日，黄达（左四）出席“谭崇台教授执教五十周年庆贺会”。左三为谭崇台。

On March 20, 1998, Huang Da (fourth from the left) attended "Congratulation on the 50th Anniversary of Prof. Tan Chongtai's Life as a Teacher." Third from the left is Tan Chongtai.

图 111 为 2008 年 11 月 25 日，黄达为谭崇台教授从教 60 周年题写贺词：“严谨庄敬，后学楷模”。

On November 25, 2008, Huang Da inscribed a congratulatory address— "Vigorous and Strict, Model for Junior Scholars"— for Prof. Tan Chongtai for the latter's 60th anniversary of being a teacher.

112

图 112 为 1985 年 11 月，黄达（右一）与谭崇台（左一）教授在武汉大学。

Huang Da (first from the right) was with Prof. Tan Chongtai (first from the left) from Wuhan University.

4-6-7>

1988 年 3 月，黄达受邀在吉林财贸学院（现吉林财经大学）和吉林省金融学会，就货币和物价问题作了三次讲演。

期间，应学生要求，黄达在一张卡片上为吉林财贸学院的学生题词：“莘莘学子，一代精英；增辉华夏，大任于斯；自勖自勉，志在请缨；无愧来者，岂逊先贤；风流倜傥，当属尔侪。”

In March 1988, Huang Da was invited to give three lectures on currency and commodity price in Jilin School of Finance and Economics (now known as Jilin University of Finance and Economics) and Jilin Society for Finance and Banking.

During the lectures, asked by a student, Huang Da inscribed "You are the elite of your generation. For the duty to prosper China, you are shouldering heavy tasks. You urge and encourage yourselves therefore, to feel no qualms to the following generations and to be the same as, even better than the past generations. You are truly with the graces " for the students of Jilin School of Finance and Economics.

右页图 ⟼

图 113 为 1988 年 3 月 21 日，黄达为吉林财贸学院（现吉林财经大学）师生作报告。

On March 21, 1988, Huang Da gave the teachers and students of Jilin School of Finance and Economics (now known as Jilin University of Finance and Economics) a report.

113

4-6-8>

1989 年 10 月中旬，中国金融学会甘肃省分会组织金融以及新闻、文化等多领域专家赴甘肃考察。

In mid October 1989, China Society for Finance and Banking Gansu Branch organized experts in finance, news and culture to go to Gansu for a visit.

114

图 114 为 1989 年 10 月，赴甘肃考察的全体专家在麦积山下合影留念。前排左六为黄达。

In October 1989, all members in the visit to Gansu took a group photo at the foot of the Maiji Mountain. The sixth one from the left in the front row is Huang Da.

115

图 115 为 1989 年 10 月，赴甘肃考察的部分专家在夏河拉卜楞寺前合影留念。左二为江其务，左五至左七分别为：黄达、俞天一、冯大麟。

In October 1989, some members visiting Gansu took a group photo in front of Labrang Monastery, Xiahe. The second one from the left is Jiang Qiwu. From the fifth to the seventh from the left are Huang Da, Yu Tianyi and Feng Dalin.

4-6-9>

其他国家政策咨询、学术活动和校外讲学

Other Policy Consulting, Academic Activities and Off-campus Lectures

116

图 116 为 1982 年，黄达在内蒙古财经学院（2012 年更名为内蒙古财经大学）讲课期间的个人留影。

This is a photo of Huang Da when he gave classes to Inner Mongolia School of Finance and Economics (renamed Inner Mongolia University of Finance and Economics in 2012) in 1982.

117

图 117 为 1982 年，黄达（后排右一）与内蒙古财经学院教师在一起。

Huang Da (first from the right in the back row) was with some teachers of Inner Mongolia School of Finance and Economics in 1982.

118

图 118 为 1984 年 4 月，黄达（左二）在陕西财经学院讲学期间，与陕西财经学院院长冯大麟（左一）、金融系主任江其务（右一）在一起。

陕西财经学院原属中国人民银行主管，后于 2000 年并入西安交通大学，更为现名西安交通大学经济与金融学院。

In April 1984, Huang Da (second from the left) was with Feng Dalin (first from the left), dean of Shaanxi School of Finance and Economics, and Jiang Qiwu (first from the right), head of the Finance Department of the same college, when he was giving lectures in Shaanxi School of Finance and Economics.

Shaanxi School of Finance and Economics was formerly and directly under the People's Bank of China. Later it was incorporated into Xi'an Jiaotong University in 2000. Now it is named School of Finance and Economics of Xi'an Jiaotong University.

119

图119为1984年10月，黄达应邀在“武汉金融中心与改革座谈会”上发言。

他以“银行管理体制应与经济体制改革和金融中心建设相适应”为题，讲述了如何改革单一纵向银行管理体制的问题。他认为，单一纵向银行管理体制是中央集权计划管理体制的必然伴生物。要走向市场经济体制，这样的单一纵向银行管理体制自然应该改革，而且原则上应是分散决策与宏观调控相结合。

In October 1984, Huang Da delivered a speech at "Wuhan Financial Centers and Reform Symposium."

He explained how to reform the single longitudinal bank management system under the title of "The bank management system shall go along with economic restructuring and the building of financial centers." He believed the single longitudinal bank management system to be a concomitant of the planning system under strong central powers, that such a single longitudinal bank management system should naturally be reformed in order to develop the market economy, following the principle of decentralized decision-making and macro control.

120

图 120 为 1986 年 8 月，黄达出席中国金融学会在长春组织的研讨会，与部分与会专家在一起。左一为黄达，左二为资耀华。

In August 1986, Huang Da attended a symposium held by China Society for Finance and Banking in Changchun, and Huang Da was with some experts. The first and second one from the left is Huang Da and Zi Yaohua respectively.

图 121 为 1986 年 8 月，黄达在会议期间游览长白山天池。

Huang Da was by the Lake of Heaven on the summit of Mount Baitou, the Changbai Mountain, in August 1986.

121

122

图 122 为 1987 年 4 月，黄达赴厦门大学讲学期间，与当时主持该校金融专业的两位教授洪文金（右一）、张亦春（左一）合影留念。

In April 1987, Huang Da was with Prof. Hong Wenjin (first from the right) and Prof. Zhang Yichun (first from the left) who were in charge of the Finance Major of Xiamen University then, and Huang Da was giving lectures in Xiamen University at the time.

4-7

博士生培养及参与博士生答辩
Cultivate PhD Students and Participate in Dissertation Defense

123

图 123 为 1988 年 11 月 25 日，1985 级博士生周慕冰（中国农业银行董事长）、王松奇（中国社会科学院金融所原党委书记、副所长）和邓乐平（西南财经大学中国金融研究中心教授）博士学位论文答辩会现场，全体答辩委员在一起。从左至右分别为：曾康霖、赵海宽、厉以宁、陈共、王庆彬、黄达。

On November 25, 1988, Zhou Mubing (director of Agricultural Bank of China), Wang Songqi (former secretary of the Party Committee and deputy director of the Institute of Finance and Banking of the Chinese Academy of Social Sciences) and Deng Leping (professor of the Institute of Chinese Finance Studies of Southwestern University of Finance and Economics), Ph.D. candidates of Class 1985, were taking the doctoral dissertation oral examination, and all the panel members were there. From the left to the right are Zeng Kanglin, Zhao Haikuan, Li Yining, Chen Gong, Wang Qingbin and Huang Da.

124

图 124 为 1988 年 11 月 26 日，黄达、王传纶与刚刚通过博士学位论文答辩的 1985 级博士生合影留念。从左至右分别为：贝多广、周慕冰、王传纶、黄达、王松奇、邓乐平。

On November 26, 1988, Huang Da and Wang Chuanlun took a group photo with the doctoral students of Class 1985 who just passed the doctoral dissertation oral examination. From the left to the right are Bei Duoguang, Zhou Mubing, Wang Chuanlun, Huang Da, Wang Songqi and Deng Leping.

125

126

图 125 为 2015 年 10 月 14 日，黄达（左一）与 1988 级博士生李焰（右一，中国人民大学商学院教授）在一起。

On October 14, 2015, Huang Da (first from the left) was with Li Yan (first from the right, a professor of the School of Business of the Renmin University of China), a Ph.D. candidate of Class 1988.

图 126 为 1999 年 7 月 26 日，黄达（右一）与 1991 级博士生王广谦（左一，中央财经大学校长）在一起。

On July 26, 1999, Huang Da (first from the right) was with Wang Guangqian (first from the left, president of the Central University of Finance and Economics), a Ph.D. candidate of Class 1991.

127

128

图 127 为 2015 年 11 月 1 日，黄达（左一）与 1990 级博士生刘振亚（右一，中国人民大学财政金融学院教授）在一起。

On November 1, 2015, Huang Da (first from the left) was with Liu Zhenya (first from the right, a professor of the School of Finance of the Renmin University of China), a Ph.D. candidate of Class 1990.

图 128 为 1998 年 6 月 3 日，黄达等与刚刚通过博士学位论文答辩的 1992 级博士生陈雨露（中国人民银行副行长）合影留念。从左至右分别为：陶湘、朱义信、黄达、陈雨露、胡代光、吴念鲁、王传纶、王林生、王克华。

On June 3, 1998, Huang Da took a group photo with Chen Yulu (deputy governor of the People's Bank of China), a Ph.D. candidate of Class 1992 who just passed the doctoral dissertation oral examination. From the left to the right are Tao Xiang, Zhu Yixin, Huang Da, Chen Yulu, Hu Daiguang, Wu Nianlu, Wang Chuanlun, Wang Linsheng and Wang Kehua.

129

131

130

132

图 129 为 1998 年 5 月 18 日，黄达等与刚刚通过博士学位论文答辩的 1995 级博士生李鹰（香港交银国际控股有限公司副首席执行官）合影留念。前排从左至右分别为：王克华、王积业、王传纶、黄达；后排从左至右分别为：李鹰、朱毅峰、李茂生、吴晓球、王广谦。

On May 18, 1993, Huang Da took a group photo with Li Ying (deputy chief executive of BOCOM International Holdings Company Limited), a Ph.D. candidate of Class 1995. From the left to the right in the front row are Wang Kehua, Wang Jiye, Wang Chuanlun and Huang Da; and from the left to the right in the back row are Li Ying, Zhu Yifeng, Li Maosheng, Wu Xiaoqiu and Wang Guangqian.

图 130 为 2015 年 10 月 26 日，黄达（左一）与 1999 级博士生郭浩（右一，河南省鹤壁市委副书记、市长）在世纪城家中。

On October 26, 2015, Huang Da (first from the left) was at home in Century Hall with Guo Hao (first from the right, Deputy Secretary and Mayor of Hebi, Henan Province), a Ph.D. candidate of Class 1999.

图 131 为 2001 年 10 月 10 日，黄达（右一）与刚刚获得博士学位的 1997 级博士生刘成（左一，国务院办公厅领导秘书）在人大校园合影留念。

On October 10, 2001, Huang Da (first from the right) took a group photo with Liu Cheng (first from the left, secretary of the General Office of the State Council), a Ph.D. candidate of Class 1997 who just got the Ph.D. degree, on the campus of the Renmin University of China.

图 132 为 2007 年 12 月 10 日，黄达（右一）与刚刚通过博士学位论文答辩的 2000 级博士生林琳（左一，中国银行纽约分行研究部助理副总裁）在一起。

On December 10, 2007, Huang Da (first from the right) was with Lin Lin (first from the left, assistant vice president of the Bank of China, New York Branch), a Ph.D. candidate of Class 2000 who had just passed the doctoral dissertation oral examination.

133

135

134

136

图 133 为 2006 年 10 月 8 日，黄达（左一）与 2000 级博士生左毓秀（右一，中央财经大学金融学院金融学系主任）在洛阳龙门石窟。

On October 8, 2006, Huang Da (first from the left) and Zuo Yuxiu (first from the right, director of the Finance Department of the Finance School of the Central University of Finance and Economics) were at Longmen Grottoes in Luoyang.

图 134 为 2007 年 4 月 29 日，黄达（右一）与 2001 级博士生李向科（左一，中国人民大学财政金融学院副教授）在一起。

On April 29, 2007, Huang Da (first from the right) was with Li Xiangke (first from the left, assistant professor of the School of Finance of the Renmin University of China), a Ph.D. candidate of Class 2001.

图 135 为 2006 年 12 月 19 日，黄达（左一）与刚刚通过博士学位论文答辩的 2001 级博士生孔燕（右一，上海票据交易所副总裁）合影留念。

On December 19, 2006, Huang Da (first from the left) took a group photo with Kong Yan (first from the right,vice president of Shanghai Commercial Paper Exchange Corporation LTD), a Ph.D. candidate of Class 2001 who just passed the doctoral dissertation oral examination.

图 136 为 2009 年 4 月 18 日，黄达（左一）与 2003 级博士生向东（右一，中国人民大学财政金融学院副教授）在一起。

On April 18, 2009, Huang Da (first from the left) was with Xiang Dong (first from the right, assistant professor of the School of Finance of the Renmin University of China), a Ph.D. candidate of Class 2003.

137

138

图 137 为 2010 年 10 月 7 日，黄达（右一）与 2006 级博士生韩文秀（左一，国务院研究室副主任）在玉泉山。

On October 7, 2010, Huang Da (first from the right) and Han Wenxiu (first from the left, deputy director of the Research Office of the State Council), a Ph.D. candidate of Class 2006, were at Yuquan Mountain.

图 138 为 1998 年 6 月 20 日，黄达（右一）与 1994 级博士后张洪涛（左一，正德人寿保险股份有限公司原董事长、总裁，中国人民大学财政金融学院保险系原主任）在一起。

On June 20,1998, Huang Da (first from the right) was with Zhang Hongtao (first from the left, former chairman of the Board and president of Zhengde Life Insurance Co., Ltd., former director of Insurance Department, School of Finance, Renmin University of China), a postdoctoral researcher of Class 1994.

139

图 139 为 1984 年 11 月，吴晓灵（左一）进行硕士学位论文答辩，黄达（右二）担任答辩委员会主席。右一为刘鸿儒。

In November 1984, Wu Xiaoling (first from the left) had an oral examination on master's degree thesis. Huang Da (second from the right) served as the chairman of the dissertation defense committee. The first from the right is Liu Hongru.

140

图 140 为 1989 年 7 月，李扬在博士学位论文答辩会结束后，与全体答辩委员合影留念。从左至右分别为：安体富、韩英杰、黄达、李扬、许毅、王传纶、张卓元、吴易风、陈共、侯梦蟾。

In July 1989, after the doctoral dissertation oral examination, Li Yang took a group photo with all the dissertation defense committee members. From the left to the right are An Tifu, Han Yingjie, Huang Da, Li Yang, Xu Yi, Wang Chuanlun, Zhang Zhuoyuan, Wu Yifeng, Chen Gong and Hou Mengchan.

141

图 141 为 1999 年 5 月 14 日，尚福林在博士学位论文答辩会结束后，与全体答辩委员合影留念。从左至右分别为：江其务、赵海宽、黄达（答辩委员会主席）、尚福林、刘诗白、吴念鲁、冯肇伯、曾康霖。

On May 14, 1999, after the doctoral dissertation oral examination, Shang Fulin took a group photo with all the dissertation defense committee members. From the left to the right are Jiang Qiwu, Zhao Haikuan, Huang Da (chairman of the dissertation defense committee), Shang Fulin, Liu Shibai, Wu Nianlu, Feng Zhaobo and Zeng Kanglin.

第五章
Chapter Five

漫展风华
20 世纪 90 年代

The Global Vision in View
in the 1990s

教研行政两不误

Neglect Neither Teaching and Research Nor Administration

走进 20 世纪 90 年代，黄达的人生翻开了更为宏伟的篇章。

1991—1994 年，黄达担任“中国人文社会科学重镇”——中国人民大学的校长。中国人民大学是黄达奋斗一生的地方，这里的一草一木都记录着他从毛头小伙到耄耋之年的奋斗历程。

能够“破例”担任校长，意味着黄达又开创了一个历史，只不过这次是在行政工作领域，而非教学科研领域。因为在这所新中国成立以来，中国共产党创办的第一所新型大学的历史上，校长和主持工作的副校长，一直由党的组织部门在校外选派合适的“革命老干部”担任。以前历任主要负责人，吴玉章、成仿吾、郭影秋、袁宝华，最低资历也是抗战爆发前后参加革命的省部级干部。黄达接任校长，意味着两个变化：其一，资历标准放开——黄达只是在解放战争初期参加革命队伍的干部；其二，开主要领导干部在校内产生之先河。

事实上，黄达担任校级领导的历程从 1983 年便已开始。1983—1985 年，担任副校长，自 1985 年起，担任主持日常工作的副校长，直到 1991 年被任命为校长。

这一年，黄达已经 66 岁。

“1985 年，袁宝华来中国人民大学当校长，我相当于常务副校长，大大小小的事情都要管，在最初的三四年写的东西就比较少。那时候，每年我都给袁校长打一份报告，说已经干了一年了，不想干了。可袁校长说，再过一段时间，我也不干了，咱俩共进退。”

“无奈”的黄达只好继续干下去，而且这一干就是 11 年。这段时间，黄达的精力不得不主要投入办学的事务之中，但他始终没有放弃“学术”。他不断尝试着如何以有限的精力来兼顾好行政与教研工作。

“再忙的时候，我坚持两条。一是晚上不开会，白天开会提高效率。管理要有方法，不要不相信别人。能干到副校长、系主任的，都是能人。依靠大家干，自己就可以挤出点时间。二是坚持每学年给学生开一次课。那时候，讲课是最优先的。只要有课，什么会都可以不去，哪怕是国家教委的。只要你讲课，就要备课，

Entering the 1990s, Huang Da opened an even grander chapter of his life.

From 1991 to 1994, he assumed the post of president of the Renmin University of China, which occupied a key position in China's humanities social sciences. Huang Da worked all his life in the Renmin University of China. Every tree and bush of the place witnessed his efforts and struggle from his youth to aged years.

In teaching and researching fields, Huang Da had made many historical records. Serving as the President of the Renmin University of China was another record created by him in the field of administration. That's because since the founding of the People's Republic of China, in the history of the first new university established by the Chinese Communist Party, its presidents and vice-presidents who took charge of the university were all selected and appointed by the organization department of the Party off campus, and usually were revolutionary veteran cadres. Former leaders such as Wu Yuzhang, Cheng Fangwu, Guo Yingqiu and Yuan Baohua were at least cadres at or above provincial and ministerial level and had joined the revolution around the era of Anti-Japanese War. Huang Da's assumption of the post of president meant two changes. Firstly, the control over criterion of qualifications and record of service was lifted. Huang Da joined the revolution in the early time of liberation war. Secondly, it was the first time that the major leader of the university was selected from inside the campus.

In fact, he started to work as a leader of the university in 1983. Between 1983 and 1985, he worked as a vice-president. From 1985, he began to take charge of routine work until 1991 when he was appointed as the president.

That year, Huang Da was 66.

"In 1985, Yuan Baohua became the president of Renmin University, and I was the executive vice-president. " said Huang, "I had to take charge of many matters—large and small. In the first three and four years, I didn't really write much. So every year, I wrote a report to President Yuan, saying that I had worked in this position for one year and hoped to quit. But he told me to wait for a longer time for his resignation together with me."

Huang Da had "no alternative " but to continue for as long as 11 years. In this period of time, he had to devote main efforts to running a university, but he didn't give up learning. He considered how he could balance administration and teaching and research!

"No matter how busy I was at the time, I adhered to two principles. " he said, "One was no meeting after dark. I tried hard to hold more efficient conferences in the daytime. Management needed to employ a right method. Trust others, because those who could reach the office of vice-president and department head are all capable brains. Relying on the intelligence and power of the team, I could find time for study. The other was to give a lecture each

就要关注学术动向，就不会丢掉专业。”

勤奋 + 效率——黄达逐渐找到了兼顾两者的好办法！

学术上，辉煌再续。

从 1983 年的《〈资本论〉和社会主义财政金融理论建设》到 1994 年的《形势 · 改革 · 资金一窥》，在担任校领导期间，他有数十篇文章发表在国家核心期刊上，内容既包括宏观调控、货币供给、财政金融体制等宏观命题，又有证券市场、企业所有权与经营权等微观理论，还多有涉及金融学科建设以及人才培养的论述。

此外，《财政信贷综合平衡导论》（中国金融出版社，1984）、《工农产品比价剪刀差》（中国社会科学出版社，1990）、《货币银行学》（四川人民出版社，1992）以及《宏观调控与货币供给》（中国人民大学出版社，1997 年初版；1999 年修订版）等四部著作或教材，见证了黄达在这一时期，虽身挑重担，却仍笔耕不辍的历程。

工作上，成效卓著。

黄达曾把成仿吾老校长比喻为华北联合大学这座革命熔炉的“掌炉人”，而他这位“掌炉人”熔铸的火候掌握得怎么样？在本书中不好作权威性的定断。换一个角度，对于他主政的一段，校内、校外人们之间的议论、人们非官方的评价为：在他的带领下，中国人民大学以教学为中心的方针，锐意进取，深化改革；在政治方面，以党的基本路线为指导，即“一个中心、两个基本点”；在学术方面，靠“双百方针”指引；通过多方努力，中国人民大学取得了可喜的进步……

依靠大家、相信大家——这是黄达的制胜法宝。在被任命校长的讲话上，他说：“有全校师生员工可以依靠：我们学校有老教师、老职工，还有关心我们工作的一千多离退休的老同志；青年教工，他们需要提高，无论是政治上还是业务上，特别是政治上。我们应该有信心团结广大青年教工把学校建设好”；在卸任校长的讲话上，他又讲道：“团结。我们这些年做了一些工作，特别是在政治风云激荡的形势下也仍然保持着正常的运作，其中，团结是一个重要的保证。团结

semester. At that time, teaching gained first priority. So long as I had a class, any meeting stepped aside, even the meeting hosted by the State Education Commission. Before a lecture, I should prepare lessons and pay close attention to academic trends. In this way, I kept up with my profession."

Industriousness and efficiency—this is how Huang Da balances teaching and research and administration.

In the academic field, he achieved more brilliant records.

During his term of office as a leader, he published dozens of articles on national core journals, such as *On Capital and the Construction on Socialist Fiscal and Financial Theories* in 1983 and *A Brief Glimpse of Situation, Reform and Capital* in 1994. The contents of those articles were related to macro-propositions such as macro-control, money supply, financial system, and microscopic theories such as stock market, enterprise ownership and management right. Besides, construction on the financial subject and personnel training were also included.

Moreover, four works or textbooks, i.e. *Introduction of General Equilibrium on Public Finance and Credit* (published by China Financial Publishing House in 1984), *Scissors Difference between Prices of Industrial and Agricultural Products* (published by China Social Sciences Publishing House in 1990), *Economics of Money and Banking* (published by Sichuan People's Publishing House in 1992), and *Macroeconomic Regulation and Money Supply* (published by China Renmin University Press in 1997; revised in 1999), witnessed Huang Da's efforts in writing despite his heavy load of administrative work.

Huang Da made remarkable achievements in his work.

Huang Da had compared Cheng Fangwu, the former president to the "Furnace-Commander " of the revolutionary furnace—North China Union University. But how was his work as the "Furnace-Commander "? This book didn't make a definitive judgment. Here is another perspective to assess his achievements from people's discussion and unofficial evaluation. Under his leadership, the Renmin University of China adhered to the teaching-centered policy, forged ahead with determination and intensified reform. Politically, the university followed the guidance of the Party's basis line, namely "one central task and two basic points ". Academically, under the "double-hundred guiding principle ", the university made satisfying progress through multiple efforts…

Trusting and relying on all others was Huang Da's winning formula for success. In his inaugural speech, he said: "With the help of the whole faculty, including senior teachers, workers, over a thousand of retired cadres who are still concerned with our work, and young faculties who need improvement both in profession and politics, politics in particular, we have faith in uniting young faculties to build a better university. " On his farewell address, he also stressed that "Unity. It is unity that ensures to the fact that we have

包括两方面，一是教学教辅人员、党政工作人员和后勤工作人员三大系统的团结，二是校领导班子的团结。”

多年以后，在《黄达文集（三续）》（中国人民大学出版社，2014）一书中，黄达用专题的形式对他在担任中国人民大学副校长和校长期间的几个重要事件，特别是在 20 世纪 80 年代围绕中国人民大学办学方向的问题，进行了系统梳理。文中提及的当年那些令人不胜唏嘘的经历，不免让人感叹那个年代办学的不易！

在经历了 20 世纪 50 年代风光无限、60 年代“失落感”渐增以及“文化大革命”期间遭遇停办等三个主要时期之后，1978 年复校的中国人民大学结束了前期主要培养“革命干部”的历史使命，正式成为以招收高中毕业生为主的综合性社会科学大学（国发 [1978]129 号文件）。然而，作为当然的“普通”大学，作为新中国创办的第一所新型正规大学，中国人民大学却在 20 世纪 80 年代围绕着“办学方向”和“领导体制”等关系学校命运的大事，经历了一段相当曲折的历程。期间，经历筹建“两院”（行政管理学院和经济管理学院）、筹建国家行政学院、“胡乔木建议”冲击、“归属”波折等等重要事件，最终，在 80 年代末期，多年事实上向综合性社会科学大学方向发展却不断受到干扰的中国人民大学，才实实在在地成为一所“普通”大学。

“实践证明，正是走了办普通大学的发展道路，而没有改组成什么高级干部培训机构，中国人民大学才可能把自己逐步升华至学问顶峰上的璀璨明珠之列。此外，也只有学问，才能为大学提供无尽的发展潜力和空间。”每每提及那段“摇摆”的岁月，黄达总是感慨良多。

made some achievements and kept normal operation amid political turbulence during the past years. Unity involves two aspects. One is the unity among teachers and teaching assistance, staff of party and government department, and logistics workers. The other means unity in the leading team of the university."

Many years later, in the *Essays of Huang Da (Extention 3)* published by China Renmin University Press in 2014, Huang Da wrote about several important events during his leadership in the Renmin University of China, especially on the educational orientation in 1980s. His remarkable experiences had people marvel at the difficulties encountered by them in running a school at that time.

As a rising shining star in the 1950s, experiencing the "sense of loss" in the 1960s, and later being suspended in the cultural revolution, the Renmin University of China, resumed class in 1978, ending its historical mission of training "revolutionary cadres", and officially turned into a comprehensive university on social sciences mainly enrolling high school graduates (as specified in Guo Fa [1978] No.129 Document). However, as a justifiable "ordinary" university, the first new formal university founded by PRC, the Renmin University of China experienced twists and turns in respect of issues concerning the destiny of the university such as the educational orientation and leadership system of the Renmin University of China in 1980s. During the period, it made preparations for building "two schools" (the School of Public Administration and the School of Economics and Management), established the National School of Administration, suffered from shocks of "Hu Qiaomu Proposal", and suffered from setbacks about "affiliation". By the end of 1980s, the Renmin University of China, which had been interfered in its progress towards a comprehensive social science university for years, finally became an "ordinary" university in a real sense.

"Practice proved that it was following the way towards an ordinary university, instead of turning into a training agency for senior cadres, which made it possible for the Renmin University of China to gradually climb up to the summit of knowledge as one of shining pearls. In addition, only knowledge can provide universities with endless potentials and space for development." Huang Da felt emotional when reminding of that period of "chop and change".

《货币银行学》

Economics of Money and Banking

20 世纪 80 年代中后期，在经历了近 10 年改革开放的洗礼之后，中国经济发展的轨迹一方面摆脱了苏联东欧模式的“航道”，另一方面则开始逐步与西方现代经济的新航线“接轨”。

这一时期，对于理论界来讲，是一次难得的思想解放、百家争鸣的好机会。更难能可贵的是，这次“思想解放”的区域已经突破了单纯的理论层面，实实在在地影响了中国经济与金融政策的制定。这个过程中的曲曲折折、风风雨雨多有值得大书特书的事件，难以尽数。不过，回到与黄达难解难分的金融，倒有一次重要的会议必须提起。

1987 年 8 月，由世界银行支持的国际研讨会——“中国财经教学计划国际研讨会”在复旦大学召开。这次会议中外著名经济学教育人士云集，会议的“焦点”聚集于经济学教学改革。

这一时期，引进西方经济学，推动经济学教学体系和课程的改革与开放已经是许多人士的共识，但怀疑、反对者也以极大的力量固守阵地。至于如何改革、如何开放也是“公说公有理，婆说婆有理”，争论不断。

这次会议上中外双方的观点针锋相对，大概能还原当时争论的“原貌”：中方学者——坚持四项基本原则，坚持以马克思主义经济学为主；外方学者——强调只应学习西方现代经济学。

第一天，双方你来我往，立论“坚定”，似乎并无调和的可能。第二天，黄达“挺身而出”，做了一个题目是“马克思的经济学要学好，非马克思的经济学也要研究”的发言。形势急转直下，“求同存异”的观点开始成为会议的主调。

前后数天的会议，在经过双方最终的“妥协”后，达成共识——拟定 10 门核心课（包括政治经济学、西方经济学、会计学、统计学、经济数学、货币银行学、财政学、发展经济学、国际贸易和国际金融）；确定各门课程的学时和比例——其中政治经济学定 6 学时、西方经济学定 4 学时，大概能量化地反映最终“妥协”与“兼顾”的程度。

Back in the middle and late period of 1980s, after nearly 10 years of reform and opening up, China's economic development got off the course of the Soviet Union and Eastern European model, and started to gradually integrate with modern Western economic model.

That period of time gave the theoretical circle an opportunity to experience ideological emancipation so that all schools of thoughts could contend for attention. Furthermore, the emancipation broke through the theoretical circle and exerted actual influence on the decision-making of China's economic and financial policies. The whole process had countless ups and downs which were worth writing in details. But, on finance issues, there was one important meeting worthy of mention here.

In August 1987, the International Symposium of China Financial and Economic Teaching Program, a symposium supported by the World Bank, was held in Fudan University. Many domestic and foreign famous public figures of the economics educational field converged at the meeting, with the focus centered on the reform of economics education.

During that period, many people reached consensus on introducing Western economics to promote the reform and opening up of economics educational system and courses. However, there was also great doubt and even opposition against it. As for how to carry out reform and opening-up, each side upheld its own viewpoints.

On the meeting, the Chinese and foreign parties stuck to each own ideas. The Chinese scholars upheld the four fundamental principles and centered on Marxist economics, while the foreign scholars stressed only learning Western modern economics.

On the first day, both sides firmly held their own viewpoints, seemingly impossible to compromise. On the next day, Huang Da stood out and made a speech named Learning Marxist Economics and Understanding Non-Marxist Economics. This brought a sudden turn of the situation. Soon, the idea of seeking common ground while reserving differences took the lead at the meeting.

Finally, both sides reached a compromise on 10 core curriculums, including political economics, western economics, accounting, statistics, economic mathematics, money and banking, public finance, development economics, international trade and international finance. Besides, the class hour for each course were determined, of which, six class hours for political economics and four class hours for western economics. So did the

会后，根据这次会议推荐的教学方案，教育部开始组织核心教材的编写。1989 年，在南开大学召开的“核心课程教学大纲编写研讨会”上，通过竞标的方式，各门教材的编写任务一一“花落各家”。其中，《货币银行学》最终确定由中国人民大学编写。

中国人民大学能够“中标”完全取决于黄达主持写出的竞标大纲。这份大纲的“巧妙”之处在于，将学苏联奠定的微观分析成果与改革开放后引进的西方宏观分析及在微观分析的发展两方面的思路，融汇成一个完整的体系。除此之外，还始终注意将针对中国现实问题的研究纳入其中。

这份大纲日后成为《货币银行学》编写的指导思想。

以后的三年中，在克服政治事件的冲击、“集体编写”带来的拖延等困难，并经过反复与同行的沟通与交流后，直到 1992 年 2 月下旬，黄达突患肺炎，高烧几天后在家闭门静养，也就是利用这段时间他才突击完成了全书的统编定稿工作。而后在春夏之交，黄达与周升业、沈伟基到北京郊区闭门通读全书才得以定稿。当年，《货币银行学》由四川人民出版社最终出版。

仔细品读这部教材，我们不仅能领略到黄达将马克思主义经济学与西方现代经济学的思想精华巧妙融合的“匠心独具”，而且能从字里行间嗅到浓浓的“中国味道”。但这部教材的鲜明特色并未使之立即走红。有不少教师埋怨“不好教”而不选用；更有许多院校因有自己编写的教材而不选用。倒是学生，不管学校选不选用，自动买来研读的人甚多。

而后，在自我开拓的进程中，各项“桂冠”亦纷至沓来。

1994 年，北京市第三届哲学社会科学优秀成果一等奖；1995 年，国家教育委员会高等学校优秀教材一等奖；1997 年，国家级教学成果奖一等奖；2002 年，教育部全国普通高等学校优秀教材一等奖。

四个“第一”，无疑是对黄达和他的团队最大的褒奖！

《货币银行学》的成功，回应了当时有关“国外已经有成熟的教科书，我们何

proportion of each course. This could reflect the degree of compromise made by them.

After the meeting, the Ministry of Education started to organize to compile core textbooks on the teaching scheme made out by this meeting. In 1989, on the Seminar on Compiling Teaching Program for Core Curriculum hosted by Nankai University, the compiling tasks for each curriculum were decided through competitive tender. The Renmin University of China gained the right to write the textbook of the *Economics of Money and Banking*.

The Renmin University of China won the bid thanks to the bidding outline mainly written by Huang Da. This outline was well-versed at integrating the micro-analysis results from learning the Soviet Union and the Western macro-analysis and the development of micro-analysis into one system. Moreover, it kept incorporating studies on China's reality.

This outline later became the guiding thought for compiling the *Economics of Money and Banking*.

In the following three years, Huang Da overcame the impact from political events and difficulties such as delay due to "collective writing", and repeatedly communicated and changed ideas with his counterparts. In late February, 1992, he did a crash job of accomplishing the final draft of the textbook when he stayed at home for a rest after suffering pneumonia and a high fever. Later, at the end of spring and the beginning of summer, Huang Da, Zhou Shengye and Shen Weiji read through the book and set the final version in the suburb of Beijing. That year, the *Economics of Money and Banking* was published by Sichuan People's Publishing House.

Reading this book, we can not only appreciate his originality of integrating the ideological essence of both Marxist economics and West modern economics, but also sense the strong Chinese flavor between lines. It didn't become popular at once. Many teachers complained that it was hard to teach and avoided using it. And many other colleges still adopted their own original textbooks. On the contrary, a great number of students went to buy and study it.

After that, crown of laurels came in flocks, such as the first prize of the 3rd Excellent Achievements in Philosophy and Social Science of Beijing in 1994; the first prize of State Education Commission for Excellent Textbook of Institution of Higher Education in 1995; the first award of State Teaching Results in 1997; and the first prize of Excellent Textbook of National General Institutes of Higher Education from the Ministry of Education in 2002.

必再编？自己能编出什么新东西来？”等具有一定影响力的思潮，证明了坚持“马克思主义与中国实际相结合”的原则，而非单纯对西方经济学的内容囫囵吞枣、照说照做的科学性与可行性。

“作为货币银行学的教学工作者，应该致力于编出：中国人，在中国大学的讲台上，为了使中国的学生掌握在中国建设中国特色社会主义的本领而传授货币银行学所需的教材。”黄达 1990 年写于《建国以来〈货币银行学〉课程发展的回顾及如何进一步建设》一文中的这段话，明确表达了他一直倡导的编写教材的基本方针，不仅今天是这样，未来更应该始终不渝地坚持下去。

从历史演进的角度来看，从衍生于“货币学”与“银行学”两门学科，到实现第一次跨越“引进宏观分析的思想”，再到第二次跨越“引进微观分析的精华”，大致可以勾勒出“货币银行学”不过百年的发展史。

如今，新时期的“货币银行学”如何实现更高层次的跨越，不仅是这个时代赋予中国金融学界的重任，更是老一代“黄达们”给予新一代中国金融学人的期许！

The four prizes as No.1 were the biggest award for Huang Da and his team!

The success of the *Economics of Money and Banking* gave a positive response to the ideological trends concerning "Why must we compile textbook since there are mature ones abroad? And what new contents could we write now? " It also proved that it was scientific and feasible to integrate the Marxist with China's reality rather than gulping down the Western economics.

"As teachers on money and banking, we should make efforts to compile textbooks for the Chinese people to teach the Economics of Money and Banking on the rostrums of Chinese universities to enable the Chinese students to grasp the skills to build socialism with Chinese characteristics in China. " These words were written in 1990 in his article Review of the Development of the Economics of Money and Banking since the Founding of the People's Republic of China and Proposed Ways to Furthur Build it. These words clearly expressed his fundamental guidelines for compiling textbooks, which he has always advocated, not only for today, but also for the future.

In retrospect, the history of the Economics of Money and Banking in less than one hundred years started from its derivation from two subjects, Economics of Currency and Economics of Banking, to the first leap of "introducing in the macro-analysis ideology ", and to the second leap of "bringing in the essence of micro-analysis ".

Today, how the Economics of Money and Banking can achieve a higher level of leap in the new age is not only an important task entrusted to China's financial circle, but also an expectation that the old generation counted on new comers.

关注广阔的金融实践

Devoted to Practice in Finance

荀子曾说，“不闻不若闻之，闻之不若见之，见之不若知之，知之不若行之。学至于行而止矣。”可见，失去了实践，理论也便没有了生命力。

对于现代大学而言，人才培养、科学研究固不可少，服务社会同样不可或缺。

对于为人师者而言，桃李满天下、著作等身与资政启民，可谓“三足鼎立”，缺一不可。

与其他为人师者的先生们一样，黄达始终不忘用平生所学去推动理论指导实践。不过，一直以来，由于体制条件，他不怎么奢望通过自己以及所在团队的努力，直接发挥类似“智囊团”和“思想库”为国家重大经济决策提供智力支持的重要作用，但为国家财经改革建言献策则始终不懈不怠。

从今天的眼光来看，黄达是个不折不扣的“全才”。他的学术研究横跨多个领域，在行业愈发细分的今天，这是很难想象的。“在历史上，不论是东方还是西方，早期的先贤哲人都是在自然和社会诸多领域具有卓越思想的综合性大家。随着社会发展和学科越来越细的划分，学者们的研究领域也逐步细分，分学科的专家越来越多，而将多学科融合一体的思想家却更显珍稀。黄达先生便是当代有重要影响的综合性大家之一。”他的弟子王广谦日后如此评价他。

正是因为在诸多领域的突出建树，20 世纪 80 年代后期以来，他曾一度集全国人大、国家机关、教育管理、社会兼职等等不同身份于一身。

第八届全国人大代表、财政经济委员会委员；

国务院学位委员会委员、经济学及应用经济学学科评议组召集人；

中国金融学会会长（1995 年，黄达“打破常规”，出任中国金融学会会长，成为迄今为止唯一一位由非中国人民银行行长担任的会长）；

中国人民银行货币政策委员会首届专家委员；

中国财政学会副会长；

中国企业管理协会副会长；

中国价格学会副会长；

According to Xunzi, "Never hearing of it is inferior to hearing of it, hearing of it inferior to seeing it, seeing it inferior to knowing it, and knowing it inferior to practicing it. The ultimate purpose of learning is practice. " Hence, without practice, theory would lose its vitality.

As for a modern university, talent training and scientific research are inevitable, but serving the society is also necessary.

As for a teacher, students, works and efforts to help manage state affairs and enlighten people are three indispensible parts.

Like other teachers, Huang Da kept his efforts to promote the guidance of practice with theory all the time. Due to the institutional conditions, he didn't expect that he and his team could act as the think tank to directly offer intellectual support for major economic decision-making by the state. However, he had never slacked at offering advice and suggestions for the national reform on finance and economics.

Huang Da is a versatile person. His academic research stretched across many fields, which is unimaginable for scholars today since industries are subdivided into many sub-industries. "In history, whether in the East or West, scholars of the past and sages were all great masters with great ideas in many fields across nature and society. " Wang Guangqian, Huang's student, said, "With the social development and the subdivision of subjects, scholars' research fields are being gradually subdivided correspondingly. The more experts on sub-discipline there are, the more valuable thinkers integrating multiple subjects are. Huang Da is one of the thinkers of great influence. "

Since the late of the 1980s, Huang Da had integrated many identities, including NPC representative, cadre of the state organs, educational administrator, member of professional affiliations, and the like as follows:

Representative of the 8th NPC and member of Financial and Economic Committee;

Member of the State Council Academic Degrees Committee and convener of the Economics and Applied Economics Disciplines Evaluation Group;

Chairman of the China Society for Finance and Banking (CFS) (in 1995, Huang Da made a breakthrough to take up the post of chairman of the CFS, becoming the only one ever in this post who was not the governor of the People's Bank of China);

Member of the first expert committee of the Monetary Policy Committee of the People's Bank of China;

Vice chairman of China Society of Public Finance;

Vice chairman of China Society of Enterprise Management;

Vice chairman of China Society of Price;

......

These duties provided him with facilities to participate in consultation on the national decision-making on finance and practice on fiscal policy.

…………

这些职务为他参与国家金融决策咨询以及金融政策实践提供了便利。

20世纪80年代初期，黄达就提出在中国改革过程中“通货膨胀”将长期存在的判断，从理论上支持在具体政策制定中把一定的物价水平上涨率考虑在内的实际做法。

1983年，时任国务院经济研究中心常务干事的徐雪寒，委托黄达约请有关单位，主要是财政部和中国人民银行的有关同志，协作研究当时的财政信贷综合平衡问题，最终形成成果“1984年2月国务院经济研究中心材料［1984］《关于加强财政信贷综合平衡的意见》”。随后，研究中心给出的按语是：“《意见》中的基本观点，值得注意。”［参见《黄达文集（三续）》。］

1993年，黄达向中央办公厅秘书局提出用“货币供给”概念代替“货币发行”概念的政策建议。作为国际货币基金组织成员，中国已经在内部进行了多年的货币供给统计，但正式按季公布则是从1994年第四季度开始。

20世纪90年代中期，金融体制改革进入深化阶段，《中华人民共和国中国人民银行法》《中华人民共和国商业银行法》《中华人民共和国保险法》等几项重要的金融立法先后颁布。黄达以全国人大财经委员会委员的身份参与了这些立法的过程。在这个阶段，他更专注于财政和金融这两个宏观调控杠杆的对比关系。他指出，改革开放后十几年的演变出现了极不正常的对比：财政收支占GDP的比重以每年约1个百分点的速度下滑，较世界各国，已经低到惊人的程度。而金融的力量虽然迅速增强，但独木支撑宏观调控，并不正常。在第八届全国人民代表大会第三次会议期间，他提出议案：“‘九五’期间必须扭转国家财政收入占GDP的比重不断下滑的局面”。当东南亚金融危机袭来之际，在财经委员会上他又明确提出，必须及时动用财政政策杠杆，包括发行公债，来应对困难局势。后来，我国财政与金融两个杠杆对比格局的逐步改善，说明了他对宏观经济问题能够立足实际，做出符合客观发展的判断。

进入新世纪以来，针对经济全面开放背景之下中国应当采取的应对政策，黄

Back in the early 1980s, Huang Da put forward the judgment that inflation would be a long standing issue in China's reform process. This provided theoretic support for the practice that taking the rising price level into consideration when making policies.

In 1983, Xu Xuehan, the executive manager of the Economic Research Center of the State Council entrusted Huang Da to invite relevant departments, mainly cadres from Ministry of Finance and People's Bank of China, to cooperate in research on comprehensive balance of financial credit at the time. Later their achievements were seen in the Opinions on Concerning Strengthening the General Equilibrium of Public Finance and Credit in Economic Research Center of the State Council in February, 1984. The editorial note said: "The basic view in the Opinions is notable."[See *Collected Works of Huang Da* (*Extension 3*).]

In 1993, Huang Da made a proposal to the Secretariat of the Central Committee of the Party that the concept of "issuance of currency " should be replaced by "money supply ". As a member of IMF, China had conducted census on money supply for many years, but it was not until the fourth quarter of 1994 that the statistics was officially made public each quarter.

In mid-1990s, the reform of financial system stepped into a deeper phase with the promulgation of major financial laws, including the Law of People's Republic of China on the People's Bank of China, Commercial Bank Law of the People's Republic of China, and Insurance Law of the People's Republic of China. As a member of the Financial and Economic Committee of NPC, Huang Da took part in the legislative procedure of these laws. In that period, he focused on the correlation between two macro-control leverages of fiscal and financial means. He pointed out that after over a decade of evolution since the reform and opening up, there was an abnormal contrast: the proportion of financial revenue in GDP decreased by one percentage point each year. Compared to other countries, it hit a striking low. On the other hand, the banking power was increasing dramatically, but it couldn't accomplish macro-control on its own. On the third Session of the 8th NPC, he proposed that "the declining situation of fiscal revenue proportion in GDP should be turned around in the Ninth Five-Year Plan Period. " When the Southeast Asian financial crisis swept over, he definitely promoted at the Financial and Economic Committee that fiscal policies should be employed to tackle the difficulties, such as issuing government bonds. Afterwards, the contrast structure of the two levers was improved, which proved that he could make proper judgment that conformed to the objective development in the light of the actual circumstances.

Entering the 21st century, Huang Da put forward many unique views on countermeasures that China should employ in the context of overall opening up in economy. In 2000, there was a saying that traditional banking services had sharply declined and finally the financial market would take the place of financial

达提出了许多自己独到的看法。2000 年，对当时在国外流行并从而也在国内流行的银行传统业务急剧衰落乃至金融市场终将代替金融中介的看法，他提出质疑："我国的银行业同样拥有开阔的发展空间和绚丽的前景。"而随后全球金融体系的演进特别是"次贷危机"对全球银行体系的冲击以及各国的政策反应充分证明了这种质疑的合理性。

2004 年，他提出，人民币发展之路一定是"非常宽阔却绝非平坦，需要在摩擦中妥协，在摩擦中协调，在摩擦中寻求合作"，同时提醒决策者，"当决策之际，必须明确并保留最后的'自我防卫手段'。"他的这些见解具有深刻的政策指引含义，加深了人们对于人民币汇率制度改革进程的理解。同时，他明确提出在那以后的相当长时期内，人民币汇率必然呈升值的走势。

2011 年，黄达在《金融评论》（第 5 期）发表了题为《通货膨胀与物价目标》的长文，对如何界定通货膨胀和如何看待通货膨胀与经济的关系等问题进行了系统阐述，并对控制物价提出了富有建设性的思路和建议。他指出应该设立一个通货膨胀区间目标，比如中期目标和年度目标。中期目标"如五年计划的目标"属于趋势估计目标、"计划"目标；年度目标可以是政府"承诺"的目标，也可以暂且是政府"争取"的目标。而通货膨胀区间目标应作为"物价总水平基本稳定"提法的具体诠释。随后，该文被《新华文摘》转载。

回过头来看，在具体的金融实践与金融决策过程中，黄达坚持认为，能否最大限度地发挥金融的积极作用而抑制其消极作用，取决于是否具备正确的金融决策理念。而正确的决策理念，则导源于对金融基本性质的如实把握。当然，要正确把握金融的基本性质，则须注重金融理论的实践检验。

经过多年参与金融决策的实践，黄达时时指出值得注意的一些倾向，诸如：一切交给市场，市场自会调节；只懂得一切仿效外国，特别是美国的模式；自觉不自觉地以计划经济思路管理和干预金融。其间，很少见他正言厉色地批判。他认为，有的过程是难以避免的，而且会长期存在，但实践会引导做出必要的纠正。

intermediaries, which prevailed both at home and abroad. He refuted the view and argued that "China's banking industry will also have a wide development space and bright future. " Later, the impact of evolution of the global financial system, especially subprime crisis on the global banking system as well as many countries' policies fully proved the rationality of his refute.

In 2004, he pointed out that the road of development of RMB was "very broad but not smooth. It needs to make concession, coordinate and seek cooperation in frictions. " Meanwhile, he reminded the decision-makers of keeping 'self-defense measures' when making decisions. His suggestions were profoundly significant and deepened people's understanding on the reform process of RMB exchange rate system. At the same time, he affirmed that RMB exchange rate was bound to appreciate in the following long period of time.

In 2011, Huang Da published a long article named Inflation and Price Target in the *Chinese Review of Financial Studies* (Vol. 5). In this article, he expounded issues such as how to define inflation and how to treat the relation between inflation and economy, and raised constructive ideas and suggestions on price control. He pointed out that there should be a goal of inflation range, such as medium-term goal and annual goal. The former, like the "goal of Five-Year Plan ", referred to the estimated target as a planned target, while the latter meant the target "promised " by the government or the target "strived for " by the government. These goals should be used as specific interpretation for the wording of "the general level of market prices is basically stable ". Later, this article was reprinted by *Xinhua Digest*.

In retrospect, in the process of financial practice and decision-making, Huang Da insisted that playing the active role of finance to the utmost and bringing down its negative effects relied on the correct concept of decision-making on finance, which resulted from the accurate understanding of the basic nature of finance. In this process, indeed, it was necessary to pay attention to the practice of financial theories.

Over years of practice of participating in financial decision-making, Huang Da often pointed out some notable tendency. For instance, everything depended on market and market would regulate it; doing everything after a foreign model, the U.S. model in particular; managing and intervening financial market with planned economic thoughts, whether conscientious or not. Yet, he didn't criticize with a severe countenance. He believed that some processes were inevitable and would exist in a long term, and practice would lead to necessary correction.

境外出访——走入更广阔的课堂

Visiting Foreign Countries — Entering a Vaster Classroom

从 20 世纪 80 年代中后期起，黄达开始进入世界经济学的大舞台。

首先值得一提的是，1987 年 9 月，黄达来到了这个舞台的中心——美国。

此次访美并不是纯粹的学术交流，而且时间短、行程长，难免走马观花。但黄达还是利用这个难得的机会，对美国的高等教育制度、生活方式、金融发展状况等等，以强烈吸纳的渴望获得了不少直接的感性认识。

为期两周的美国之行，除了实地考察金融部门、参观高等学府和研究机构以外，他主要是肩负着一个重要的使命——参加中美经济学教育交流委员会（简称“中方委员会”）与美中经济学教育与研究委员会（简称“美方委员会”）第二次联席会议；那时他拥有一个重要的头衔——“中方委员会”主席。美方委员会主席则由普林斯顿大学的邹至庄教授和哈佛大学的帕金斯教授共同担任，而邹至庄教授作为美国华人经济学者当中的佼佼者，是最早参与推动中美经济学教育交流的学者之一，也是该项目的首倡者。黄达与邹至庄因此“结缘”，而后两位经济学家携手推动中美经济学教育交流的故事被经济学界广为传颂。

中美两个委员会是“中美经济学教育交流项目”分设在中美两国的执行机构，联席会议是要为双方提供一个协商重大事宜的平台。该项目始于 1985 年，得到了教育部和美国福特基金会的鼎力支持，习惯被称作“福特项目”。中美双方的委员会每两年召开一次年会，从 1985 年至 1994 年共召开了 5 次，第一、三、五次在北京，这次黄达赴美参加的正是在纽约召开的第二次会议，而后的第四次会议在华盛顿举行。

“福特项目”包含学制一年的西方经济学培训班，暑期经济学研讨班，派出研究生、青年教师赴北美攻读博士学位，美方资助中方访问学者赴北美访学，派遣经济学家小组赴美考察，资助留学生回国讲学项目以及经济学科文献交流 7 个子项目。其中最为有名的是“福特班”——学制一年的西方经济学培训班。这在当时的中国经济学界可谓无人不知、无人不晓。

项目执行的 10 年间，多位来自欧美的著名经济学教授前来授课。前后总计培养的 618 位学员，除其中的一小部分在国外发展、成就显著之外，大部分则成长为中

Since the middle and late 1980s, Huang Da has come into the arena of economics in the world.

In September 1987, Huang Da came to the arena center—the United States—for a second time.

His visit was not just for academic exchange. The visit was short while their travel distance was long, so he only took a brief look. But he took the opportunity to gain perceptual knowledge about American higher educational system, life style and financial development.

Within two weeks of his trip in the U.S., apart from investigating American financial institutions on the spot and visiting higher education institutions and research institutes, Huang Da had an important mission, namely, to attend the joint conference of China-US Economics Educational Exchanges Committee (CU-committee for short) and US-China Economics Educational Exchanges Committee (UC-committee for short). At that time, he was the president of CU-committee, while his counterparts were Professor Gregory Chow of Princeton University and Professor Dwight Perkins of Harvard University. As an outstanding person among Chinese-American economists, Gregory Chow was the earliest participator in promoting economics educational exchanges between China and the U.S., and was also an initiator of this program. The story that Huang and Chow promoted China-U.S. economics educational exchanges was widely spread in the economics circle.

The two committees were two executive bodies established respectively in two countries for the China-US Economics Educational Exchanges Programs, and the joint conference was to provide a platform for negotiating major issues. Starting from 1985, the program gained full support from the Ministry of Education and Ford Foundation, hence the name "Ford Program ". The two committees held an annual meeting once every two years. From 1985 to 1994, they had five meetings, among which the first, third and fifth meetings were held in Beijing. And this time Huang went to New York to join the second meeting, and the fourth was held in Washington.

"Ford Program" contained seven sub-projects, such as one-year training course on Western economics, a summer seminar on economics, sending postgraduates and young teachers to study in Northern America for doctor's degree, the American side sponsored Chinese visiting scholars to study in North America, sending economist teams to investigate in the U.S., supporting returned students to give lectures and the exchange of literature of economics. Of these, the one-year training course on Western economics was the most notable. It was also known as Ford Class, which was well-known to the whole economics circle of China.

Within the decade of the program, many famous

国经济学界和业界的中坚力量。

事实上，美国之行并不是黄达第一次走出国门。1986 年 5 月，作为中国“行政干部培训政策”代表团团长率团赴法国访问——这是他首次境外出访，也是他“走入更广阔课堂”的起点。

从那以后，古巴、苏里南、日本、匈牙利、波兰、俄罗斯、意大利、法国、英国、加拿大、澳大利亚、中国香港、中国台湾、瑞典、阿根廷和墨西哥等国家和地区，都留下了黄达的足迹。

其中，与中国台湾金融业界和学界 6 年的直接交往尤其值得怀念。“虽然参与两岸金融学术交流不过短短六年，也无大惊大险，但跌宕起伏，内容颇为丰富，无论如何是值得纪念的。”

1995 年 5 月，在北京，以中国金融学会会长身份接待台湾“中央银行”原行长、时任“总统府”顾问的谢森中先生，算是黄达与台湾的第一次“接触”。

转年的 11 月，黄达以中国金融学会会长的身份率团出席在台北召开的“第三届两岸金融学术研讨会”。会后，黄达有感而发，写就一首七绝：“抽刀断水水更流，金融似水贯九洲，分财布利足天下，自可欢聚酣高楼”。套用李白诗句，朴实无华而又意味深长，字里行间既蕴含了统一不可抗拒之意，又突出“金融似水”，必须积极疏通。

“两岸金融学术研讨会”是两岸交流的重要平台，有着极其旺盛的“生命力”。该会议由中国金融学会、台北金融研究发展基金会以及“中华经济研究院”联合举办，从 1994 年开始，交替在大陆和台北召开，除个别年份，一直持续未断。事实证明，会议的举办为两岸金融理论与实务界的交流做出了不可估量的贡献。

economics professors from Europe and America came to give lectures. The course trained 618 students in total. Some of them went abroad and made great achievements, but most became the hard core of China's economics circle and industries.

The trip to America was not Huang Da's first visit abroad. In May 1986, he paid a visit to France as the head of Chinese delegation of Administrative Staff Training Policies. This was his first time to visit another country, and also the starting point for him to enter a vaster classroom.

After then, he visited many countries and regions, including Cuba, Surinam, Japan, Hungary, Poland, Russia, Italy, France, the UK, Canada, Australia, Hong Kong of China, Taiwan of China, Sweden, Argentina and Mexico.

Huang Da cherished the memory of the six-year direct contact with Taiwan financial industry and educational circles during that period. "The cross-straits financial academic exchange lasted for no more than six years," he said, "we had no thrilling moments, but there were rich contents with many ups and downs. It was worthy of remembering."

In May 1995, as the chairman of the China Society for Finance and Banking, Huang Da received Xie Senzhong, former president of Taiwan's "Central Bank" and the then adviser of "Presidential Palace", which was his first "contact" with Taiwan.

In the next November, Huang Da led a delegation to join the 3rd Cross-straits Finance Symposium in Taipei. After the meeting, he was inspired to write down a four-line poem with seven characters to a line, which read: "Water still flows, though we cut it with our swords; And finance is like water connecting us across the straits; When the nation has ample funds countrywide, we can enjoy happy gathering and drinking." By imitating Li Bai's poem, he expressed a profound sense with simple and unadorned words, meaning that the unity of two sides of the Straits is inexorable and finance, like water, needs to dredge.

The Symposium provided an important platform with good vitality. It was jointly held by China Society for Finance and Banking, Taipei Foundation of Finance and "Chung-Hua Institution for Economic Research." Since 1994, it was held in mainland and Taipei in turn. With few exceptions in some particular years, it has kept on till now. Facts proved that the Symposium made immeasurable contributions to the exchanges of financial theory and practice between both sides of the Straits.

5-1

《货币银行学》
Economics of Money and Banking

最晚于20世纪20年代，货币银行学课程就已经从西方引进开设。新中国成立之后，货币银行学课程也一直被列入教学计划之中。但是，直到改革开放之后，我们依然没能编写出一部真正符合中国实际的货币银行学教材：现行的本土教材内容陈旧，引进的国外教材又脱离中国国情。因此，编写出“中国人，在中国大学的讲台上，为了使中国的学生掌握在中国建设中国特色社会主义的本领而传授货币银行学所需的教材”成为亟待解决的问题。

1987年8月下旬，“中国财经教学计划国际研讨会”在复旦大学召开。这次会议是列入世界银行对中国的软贷款“中国大学发展项目Ⅱ”的一个项目。会上，包括在中国讲学的国外知名教授、国内知名教授、世界银行专家和国家教委工作人员等在内的二三十位中外专家学者，经过不同见解的冲突和妥协，最终提出了关于中国财经学科教学计划的建议。其中，货币银行学、政治经济学、西方现代经济学、会计、统计、经济数学、财政学、发展经济学、国际贸易和国际金融10门课程被确定为核心课程。

随后，1989年10月，国家教委在南开大学召开“核心课程教学大纲编写研讨会”，通过招标方式逐一确定10门核心课程的编写单位。中国人民大学金融系由黄达主持编写的《货币银行学》大纲中标。中标后，中国人民大学金融系的周升业、王松奇、李焰、沈伟基等先后参加了大纲和教材初稿的编写。

1991年7月底到8月上旬，在长春金融管理干部学院召开《货币银行学》教材编写研讨会，全国金融教学界的领军人士和崭露头角的新秀积极与会，提出了许多有利于进一步编写的建议。

然而编写的进度并不理想。1992年2月下旬，黄达利用突患肺炎后在家静养期间，突击完成了全书的统编定稿。大约在春夏之交，他与周升业、沈伟基在北京郊区“闭关”几日，最终通读定稿。当年9月，前后历时三年的《货币银行学》由四川人民出版社出版，同时被纳入“高等学校财经类专业核心课程教材”。1999年，经较大修改而成的《货币银行学（第二版）》，纳入“国家级重点教材”系列，改由中国人民大学出版社出版。这个修订版本在该出版社当年的畅销书中位列首位。2000年，该教材又被纳入“教育部面向21世纪经济、管理类核心课程教材”系列。

21世纪之交，金融学科的建设必须跨上一个新的台阶，成为中国金融学界的共识。为此，自1997年起，一些设有知名金融专业的高校，相继组织召开全国性的研讨会，讨论新世纪金融学科建设的方向、重点和规划。2000年4月，中国人民大学财政金融学院邀请兄弟院校金融教学骨干，讨论建设金融学科和重新编写货币银行学教材的指

As late as the 1920s, the course of the Economics of Money and Banking has been introduced from the West and opened. After the founding of new China, the course of the Economics of Money and Banking has been included in the teaching program. However, China had not compiled a textbook of the Economics of Money and Banking that truly conformed to the reality of China after it adopted the reform and opening-up policy—the textbook currently in use was out of date, and the textbook introduced from abroad did not conform to the national conditions of China. Therefore, it became urgent to compile "textbooks for the Chinese people to teach the Economics of Money and Banking on the rostrums of Chinese universities to enable the Chinese students to grasp the skills to build socialism with Chinese characteristics in China."

In late August 1987, "International Workshop on China's Public Finance and Economics Teaching Plan " was held in Fudan University. The meeting was on the agenda of "China Universities Development Program Ⅱ " that was financed by the World Bank with soft loans. At the meeting, twenty to thirty Chinese and foreign experts and scholars, including well-known Chinese and foreign professors, experts of the World Bank and staff of the State Education Commission, despite conflicts and compromises for holding different opinions, finally made suggestions on the teaching program of courses of finance and economics in China. Ten courses, namely Money and Banking, Political Economy, Modern Economics in the West, Accounting, Statistics, Economic Mathematics, Public Finance, Developmental Economics, International Trade and International Finance were set to be core courses.

Later, in October 1989, the State Education Commission held "Core Courses Syllabi Compilation Seminar " in Nankai University, and determined the syllabus compilers of the ten core courses one by one through invitation to bid. The syllabus of *Economics of Money and Banking* compiled by the Department of Finance of the Renmin University of China under the leadership of Huang Da got the bid. After that, Zhou Zhengye, Wang Songqi, Li Yan and Chen Weiji from the Department of Finance of the Renmin University of China participated in the compilation of the syllabus and the first draft of the textbook.

At the turn of July and August 1991, the *Economics of Money and Banking* Textbook Compilation Seminar was held in Changchun Financial Management Cadre Institute. The leading figures in the finance teaching circles and the promising young attended the meeting actively, and made many suggestions for the further compilation of the textbook.

However, the compilation progress was not ideal. In late February 1992, Huang Da was convalescing from pneumonia, and crashed to complete the finalization of the whole book. It was about at the turn of spring and summer that he and Zhou Shengye and Shen Weiji "secluded " themselves in the suburbs of Beijing, and read the draft through and finalized it. In September of the same year, *Economics of Money and Banking* was published by Sichuan People's Publishing House, and was included in "Core Textbooks for Majors of Finance and Economics in Universities. " In 1999, the second edition of *Economics of Money and Banking*, which had been greatly revised, was included in "National Priority Textbooks " and was published by China Renmin University Press. The revised *Economics of Money and Banking* topped the bestsellers of the year of China Renmin University Press. In 2000, it was included in "Core Economics and Management Textbooks Facing the 21st Century of the Education of China. "

At the turn of the 21st century, it had become the consensus of the Chinese financial circles that the building of financial disciplines must step on a new stage. Since 1997, some universities having well-known majors of money and finance held national seminars in succession to discuss the direction and priorities of and planning for developing the majors of money and finance in the new century. In April 2000, the School of Finance of the Renmin University of China invited capable teachers of economics of money and finance from sister universities to discuss the guiding ideology of building

导思想。会后，学院决定着手编写《货币银行学》的“升级版”——《金融学》[《货币银行学(第三版)》]。此后，担任主编的黄达，历访多所兄弟院校的经济、金融院系，研讨编写所遇到的原则性问题。前后又历时 3 年，《金融学》最终由中国人民大学出版社出版。

在《金融学》出版之后，黄达决定“退出江湖”。《金融学》的修订工作落到了沈伟基教授和张杰教授肩上。两位教授分别主持修订的《金融学（第二版）》[《货币银行学（第四版）》]与《金融学（第三版）》[《货币银行学（第五版）》]，于 2008 年和 2012 年由中国人民大学出版社先后出版。

142

图 142 为 1987 年 8 月 24 日，“中国财经教学计划国际研讨会”在复旦大学召开。全体与会专家合影留念。前排右三为黄达，右十为时任复旦大学校长谢希德。

On August 24, 1987, the "International Workshop on China's Public Finance and Economics Teaching Plan" was held in Fudan University. All the attendees took a group photo. The third from the right in the front row is Huang Da; and the tenth from the right in the front row is Fudan University President Xie Xide.

financial disciplines and recompiling the textbook of money and banking. After the meeting, the School of Finance decided to start out compiling the "upgraded" edition of *Economics of Money and Banking—Economics of Money and Finance* (*Economics of Money and Banking*, 3rd Edition). Huang Da, the editor-in-chief, then visited the economics and finance schools and departments of many sister universities, and discussed with the latter the principle problems he met during compilation. It took another three years before *Economics of Money and Finance* was published by China Renmin University Press.

After the publishing of *Economics of Money and Finance*, Huang Da decided to "withdraw". The task to revise *Economics of Money and Finance* fell to Prof. Shen Weiji and Prof. Zhang Jie. The two professors presided over revising *Economics of Money and Finance* (2nd Edition) *(Economics of Money and Banking, 4th Edition)* and *Economics of Money and Finance* (3rd Edition) *(Economics of Money and Banking*, 5th Edition*)*, respectively. The two books were published by China Renmin University Press in 2008 and 2012, respectively.

143

图 143 为 1989 年 10 月 28 日，“核心课程教学大纲编写研讨会”在南开大学召开。全体与会专家合影留念。前排左六为黄达。

On October 28, 1989, the "Core Courses Syllabi Compilation Seminar" was held in Nankai University. All the attendees took a group photo. The sixth from the left in the front row is Huang Da.

144

图 144 为 1991 年 7 月 26 日，“《货币银行学》教材编写研讨会”在长春金融管理干部学院召开。全体与会专家合影留念。前排左五为黄达。

期间，黄达曾应邀题词。

On July 26, 1991, the "The *Economics of Money and Banking* Textbook Compilation Seminar" was held in Changchun Financial Management Cadre Institute. All the attendees took a group photo. The fifth from the left in the front row is Huang Da.

During the seminar, Huang Da wrote an inscription on invitation.

图 145 为 1991 年 8 月 2 日，“《货币银行学》教材编写研讨会”期间，黄达（右二）、王广谦（左一）、查卫平（左二）和夏德仁（右一）在一起。

On August 2, 1991, during the "The *Economics of Money and Banking* Textbook Compilation Seminar," Huang Da (second from the right), Wang Guangqian (first from the left), Zha Weiping (second from the left) and Xia Deren (first from the right) were together.

145

146

148

147

149

图 146 为《货币银行学》（四川人民出版社 1992 年初版）。

Economics of Money and Banking (First Edition, Sichuan People's Publishing House, 1992)

图 147 为《货币银行学》（中国人民大学出版社 1999 年修订版）。

Economics of Money and Banking (Revised Edition, China Renmin University Press, 1999)

图 148 为《货币银行学》（四川人民出版社 1992 年再版）。

Economics of Money and Banking (Second Edition, Sichuan People's Publishing House, 1992)

图 149 为《货币银行学》（中国人民大学出版社 2000 年第二版）。

Economics of Money and Banking (Second Revised Edition, China Renmin University Press, 2000)

5-2

打破惯例，出任中国人民大学校长

Break Fresh Ground to Take Up the Post of the President of the Renmin University of China

1989年秋冬之交，时任中国人民大学校长袁宝华向国务院提请辞去校长一职，并推荐黄达接任校长职务。按照惯例，中国人民大学校长一直由组织部门在校外选派合适的“革命老干部”担任。以前历任主要负责人，包括袁宝华校长，最低资历是抗日战争爆发前后参加革命的省部级干部。如果由黄达接任，意味着在中国人民大学校长人选上出现两个变化：一是资历标准放开——黄达只是解放战争初期参加革命队伍的干部；二是开主要领导干部在校内产生之先河。

除去这样的改变，加之其他种种原因，经过1990、1991两年的考察、酝酿，1991年12月16日，黄达才正式被任命为中国人民大学校长。

在担任校长两年多之后，1994年7月11日，国家教委主任朱开轩等有关领导来中国人民大学宣布学校领导班子换届的决定，校党委书记李文海接替黄达担任中国人民大学校长。会上，黄达对于上上下下、方方面面，以及“同学们”在他任职期间给予的支持表达了感激。之所以对“同学们”表示感谢，一方面，黄达任职期间经历了当时特殊事件的前后几年，因此对于学生的感激并不仅仅限于客套话，而是有着较为特殊的意味。另一方面，即使不在非常年代，充分发挥学生的主动性和创造性，教与学相辅相成本身也应当是学校日常工作中极其重要的部分。

At the turn of autumn and winter in 1989, the then president of the Renmin University of China Yuan Baohua applied to the State Council of China for resigning his post as the president of the Renmin University of China, and recommended Huang Da to be the new president. By convention, the president of the Renmin University of China had been some "revolutionary senior cadre " selected by the organization department from outside the university. The main persons in charge of the Renmin University of China in the past, including president Yuan Baohua, were principal and ministerial level cadres, who took part in revolution around the outbreak of the Anti-Japanese War, at the lowest level. If Huang Da were to take the post, it would indicate two changes in the selection of president of the Renmin University of China: first, the requirements in qualifications were loosened—Huang Da was a cadre who took part in revolution in the early days of China's war of revolution; second, it may begin to select major leading cadres from inside the Renmin University of China ever since.

Given such changes and other reasons, Huang Da was not officially appointed the president of the Renmin University of China till December 16, 1991 after two years of observation and preparation in 1990 and 1991.

More than two years after he took the post of the president of the Renmin University of China, Zhu Kaixuan, the then Minister of the State Education Commission, and other related personnel went to the Renmin University of China to announce the decision to change the university leadership, and decided to appoint Li Wenhai, secretary of the Party Committee of the Renmin University of China, to take the place of Huang Da as the president of the Renmin University of China. During the meeting, Huang Da expressed his gratitude for all, and for the support the "students " gave him during his term. He thanked the "students " because he held the post in the years after the special incident (the 1989 political incident) and it was not only polite formula, but had a special meaning; and because giving full play to the students' initiative and creativeness and having teaching and learning complemented is always an important part in the daily work of the university.

任命机关：中华人民共和国国务院
任命文号：国任字[1991] 144 号

第1000315号

任命黄达为
中国人民大学
校长

国务院总理 李鹏

1991 年 11 月 24 日

150

图 150 为 1991 年 11 月 24 日，国务院总理李鹏签发的黄达担任中国人民大学校长的任命书。

On November 24, 1991, the then Premier of the State Council Li Peng signed and issued the letter of appointment as the president of the Renmin University of China to Huang Da.

图 151 为 1991 年 12 月 16 日，国家教委副主任何东昌到中国人民大学宣布校长任免，向黄达递交校长任命书。右为何东昌，左为黄达。

On December 16, 1991, He Dongchang, deputy director of the State Education Commission, went to the Renmin University of China, to announce the appointment and dismissal of the president of the Renmin University of China, and sent the letter of appointment to Huang Da. The right is He Dongchang and the left is Huang Da.

151

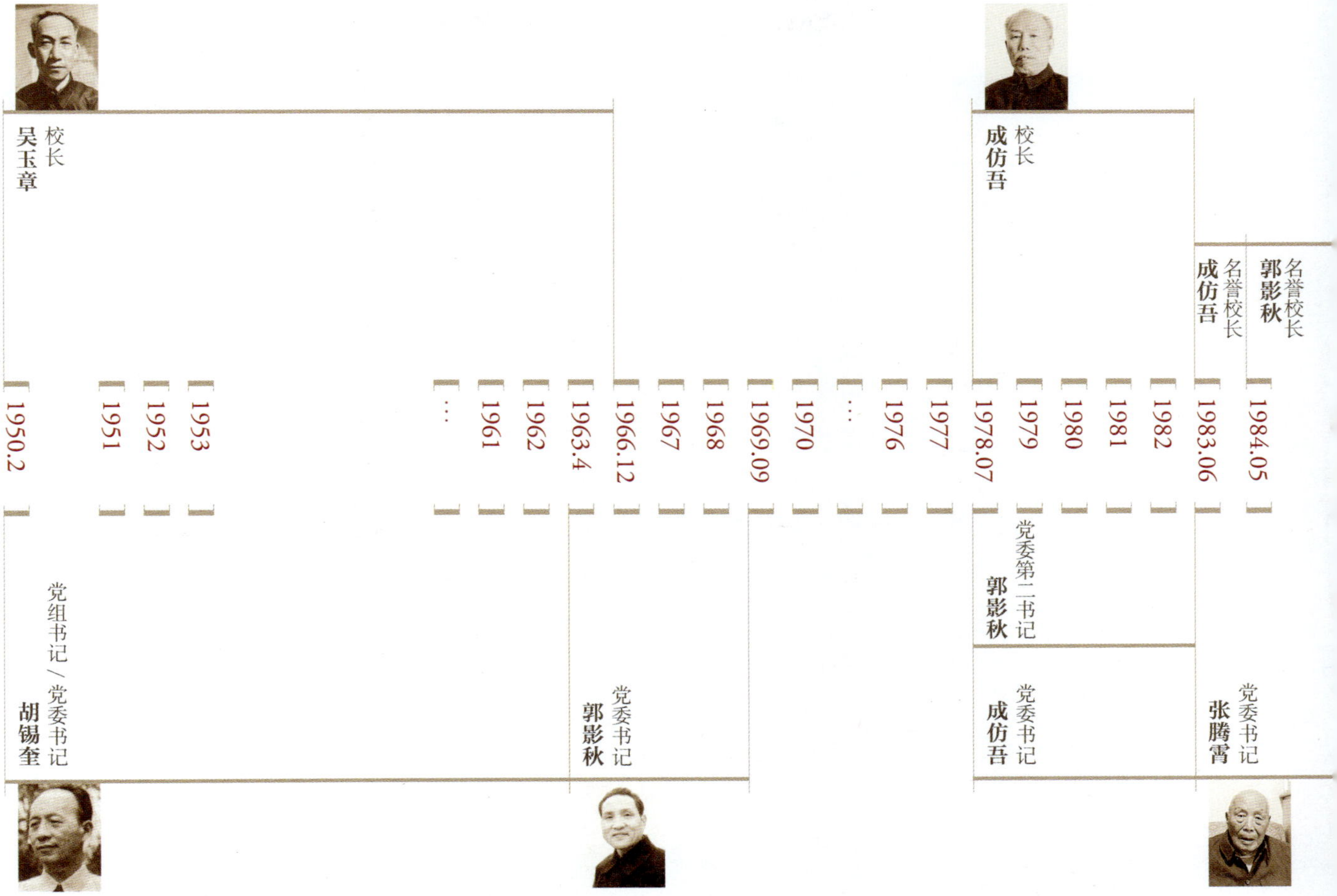

152

图 152 为中国人民大学历任校长和党组书记、党委书记。黄达于 1991 年 11 月—1994 年 6 月担任中国人民大学校长。现任中国人民大学党委书记、校长分别为靳诺、刘伟。

This is a picture of the past presidents, secretaries of the leading Party group, and secretaries of the Party Committee of the Renmin University of China. Huang Da served as the president of the Renmin University of China during November 1991 and June 1994. The current secretary of the Party Committee and president of the Renmin University of China are Jin Nuo and Liu Wei respectively.

5-2-1>

“这是一段长达八九年的乐章。可以称得上是美妙的华彩乐章，但可惜最终没有纳入人民大学交响乐的总谱之内。”关于从20世纪80年代初期开始，中国人民大学筹建国家行政学院一事，黄达曾在《黄达文集》（三续）中如此叙述。

“从1982年‘中发41号文件’到1990年中国人民大学的同志从国家行政学院的最终撤出，先后持续七八年，在循着以文科为主的综合性大学这条轨道办学的同时，一直伴随着将会使人民大学受到特殊关照的‘诱惑’——筹建好像只有人民大学才有资格筹建的‘两院’（指行政管理学院和经济管理学院）和国家行政学院。人民大学里的一些同志和与人民大学有历史渊源的一些同志，往往出于对人民大学在建国之初风光无限的怀念和希望人民大学重现雄风的愿望，对筹建‘两院’乃至筹建国家行政学院寄予过大的期望，认为这是人民大学能否发展的主要机缘和决定性的关键。然而事实却是：受当时副总理兼教委主任支持的‘两院’竟然未能立项；而迅速立项的国家行政学院，却瞬息之间就与指定负责筹建的人民大学脱钩。人民大学都是白忙乎了一阵。假设把主要的希望寄托在筹建‘两院’和筹建国家行政学院上面，那么人民大学在这个过程中所受到的精神上的打击和工作上的损失是可以设想的。然而，有幸的是，在这个‘诱惑’刚刚摆在面前之际，也就是1982年、1983年之交，与人民大学相伴成长的骨干，保持了清醒的头脑，形成了正确办学方针的基本共识。”

| 右页图 |—>

图155为1990年6月14日，国家行政学院筹建领导小组成员合影。左二至左十分别为：力康泰、黄达、刘积斌、郝建秀、赵东宛、袁宝华、刘宗德、程联昌、李文海。

On June 14, 1990, members of the leading group for the preparation to set up National School of Administration took a group photo. From the second to the tenth from the left are Li Kangtai, Huang Da, Liu Jibin, Hao Jianxiu, Zhao Dongwan, Yuan Baohua, Liu Zongde, Cheng Lianchang and Li Wenhai.

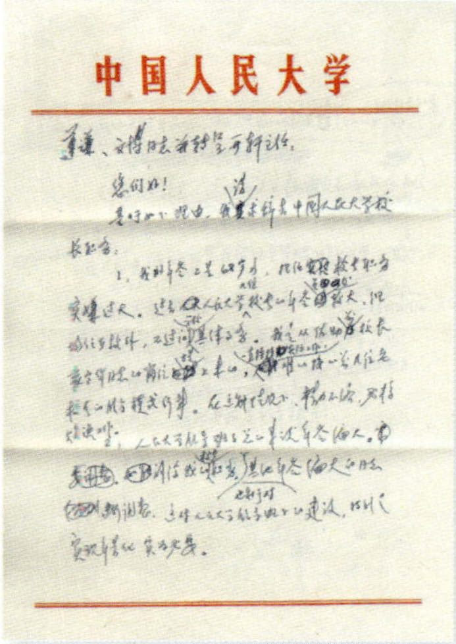
中国人民大学

153

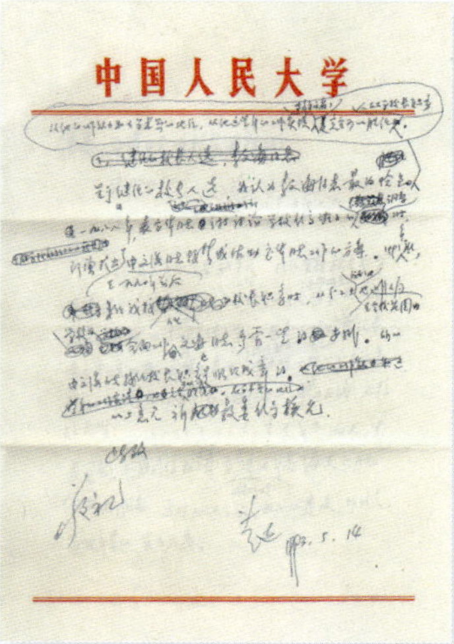
中国人民大学

154

图 153 和图 154 为 1993 年 5 月 14 日，黄达向国家教委递交的辞职报告（底稿）。

“遵谦、文博同志并转呈开轩主任：您们好！基于如下理由，我请求辞去中国人民大学校长职务：1. 我的年龄已是 68 岁多，担任校长职务实嫌过大。过去人民大学几位校长的年龄虽然较大，但均住在校外，不过问学校具体事务。我是从佐助前校长袁宝华同志的岗位上提上来的，一直操持实际工作，难以按照前几位老校长的工作模式行事。在这种情况下，精力不济，必将贻误工作。2. 人民大学领导班子总的来说年龄偏大。解除我的校长职务，也利于对其他年龄偏大的同志进行调整，这对人民大学领导班子的建设，特别是实现年轻化实为必要。关于继任的校长人选，我认为李文海同志最为恰当。从他的工作能力和在学术界的地位，从他这些年的工作实效等多方面来看，完全可以胜任人民大学校长职务。1988 年，袁宝华同志主持讨论学校领导班子的调整时，即曾提出在 1990 年前后，由文海同志接替我佐助宝华同志工作的方案。1991 年底，委任我接任校长职务时，从分工上我们也在全校范围内明确学校全面工作由文海同志多管一些的安排，所以由文海同志接任校长职务也是顺理成章的。黄达，1993 年 5 月 14 日。”

On May 14, 1993, Huang Da submitted a resignation report (draft) to the State Education Commission.

"To Comrade Zun Qian, Wenbo and Minister Kaixuan, For the following reasons, I now request to resign the post as president of the Renmin University of China. Firstly, I am more than 68 years old, and too old for the post. Several presidents of the university were old, but they did not live on the campus or get involved in specific administration. I was promoted from the assistant of former president Yuan Baohua, and have been working concretely. So it is hard for me to follow the working style of the former several presidents. I feel tired, which will bungle the job. Secondly, the leading cadres of the Renmin University of China are old in general. Removing me from my post is conducive to adjusting the posts of other old comrades, which is necessary for the building of the leadership of the Renmin University of China and for promoting younger staff. As for the candidate for the next president, I personally recommend Li Wenhai. His capabilities, his status in the scholars, and his performance in work in these years all indicate that he is totally competent for the post. In 1988, when Yuan Baohua presided over a discussion on adjusting the university leadership, he mentioned the plan to let Wenhai take the place of me as the assistant of Baohua till around 1990. At the close of 1991 when I was appointed the president of the Renmin University of China, we made clear the arrangement of letting Wenhai take charge of more school work around the university. So it is rational that Wenhai takes the post of president. Huang Da, on May 14, 1993."

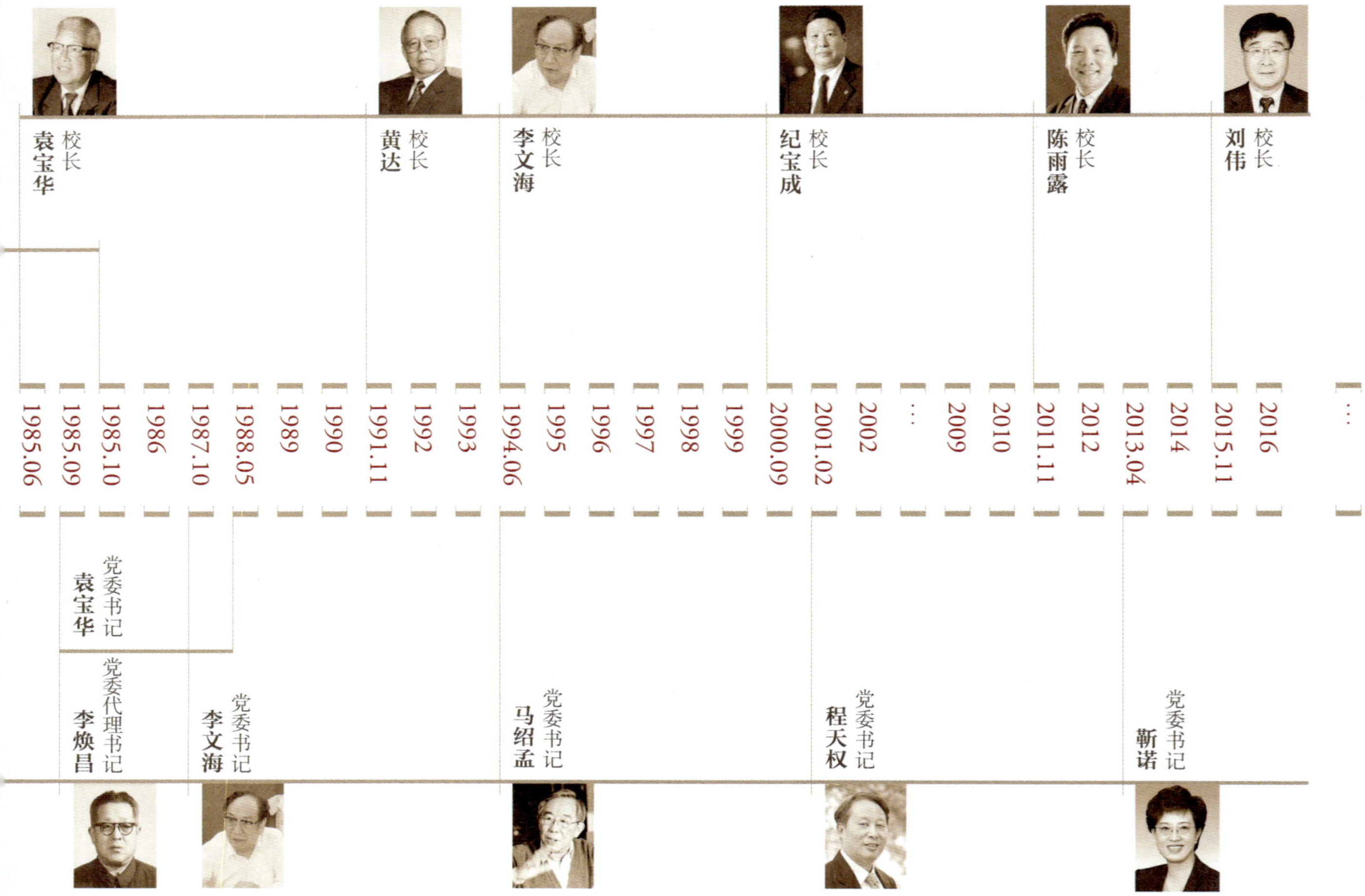
校长 袁宝华
校长 黄达
校长 李文海
校长 纪宝成
校长 陈雨露
校长 刘伟
1985.06
1985.09
1985.10
1986
1987.10
1988.05
1989
1990
1991.11
1992
1993
1994.06
1995
1996
1997
1998
1999
2000.09
2001.02
2002
…
2009
2010
2011.11
2012
2013.04
2014
2015.11
2016
…
党委书记 袁宝华
党委代理书记 李焕昌
党委书记 李文海
党委书记 马绍孟
党委书记 程天权
党委书记 靳诺

"It is a movement that lasted eight or nine years. It can be called a dulcet and gorgeous movement. However, it is unlucky that it was not involved in the score of the symphony of the Renmin University of China. " On preparing to set up National School of Administration, Huang Da dedicated a statement of it in *Essays of Huang Da (Extention 3).*

"For seven to eight years from 'Zh. F. No.41 file' in 1982 to the final pull-out of the comrades of the Renmin University of China from National School of Administration in 1990, the Renmin University of China, while following the route to develop itself into a comprehensive university that focused on liberal arts, was filled with the 'allure' that it might be given special concern—preparing to set up 'two schools' (National School of Public Administration and National School of Economic Management), which it seemed that only the Renmin University of China had the qualification to do. Some people in the Renmin University of China and some people who were related to the Renmin University of China expected too much from the preparation for building 'two schools,' even National School of Administration out of the yearning for the glory of the Renmin University of China in the early years of the founding of New China and the wish that the Renmin University of China could stand up again in a gallant and stately manner. They thought it to be a major lucky chance for, and a decisive key to the development of the Renmin University of China. The fact is: the 'two schools' project supported by the then vice premier of China who was concurrently in charge of the State Education Commission was not approved; the project of National School of Administration which was soon approved unhooked with the Renmin University of China that was designated to take charge of the preparatory work over a blink. The Renmin University of China was busy for a while for nothing. Suppose the Renmin University of China set its hope on preparing to build 'two schools' and National School of Administration, the shock to it and the loss it suffered in work in the process could be imagined. However, it is lucky while the 'allure' was just in front of it, that is, at the turn of 1982 and 1983, the backbone cadres who grew along with the Renmin University of China kept sober and reached a consensus on the right guideline for running the university. "

155

5-2-2>

从抗日烽火中陕北公学的建校，到挺进敌后开展国防教育的华北联合大学，到迎接新中国的华北大学，到为新中国经济建设而创办并经历风风雨雨迎来改革开放的中国人民大学，不论时代如何变迁，历史如何推进，自始至终贯穿的红线，自始至终鼓舞中国人民大学不断前进的奋斗目标和动力是什么？

中国人民大学五十五周年校庆之际，这个长期萦绕在黄达心中的目标和动力逐渐明确起来——“永远奋进在时代前沿！”为此，黄达在校庆大会上专门以“永远奋进在时代前沿”为题发表了讲话。

此外，校庆前夕，“实事求是”还被正式确定为中国人民大学校训。

The Renmin University of China has transformed from the Shanbei Public School in the Anti-Japanese War, to North China Union University which went deep to the enemy's rear area to provide national defense education, to North China University which welcomed the founding of new China, and finally to the Renmin University of China which was built for the economic development of new China and ushered in the reform and opening up through hardships. Despite of the vicissitudes and historical evolution, what is the red line and what is the goal and motivation that has been running through the development of the Renmin University of China?

At the celebration of the 55th anniversary of the Renmin University of China, the goal and the motivation which had long been in the mind of Huang Da became clear—"to always advance bravely ahead of the times! " Therefore, Huang Da delivered a speech with the title of "Always Advance Bravely ahead of the Times! "

Besides, on the eve of the celebration, "To Seek Truth from Facts " was officially made the school motto of the Renmin University of China.

156

图 156 为 1992 年 11 月 1 日，黄达在庆祝中国人民大学建校五十五周年大会上致辞。

On November 1, 1992, Huang Da addressed the 55th anniversary of the founding of the Renmin University of China.

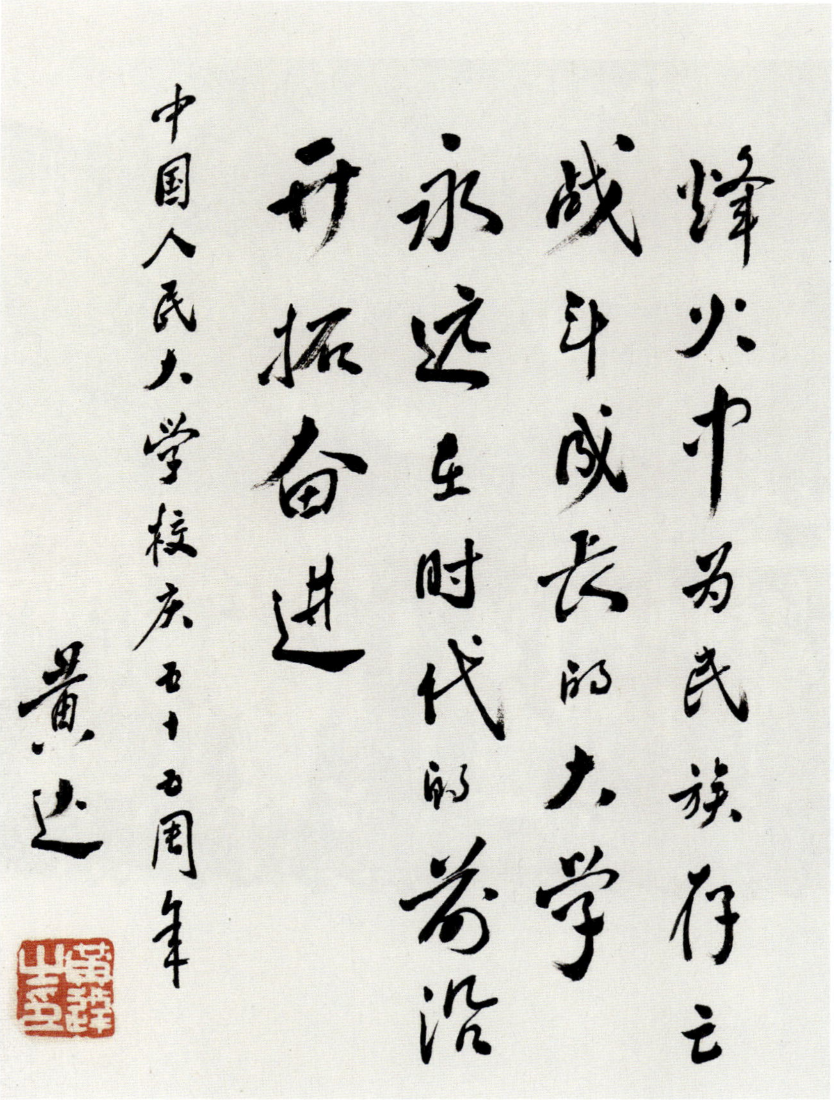

157

图 157 为 1992 年 10 月 17 日，黄达为校刊题词祝贺中国人民大学校庆五十五周年。

On October 17, 1992, Huang Da inscribed the university journal for the 55th anniversary of the founding of the Renmin University of China.

158

图 158 为 1997 年 11 月 1 日，庆祝中国人民大学建校六十周年暨第三届吴玉章奖金颁奖大会隆重举行。全体与会嘉宾合影留念，前排右四为黄达。

On November 1, 1997, the 60th anniversary of the founding of the Renmin University of China and the 3rd Wu Yuzhang Prize Presentation was held. All the guests there took a group photo. The fourth from the right in the front row is Huang Da.

159

图 159 为 1997 年 11 月 1 日，从左至右在大会主席台就座的为：张腾霄、宋涛、吴树青、黄达、马绍孟。

On November 1, 1997, the seated ones from the left to the right on the rostrum are Zhang Tengxiao, Song Tao, Wu Shuqing, Huang Da and Ma Shaomeng.

5-2-3>

1992 年，邓小平南方谈话之后，改革又迸发出新一轮的激情。在学校里，先是一段集中于管理体制的改革，随后逐渐深入到学科建设。

对于中国人民大学而言，最让人感到巨大压力的是如何直接触及马克思主义这个政治敏感问题。在这种情况下，黄达坚持的立场是：应从探寻正确思维的角度而不是从现实的世俗政治斗争角度出发，既不应教条地固守不该固守的阵地，又反对无知地反对人类精神文明发展历程中的巅峰。但究竟如何对此问题进行全面总结并予以明确表达，在黄达自己看来直到今天也尚需努力理清。

After Deng Xiaoping's remarks on reform during his southern tour of China in 1992, the reform and opening up in China became fervent again. In schools, there was a period of time dedicated to reforming the management system, and then the building of courses.

For the Renmin University of China, the issue that brought the greatest pressure to it was how to directly touch the politically sensitive problem of Marxism. In such situation, Huang Da insisted on the perspective of searching the correct way of thinking instead of that of secular political struggles. He thought it to be wrong to stick to a position that should not be stuck to, or to ignorantly object the development peak of human spiritual civilization. As for how to comprehensively sum up and clearly express such issue, Huang Da thinks that efforts have to be made to rationalize that even today.

| 右页图 |—>

图 160 为 1992 年，黄达有关改革的讲话手稿。

在这篇讲话中，黄达提出改革的基本指导思想：马列主义实质是实事求是；教学改革，重视渐变。同时，他还谈到学科建设目标（解决用什么东西教学生）、教学体制的改革（解决通过什么方式把我们所要教的教给学生）以及管理体制改革三个主要问题。

These pictures record the manuscript of Huang Da's speech on reform in 1992.

In the speech, Huang Da put forward the basic guiding philosophy of reform—the essence of Marxism-Leninism is to seek truth from facts; the reform of teaching shall be progressive. Meanwhile, he talked about three major issues in this speech, namely the goal of the construction of courses (to solve the problem of teaching materials), reform of the teaching system (to solve the problem of the ways of teaching) and reform of the management system.

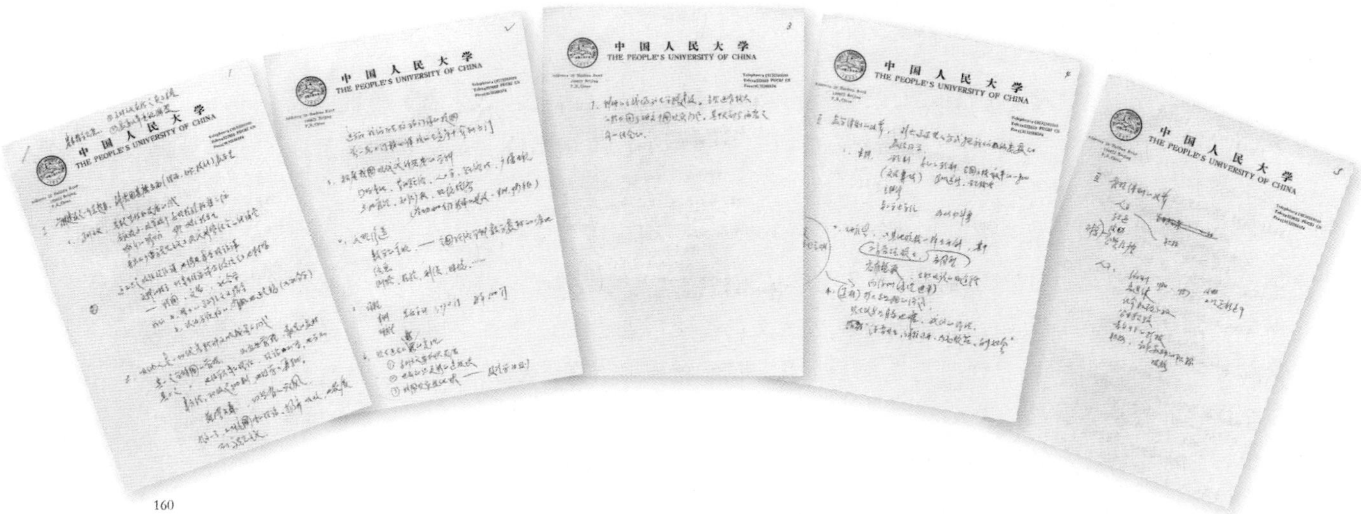

160

5-2-4>

1993 年初，处于改革关键期的中国人民大学，却因为一桩“放弃马克思主义”公案而成为当时国内外舆论关注的热点。

1 月 7 日，《光明日报》发表了题为《主动接轨、深化改革，中国人民大学调整专业》的报道，就中国人民大学“增设一批专业，停招一批专业”的事件进行了陈述。

1 月 29 日，《人民日报》发表了题为《加快教育改革适应社会主义市场经济体制，中国人民大学大幅度调整学科》的报道并配以短评《抓住大学改革的“龙头”》。该报道是一篇符合学校改革实际的正面新闻。但是，报道中的统计数字“今年停止招生的专业和新设的专业，合起来占原有专业总数的 60%”，却由于统计方法不同，与实际 20% 的比例相比被严重夸大了。

2 月 2 日，《中国青年报》在《经济蓝讯》发表了题为《人大拎起泳衣》的报道，提到中国人民大学“拟停招马克思主义基础专业学生”，用词比较“俏皮”，至于报道事实并没有太大出入。

由于中国人民大学是中国共产党创办的大学，是传播马克思主义理论的重要阵地，因此改革开放以来，对中国共产党及马克思主义持对立意见的人们，就有这样的思路：丑化、搬倒中国人民大学，会是对马克思主义的沉重一击；如能论证中国人民大学也要放弃马克思主义，则可说明马克思主义在中国已经动摇，等等。因此，上述报道随即在国内外舆论界引起很大反响。“美国之音”、英国的“BBC”等广播电台，《明报》（中国香港）、《金融时报》（英国）等报刊纷纷以中国人民大学“放弃马克思主义”及“取消马克思主义课程”为内容进行了专门报道。国内理论界、教育界、知识界的人士纷纷通过各种渠道向学校了解事情真相。

为了消除不良舆论影响，中国人民大学从 2 月下旬起陆续在北京广播电台、《人民日报》、《光明日报》、《中国教育报》等媒体发表了关于学校教学改革的正面专题报道。3 月 29 日，国务委员兼国家教委主任李铁映在答美国《新闻周刊》记者问中，专门谈到中国人民大学专业调整问题。这次权威的解答在引导舆论正确认识中国人民大学教学改革的同时，也为“放弃马克思主义”这桩公案画上了句号。

现将这次问答摘录如下：

问：某些大学（如中国人民大学）正调整其教学课程以适应中国变化着的形势，那些从前以马列思想为主要教学内容的（系）也正在解散，为什么？

答：最近一个时期，每个高等学校的教学改革，尤其是文科教学结构的调整和课程设置、教学内容改革的步伐在加快。改革的目的，是要使文科教育更好地适应社会主义市场经济体制的需要，更好地服务于社会主义政治、经济、文化建设。据我所知，中国人民大学有 14 个社会急需的新专业准备在今年秋季招生，另有 17 个专业今年暂停招生。在暂停招生的专业中，有些专业，如科学社会主义、国际共产主义运动专业，一直采取隔年招生的办法；另一些专业，主要是由于社会需求方面的原因今年暂时停招；还有一些专业，如马克思主义原理、中国革命史等主要培养高校理论师资的专业，

At the beginning of 1993, the Renmin University of China at the crucial stage of reform became the focus of domestic and foreign public opinions for a legal case of "Abandon Marxism. "

On January 7, *Guangming Daily* published a report titled Take the Initiative, Deepen the Reform—the Renmin University of China Adjusts its Majors to report the event of "opening some new majors, and stopping enrolling students to some old majors. "

On January 29, *People's Daily* published a report titled Accelerate Educational Reform to Adapt to the Socialist Market Economic System—the Renmin University of China Substantially Adjusts Disciplines with a short comment titled Take the "Head " of University Reform. The report was a piece of active news that conformed to the reform reality of the Renmin University of China. But the report read, "The majors that stopped enrolling students and the newly opened majors this year take up for 60% of the total number of majors in the past, " which was exaggeration of 20%, the actual percentage, due to different calculation methods.

On February 2, *China Youth Daily* published a report titled The Renmin University of China Picked Up the Swimming Wear, in which it mentioned that the Renmin University of China "planned to stop enrolling students for the major of Marxist basics " in "witty " words. The fact reported was not too far from the truth.

Because the Renmin University of China was founded by the Communist Party of China, and was an important battlefield for spreading the Marxist theories, those who were against the Communist Party and Marxism thought that smearing the image of and pulling down the Renmin University of China would be a heavy blow to Marxism; that if the Renmin University of China was proved to abandon Marxism, it would explain that Marxism had been vacillated in China, etc. Therefore, the above report had great repercussion in the domestic and foreign media. VOA, BBC, *Ming Pao Daily News* (Hong Kong of China), *Financial Times* (UK) etc. all had special reports on "abandoning Marxism," "canceling Marxist courses" by the Renmin University of China. The theorists, the educational circles and the intellectuals all tried to get the truth from the Renmin University of China through various channels.

In order to get rid of the impact of adverse public opinions, the Renmin University of China broadcast and published special positive reports on its education reform through Radio Beijing, *People's Daily, Guangming Daily, and China Education Daily* in succession since late February. On March 29, Li Tieying, member of the State Council and director of the State Education Commission, especially mentioned the quantitative issue of readjusting the specialties offered by the Renmin University of China when answering the questions of the journalist of *Newsweek*. His authoritative answer guided the media to correctly understand the reform in education of the Renmin University of China, and put an end to the complicated case of "abandoning Marxism. "

Below is an extract of the Q&A.

Question: Some universities (like the Renmin University of China) are adjusting their courses to adapt to the changing situation in China. The departments mainly focusing on Marxism-Leninism in teaching are being dissolved. Why?

Answer: Recently, Chinese universities are accelerating the reform in education, especially the adjustment of educational structure of liberal arts, course setting and teaching contents. The aim of it is to make the education of liberal arts more adaptive to the requirements of the socialist market economic system, and better serve socialist politics, economy and culture. As far as I know, the Renmin University of China planned to enrolled students to 14 new majors that are badly needed by the society, and to temporarily stop enrolling students to another 17 majors. Of the latter majors, some like scientific socialism and international communist movement have been enrolling students every another year; some temporarily stopped enrolling students mainly for social demand; and some like Marxist theories, history of revolution in China, which mainly cultivate teachers of theories for universities, will mainly enroll postgraduate students. Of these majors, except the major of price theory that has been revoked, and that of national economic planning, which has been changed into the major of national economic management, the rest are not revoked, nor the organizational structure of any department. As regards the reform in education, we highlight the guidance of the theory of building socialism with Chinese characteristics, the adjustment and enrichment of the teaching contents in combination with major features; and actively guide the students to analyze and study the new situations, new experience and new topics

今后主要培养研究生层次的人才。这些专业中，除价格学专业已经撤销、国民经济计划学专业改为国民经济管理专业以外，并没有撤销其他专业，更没有取消任何一个系的建制。在教学改革上，我们强调在建设有中国特色社会主义理论指导下，结合各专业特点，调整、充实教学内容，积极引导学生分析、研究改革开放中出现的新情况、新经验和新课题，这不是削弱马克思主义理论，而是使马克思主义理论教育与经济建设结合得更加紧密，更加贴近现实生活，更具时代感。顺便说一句，前段时间，国内外有的新闻单位关于中国人民大学专业调整和教学改革的报道，是不够准确的。

积极稳妥推进学科改革与建设

中国人民大学校长 黄达

161

图 161 为 1993 年 3 月 16 日，《中国教育报》刊登的由黄达撰写的《积极稳妥推进学科改革与建设》一文。

文中，作为校长的黄达不是辩解人民大学有没有所谓的“放弃”马克思主义，而是正面阐明学校对马克思主义的态度。其中专门讲到了教育改革的全局性问题：如对改革一般和教育改革本身特点如何结合的理解；如尊重人民大学的历史和跟上形势如何统一的理解；如哲学社会科学、人文科学吸取外国的文明成果往往碰到带有政治性的敏感问题以及当时对学习西方经济理论的自我封闭倾向；如人民大学已有的改革成绩和今天的差距；如为什么中国人民大学必须把学科建设提到一切工作的首位；等等。同时，还讲到了无论上下左右有多大的压力，学校自始至终坚持着革命激情和冷静稳妥相结合的方针。

On March 16, 1993, *China Education Daily* published an article written by Huang Da—Advance Disciplinary Reform and Construction Actively and Steadily.

In the article, Huang Da, as the president, did not try to explain if the Renmin University of China "abandoned" Marxism or not, but explained the attitude of the Renmin University of China toward Marxism. He mentioned the global issues of the education reform in China like the understanding of the ways to combine the reform with the characteristics of education; that of integrating the respect for the history of the Renmin University of China and the efforts made to cope with the situation; the fact that philosophical and social sciences and human studies would more than often meet politically sensitive issues when absorbing foreign civilization achievements; the then self-containment tendency towards studying Western economic theories; the gap between the achieved reform results of the Renmin University of China and that today; the reasons why the Renmin University of China must give top priority to disciplinary construction. Meanwhile, he said that, regardless of all pressure, the Renmin University of China would always stick to the guideline of being enthusiastic, and calm and steady.

emerging in the reform and opening up. It is not to weaken the Marxist theories, but to bring the education of Marxist theories closer to economic construction and to the real life, and make it more up-to-date. By the way, the coverage, by some domestic and foreign news media, on the disciplinary adjustment and reform in education of the Renmin University of China recently was not accurate enough.

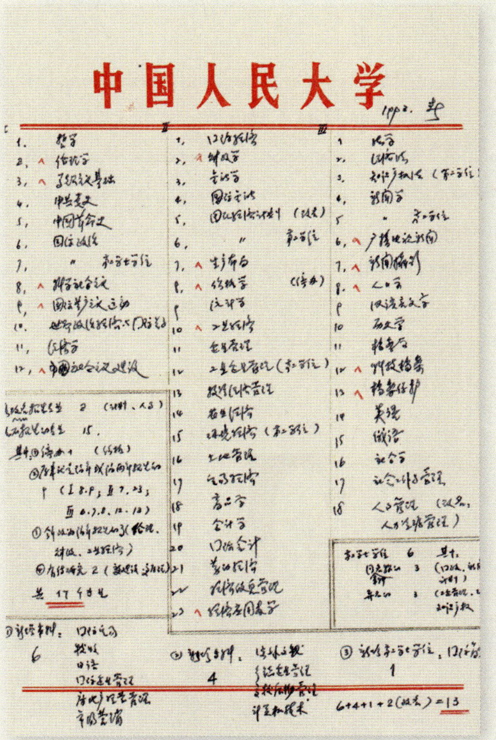
中国人民大学

162

图 162 为 1993 年初，为了弄清中国人民大学本科专业的设置变动，同时也为了厘清专业调整与所谓的“放弃马克思主义”舆论的关系，黄达专门作了一份本科专业的统计图。

At the beginning of 1993, in order to figure out the changes in the setting of majors for undergraduates of the Renmin University of China, and to clarify the relationship between the adjustment of majors and the public opinion of the so-called "abandoning Marxism," Huang Da specially made a cartogram of the majors for undergraduates.

5-2-5>

1995 年 12 月，中国陕北公学华北联合大学校友会（简称“陕公联大校友会”）正式成立。原中共中央政法委员会委员、国家安全部党组书记、部长凌云同志担任会长，李贵、云世英、张腾霄、黄达等同志担任副会长。后于 2005 年 4 月，陕公联大校友会一致表决通过，更名为中国人民大学校友会。2008 年 10 月，民政部审批同意中国陕北公学华北联合大学校友会更名为中国人民大学校友会。

黄达积极参与了校友会的相关组织工作，为校友会发展壮大，逐步走向规范化和制度化做出了一定贡献。

In December 1995, Alumni Association of Shanbei Public School and North China Union University was set up officially. Ling Yun, former member of the Politics and Law Committee of the CPC Central Committee, secretary of the leading Party group and minister of Ministry of State Security, served as the chairman; Li Gui, Yun Shiying, Zhang Tengxiao and Huang Da served as the vice chairman. In April 2005, Alumni Association of Shanbei Public School and North China Union University unanimously voted to change its name into the Alumni Association of the Renmin University of China. In October 2008, the Ministry of Civil Affairs approved the change.

Since the initiation of the Alumni Association, Huang Da had actively participated in organizations and contributed to the development and normalization of the Alumni Association.

163

图 163 为 1986 年春节，黄达与原华北联合大学财经系在北京的老同学聚会。前排从左至右分别为：尹永平、李光宇、贾文灏、谢静修、陈中、黄达；后排从左至右分别为：耿树平、阮若坤、陆迅、刘佩弦、罗扬。

In the spring festival of 1986, Huang Da got together with his classmates of former Department of Finance and Economics of the North China Union University. From the left to the right in the front row are Yin Yongping, Li Guangyu, Jia Wenhao, Xie Jingxiu, Chen Zhong, Huang Da; from the left to the right in the back row are Geng Shuping, Ruan Ruokun, Lu Xun, Liu Peixian and Luo Yang.

164

图 164 为 1995 年 12 月 14 日，陕公联大校友会在中国人民大学成立，全体与会老校友在图书馆前合影留念。最后排左一为黄达。

On December 14, 1995, the Alumni Association of Shanbei Public School and North China Union University was founded in the Renmin University of China. All the alumni present took a group photo in front of the library. The first from the left in the back row is Huang Da.

165

166

图 165 为 1996 年 5 月 21 日，陕公联大校友会举办敬老祝寿联谊会。左一为李光宇，右一和右二分别为黄达、许植。

On May 21, 1996, Alumni Association of Shanbei Public School and North China Union University held a sociable to venerate the elderly and celebrate the birthday. The first from the left is Li Guangyu, the first and second from the right are Huang Da and Xu Zhi, respectively.

图 166 为 1999 年 4 月 18 日，陕公联大校友会敬老祝寿联谊会在中山公园举行。从左至右分别为：吴炯、佘涤清、路地、余飘、张西帆、黄达。

On April 18, 1999, the sociable of the Alumni Association of Shanbei Public School and North China Union University was held in Zhongshan Park. From the left to the right are Wu Jiong, She Diqing, Lu Di, Yu Piao, Zhang Xifan and Huang Da.

167

图 167 为 1998 年 4 月 23 日，陕公联大校友会敬老祝寿联谊会在中国人民大学举行。全体与会老校友在图书馆报告厅前合影。最后排右一为黄达。

On April 23, 1998, Alumni Association of Shanbei Public School and North China Union University held a sociable in the Renmin University of China. All the alumni present took a group photo in front of the library. The first from the right in the back row is Huang Da.

168

图 168 为 2000 年 9 月 6 日，陕公联大校友会会长会在中国人民大学举行。从左至右分别为：路地、李源、张腾霄、凌云、李贵、云世英、缪文、黄达、王建华。右一为刘平。

On September 6, 2000, chairmen's conference of the Alumni Association of Shanbei Public School and North China Union University was held in the Renmin University of China. From the left to the right are Lu Di, Li Yuan, Zhang Tengxiao, Ling Yun, Li Gui, Yun Shiying, Miao Wen, Huang Da and Wang Jianhua. The first from the right is Liu Ping.

169

图 169 为 2001 年 4 月 20 日，陕公联大校友会会长会在国家安全部招待所举行。前排从右至左分别为：王建华、刘平、李贵、凌云、缪文；后排从左至右分别为：李源、云世英、黄达、张腾霄、路地。

On April 20, 2001, chairmen's conference of the Alumni Association of Shanbei Public School and North China Union University was held in the guest house of the Ministry of State Security. From the right to the left in the front row are Wang Jianhua, Liu Ping, Li Gui, Ling Yun and Miao Wen; from the left to the right in the back row are Li Yuan, Yun Shiying, Huang Da, Zhang Tengxiao and Lu Di.

170

图 170 为 2003 年 8 月 24 日，陕公联大校友会会长会在国家安全部招待所举行。从左至右分别为：缪文、黄达、凌云、云世英、刘平、李源、王建华、路地。

On August 24, 2003, chairmen's conference of the Alumni Association of Shanbei Public School and North China Union University was held in the guest house of Ministry of State Security. From the left to the right are Miao Wen, Huang Da, Ling Yun, Yun Shiying, Liu Ping, Li Yuan, Wang Jianhua and Lu Di.

171

图 171 为 2001 年 6 月 14 日，陕公联大校友会隆重举办庆祝中国共产党成立 80 周年大会，会议由黄达（主席台左一）主持。

会上，校友会会长凌云代表全体老同志表示，总结 80 年的经验，集中到一点就是：中国共产党是全中国人民的领导核心，没有共产党，就没有新中国；没有共产党，就没有建设有中国特色社会主义的新道路；这是中国百年巨变的必然结论，这是历史的抉择，这是人民的抉择。

On June 14, 2001, the Alumni Association of Shanbei Public School and North China Union University held the 80th anniversary celebration of the Communist Party of China, and the celebration was presided over by Huang Da (first from the left on the rostrum).

At the meeting, Ling Yun, head of the Alumni Association, expressed on behalf of all the old Party associates that, the experience in the past 80 years could be generalized as the follows: The Communist Party of China is the leading core of the Chinese people; without the Communist Party of China, there wouldn't be New China; without the Communist Party of China, there would not be the new path to socialism with Chinese characteristics; the Communist Party of China is the natural conclusion of the tremendous changes in China in the past century, a historical choice and the choice of the people.

172

图 172 为 2005 年 6 月 12 日，陕公联大校友会隆重举办庆祝抗日战争胜利六十周年大会，会议由黄达（主席台左一）主持。

会上，校友会会长凌云在讲话中回顾了中国人民的抗日战争史，总结了校友会从 1995 年来的各项工作。在谈到中国陕北公学华北联合大学校友会今后的运作时，表示将由中国人民大学校友会统筹安排。艺术家田华作为 1941 年在华北联合大学文艺九队学习过的校友，怀念了在战争中牺牲了的战友，揭露了战争的残酷，表达了在晚年要为祖国的文化事业做贡献的愿望。画家李琦和夫人冯真在台上合唱了当年华北联大的校歌。中央歌舞团原团长孟云校友与著名表演艺术家前民校友演唱了《二月里来》《在太行山上》《白毛女》等歌曲。另外，会上发放的由校友们共同制作的《中国延安陕北公学华北联合大学校友永久纪念》书画册，收录了大量珍贵的历史照片，反映了许多老校友的精神风貌。

On June 12, 2005, the Alumni Association of Shanbei Public School and North China Union University held a conference to celebrate the 60th anniversary of the success of the Anti-Japanese War. The conference was presided over by Huang Da (first from the left on the rostrum).

At the conference, Ling Yun, chairman of the Alumni Association, reviewed the history of the Anti-Japanese War by the Chinese people, summarized the work of the Alumni Association since 1995. Speaking of the running of the Alumni Association of Shanbei Public School and North China Union University in the days to come, he expressed that the Alumni Association of the Renmin University of China would make overall arrangements of it. Artist Tian Hua, as an alumnus who once studied in Performance Team 9 of North China Union University, commemorated his comrades in the war; revealed the cruelty of the war ; and expressed the wish to contribute to China's cause of culture in his senior years. Painting artist Li Qi and his wife Feng Zhen sang the school song of North China Union University in those years together. Meng Yun, former head of Central Ensemble of Songs and Dances, and Qian Min, a famous performing artist, sang such songs as In February, On the Taihang Mountains and The White Haired Girl. Besides, the album for everlasting memory of the alumni of Shanbei Public School and the Alumni of North China Union University made by the alumni together collected a lot of precious photos, and reflected the spirit of many alumni.

173

174

图 173 为 2008 年 10 月 12 日，陕公联大校友会敬老祝寿联谊会在中国人民大学举行。黄达（后排左一）与不同时期老校友在一起。

On October 12, 2008, the Alumni Association of Shanbei Public School and North China Union University held a sociable in the Renmin University of China. Huang Da (first from the left in the back row) was with the alumni of the Renmin University of China.

图 174 为 2009 年 9 月 26 日，陕公联大校友会敬老祝寿联谊会在中国人民大学举行，黄达出席会议并担任主持。会上，在 60 余名年逾八九十岁的老校友的见证下，陕公联大校友会秘书长李源将原陕公联大校友会的重要资料正式移交给中国人民大学校友会。

On September 26, 2009, the Alumni Association of Shanbei Public School and North China Union University held a sociable in the Renmin University of China. Huang Da presided over it.

At the meeting, witnessed by more than 60 alumni and alumna of over 80, even 90 years old, Li Yuan, secretary-general of the Alumni Association of Shanbei Public School and North China Union University, officially handed important materials of the Alumni Association over to the Alumni Association of the Renmin University of China.

175

图 175 为 1985 年 9 月 29 日，中国人民大学福建校友会成立大会在福州隆重举行。全体与会校友合影留念。前排左七为黄达。

On September 29, 1985, the inauguration meeting of Fujian Alumni Association of the Renmin University of China was held in Fuzhou. This is a group photo of the alumni present at the meeting. The seventh from the left in the front row is Huang Da.

图 176 为 1985 年 9 月 29 日，时任中国人民大学副校长黄达（右二）代表学校在大会上致辞。

On September 29, 1985, Huang Da, the then vice president of the Renmin University of China (second from the right), addressed the meeting.

176

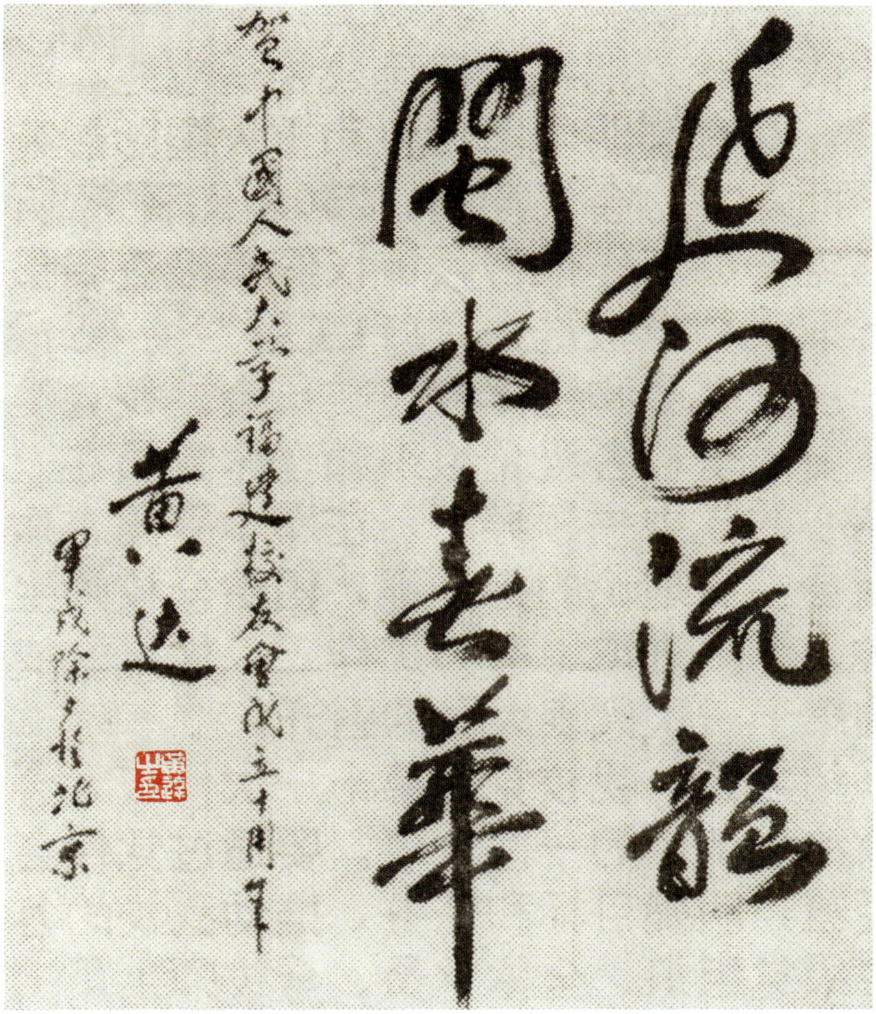

177

图 177 为 1994 年底，黄达为中国人民大学福建校友会成立十周年题写贺词。

At the end of 1994, Huang Da inscribed for the 10th anniversary of Fujian Alumni Association of the Renmin University of China.

178

图 178 为 1991 年 10 月 12 日，黄达（前排左十三）在广西南宁出席中国财政学会组织的会议期间，看望当地华北大学校友并与大家合影留念。

On October 12, 1991, Huang Da (13th from the left in the front row), taking the chance of attending the meeting organized by China Finance Society in Nanning, Guangxi, visited the alumni of North China University, and took a group photo with them.

图 179 为 1986 年 1 月 20 日，黄达向中国人民大学广西校友聚会发电报致贺。

On January 20,1986, Huang Da sent a telegram to congratulate the get-together of the Guangxi alumni of the Renmin University of China.

图 180 为 1996 年 2 月 7 日，黄达为中国人民大学广西校友会成立题写贺词。

On February 7, 1996, Huang Da inscribed his congratulations for the inauguration of Guangxi Alumni Association of the Renmin University of China.

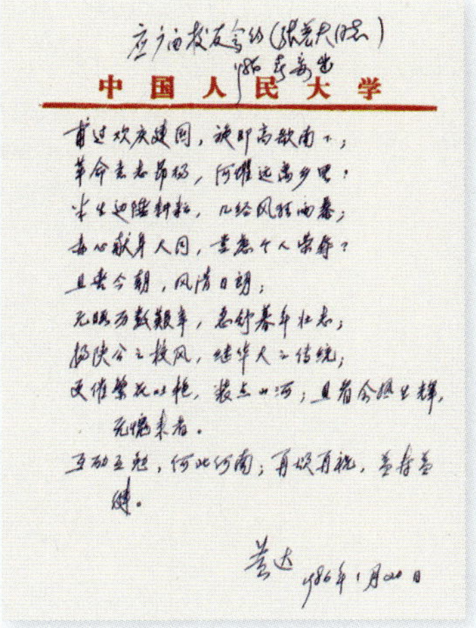

179

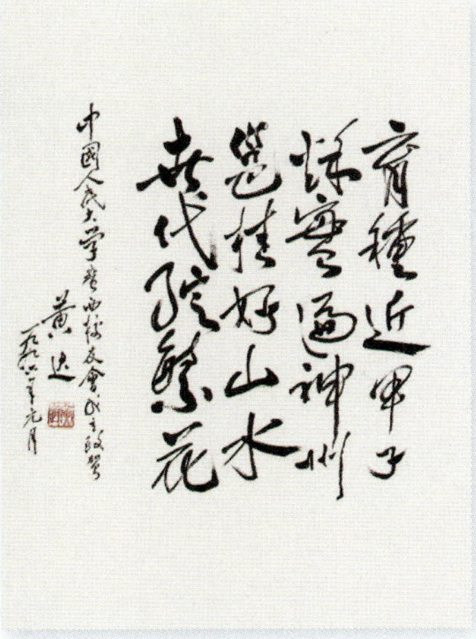

180

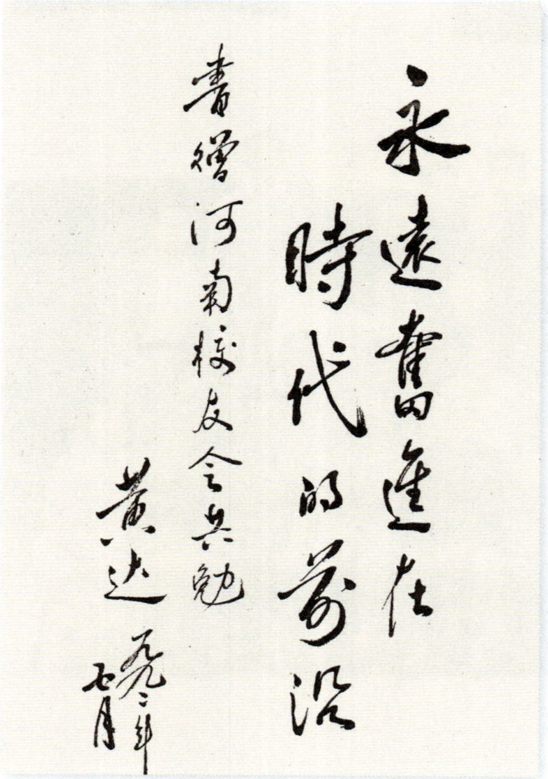

181

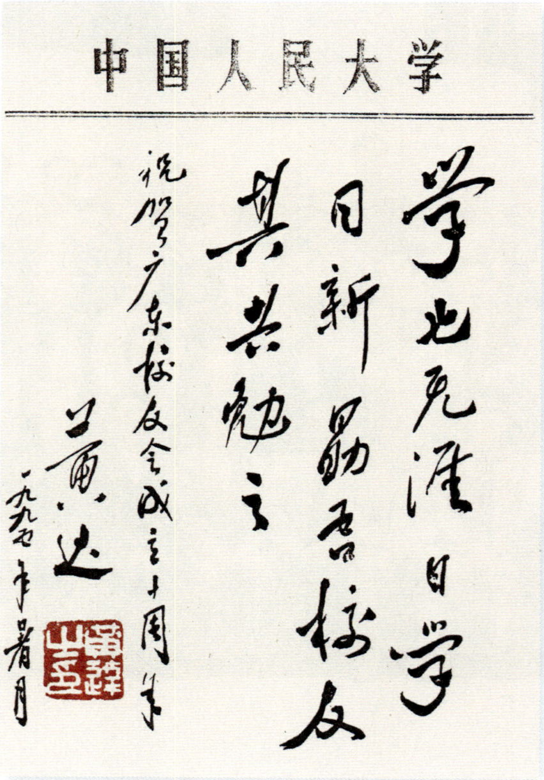

182

图 181 为 1992 年 5 月 4 日，黄达为中国人民大学河南校友会纪念册题词。

On May 4, 1992, Huang Da inscribed on the commemorative album of Henan Alumni Association of the Renmin University of China.

图 182 为 1995 年暑月，黄达为中国人民大学广东校友会成立十周年题写贺词。

In the summer of 1995, Huang Da inscribed his congratulations to the 10th anniversary of the founding of Guangdong Alumni Association of the Renmin University of China.

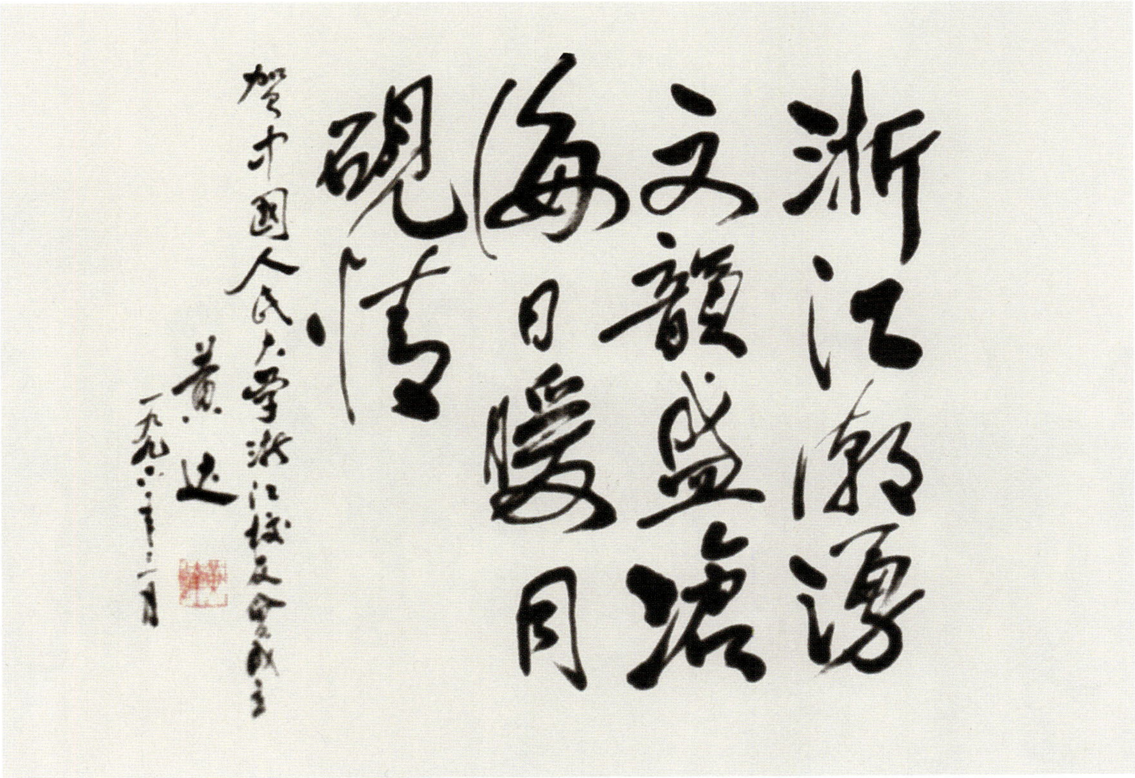

183

图 183 为 1996 年 3 月 30 日，黄达为中国人民大学浙江校友会成立题写贺词。

On March 30, 1996, Huang Da inscribed his congratulations to the founding of Zhejiang Alumni Association of the Renmin University of China.

5-2-6>

校长“杂事”多

The President Has Plenty of Trivial Matters to Deal with

184

图 184 为 1990 年 4 月 28 日，黄达（前排左四）代表中国人民大学出席中国大学生体协篮球协会筹备会。

On April 28, 1990, Huang Da (fourth from the left in the front row) attended the Preparatory Meeting of the Basketball Association of Chinese College Students Sports Association as a representative of Renmin University of China.

185

图185为1991年11月，中国人民大学举行第一次政府特殊津贴证书颁发仪式。全体与会教师合影留念。前排左二为吴大琨，左四至左八分别为：戴世光、袁宝华、宋涛、苗力田、甘惜分，右一为高鸿业；后排左一至左十五分别为：郑杭生、阎达五、塞风、钟契夫、许征帆、吴易风、刘佩弦、邬沧萍、罗国杰、黄达、李震中、彭明、方汉奇、肖前、陈共，后排右一和右二分别为高铭暄、陈先达。

国务院政府特殊津贴是国务院对于高层次专业技术人才和高技能人才的一种奖励制度，于1990年开始向做出突出贡献的专家、学者、技术人员发放。

In November 1991, the Renmin University of China held the first ceremony to issue certificates of special government allowances. All the attended teachers took a group photo. The second from the left in the front row is Wu Dakun; the fourth to the eighth from the left are Dai Shiguang, Yuan Baohua, Song Tao, Miao Litian and Gan Xifen; the first from the right is Gao Hongye; the first to the fifteenth from the left in the back row are Zheng Hangsheng, Yan Dawu, Sai Feng, Zhong Qifu, Xu Zhengfan, Wu Yifeng, Liu Peixian, Wu Cangping, Luo Guojie, Huang Da, Li Zhenzhong, Peng Ming, Fang Hanqi, Xiao Qian, Chen Gong, the first to the second from the right in the back row are Gao Mingxuan and Chen Xianda.

The special government allowances of the State Council are a system to reward high-level professional technicians and highly-skilled talented people, and have been issued since 1990 to the experts, scholars and technicians with outstanding contributions.

186

图 186 为 1991 年 12 月 30 日，中国人民大学首届工商管理硕士 90 名 MBA 合影留念。前排右七为黄达。

On December 30, 1991, the first MBAs of the Renmin University of China, altogether 90, took a group photo. The seventh from the right in the front row is Huang Da.

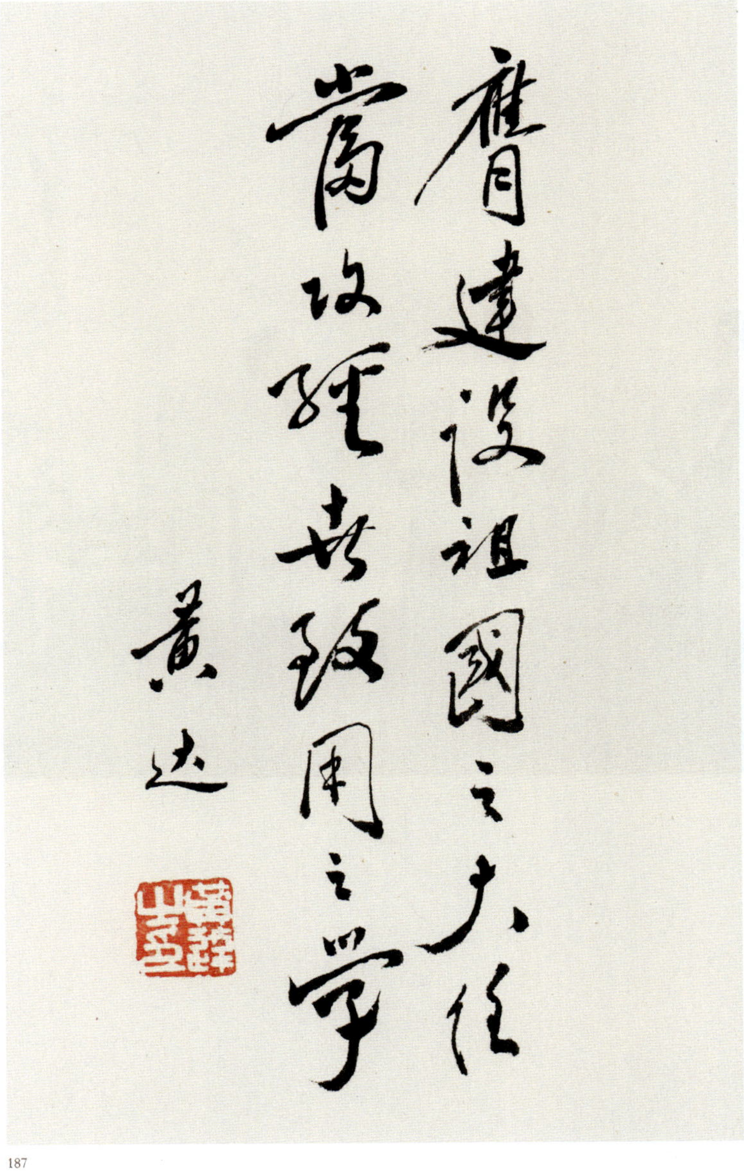

187

图 187 为 1992 年 4 月，黄达为中国人民大学招生办公室拟印刷的招生简章题写校长寄语。

In April 1992, Huang Da wrote a president's message to the Admissions Office of the Renmin University of China on the admission brochure to be printed.

188

图 188 为 1992 年 8 月 3 日，黄达（右二）在中国人民大学校部贵宾室（位于现教学二楼）接待外宾。

On August 3, 1992, Huang Da (second from the right) was receiving foreign guests in the VIP room of the Renmin University of China (now in No. 2 Teaching Building).

189

图 189 为 1992 年夏，黄达应中国人民大学原副校长杨德福之请，为新落成的图书馆前立石题写“业精于勤”。

这块立石如今依然是人大学生毕业留影的必到场所，也是黄达留在人大校园为数不多的手迹之一。

In the summer of 1992, at the invitation of former Vice President Yang Defu, Huang Da inscribed "Practice Makes Perfect" on the stone in front of the newly established library.

The stone, one of the few handwritings that Huang Da left on campus, is a destination that graduates must go to take group photos.

190

图 190 为 1992 年 10 月中旬，北京市教委举行北京高校文明校园评比。经过一番比拼，清华大学最终获得第一，中国人民大学与北京大学并列第二。黄达（第二排右五）与部分学校领导干部、评比组成员在一起。

In mid October 1992, Beijing Municipal Education Commission held an evaluation of universities in Beijing with civilized campus. After comparison, Tsinghua University ranked the first, and the Renmin University of China and Peking University ranked the second. Huang Da (fifth from the right in the second row) was with the leading cadres of some universities and members of the evaluation team.

191

图 191 为 1992 年 10 月 13 日，黄达（前排右二）与英国杜伦大学校长艾波斯沃思教授（前排左一）签署两校合作协议书。

On October 13, 1992, Huang Da (second from the right in the front row) signed an intercollegiate cooperation agreement with Prof. Evelyn Ebsworth (first from the left in the front row), the then president of Durham University.

192

图 192 为 1993 年 4 月 6 日，黄达（右一）会见委内瑞拉前总统拉斐尔·卡尔德拉（左一）。1916 年 1 月 24 日，拉斐尔·卡尔德拉出生于委内瑞拉亚拉奎州首府圣费利佩市。1969—1974 年、1994—1999 年先后两次当选委内瑞拉总统。

On April 6, 1993, Huang Da (first from the right) met Rafael Caldera Rodríguez (first from the left), former president of Venezuela.

President Rafael Caldera Rodríguez was born on January 24, 1916 in the city of San Felipe, the capital of the State of Yaracuy. He was the president of Venezuela in 1969—1974 and 1994—1999 respectively.

193

图193为1993年4月7—8日，中英大学校长研讨会在中国人民大学召开。左三为黄达，左五为会议主持人、时任中国人民大学副校长郑杭生。

During April 7 and 8, 1993, the British-Chinese Vice Chancellor Symposium was held in the Renmin University of China. The third from the left is Huang Da; and the fifth from the left is Zheng Hangsheng, workshop presider and the then deputy president of the Renmin University of China.

194

图 194 为 1994 年 1 月 29 日，中国人民大学新老校领导寒假期间在一起。前排从左至右分别为：黄达、袁宝华、李文海；后排从左至右分别为：杜厚文、陈光、杨德福、马绍孟、李昭公、郑杭生。

On January 29, 1994, leaders of the Renmin University of China were together in the winter vacation. From the left to the right in the front row are Huang Da, Yuan Baohua and Li Wenhai; from the left to the right in the back row are Du Houwen, Chen Guang, Yang Defu, Ma Shaomeng, Li Zhaogong and Zheng Hangsheng.

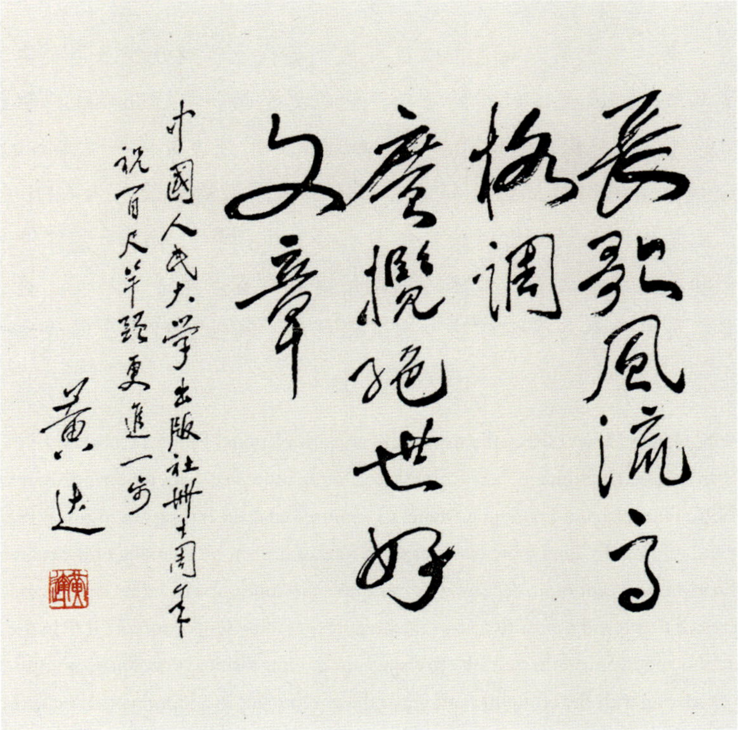

195

图 195 为 1994 年 9 月，黄达为中国人民大学出版社成立四十周年题词。

In September 1994, Huang Da inscribed for China Renmin University Press for its 40th anniversary.

5-3

当选第八届全国人民代表大会代表
Selected as a member of the 8th National People's Congress

5-3-1>

1993—1998年，黄达当选第八届全国人民代表大会代表、财政经济委员会委员。五年期间，特别是参与全国人大财经委的活动，使他更全面、更近距离地感触到全国经济发展和改革的脉搏，从而推动了对于经济金融理论和财经决策进一步深入的思考。如对于宏观经济分析方法的继续提炼；如建言必须扭转国家财政收入占GDP的比重不断下滑的局面，反复论述必须改变财政只应力求自身平衡和力求不干预经济的指导思路；在东南亚金融危机袭来之后，力陈必须动用财政政策；等等。期间，黄达还以经济学者的财经委委员身份参与了证券法、人民银行法、商业银行法、保险法、外汇法等立法活动。

During 1993 and 1998, Huang Da was selected a member of the 8th National People's Congress (NPC) and a member of the NPC Financial and Economic Affairs Committee.During those five years, especially his involvement in the activities of the NPC Financial and Economic Affairs Committee enabled Huang Da to touch the pulse of economic development and reform of China more closely, and to further deepen his thinking of the economic and financial theories and financial and economic decisions. For example, he continued to refine the macroeconomic analytic techniques; suggested that it was a must to reverse the situation of falling proportion of GDP in the national financial revenue; repeatedly expounded on the necessity to change the guiding ideology that finance should primarily be balanced, instead of interfering with the economy; and urged the government to adopt financial policies after the outbreak of the financial crisis in Southeast Asia, etc. During the same period, he participated in the legislation of the securities law, the law on People's Bank of China, the law of commercial banks, the insurance law, and the foreign exchange law as an economist.

| 右页图 |→

图196为1993年3月15日，黄达在第八届全国人大第一次会议上投下庄严的一票。

On March 15, 1993, Huang Da voted solemnly at the 1st plenary session of the 8th National People's Congress.

196

197

图 197 为 1994 年 6 月 1 日，第八届全国人大财经委赴江西南昌进行《统计法》执法检查。黄达在座谈会上发言。

On June 1, 1994, the Financial and Economic Affairs Committee of the 8th National People's Congress went to Nanchang, Jiangxi, to check the enforcement of The Law of Statistics. Huang Da delivered a speech at the symposium.

198

图 198 为 1994 年 6 月 9 日，第八届全国人大财经委赴广东顺德进行《统计法》执法检查。黄达（右一）与时任第八届全国人大财经委副主任李灏（左一）在一起。

On June 9, 1994, the Financial and Economic Affairs Committee of the 8th National People's Congress went to Shunde, Guangdong, to check the enforcement of The Law of Statistics. Huang Da (first from the right) was with Li Hao (first from the left), the then deputy director of the Financial and Economic Affairs Committee of the 8th National People's Congress.

199

图 199 为 1997 年 11 月 27 日，第八届全国人大财经委赴浙皖进行《银行法》执法检查。黄达（前排左五）为该检查组负责人。

On November 27, 1997, the Financial and Economic Affairs Committee of the 8th National People's Congress went to Zhejiang and Anhui to inspect the enforcement of the Banking Law. Huang Da (fifth from the left in the front row) was the person in charge of the inspection group.

200

图200为1997年11月27日，黄达（右一）与陆燕荪（左一）在浙江嘉兴南湖。

On November 27, 1997, Huang Da (first from the right) and Lu Yansun (first from the left) were by the South Lake, Jiaxing, Zhejiang.

201

图 201 为 1997 年 3 月 14 日，第八届全国人大财经委员会全体委员和工作人员合影留念。第二排左一为黄达。

On March 14, 1997, all the members of the Financial and Economic Affairs Committee of the 8th National People's Congress and the staff took a group photo. The first from the left in the second row is Huang Da.

202

图 202 为 1998 年 8 月 14—18 日，西北五省区人大财经工作座谈会在宁夏银川召开。黄达（前排左七）作为全国人大财经委代表与会。

During August 14 and 18, 1998, the people's congresses of five provinces and autonomous regions in northwestern China held a financial and economic affairs symposium in Yinchuan, Ningxia. Huang Da (seventh from the left in the front row) attended the symposium as a representative of the NPC Financial and Economic Affairs Committee.

5-3-2>

1995年11月21日—12月7日，全国人民代表大会财经委员会组团访问瑞典、意大利和中国香港，考察外汇立法和外汇管理。团长由全国人大常委会委员、全国人大财经委员会副主任委员、《外汇管理法》起草领导小组组长戴杰担任，黄达以全国人大代表、全国人大财经委员会委员、《外汇管理法》起草领导小组成员的身份参与考察。其余团员包括全国人大财经委员会《外汇管理法》起草工作小组组长、研究员王中等六位。

During November 21 and December 7, 1995, the NPC Financial and Economic Affairs Committee formed a delegation to visit Sweden, Italy and Hong Kong of China to observe their foreign exchange legislation and foreign exchange administration. Dai Jie, member of the NPC Standing Committee, deputy director of the NPC Financial and Economic Affairs Committee, and head of the leading group of the drafting of the Law of Foreign Exchange Administration (of the People's Republic of China), served as the head of the delegation. Huang Da was a member of the delegation as an NPC member, a member of the NPC Financial and Economic Affairs Committee, and a member of the leading group of the drafting of the Law of Foreign Exchange Administration. The delegation also had another six members, including Wang Zhong, head and researcher of the working group for drafting Law of Foreign Exchange Administration of the NPC Financial and Economic Affairs Committee.

| 右页图 |⟶

图203为1995年11月23日，考察团访问瑞典中央银行。左四至左六分别为戴杰、王中和黄达。

在瑞典中央银行，考察团听取了有关IMF和OECD外汇管理规定、瑞典外汇管理历史及立法、瑞典对外收付放开后的外汇管理、放开外汇市场应注意的问题以及起草支付法的构思和建议等问题的介绍。随后，考察团参观了瑞典外汇交易室和印钞厂。

On November 23, 1995, the delegation visited Sveriges Riksbank (namely Sweden Central Bank). From the fourth to the sixth from the left are Dai Jie, Wang Zhong and Huang Da.

In Sveriges Riksbank, the delegation listened to the IMF and OECD management provisions on foreign exchange, Swedish foreign exchange management history and legislation, Swedish foreign exchange management after Sweden unlashed foreign collection and payment, the problems that deserved attention if the foreign exchange market was opened, the idea to draft the payment law and suggestions. After that, the delegation visited Swedish foreign exchange dealing rooms and bill printing factory.

203

204

图 204 为 1995 年 11 月 29 日，考察团访问米兰交易所。左二为黄达。此前，考察团还先后与意大利外汇管理局、意大利国家银行（中央银行）以及意大利商业银行等进行了座谈。

On November 29, 1995, the delegation visited Milan Stock Exchange. The second from the left is Huang Da.

Before that, the delegation held symposiums with Italian Administration for Foreign Exchange, National Bank of Italy (Central Bank) and Italian Commercial Bank in succession.

205

图 205 为 1995 年 11 月 29 日，黄达在米兰教堂前。

On November 29, 1995, Huang Da was in front of Milan Cathedral.

图 206 为 1995 年 11 月 29 日，黄达参观庞贝古城。

On November 29, 1995, Huang Da visited the ancient ruins of Pompeii.

206

5-3-3>

1996年12月8—21日，全国人大财经委员会组团访问南美阿根廷和墨西哥两国，考察税法。团长由全国人大财经委员会副主任委员迟海滨担任。团员除黄达之外，还有全国人大财经委计划预算室副主任姚胜、经济法室副处长刘修文、国家税务总局法规司副司长马林、财政部税政司副处长王刚、翻译金菁。

During December 8 and 21, 1996, the Financial and Economic Affairs Committee of the National People's Congress formed a delegation to visit Argentina and Mexico in South America to observe their tax laws. The head of the delegation was Chi Haibin, deputy director of the Financial and Economic Affairs Committee of the National People's Congress. Besides Huang Da, the delegation also included Yao Sheng, deputy director of the Planned Budget Office of the Financial and Economic Affairs Committee of the National People's Congress, Liu Xiuwen, deputy head of the Economics Law Office of the Financial and Economic Affairs Committee of the National People's Congress, Ma Lin, deputy chief of State Administration of Taxation Policy & Regulations Department, Wang Gang, deputy head of the Department of Taxation under the Ministry of Finance, and interpreter Jin Jing.

207

图207为1996年12月9日，阿根廷总理（左七）会见考察团一行。左三为黄达。

On December 9, 1996, Argentina Premier (seventh from the left) met the delegation. The third from the left is Huang Da.

208

图 208 为 1996 年 12 月 9 日，阿根廷参议院外事委员会主席（右一）会见考察团一行。左二为黄达，右二为迟海滨。

On December 9, 1996, chairman of the Foreign Affairs Committee of the Argentine Senate (first from the right) met the delegation. The second from the left is Huang Da, and the second from the right is Chi Haibin.

209

右页图

图 209 为 1996 年 12 月 13 日，黄达在访问期间参观伊瓜苏大瀑布。

On December 13, 1996, Huang Da toured and visited Iguacu Falls.

图 210 为 1996 年 12 月 16 日，墨西哥财政部副部长（前排左三）会见考察团一行。前排左二为黄达，左四为迟海滨。

On December 16, 1996, Vice Minister of Finance of Mexico (third from the left in the front row) met the delegation. The second from the left in the front row is Huang Da; the fourth from the left is Chi Haibin.

5-3-4>

1997 年 5 月 10—12 日，全国人大财经委员会组团赴美考察。团长、副团长分别由全国人大常委、财经委主任委员柳随年和全国人大常委、财经委副主任委员董辅礽担任。团员包括黄达、全国人大财经委委员陆燕荪和财经委办公室李命志。本次访问的目的主要是了解美国国会对政府财政经济工作的监督和经济立法，以及美国国会及其专门委员会的机构设置和运转等情况。

During May 10 and 12, 1997, the Financial and Economic Affairs Committee of the National People's Congress formed a delegation to go to the United States for an investigation. The head and deputy head of the delegation were Liu Suinian, member of the Standing Committee of the National People's Congress and head of the Financial and Economic Affairs Committee of the National People's Congress, and Dong Fureng, member of the Standing Committee of the National People's Congress and deputy head of the Financial and Economic Affairs Committee of the National People's Congress, respectively. Members of the delegation included Huang Da, Lu Yansun, member of the Financial and Economic Affairs Committee of the National People's Congress, and Li Mingzhi from the office of the Financial and Economic Affairs Committee of the National People's Congress. Through the visit, the Chinese delegation was mainly to understand the supervision of government's financial and economic work and the economic legislation by the US Congress, the organizational structure and operations of the US Congress and its special committees.

| 右页图 ⟼

图 211 为 1997 年 5 月 12 日，美国参议院拨款委员会主席会见考察团一行。左一至左五分别为：黄达、董辅礽、美国参议院拨款委员会主席、柳随年、陆燕荪。

On May 12, 1997, chairman of the United States Senate Committee on Appropriations met the Chinese delegation. The first to the fifth from the left are Huang Da, Dong Fureng, chairman of the United States Senate Committee on Appropriations, Liu Suinian and Lu Yansun.

211

5-4

身兼数职，倾力推动中国经济金融学科发展

Promote the Development of Economic and Financial Disciplines

自 20 世纪 80 年代后期开始，黄达先后担任国务院学位委员会第二届、第三届委员（1987—1999 年），经济学学科评议组邀请成员、成员、召集人（1981—1997 年），应用经济学学科评议组召集人（1997—2002 年）；全国哲学社会科学研究基金“八五”规划经济学学科规划小组成员、部门经济学学科评审组召集人（1991—1998 年），“九五”规划应用经济学学科规划小组和学科评审组成员（1998—2002 年）；全国博士后管理委员会经济学学科评议组召集人（1993—1997 年）；国家教委人文社会科学研究专家咨询委员会主任委员（1997—2004 年）；教育部社会科学委员会顾问（2004 年 6 月至今）；以及孙冶方经济科学基金会评奖委员会荣誉委员等职务。

担任上述职务，不仅为黄达理论联系实际提供了便利，而且让他有机会直接参与学科规划、研究和建设，以此进一步推动中国金融学科发展。

Since the late 1980s, Huang Da was a member of the 2nd, and then the 3rd State Council Academic Degrees Committee (1987—1999); member or convener of the Economics Discipline Evaluation Group (1981—1997); convener of Applied Economics Discipline Evaluation Group (1997—2002); member of the Subcommittee for the Planning of the Economics Discipline during the "8th Five-year Plan" Period supported by the National Philosophy and Social Science Research Fund and convener of the Discipline of Department Economics Evaluation Group (1991—1998); member of the Subcommittee for the Planning of the Discipline of Applied Economics during the "9th Five-year Plan" Period, and of the Discipline of Applied Economics Evaluation Group (1998—2002); convener of the Evaluation Group of the Discipline of Economics, National Postdoctoral Positions Management Committee (1993—1997); director of the Expert Advisory Council of Studies in Humanities and Social Science under the State Education Commission (1997—2004); consultant of the Social Sciences Committee under the Ministry of Education (since June 2004); and honorary member of the Awarding Subcommittee of Sun Yefang Economic Science Foundation.

Taking these positions offered Huang Da the convenience to link theory with practice, enable him to participate in the planning, research and construction of the disciplines and promote the development of China's financial disciplines.

212

图 212 为 1992 年 6 月 9—12 日，国务院学位委员会经济学博士、硕士学科、专业简介定稿会议在青岛召开。全体与会专家合影留念。前排左四为会议召集人、中国人民大学老教授宋涛，左五为黄达，左六为会议具体组织者军委后勤学院张振龙教授。

During June 9 and 12, 1992, the meeting of the State Council Academic Degrees Committee to finalize the brief introduction to the discipline and majors of masters and doctors of economics was held in Qing Dao. All attendees took a group photo. The fourth from the left in the front row is Song Tao, the convener of the meeting and senior professor of the Renmin University of China. The fifth from the left is Huang Da.The sixth from the left is the organizer, Professor Zhang Zhenlong, from the Logistics College of Central Military Commission.

图 213 为 1992 年 6 月 9 日，黄达（右一）与宋涛（右二）、张振龙（右三）在一起。

On June 9, 1992, Huang Da (first from the right) was with Song Tao (second from the right) and Zhang zhenlong (third from the right).

213

214

图 214 为 1993 年 9 月 21—29 日，国务院学位委员会学科评议组第五次会议在北京京西宾馆召开。全体与会专家合影留念。后排左六为黄达。

During September 21 and 29, 1993, the Discipline Evaluation Group under the State Council Academic Degrees Committee held its fifth meeting in Jingxi Hotel, Beijing. All attendees took a group photo. The sixth from the left in the back row is Huang Da.

215

图 215 为 1996 年 1 月 6—11 日，国务院学位委员会在郑州、北京两地分别召开学科评议组会议。黄达（最后排左二）作为经济学学科评议组召集人出席郑州会议。

During January 6 to 11, 1996, the State Council Academic Degrees Committee held meetings of the discipline evaluation groups in Zhengzhou and Beijing, respectively. Huang Da (second from the left in the last row) attended the meeting in Zhengzhou as the convener of the Discipline of Economics Evaluation Group.

216

图 216 为 1992 年 12 月 19—25 日，国家教委在复旦大学组织召开“高等学校‘八五’人文、社会科学研究规划项目评审会议”。北京大学、中国人民大学、复旦大学、吉林大学、武汉大学等高校的二十余位校（院）长参加了会议。前排右六为黄达。

During December 19 and 25, 1992, the State Education Commission held "Universities Evaluation of Projects on Humanities and Social Sciences Studies during the '8th Five-year Plan' Period" in Fudan University. More than 20 presidents of universities (schools), including Peking University, the Renmin University of China, Fudan University, Jilin University and Wuhan University, attended the conference. The sixth from the right in the front row is Huang Da.

217

图 217 为 1995 年 7 月 16 日，国家教委人文社会科学研究优秀成果奖专家评审会在长春召开。黄达（前排左三）作为经济小组召集人，与来自全国 49 所高校的 140 位专家一起参加了会议。

On July 16, 1995, the Expert Advisory Council of the State Education Commission of Prizes for Outstanding Humanities and Social Science Achievements was held in Changchun. Huang Da (third from the left in the front row) as the convener of the economics group attended the council along with 140 experts from 49 Chinese universities.

218

图 218 为 2009 年 9 月 18 日，“教育部社会科学委员会经济学学部 2009 年工作会议暨国际金融危机对中国民营经济影响研讨会”在杭州召开。部分与会专家合影留念。左六为黄达。

On September 18, 2009, the "2009 Work Conference of the Economics Section, Department of Social Science of the Chinese Ministry of Education and Symposium on the Influences of the International Financial Crisis over China's Privately-run Sector of the Economy" was held in Hangzhou. Some of the attendees took a group photo. The sixth from the left is Huang Da.

219

220

图219为2010年6月8日，“教育部社会科学委员会经济学学部2010年工作会议暨世博会、长三角与中国经济发展研讨会”在上海举行。全体与会专家合影留念。前排右五为黄达。

On June 8, 2010, the "2010 Work Conference of the Economics Section, Department of Social Science of the Chinese Ministry of Education and Symposium on the World Expo, the Yangtze River Delta Economic Zone and China's Economic Development" was held in Shanghai. All the present experts took a group photo. The fifth from the right in the front row is Huang Da.

图220为2012年5月12日，“2012年教育部社会科学委员会经济学学部工作会议”在南京召开。全体与会专家合影留念。前排左五为黄达。

On May 12, 2012, "2012 Work Conference of the Economics Section, Department of Social Science of the Chinese Ministry of Education" was held in Nanjing. All the present experts took a group photo. The fifth from the left in the front row is Huang Da.

221

图 221 为 1996 年 4 月 22—28 日，全国哲学社会科学研究“九五”规划工作暨项目评审会议期间，国家社科基金应用经济学评议组全体成员合影留念。前排左四为评议组召集人黄达。

时任全国哲学社会科学规划领导小组秘书长、中宣部副部长刘云山代表领导小组讲话，会议由王忍之主持。28 日下午，时任中共中央政治局委员、书记处书记、中宣部部长、全国社科规划领导小组组长丁关根到会同参加会议的各学科规划评审组负责人座谈并作了重要讲话。

During April 22 and 28, 1996, during the National Conference on the Studies in Philosophy and Social Sciences during the "9th Five-year Plan" Period and Project Evaluation Meeting, members of the Discipline of Applied Economics Evaluation Group took a group picture. The fourth from the left is Huang Da.

Liu Yunshan, the then secretary-general of the leading group of National Planning for Philosophy and Social Sciences and vice minister of Central Propaganda Department, addressed the conference on behalf of the leading group. Wang Renzhi presided over the conference. In the afternoon of April 28, Ding Guangen, the then member of the Political Bureau of the Central Committee of the Communist Party of China, secretary of the Secretariat of the Central Committee of the Communist Party of China, minister of the Central Propaganda Department and leader of the National Social Sciences Planning Leading Group, had a seminar with the persons in charge of the planning for different subjects and delivered an important speech.

222

图 222 为 2001 年 4 月 8—12 日，国家社科基金项目评审会在北京举行。全体与会专家合影留念。前排右四为黄达。

During April 8 and 12, 2001, National Fund in Social Science Projects Evaluation Meeting was held in Beijing. All the present experts took a group photo. The fourth from the right in the front row is Huang Da.

223

图 223 为 2001 年 5 月 31 日，孙冶方经济科学基金会评奖委员会在北京大学召开会议。全体与会专家合影留念。最后排左二为黄达。

On May 31, 2001, the Awarding Subcommittee of Sun Yefang Economic Science Foundation held a meeting in Peking University. All the present experts took a group photo. The second from the left in the back row is Huang Da.

224

图 224 为 2003 年 12 月 3 日，“第十届孙冶方经济科学奖颁奖大会”在深圳召开。主席台就座的颁奖嘉宾与获奖者合影留念。前排右三为黄达。

On December 3, 2003, the "10th Sun Yefang Award for Economic Science Presentation Ceremony" was held in Shenzhen. The award presenters on the rostrum and the award winners took a group photo. The third from the right in the front row is Huang Da.

225

图 225 为 2013 年 12 月 8 日，孙冶方经济科学基金会三十周年纪念会暨第十五届孙冶方经济科学奖颁奖大会在北京召开。全体与会专家合影留念。前排左六为黄达。

On December 8, 2013, the 30th Anniversary of Sun Yefang Economic Science Foundation and the 15th Sun Yefang Award for Economic Science Presentation Ceremony was held in Beijing. All the present experts took a group photo. The sixth from the left in the front row is Huang Da.

226

图 226 为 2015 年 11 月 8 日，第十六届孙冶方经济科学奖颁奖大会暨孙冶方经济科学奖文献馆开馆仪式在浙江财经大学举行。全体与会专家合影留念。前排左八为黄达。

On November 8, 2015, "the 16th Sun Yefang Award for Economic Science Presentation Ceremony and the Opening Ceremony of Sun Yefang Economic Science Literature Hall" was held in Zhejiang University of Finance & Economics. All the attendees took a group photo. The eighth from the left in the front row is Huang Da.

227

图 227 为 2015 年 11 月 8 日，颁奖大会结束后，黄达（前排右三）出席随后举行的孙冶方经济科学奖文献馆开馆仪式。

On November 8, 2015, Huang Da (third from the right in the front row) attended the "Opening Ceremony of Sun Yefang Economic Science Literature Hall".

5-5

“破例”担任中国金融学会会长

Break the Tradition and Take up the Post of Chairman of China Society for Finance and Banking

在1995年初之前，中国金融学会会长曾长期缺位。按照惯例，中国人民银行行长是中国金融学会会长的当然人选。但是，由于当时的中国人民银行行长由朱镕基总理兼任，总理担任学会会长没有先例，而且新任中国人民银行行长的确定还需时日，因此，当难以再行推迟召开中国金融学会代表大会和选出第五届会长之际，黄达于1995年4月打破惯例出任中国金融学会会长。

在此前后，黄达还担任了中国人民银行货币政策委员会委员（1997—2000年），中国证券监督管理委员会股票发行审核委员会第四、五届委员（1999年9月—2003年12月），中国财政学会副会长，中国国际金融学会副会长，中国价格学会副会长，中国企业联合会（原名企业管理协会）副会长以及中国证券业协会副会长等职，为推动新中国财政金融改革与发展做出了应有的贡献。

Before the beginning of 1995, China Society for Finance and Banking did not have a chair. By convention the governor of the People's Bank of China is the most likely candidate for the position. However, the governor of the People's Bank of China then was Premier Zhu Rongji, and there was no precedent that the premier served as the chairman of the society. Besides, it took some time to determine the new governor of the People's Bank of China. Therefore, Huang Da broke the tradition and took up the post of chairman of China Society for Finance and Banking in April 1995 when it was hard to postpone the congress of China Society for Finance and Banking once again and the new chairman was yet to be elected.

Besides, Huang Da also served as a member of the Monetary Policy Commission of the People's Bank of China (1997—2000); member of the 4th and the 5th Public Offering Review Committee of China Securities Regulatory Commission (from September 1999 to December 2003); vice chairman of China Society of Public Finance; vice chairman of China International Finance Society; vice chairman of China Society of Price; vice chairman of China Enterprise Confederation (formerly known as China Society of Enterprise Management) and vice chairman of Securities Association of China, making his due contribution to pushing forward the financial reform and development of new China.

5-5-1>

与台湾长达六年的交往是黄达担任中国金融学会会长期间开展的最为重要的活动之一。双方联合发起的“两岸金融学术研讨会”，采取中国金融学会和台北金融研究发展基金会每年轮流主办的模式，截至目前已经连续举办 19 届，为两岸金融合作做出了突出贡献。

1994 年 5 月，第一届研讨会在台北召开，黄达未能出席。1995 年 7 月 31 日—8 月 2 日，在北京召开的第二届研讨会上，黄达首次以中国金融学会会长和大陆代表团团长的身份出席。

对比前两届会议，第一届偏重“学术性”交往，而第二届“官方背景”极其明显。台湾“财政部”原部长陆润康担任团长，台湾“中央银行”原行长、时任“总统府”顾问和“中央银行”顾问的谢森中以“中国信托商业银行决策咨询委员会总裁”身份出席第二届会议。其他成员还包括台湾“中央银行”经济研究处副处长简济民和“财政部”金融管理局组长庄有德等。中方会议组织主要由时任中国人民银行副行长陈元负责。如此规格在当时实属两岸金融界最高级别交往。

Keeping the exchanges with Taiwan for six years was one of the most important activities held when Huang Da served as the head of China Society for Finance and Banking. Held annually by China Society for Finance and Banking and Taipei Foundation of Finance by turns, the two parties jointly launched "Cross-Straits Finance Symposium ". Up to now, Cross-Straits Finance Symposium has been held 19 times, making a major contribution to the cooperation of Mainland China and Taiwan in the financial sector.

The first symposium was held in Taipei in May 1994, Huang Da was unable to attend.The second was held in Beijing during July 31 and August 2, 1995, to which Huang Da attended as chairman of China Society for Finance and Banking and head of the delegation of Mainland China.

Comparatively speaking, the first symposium focused on "scholarly" exchanges, and the second one had a very significant "government background. " Seen from the members of the Taiwan delegation, it was headed by Lu Runkang, the former "minister of finance" of Taiwan; and Xie Senzhong, the former governor of "Central Bank of China" [a.k.a. "Central Bank of the Republic of China (Taiwan)" since 2000], and the then consultant of Taiwan "Presidential Office " and of Taiwan "Central Bank", attended the symposium as "President of Chinatrust Commercial Bank Limited Decision-making Advisory Committee. " The other members of the delegation included Jian Jimin, the then deputy chief of Economic Division of "Central Bank of China ", and Zhuang Youde, head of the Monetary Authority of the "Ministry of Finance". Chen Yuan, the then deputy governor of the People's Bank of China was responsible for holding the symposium in China. The symposiums were indeed the highest level exchanges in the financial circles between Mainland China and Taiwan.

228

图 228 为 1995 年 8 月 2 日，台湾代表团举办“第二届两岸金融学术研讨会”回请晚宴。站立者从左至右分别为：荣鸿庆、陈元、黄达、陆润康、谢森中、李飞、周吴添。

On August 2, 1995, the delegation of Taiwan held a return banquet during the 2nd Cross-Straits Finance Symposium. Those who were standing from the left to the right are Rong Hongqing, Chen Yuan, Huang Da, Lu Runkang, Xie Senzhong, Li Fei and Zhou Wutian.

图 229 为 1995 年 8 月 2 日，大陆代表团团长黄达（右一）与台湾代表团团长陆润康（左一）互赠礼物。

On August 2, 1995, Huang Da (first from the right), head of the delegation of Mainland China, exchanged gifts with Lu Runkang (first from the left), head of the delegation of Taiwan.

229

5-5-2>

1996 年 11 月 4—14 日，“第三届两岸金融学术研讨会”在台北召开。黄达作为团长率大陆 25 人代表团首次踏上宝岛台湾。中国人民银行原常务副行长、时任光大集团名誉董事长邱晴担任代表团顾问；中国人民银行原办公厅主任、时任中信银行董事长洪允成，时任国家外汇管理局副局长吴晓灵，时任中国人民银行金融研究所所长秦池江担任副团长；时任中国人民银行银行司司长蔡鄂生担任秘书长；时任中国人民银行外资金融机构管理司副司长金琦和金融研究所副所长谢杭生担任副秘书长。

赴台期间，大陆代表团与台湾金融界人士面对面接触交流，向他们介绍祖国大陆金融体制改革开放的情况，宣传“九七”后大陆对港金融政策，宣传钱其琛副总理宣布的有关香港涉台问题 7 条原则及对台金融政策。同时，通过到不同类型的金融机构调研，进一步加深了对台湾金融制度及市场的了解。

此外，作为本次台湾之行的核心任务，“第三届两岸金融学术研讨会”将两岸学术交流活动引向实务交流，为今后深入开展对台金融交流工作打下了比较好的基础。研讨会在台湾经济、金融、新闻界引起了较大反响，基本上达到了“促进两岸金融界相互了解，发展两岸金融关系”的目的，取得了比较圆满的成果。

During November 4 and 14, 1996, the 3rd Cross-Straits Finance Symposium was held in Taipei. Huang Da led a delegation of 25 people to set foot on Taiwan for the first time. Qiu Qing, former executive deputy governor of the People's Bank of China and the then honorary director of the board of China Everbright Group, served as the consultant of the delegation. Hong Yuncheng, former director of the General Office of the People's Bank of China and the then director of the board of China CITIC Bank, Wu Xiaoling, the then deputy director of the State Administration for Foreign Exchange, and Qin Chijiang, the then head of Finance Institute of the People's Bank of China, served as the deputy heads of the delegation. Cai Esheng, the then director-general of the Department of Banks of the People's Bank of China, served as the secretary-general of the delegation. Jin Qi, the then deputy director-general of Foreign-capital Financial Institutions Management Department of the People's Bank of China, and Xie Hangsheng, deputy head of Finance Institute of the People's Bank of China, served as the deputy secretary-generals of the delegation.

In the visit to Taiwan, figures in the financial circles from Mainland China and Taiwan had the chance to exchange ideas face to face. The delegation of Mainland China introduced the reform and opening up of the financial system in Mainland China; publicized China's financial policies toward Hong Kong after the return of Hong Kong to China in 1997, as well as the seven principles to be followed by Hong Kong in Taiwan-related issues that were announced by Vice Premier Qian Qichen and China's financial policies toward Taiwan. Meanwhile, by investigating different types of financial institutions in Taiwan, the delegation brought its understanding of Taiwan's financial system and market deeper.

The 3rd Cross-Straits Finance Symposium led the scholarly exchanges between Mainland China and Taiwan to practice, and laid a solid foundation for deepening the financial exchanges with Taiwan, causing a great sensation in the economic and financial circles and the media of Taiwan. The aim of "promoting the financial circles of Mainland China and Taiwan to understand each other, and developing the financial relations between Mainland China and Taiwan " was realized; and satisfying results were achieved.

230

图 230 为 1996 年 11 月 4 日，大陆代表团抵达台湾桃园机场，与在机场迎接的台湾专家合影留念。右十二为黄达。

On November 4, 1996, the delegation of Mainland China reached Taoyuan Airport in Taiwan and took a group photo with the experts of Taiwan. The twelfth from the right is Huang Da.

231

图 231 为 1996 年 11 月 4 日，大陆与台湾双方专家在欢迎晚宴前亲切交流。从左至右分别为：蔡鄂生、周吴添、洪允成、谢森中、郭新容、邱晴、黄达、吴晓灵、陆润康、荣鸿庆、金琦、秦池江。

On November 4, 1996, experts of both sides chatted before the welcoming banquet. From the left to the right are Cai Esheng, Zhou Wutian, Hong Yuncheng, Xie Senzhong, Guo Xinrong, Qiu Qing, Huang Da, Wu Xiaoling, Lu Runkang, Rong Hongqing, Jin Qi and Qin Chijiang.

232

图 232 为 1996 年 11 月 4 日，大陆与台湾双方代表在欢迎晚宴上互赠礼物。从左至右分别为：黄达、谢森中、周吴添。

On November 4, 1996, representatives of both sides exchanged gifts at the welcoming banquet. From the left to the right are Huang Da, Xie Senzhong and Zhou Wutian.

233

图 233 为 1996 年 11 月 5 日，黄达在会议期间接受台湾媒体专访。

On November 5, 1996, Huang Da received an interview with Taiwan media.

234

图 234 为 1996 年 11 月 6 日，出席“第三届两岸金融学术研讨会”闭幕式的部分专家合影留念。主席台从左至右分别为：秦池江、周添城、戴立宁、荣鸿庆、邱晴、黄达、洪允成、吴晓灵。

On November 6, 1996, some attendees at the closing ceremony of the symposium took a group photo. From the left to the right on the rostrum are Qin Chijiang, Zhou Tiancheng, Dai Lining, Rong Hongqing, Qiu Qing, Huang Da, Hong Yuncheng and Wu Xiaoling.

图 235 为 1996 年 11 月 5 日，出席“第三届两岸金融学术研讨会”开幕式并在主席台就座的专家合影留念。从左至右分别为：周吴添、陆润康、黄达、谢森中、邱晴、荣鸿庆。

On November 5, 1996, the experts sitting on the rostrum took a group photo at the symposium. From the left to the right are Zhou Wutian, Lu Runkang, Huang Da, Xie Senzhong, Qiu Qing and Rong Hongqing.

235

236

237

图236为1996年11月7日，大陆代表团访问台北金融研究发展基金会。左三为黄达。

On November 7, 1996, the delegation of Mainland China visited Taipei Foundation of Finance. The third from the left is Huang Da.

图237为1996年11月8日，大陆代表团参观台湾证券交易所。前排左三为黄达。

On November 8, 1996, the delegation of Mainland China visited Taiwan Stock Exchange. The third from the left in the front row is Huang Da.

238

图 238 为 1996 年 11 月 11 日，大陆代表团全体成员游览垦丁。

On November 11, 1996, the delegation of Mainland China toured and visited Kenting.

239

图 239 为 1996 年 11 月 13 日，黄达在大陆代表团答谢宴会上致辞。

宴会上，大陆代表团向台湾地区的主办、协办单位赠送题有“万里同风舞，众煦漂山移”的纪念牌。

On November 13, 1996, Huang Da addressed the thank-you banquet held by the delegation of Mainland China.

At the banquet, the delegation of Mainland China sent a souvenir metal to the host and sponsoring units in Taiwan.

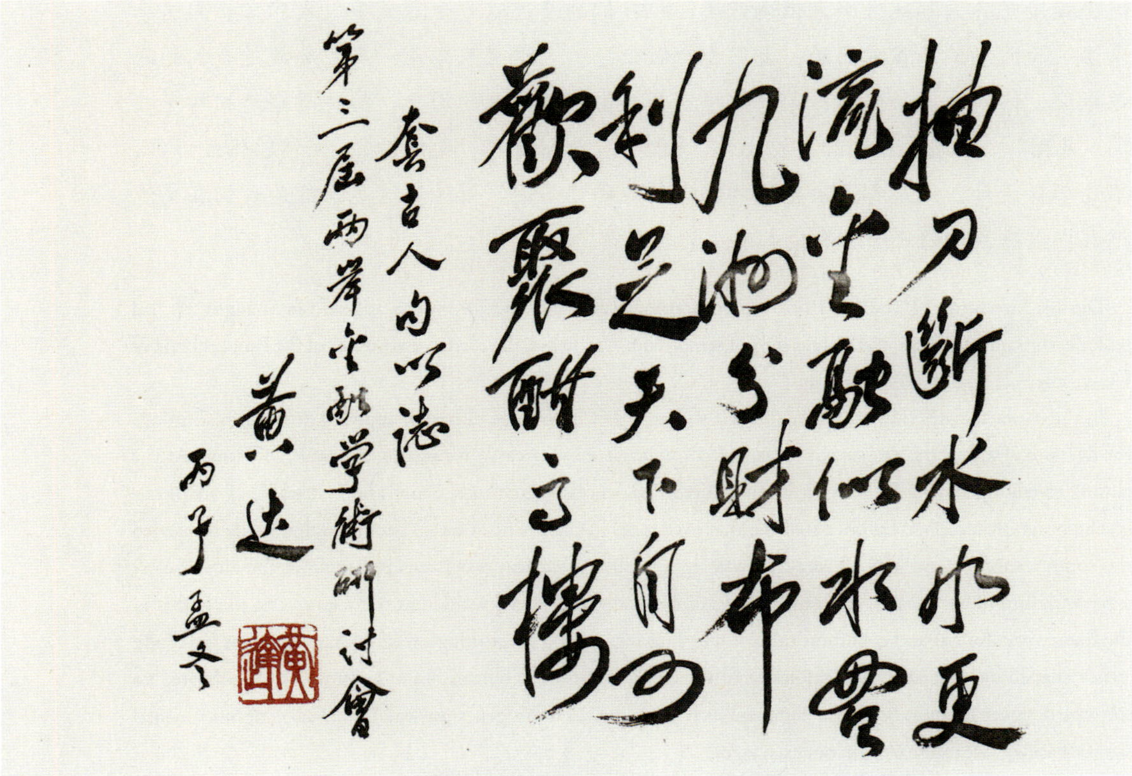

240

图 240 为本次研讨会后不久，应周吴添编印第三届两岸金融学术研讨会纪念册之请，黄达套用李白诗句，题写了一首七绝：“抽刀断水水更流，金融似水贯九洲；分财布利足天下，自可欢聚酣高楼。”既寓统一不可抗拒的意思，同时更突出“金融似水”的本质，必须积极疏通。

Soon after the conference, at the invitation of Zhou Wutian in the printing of souvenir album of the 3rd Cross-Straits Finance Symposium, Huang Da wrote a poem—to indicate the irresistible trend of unification of Taiwan and Mainland China, and to highlight the "watery" nature of finance, which calls for active communication.

5-5-3>

1997 年 11 月 11—12 日，“第四届两岸金融学术研讨会”在上海召开。本次研讨会的规格和范围与上一届基本一致。中方主要由时任中国人民银行副行长殷介炎负责。

通过前后几次与台湾方面的接触，黄达深切感受到尽管双方有近半个世纪处于不同体制之下，但华夏一脉，相互交流，极易沟通。为此他在闭幕式上专门讲道：“学术交流有益于双方自不待言，但意义似更深远。陆润康团长曾对我说，金融方面的交流无疑应对各国各地区全方位地开展，但我们的交流双方受益最多。我非常赞同这个看法。原因当然是多方面的，大家都会做出分析。这里只想谈一点，那就是我们的思维框架、格式、认知规则等等，似乎有某些由中华民族的历史、传统所塑造的特定共同‘基因’。如果把我们的大脑比作‘软体’（大陆译作‘软件’），任何软体设计师，不论怎样设计，像是都无法把这些特定的共同‘基因’排除。这是否就是我们在交流过程中倍感亲切的一个具有根本意义的原因？”

During November 11 and 12, 1997, the 4th Cross-Straits Finance Symposium was held in Shanghai. It had basically the same standards and scale as the last symposium. Yin Jieyan, the then vice governor of the People's Bank of China, was in charge of the symposium.

In the contacts with Taiwan, Huang Da felt so much that both sides, although applying different institutions for nearly half a century, exchanged ideas and communicated very easily for having the same ancestors. At the closing ceremony, Huang Da said, "It is self-evident that scholarly exchanges benefit both sides. They are of far-reaching significance. Mr. Lu once told me that exchanges in the financial sector should undoubtedly be carried out comprehensively and with all countries and regions, but the exchanges between us benefit us the most. I can't agree with him more. Reasons are many, and we can all analyze it. Here I would like to focus on one thing, that is, the framework, format and cognition rules of our thinking, among other things, seem to have the same particular 'genes' shaped by the history and traditions of the Chinese nation. If human brain is compared to 'software,' no software designer seems to be able to eliminate such particular common 'genes' anyway. Is it a reason of fundamental significance why we feel so close in our exchanges? "

241

图 241 为 1997 年 11 月 11 日，“第四届两岸金融学术研讨会”期间，黄达（居中）与戴立宁（左一）、李柄才（右一）在一起。

On November 11, 1997, Huang Da (middle) was with Dai Lining (first from the left) and Li Bingcai (first from the right) during the 4th Cross-Straits Finance Symposium.

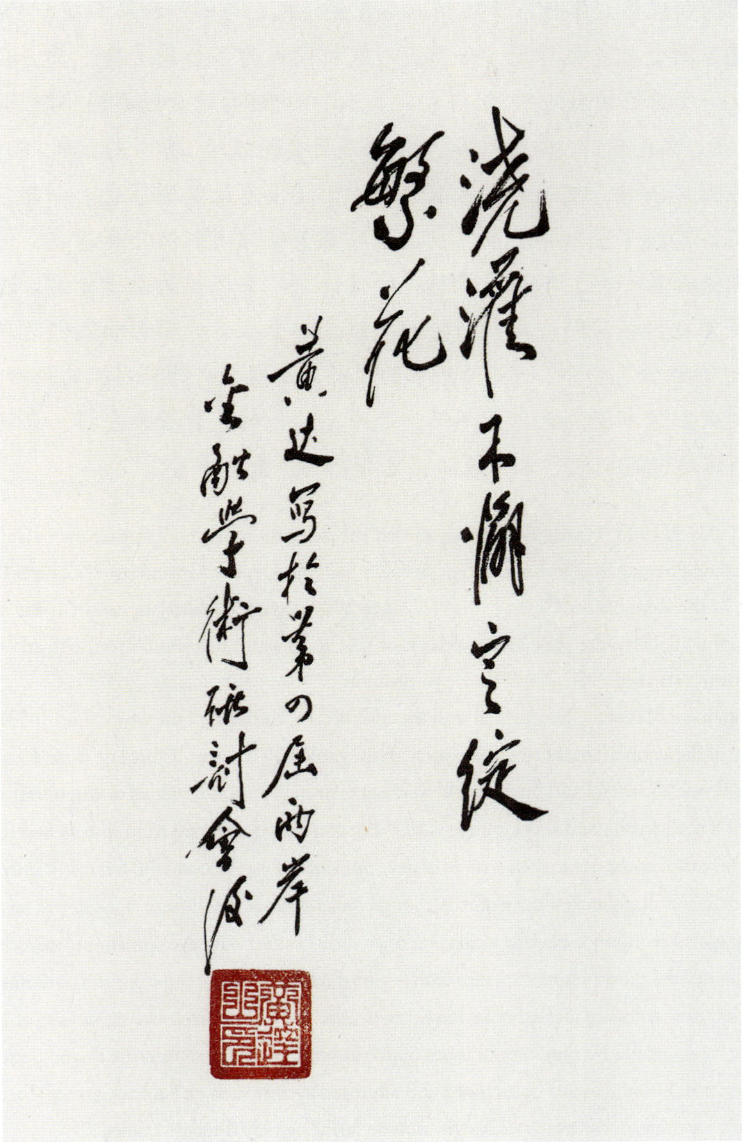

242

图 242 为 1997 年 11 月 12 日，黄达为“第四届两岸金融学术研讨会”题词：“浇灌不懈，定绽繁花”。

On November 12, 1997, Huang Da inscribed "Application and Perseverance Give Results" for the 4th Cross-Straits Finance Symposium.

5-5-4>

1998年11月2—9日，黄达再次以团长身份率团赴台，出席“第五届两岸金融学术研讨会”。除了台湾“中央银行”许嘉栋副总裁以台湾经济学会理事长身份与会之外，本次研讨会参会范围和规格大体与第三届相当，开会模式也与第一和第三届相同。

本次会议恰逢亚洲金融危机期间，如何应对危机便成为了会议主题。黄达在开幕致辞中就此问题表达了自己的看法：“记得大前年，我在欢迎台湾金融界同仁时曾说过，金融‘时而疾风骤雨，雷霆万钧，震撼九州’。但这是历史的经验，旁人的教训。而那时，我们正是沐浴在东亚经济神奇发展的醉人熏风之中，还没有切身的感受。今天，去年开始的金融风暴已经震撼了全世界。虽然我们两岸都未使惊涛骇浪登岸肆虐，但全球的经济走势，特别是今后一年，不论是最悲观的估计——全球性的通货紧缩，还是最乐观的估计——有望扭转颓势而迎接新一轮的高涨，都会从多方面影响我们两岸的发展前景。而且，在世界性的震动中，一些最基本的经济学论题又成为世界性的论辩热点。显然，我们两岸的金融学术交流也不能不环绕这个全局性的大背景来安排、来推进。面对接踵而来的新课题，我们的学术交流必将更加充实、更加丰富。”

During November 2 and 9, 1998, Huang Da once again led the delegation of Mainland China to Taiwan to attend the 5th Cross-Straits Finance Symposium. Except that Xu Jiadong, Deputy Governor of "Central Bank of China "["Central Bank of the Republic of China (Taiwan)" since 2000], attended the symposium as the director general of Taiwan Economic Society, the scale and standards of this symposium was similar to the third one, and the mode of it was the same as that of the first and third symposiums.

It was during the Asian financial crisis, so how to deal with the crisis became the topic of the symposium. In his speech at the opening ceremony of the symposium, Huang Da expressed his opinions, "The year before last when I welcomed the fellows in the Taiwan financial circles, I said that finance 'experiences strong winds and sudden downpours from time to time, with the force of a thunderbolt and shocking the world.' But it is a lesson learned from history and from the others. Back then, we were bathed in the miraculous economic development of East Asia, and did feel it so keenly. Today, the financial storm since last year has shocked the world. Although either Mainland China or Taiwan was ravaged by the perilous situation, the global economy, especially in the year to come, will affect our development prospects in many aspects, considering no matter the most pessimistic estimation—global inflation, or the most optimistic estimation—the hope to reverse the declining tendency and usher in a new boom. And in worldwide economic vacillation, some of the most basic economic topics would become central issues of debate worldwide. Obviously, the financial exchanges between Mainland China and Taiwan have to be arranged and advanced against such global background. Faced with new topics coming one after another, our scholarly exchanges must be further enriched and diversified."

243

图243为1998年11月2日，“第五届两岸金融学术研讨会”期间，黄达（右二）与邹至庄（左二）、殷介炎（左一）和周吴添（右一）在一起。

On November 2, 1998, Huang Da (second from the right) was with Gregory Chow (second from the left), Yin Jieyan (first from the left) and Zhou Wutian (first from the right) at the 5th Cross-Straits Finance Symposium.

图 244 为 1998 年 11 月 2 日，大陆与台湾双方专家在欢迎晚宴前交流。从左一至左四分别为：陆润康、黄达、殷介炎、荣鸿庆。

On November 2, 1998, experts of both sides communicated with one another before the welcoming banquet. From the first to the fourth from the left are Lu Runkang, Huang Da, Yin Jieyan and Rong Hongqing.

244

图 245 为 1998 年 11 月 3 日，出席“第五届两岸金融学术研讨会”开幕式的部分专家合影留念。前排左一和左二分别为邹至庄和黄达，后排左二为许嘉栋，左五为谢平。

On November 3, 1998, some attendees took a group photo at the opening ceremony of the 5th Cross-Straits Finance Symposium. The first and second from the left in the front row are Gregory Chow and Huang Da seperately. The second from the left in the back row is Xu Jiadong. The fifth from the left in the back row is Xie Ping.

245

246

图 246 为 1998 年 11 月 4 日，出席“第五届两岸金融学术研讨会”闭幕式的部分专家合影留念。前排左九为黄达。

On November 4, 1998, some attendees were at the closing ceremony of the 5th Cross-Straits Finance Symposium. The ninth from the left in the front row is Huang Da.

图 247 为 1998 年 11 月 4 日，双方专家在“第五届两岸金融学术研讨会”间歇期间进行学术交流。从左至右分别为：黄达、谢平、周吴添、谢森中。

On November 4, 1998, during the 5th Cross-Straits Finance Symposium, experts of both sides had scholarly exchanges. From the left to the right are Huang Da, Xie Ping, Zhou Wutian and Xie Senzhong.

247

248

图 248 为 1998 年 11 月 5 日，黄达在大陆代表团回请晚宴上致辞。

On November 5, 1998, Huang Da addressed the return banquet held by Mainland China delegation.

5-5-5>

由于两岸紧张的政治形势，本应于 1999 年举办的“第六届两岸金融学术研讨会”推迟一年，于 2000 年 10 月底在北京召开。刚刚卸任中国金融学会会长的黄达仍以贵宾身份出席开幕式并致辞。从这次研讨会之后，黄达很快从两岸学术交流的活动中淡出。只是“第八届两岸金融学术研讨会”在北京召开时，他曾出席开幕式，见见老朋友。

在黄达看来，虽然参与两岸金融学术交流不过短短六年，也无大惊大险，但跌宕起伏，内容颇为丰富，无论如何是值得纪念的！

Due to the tense political relations between Mainland China and Taiwan, the 6th Cross-Straits Finance Symposium was postponed a year, and was not held till the end of October 2000. Huang Da who just left off the post as the chairman of China Society for Finance and Banking, attended and addressed the symposium as a distinguished guest. After the symposium, Huang Da faded away from the academic exchanges between Mainland China and Taiwan. He attended the opening ceremony of the 8th Cross-Straits Finance Symposium to meet old friends when it was held in Beijing.

To Huang Da, although his involvement in the exchanges between Mainland China and Taiwan in finance lasted for only six years, and was undisturbed, it is lumpy and with rich contents, and is therefore to be remembered.

249

图 249 为 2000 年 10 月 30 日，“第六届两岸金融学术研讨会”欢迎晚宴前，黄达（左一）与陆润康（右一）握手致意。

On October 30, 2000, before the reception dinner of the 6th Cross-Straits Finance Symposium, Huang Da (first from the left) was shaking hands and talking with Lu Runkang (first from the right) before the welcoming banquet.

250

图 250 为 2000 年 10 月 30 日，“第六届两岸金融学术研讨会”欢迎晚宴前，黄达（右一）与刘鸿儒（左一）、谢森中（居中）在一起。

On October 30, 2000, before the reception dinner of the 6th Cross-Straits Finance Symposium, Huang Da (first from the right) was with Liu Hongru (first from the left) and Xie Senzhong (middle) before the welcoming banquet.

| 右页图 ⟼

图 251 为 2003 年秋，应台北金融发展研究基金会之请，黄达为纪念两岸金融学术交流十周年写了一帧横幅："筚路蓝缕，开拓有方；承之继之，不懈不怠；箕土跬步，恒且化坚；喜看今朝，更望来日。"

十周年之际，黄达借此表达了自己对于两岸金融学术交流的肯定和期许。

In the autumn of 2003, at the invitation of Taipei Foundation of Finance, Huang Da wrote a banner for the 10th anniversary of academic exchanges on finance between Mainland China and Taiwan—"Despite the hardships, you pioneer; you never stop carrying it forward; you are persistent and even more determined; today, we happily see you make achievements, and we look forward to seeing you make greater achievements tomorrow." By the chance, Huang Da made a neat summary of the event.

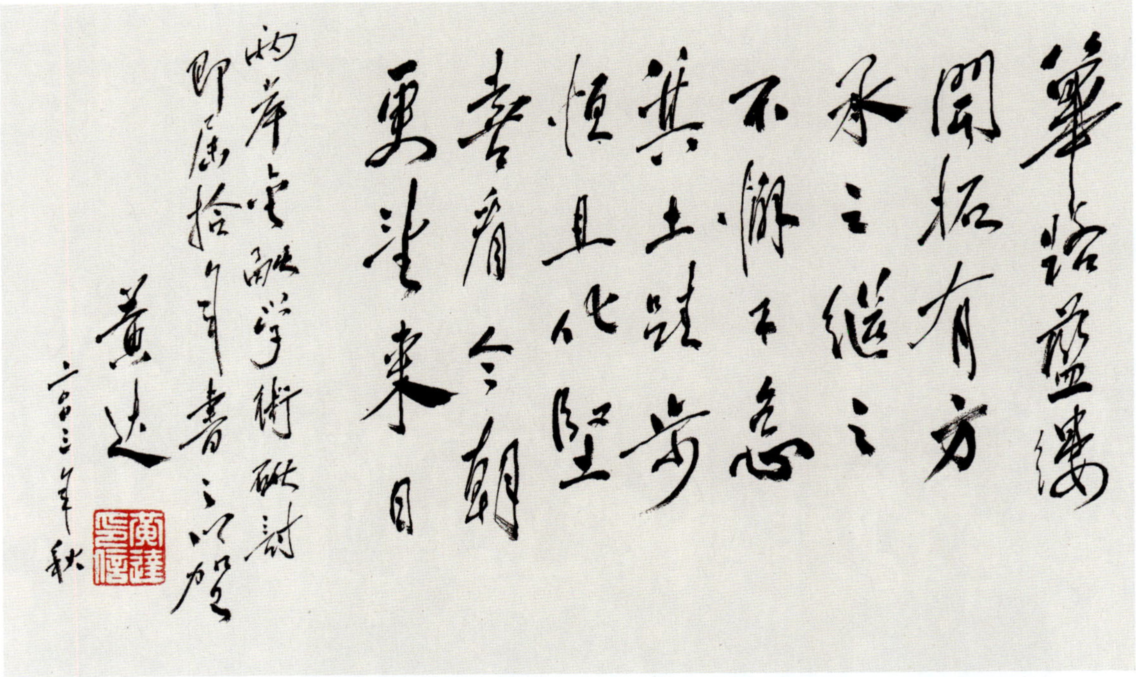

251

5-5-6>

以中国金融学会会长身份参加的其他相关活动

Other Activities Attended as the Chairman of China Society for Finance and Banking

252

图 252 为 1992 年 10 月 6 日，“92 中国金融学术研讨暨优秀论文颁奖大会”在北京召开。全体与会专家合影留念。前排左四为黄达，左七为著名经济学界前辈陈岱孙，左八为中国金融学会副会长乔培新。

On October 6, 1992, "1992 China Symposium on Finance and Excellent Papers Award Presentation Meeting" was held in Beijing. All the present experts took a group photo. In the front row, the fourth from the left is Huang Da; the seventh from the left is Chen Daisun, a famous senior economist; and the eighth from the left is Qiao Peixin, vice chairman of China Society for Finance and Banking.

253

图 253 为 2000 年 7 月 27 日中国金融学会第六次代表大会在北京召开。大会选举了理事会、常务理事会，通过了由著名专家、教授组成的中国金融学会第三届学术委员会。时任中国人民银行行长戴相龙（左一）接替黄达（左二）当选中国金融学会新一届会长。

On July 27, 2000, the 6th congress of China Society for Finance and Banking was held in Beijing. The congress elected the council and the standing council; and approved the third academic committee of China Society for Finance and Banking that was made up of famous experts and professors. Dai Xianglong (first from the left), the then governor of the People's Bank of China, took the place of Huang Da (second from the left) and became the new chairman of China Society for Finance and Banking.

5-6

“福特项目”
The Ford Program

从1985年到1995年的十年时间里，由中国教育部，著名华人经济学家、普林斯顿大学教授邹至庄以及美国福特基金会联合推动的“中美经济学教育交流项目”，为培养既精通马列主义又懂得现代经济学的人才做出了突出贡献。该项目的全称为“美国福特基金会支持的美中经济学教育与研究委员会同中国国家教委（教育部）支持的中美经济学教育交流委员会合作执行的中美经济学教育交流项目”，而“福特项目”的简称更为大家熟知。

“中美经济学教育交流委员会”（简称“中方委员会”）以及“美中经济学教育与研究委员会”（简称“美方委员会”）是分别承担中美双方各自项目执行工作的机构。“中方委员会”于1985年6月25日成立，由中国人民大学黄达、北京大学洪君彦、南开大学熊性美、武汉大学谭崇台、复旦大学陈观烈、吉林大学刘传炎、厦门大学刘平等7所教育部指定高校派出的代表，以及教育部两位代表（先是美大处处长王复苏和财经政法处处长王泽农，后由郭懿清替代王复苏）组成，黄达担任主席。按照黄达自述，他是在教育部“授意”之下由其他委员鼓掌通过的。该委员会的办事机构设在中国人民大学，先后由中国人民大学宋立刚和黄卫平担任秘书长并兼任经济学培训中心主任。“美方委员会”于1985年初成立，由邹至庄教授和哈佛大学教授帕金斯共同担任委员会主席，成员包括 Robert Dernberger、D. Gale Johnson、Lawrence R. Klein、Herbert A. Simon 和刘遵义。该委员会的办事机构设在位于华盛顿的美中学术交流委员会，由姜士德博士于1986—1991年间担任执行主任。

按照约定，“中方委员会”与“美方委员会”每年各自召开一次年会，会后向对方通报年会情况。同时双方每两年召开一次联席会议。从1985年6月第一次联席会议到1994年6月第五次联席会议，共召开了5次。其中，第一、三、五次会议地点在北京，第二次在纽约，第四次在华盛顿。

在双方委员会的共同推动下，该项目举办了一年制经济学培训班，暑期经济学研讨班，派出研究生、青年教师赴北美攻读博士学位或做访问学者，派遣经济学家小组赴美考察，资助留学生回国讲学以及经济学科文献交流等活动。其中，一年制经济学培训班是项目的核心。从1985年起，在中国人民大学共举办了十期现代经济学基础理论培训班。先后有417名在学硕士生和青年教师参加；从1987年起，复旦大学举办了五期侧重国际经济学的培训班，共有201名在学硕士生和青年教师参加。在此期间，美方委员会共选派了70名外籍教授（80人次）到中国人民大学和复旦

In the decade from 1985 to 1995, the "Sino-US Educational Exchange Program in Economics " jointly promoted by the Chinese Ministry of Education, Gregory Chow—famous Chinese economist and professor of Princeton University, and the Ford Foundation, did outstanding contribution to cultivating talented people having a good command of Marxism-Leninism and well understanding economics. Its full name was "Sino-US Economics Educational Exchange Program in Economics Jointly Executed by the Chinese and US Educational Exchange Commissions, and Sponsored by Ford Foundation and Supported by the State Education Commission of China (the Chinese Ministry of Education). " "The Ford Program " is even more familiar to people.

Chinese Committee on Economics Education Exchange with the U.S., referred to as "the Chinese Committee," CEEEUS in short, and American Committee on Economics Education and Research in China, referred to as "the US Committee, " CEERC in short, were the Chinese and US agencies to execute the program. The Chinese Committee was established on June 25, 1985, and made up of Huang Da from the Renmin University of China, Hong Junyan from Peking University, Xiong Xingmei from Nankai University, Tan Chongtai from Wuhan University, Chen Guanlie from Fudan University, Liu Chuanyan from Jilin University and Liu Ping from Xiamen University, that is, representatives of seven universities designated by the Ministry of Education, as well as two representatives from the Ministry of Education (Wang Fusun from the MOE Department of International Cooperation and Exchanges and Wang Zenong from the MOE Department of Finance; Guo Yiqing later substituted Wang Fusun). Huang Da was the chairman of the committee. In his own words, Huang Da was elected by the other committee members who clapped under the "incitation " of the Ministry of Education. The office of the committee was in the Renmin University of China. Song Ligang, and then Huang Weiping, both from the Renmin University of China, served as its secretary-general and were in charge of the Economics Training Center. The US Committee, established in early 1985, was chaired by Prof. Gregory Chow and Prof. Dwight Perkins, a Harvard University Professor, and made up of Robert Dernberger, D. Gale Johnson, Lawrence R. Klein, Herbert A. Simon and Lawrence J. Law. The committee had its office in the Washington-headquartered Committee on Scholarly Communication with China, and was headed by Dr. Todd Johnson during 1986—1991.

As contracted, the Chinese Committee and the US Committee each held a meeting annually, and informed the other party of the annual meeting after it was closed. Meanwhile, both held a joint meeting every two years. From June 1985 to June 1994, altogether five joint meetings were held, of which the first, third and fifth meetings were held in Beijing, the second in New York and the fourth in Washington.

Promoted by both committees, the Ford Program held such activities as one-year economics training classes; economic seminars during summer vacation; sending graduates and young teachers to North America for the Ph.D. program or as visiting scholars; sending an economist group to the US for inspection; funding overseas Chinese students to come back and give lectures and for exchanges of documents of economics, of which the one-year economics training classes were the program core. Since 1985, a total of 10 training classes of basic theories of modern economics were held, and attended by 417 active graduates and young teachers. Since 1987, Fudan University held five training classes focusing on international economics, and attracted altogether 201 active graduates and young teachers. During the period, the US Committee selected before designating 70 foreign professors (80 persons) to coach the two training classes, in the Renmin University of China and Fudan University, respectively. They taught nearly 20 courses,

大学的两个培训班任教。先后讲授了宏观经济学（中高级）、微观经济学（中高级）、发展经济学、计量经济学、国际金融、国际贸易、货币银行学、工业经济学、劳动经济学、应用统计学、投资经济学、技术经济学、公共财政和对策论等近二十门课程。该项目培养出的学员，部分在国外发展，大部分成为中国经济学界和业界的中坚力量。

| 右页图 |⟶

图 254 为 1985 年初，黄达以中国人民大学副校长的身份参与“福特项目”的筹备工作。1 月 23 日晚，教育部王泽农处长向几所大学吹风：有一个由美福特基金会资助的美中经济学教育交流项目，内容包括：办讲习班；由第一流的专家讲学 3 个月、半年，培养硕士研究生；青年学者出国读学位；交换图书资料；派代表团考察美国经济学教育等。3 月 4 日，教育部正式发文，要求中国人民大学等七所大学接待美方派来论证培训可行性的人士。3 月 5 日，时任中国人民大学外事处长刘幼勤传达教育部要求中国人民大学负责组织接待事宜。自此，黄达开始了直接参与这项交流的十年历程。

黄达在笔记本里保存的参加 1985 年 1 月 23 日和同年 3 月 5 日两次相关会议的记录。

In early 1985, Huang Da participated in the preparation of "the Ford Program" as vice president of the Renmin University of China. In the evening of January 23, Wang Zenong, a director at Ministry of Education, introduced "the Ford Program" to several universities: a Sino-US Educational Exchange Program in Economics was sponsored by Ford Foundation; the program encompasses study group, cultivation of master's students taught by first-tier experts for 3 months or half a year, young scholars studying overseas for academic degrees, books exchange, sending a delegation to investigate education in economics in the US, etc. On March 4, the Ministry of Education officially required seven universities including Renmin University of China to receive the delegation from the US to analyze the feasibility of the program. On March 5, Liu Youqin, the then director of Foreign Affairs of Renmin University of China, passed on the requirement of the Ministry of Education. From then on, Huang Da started the 10-year experience of participating in this program.

Minutes of two respective meetings related to the program on January 23 and March 5, 1985, kept in Huang Da's notebook.

including macroeconomics (intermediate and advanced level), microeconomics (intermediate and advanced level), development economics, econometrics, international finance, international trade, monetary economics and banking, industrial economics, labor economics, applied statistics, investment economics, technical economics, public finance and the theory of games. Some students of the program sought development abroad, and some became the backbone force in the economics and the industry.

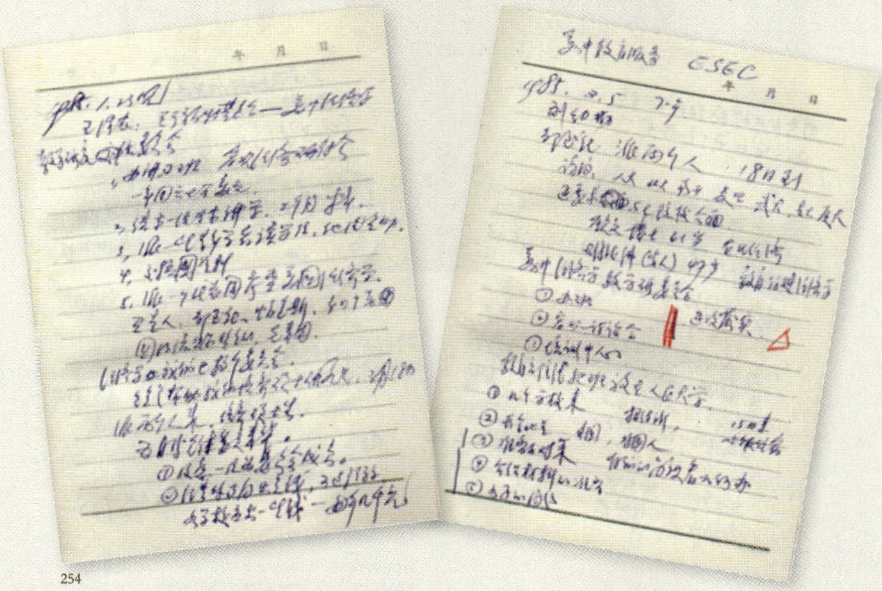

254

255

图 255 为 1986 年 3 月 20 — 25 日，“中方委员会”第二次年会在复旦大学召开。部分与会专家合影留念。前排从左至右分别为: 王泽农、黄达、谭崇台、刘传炎、熊性美；后排从左至右分别为：王百哲、洪君彦、陈观烈、刘平。

During March 20 and 25, 1986, the second annual meeting of the Chinese Committee was held in Fudan University. This is a group photo of some of the present experts. From the left to the right in the front row are Wang Zenong, Huang Da, Tan Chongtai, Liu Chuanyan and Xiong Xingmei; from the left to the right in the back row are Wang Baizhe, Hong Junyan, Chen Guanlie and Liu Ping.

256

图256为1988年4月25—27日，“中方委员会”第四次年会在中国人民大学黄山学术交流中心召开。与会专家合影留念。从左至右分别为：李键聪、刘平、王泽农、洪文达、谭崇台、黄达、刘传炎、洪君彦、熊性美。

During April 25 and 27, 1988, the Chinese Committee held the fourth annual meeting in Huangshan Scholarly Exchange Center, the Renmin University of China. From the left to the right are Li Jiancong, Liu Ping, Wang Zenong, Hong Wenda, Tan Chongtai, Huang Da, Liu Chuanyan, Hong Junyan, and Xiong Xingmei.

257

图 257 为 1987 年 9 月 9 日，“中美双方委员会第二次联席会议”在纽约召开。全体与会专家合影留念。前排从左至右分别为：翻译、郭懿清、刘平、帕金斯、黄达、邹至庄。

On September 9, 1987, the second joint meeting of the Chinese and the US Committee was held in New York. This is a group photo of all the attendees. From the left to the right in the first row are the interpreter, Guo Yiqing, Liu Ping, Perkins, Huang Da and Gregory Chow.

258

图 258 为 1987 年 9 月 9 日，中美双方委员会第二次联席会议期间，黄达（左二）与邹至庄（左一）和帕金斯（右一）一起交谈。

On September 9, 1987, during the second joint meeting of the Chinese and the US Committee, Huang Da (second from the left), Gregory Chow (first from the left) and Perkins (first from the right) were talking.

259

图 259 为 1987 年 9 月，斯坦福大学教授为中方代表团举行家宴。期间，黄达（左四）与著名经济学家约翰·泰勒（右二）等人交谈。

In September 1987, professors from Stanford University held a family feast to welcome the Chinese delegation. Huang Da (fourth from the left) was talking with famous economist John Taylor (second from the right) et al.

260

图 260 为 1987 年 9 月，中方代表团访问普林斯顿大学。从左至右分别为：刘平、熊性美、王泽农、黄达、邹至庄、谭崇台、刘传炎、陈观烈、洪君彦、Todd Johnson、郭懿清。

In September 1987, the Chinese delegation visited Princeton University. From the left to the right are Liu Ping, Xiong Xingmei, Wang Zenong, Huang Da, Gregory Chow, Tan Chongtai, Liu Chuanyan, Chen Guanlie, Hong Junyan, Todd Johnson and Guo Yiqing.

261

图 261 为 1989 年 8 月 23 日，“中美双方委员会第三次联席会议”在北京召开。与会专家在会议茶歇期间交流。从左至右分别为：帕金斯、陈良焜、刘遵义、福特基金会代表彼得·盖特纳、黄达、盖尔·约翰逊。

1989 年政治风波极大地冲击了对外交流，中美经济学教育交流也不例外。为了防止项目中断，并借该项目来突破政治风波之后已经陷入全面停顿状态的中美民间交流，经中美双方努力，美方委员会代表团于 8 月 23 日来华，参加第三次联席会议。这是当年政治风波之后第一个来华的美国学术界代表团，受到了领导高度重视。江泽民总书记在会议期间专门接见了邹至庄、黄达等。

On August 23, 1989, the third joint meeting of the Chinese and the US Committee was held in Beijing. Some Chinese and foreign attendees were together during tea break. From the left to the right are Perkins, Chen Liangkun, Lawrence J. Law, the Ford Foundation representative Peter F. Geithner, Huang Da, and Gale Johnson

The political incident of 1989 greatly shocked China's foreign exchange, with no exception of Sino-US educational exchange in economics. To prevent the program from being interrupted, and to break the icy Sino-US non-governmental exchange after the political incident, with the efforts of both sides, the US Committee delegation came to China on August 23 for the third joint meeting. Being the first US delegation of scholars coming to China after the political incident of 1989, it received close attention from the Chinese leaders. Secretary General Jiang Zemin received Gregory Chow, Huang Da and others during the conference.

262

263

图 262 为 1990 年 4 月 17 日，“中方委员会”第六次年会在武汉大学召开。黄达（右三）与与会专家讨论相关问题。

On April 17, 1990, the 6th annual meeting of the Chinese Committee was held in Wuhan University. Huang Da (third from the right) was discussing with other participants.

图 263 为 1991 年 4 月 11 日，“中方委员会”第七次年会在南开大学召开。全体与会专家合影留念。前排从左至右分别为：熊性美、王泽农、陈观烈、谭崇台、黄达、王百哲、周光亚、钱伯海、钱玉麟；后排右四为中国人民大学培训中心主任黄卫平。

On April 11, 1991, attendees of the seventh annual meeting of the Chinese Committee were held in Nankai University. All attendees took a group photo. From the left to the right in the front row are Xiong Xingmei, Wang Zenong, Chen Guanlie, Tan Chongtai, Huang Da, Wang Baizhe, Zhou Guangya, Qian Bohai and Qian Yulin; the fourth one from the right in the back row is Huang Weiping, director of the training center of the Renmin University of China.

264

265

图264为1992年9月，中方五人代表团赴美出席“中美双方委员会第四次联席会议”。期间，他们游览了华盛顿。照片为黄达在白宫外的个人照。

In September 1992, five Chinese delegates visited the US and attended the fourth joint meeting held by the Chinese and the US Committee. During their stay there, they visited Washington. This is a personal picture of Huang Da outside the White House.

图265为1993年3月9日，“中方委员会”第九次年会在厦门大学召开。全体与会专家合影留念。第二排左五为黄达。

On March 9, 1993, the 9th annual meeting of Chinese Committee was held in Xiamen University. All participants took a group photo. The fifth from the left in the second row is Huang Da.

266

图 266 为 1994 年 6 月 13 日，“中美双方委员会第五次联席会议”在北京召开。全体与会专家合影留念。前排从左至右分别为：陈观烈、盖尔·约翰逊、邹至庄、黄达、帕金斯、罗伯特·顿伯格、王泽农。

当时，主要由于福特基金会的原因，“福特项目”的核心部分——经济学一年制培训班将告结束。所以本次会议实际上是中美双方总结十年合作并宣告结束合作的会议。

On June 13, 1994, delegates to the fifth joint meeting of the Chinese and the US Committee were held in Beijing. From the left to the right in the first row are Chen Guanlie, Gale Johnson, Gregory Chow, Huang Da, Perkins, Robert F. Dernberger and Wang Zenong.

Primarily for the reason of the Ford Foundation, the core part of "the Ford Program"— the one-year economics training class was soon to end. The fifth joint meeting held in Beijing was actually a meeting on which both China and the US summarized their 10-year-long cooperation and announced the conclusion of their cooperation.

267

268

图 267 为 1996 年 8 月 29 日，黄达（右一）与原美方委员会委员刘遵义（左一）在北京友谊宾馆会面。

On August 29, 1996, Huang Da (first from the right) was with Lawrence J. Law (first from the left), a member of the US Committee.

图 268 为 2008 年 5 月 15 日，黄达（左一）在中国人民大学会见来访的原美方委员会主席帕金斯（右一）。

On May 15, 2008, Huang Da (first from the left) was with Perkins (first from the right), chairman of the US Committee.

269

图 269 为 1997 年 12 月 19 日，黄达（右一）与原美方委员会主席邹至庄（左一）在一起。

On December 19, 1997, Huang Da (first from the right) was with Gregory Chow (first from the left), chairman of the US Committee.

图 270 为 2010 年 6 月 23 日，黄达专门为邹至庄 80 寿辰题字：“力促交流，瞻远信笃，不移不懈，壮哉夫子。”以感谢邹至庄教授数十年如一日地关怀中国经济学教育发展。

On June 23, 2010, Huang Da inscribed "Dedicated to Mutual Exchange, Forward-looking and Resolute, Persistent—A Great Master" for the 80th birthday of Gregory Chow to express gratitude for Professor Gregory Chow for his decades of attention to the development of education of economics in China.

270

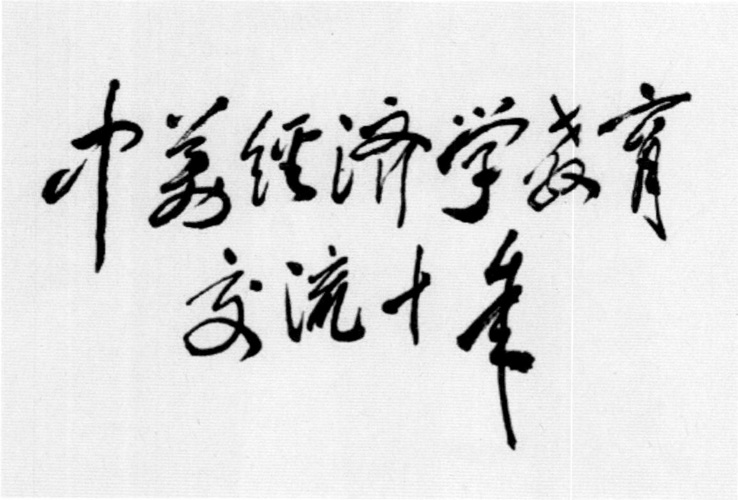

271

图 271 为 2008 年 7 月，黄达应邀为《中美经济学交流十年》画册题字。

In July 2008, Huang Da inscribed for album *Ten Years of Communication and Exchange in Economics between China and the US.*

272

图 272 为 2010 年 6 月 23 日，中国人民大学实施中美经济学教育交流项目 25 周年纪念大会召开。中方委员会主席黄达（第一排右十），美方委员会主席邹至庄（第一排左十）、帕金斯（第一排右九）等出席会议并致辞。

会上，黄达回顾了中美经济学教育交流项目的发展历程，他将这个项目比作中西方文化交流的一朵小的“浪花”，是两种语言、两种概念体系之间的碰撞、交流与融合。“尽管中美经济学教育交流项目已经结束，但在这为期十年的西学东渐过程中，两种语言和概念体系交流融合，体现出的海纳百川、滋养中华民族文化传统的品德值得纪念。”

On June 23, 2010, the Commemoration of the 25th Anniversary for the Sino-US Educational Exchange Program in Economics was held. Huang Da (tenth from the right in the first row), chairman of the Chinese Committee, Gregory Chow (tenth from the left in the first row), chairman of the US Committee, and Perkins (ninth from the right in the first row) presented and addressed the meeting.

Huang Da reviewed the development of the Sino-US educational exchange program in economics; compared it to a small "spray" in the scholarly exchanges between the West and the East; and thought it to be collision, exchange and integration of two languages and two systems of concepts. "Although the program has been closed, the last decade saw the exchange and integration of two languages and systems of concepts. The tolerance of it and the virtues that nourish the cultural traditions of the Chinese nation are to be remembered."

5-7

欧洲之行
The Travels to Europe

5-7-1>

1985 年 5 月 21—30 日，黄达以中国人民大学副校长的身份，作为考察“行政干部培训政策”代表团团长，赴法国访问。团员包括中国人民大学副校长李文海、外事处处长刘幼勤以及人事部一位干部。

本次法国之行是黄达第一次走出国门，当时已逾六十一岁。其背景是，李鹏副总理在访法时，与时任法国总理商定组建一个考察法国高级行政干部（法国习惯用“文官”一词）培训制度和政策的代表团，重点考察法国国立行政学院。因此，这项活动被列入国家教委 1986 年中法文化交流执行计划之中。

通过十天的访问，除了对法国行政管理制度与高级公务员的培训有了初步了解之外，法国的社会制度与风土人情给黄达留下了深刻的印象，同时也让他开始意识到走出国门、开阔眼界的重要性。

During May 21 and 30, 1985, Huang Da, as the vice president of the Renmin University of China and head of the delegation which was to observe "the training policies of administrative cadres, " went to visit France. Members of the delegation included Li Wenhai, the then vice principal of the Renmin University of China, Liu Youqin, head of the Foreign Affairs Division of the Renmin University of China, and a cadre of the HR Department of the Renmin University of China.

The travel to France was the first time Huang Da ever went abroad, and he was more than 61 years old. They had the travel to France because the then Chinese Vice Premier Li Peng, when visiting France, negotiated with the then French Premier about setting a delegation to observe the system for and policies on training senior administrative cadres (more than often "civilians" in France) in France, with the priority to observing the French National School of Administration. The activity was included in 1986 Sino-French cultural exchange execution plan by the State Education Commission.

During the ten-day visit, besides getting preliminary understanding of the administration system and training of senior civil servants in France, Huang Da was deeply attracted by the social system and local customs of France. The travel made him realize the importance of going abroad and broadening his horizons.

273

图 273 为 1986 年 5 月 21 日，黄达一行访问法国国立行政学院。右二为黄达，右三为李文海，左二为时任法国国立行政学院副院长。

On May 21, 1986, Huang Da and the delegation visited the French National School of Administration. The second from the right is Huang Da; the third from the right is Li Wenhai; and the second from the left was the then deputy dean of the French National School of Administration.

274

图 274 为 1986 年 5 月 25 日，黄达参观凡尔赛宫。

On May 25, 1986, Huang Da visited Versailles.

5-7-2>

20 世纪五六十年代之交，中苏关系开始恶化，两国的交流陷于停滞。即使在改革开放之后，中国开始不断开拓与西方经济文化交流的渠道，而与苏东的交流却始终保持在极低的水平。从 80 年代后期开始，中国人民大学尝试通过自身的努力来改变这种状态。

1988 年 10 月 27 日—11 月 16 日，中国人民大学代表团访问匈牙利、波兰，并在莫斯科作短暂停留。代表团除了黄达之外，还包括苏联东欧研究所副所长赵大伦、苏联东欧研究所兼职研究员苗华寿和中国人民大学外事处处长金戈。本次访问的任务是与匈牙利、波兰的相关教学单位商谈交流问题。但给黄达留下最为深刻印象的却是对苏东国家的第一印象以及这些国家在巨大政治风云变幻前夕山雨欲来风满楼的氛围。

At the turn of the 1950s and 1960s, Sino-Soviet relationship began to deteriorate, and bilateral exchanges were stuck in stagnation. Even if China began to extend channels of economic and cultural exchanges with the West after taking the reform and opening-up policy, its exchange with the Soviet Union and Eastern Europe was as cool as before. Since the late 1980s, the Renmin University of China tried to change the situation with its efforts.

During October 27 and November 16, 1988, the delegation of the Renmin University of China visited Hungary, Poland and stayed briefly in Moscow. Besides Huang Da, Zhao Dalun, deputy director of the Soviet Union and Eastern Europe Research Institute, Miao Huashou, part-time researcher of the Soviet Union and Eastern Europe Research Institute, and Jin Ge, head of the Foreign Affairs Department of the Renmin University of China, were also members of the delegation. The task of the travel was to negotiate with related teaching units in Hungary and Poland about exchange, but the deepest impression on Huang Da was the first impression of the Soviet Union and Eastern European countries and the atmosphere before huge political turmoil in these countries.

275

图 275 为 1988 年 10 月 30 日，黄达在布达佩斯街头。

Huang Da was on the street of Budapest on October 30, 1988.

276

图 276 为 1988 年 10 月 31 日，黄达（右一）与匈牙利卡尔·马克思经济大学校长（左一）一起交谈。

中国人民大学代表团于 10 月 29 日 — 11 月 3 日访问了该校，双方签署了学术交流协议，并商定了 1989 年两校交流计划。

On October 31, 1988, Huang Da (first from the right) was with the president of Karl Marx University of Economic Sciences in Hungary (first from the left).

The Renmin University of China delegation visited it during October 29 and November 3. Both sides signed an agreement on scholarly exchange, and decided on the mutual exchange plan in 1989.

图 277 为 1988 年 11 月 4—10 日，代表团在波兰华沙访问一周，与华沙大学商定了 1989 年双方的交流计划。期间，黄达（左四）一行到加克家里做客。加克是一位经常与中国联系的波兰统一工人党人士。

During November 4 and 10, 1988, the delegation visited Warsaw, Poland, for a week, and negotiated with Warsaw University about the mutual exchange plan in 1989. During their visit, Huang Da (fourth from the left) and the other delegation members visited a member of Polish United Workers' Party who contacted China very often.

277

图 278 为 1988 年 11 月 14 日，代表团成员与莫斯科普列汉诺夫国民经济学院院长会谈。左一为黄达。

此外，在莫斯科停留期间，代表团还访问了苏联科学院远东研究所。

On November 14, 1988, members of the delegation talked with head of the Moscow Plekhanov Institute of National Economy. The first one from the left is Huang Da.

Besides, during the stay in Moscow, the delegation also visited the Far East Research Institute of the Soviet Union Academy of Social Sciences.

278

5-7-3>

1992 年 5 月 10—18 日，以黄达为团长的中国人民大学代表团访问奥地利。成员包括法学院副院长王益英、曾宪义，国际政治系教授苗华寿，法学院讲师何家弘等。代表团主要访问了维也纳大学和格拉茨大学，并与这两所大学的法学院建立交流联系。

本次奥地利之行让黄达感受最深的是西方世界与中国之间的隔阂。究其原因，他认为，深层次的应是东西方不同的历史文化传统。但在近半个世纪以来，双方的隔阂主要来自列宁的布尔什维克与西欧社会民主党从意识形态到政策实践的对立，以及西藏问题和 1989 年政治风波等问题。

During May 10 and 18, 1992, the Renmin University of China delegation led by Huang Da visited Austria. Wang Yiying and Zeng Xianyi, deputy deans of the School of Law, Miao Huashou, professor of the Department of International Politics, He Jiahong, lecturer of the School of Law, etc. were also members of the delegation. The delegation mainly visited the University of Vienna and Graz University, and built a connection with the schools of law of these two universities.

What stroke Huang Da the most in the travel to Austria was the gulf between the West and China, which was deep-rooted different historical and cultural traditions in the East and the West. However, in the past nearly half a century, the gulf between the West and China was mainly caused by the confrontation, from ideology to practical policies, of Lenin's Bolshevik and the social-democratic parties in Western Europe, the issue of Tibet, the 1989 political incident, etc.

279

280

281

图 279 为 1992 年 5 月 11 日，黄达（右一）在奥地利维也纳街头。

Huang Da (first from the right) was on the street of Vienna, Austria, on May 11, 1992.

图 280 为 1992 年 5 月 14 日，黄达（右一）与维也纳大学校长（右二）交谈。

Huang Da (first from the right) was talking with the principal of the University of Vienna (second from the right) on May 14, 1992.

图 281 为 1992 年 5 月 14 日，黄达在维也纳音乐家之墓前。这里是奥地利的先贤祠，也是全世界音乐爱好者心中的圣地。

Huang Da was in front of Vienna Central Cemetery on May 14, 1992. It is Pantheon in Austria, also a sacred place in the heart of music fans around the world.

| 右页图 |→

图 282 为 1992 年 5 月 14 日，黄达（右一）与苗华寿（左一）在维也纳附近的一个小镇漫步。

Huang Da (first from the right) was stroking with Miao Huashou (first from the left) in a town near Vienna.

EKE

5-7-4>

1993 年 4 月 25 日—5 月 4 日，由黄达担任团长的中国人民大学代表团先后访问了意大利那不勒斯东方大学、法国巴黎第十大学和英国杜伦大学。本次出访属于学校开展校际交流的外事活动。学校外事处副处长王清源陪同出访。

4 月 25—27 日黄达一行访问意大利那不勒斯东方大学，一起访问的还有曾在该校留学的黄卫平教授。那不勒斯东方大学是意大利面对东方的一所窗口大学。自 1987 年起，中国人民大学就与该校建立了涵盖学者互换等在内的校际合作关系。本次访问该校主要是商谈续约和签署延期协议等事宜。

4 月 28 日下午，黄达一行从意大利飞抵巴黎。本次巴黎之行是应巴黎第十大学副校长、科学哲学教授拉比卡的邀请，一来为授予拉比卡教授中国人民大学名誉教授称号，二来为探索建立与巴黎第十大学的校际合作关系。在这次访问中，黄达不停地思考浪漫的法国如何能够创造工业奇迹？法国的力量源泉到底在哪里？"有法国大革命的自由平等博爱传统；有拿破仑叱咤风云所依靠的民族传统。这些应是无疑的，但都嫌过分笼统。也许并非一两句话可以概括。但有一点是清楚的：当我们戴着有色眼镜，而且是质量有问题的眼镜，来观察世界时，是不能如实地把握世界的。你总是片面地解读旁人，旁人依然是旁人自己而不会因你的片面解读而缺胳膊少腿；归根结底，真正受伤害的是你自己——必将为有意无意地片面理解自己生活的世界而付出代价。"

5 月 2 日下午，黄达一行从巴黎飞抵纽卡斯尔。本次英国之行主要是访问杜伦大学并顺访新堡大学。杜伦大学从 1983 年就开始向中国人民大学派遣学习中文的留学生并聘请汉语教师到该校任教。此次访问属于正式的校际访问，以期巩固已有的交流成果和寻求进一步扩大合作范围的可能。新堡大学也曾派遣留学生到中国人民大学学习语言。在完成两校的访问之后，黄达一行于 5 日傍晚到达伦敦，并有机会作短暂停留。在英国期间，黄达零距离、多视角地观察到了英国人的安逸生活，而后终于摆脱了朦胧感受的困扰并使他明明白白地给自己找出了全然不难理解的判断：中国人生活得太辛苦了！

283

图 283 为 1993 年 4 月 27 日，黄达（右二）与那不勒斯东方大学校长罗西（左二）签署合作协议。

On April 27, 1993, Huang Da (second from the right) and Rossi (second from the left), the then principal of University of Naples "L'Orientale" in Italy, signed an agreement.

During April 25 and May 4, 1993, the Renmin University of China delegation led by Huang Da visited University of Naples "L'Orientale" in Italy, Université de Paris 10 Nanterre in France and Durham University in UK in succession. The visit was an activity in connection with foreign affairs which involved launching intercollegiate exchanges. Wang Qingyuan, deputy head of the Foreign Affairs Department of the Renmin University of China travelled with the delegation.

During April 25 and 27, Huang Da and his delegation visited University of Naples "L'Orientale " in Italy. Professor Huang Weiping, who was once a student of the university, was with Huang Da and the delegation. University of Naples "L'Orientale " in Italy is a window university in Italy to the East. Since 1987, the Renmin University of China has established intercollegiate cooperation, including exchanging scholars, with the university. In the visit, Huang Da and the delegation were mainly talking about renewing the contract and signing an extension agreement with the university.

In the afternoon of April 28, Huang Da and his delegation flew to Paris at the invitation of George Labica, the then vice principal and professor of philosophy of science of Université de Paris 10 Nanterre, to present Prof. Labica the title of honorary professor of the Renmin University of China and to explore to build intercollegiate cooperation with Université de Paris 10 Nanterre. During the visit, Huang Da kept thinking why romantic France could make an industrial miracle, where the source of power for France was. "It is the tradition of freedom, equality and universal love of the French Revolution; the national tradition Napoleon relied on for sure, but it is too rough, and can't easily explained. One thing is for sure: If we observe the world stereotypically, we can't truthfully understand the world. If one always interprets the others partially, he would eventually hurt himself instead of the others, because the others do not lose an arm or leg for his partial interpretation, but he will pay a price for partially, consciously or unconsciously, understanding the world he lives in."

On the afternoon of May 2, Huang Da and his delegation flew from Paris to Newcastle for the main purpose of visiting Durham University and stopping by Newcastle University. Durham University has been sending students to the Renmin University of China to learn Chinese and hired Chinese language teachers to teach its students Chinese. It was an official intercollegiate visit to consolidate the established exchange results and seek the possibility of further expanding the scope of cooperation. Newcastle University was also a university sending students to acquire language skills in the Renmin University of China. After visiting the two universities, Huang Da and his delegation reached London on the evening of May 5, and had a chance to stay there briefly. There and then, Huang Da observed the comfortable life of British people face to face and from multiple angles. Later he got rid of the harassment of a vague feeling, and made a judgment that was easy to understand: The life of the Chinese people was too hard.

284

图 284 为 1993 年 4 月 28 日，黄达（左二）向巴黎第十大学副校长拉比卡教授（左三）颁发中国人民大学名誉教授聘书。

On April 28, 1993, Huang Da (second from the left) presented the letter of appointment to Prof. Labica (third from the left), vice president of Université de Paris 10 Nanterre, as an honorary professor of the Renmin University of China.

285

图 285 为 1993 年 5 月 4 日，黄达（右一）与杜克大学校长（左一）互换礼物。

On May 4, 1993, Huang Da (first from the right) exchanged gifts with the president of Duke University (first from the left).

图 286 为 1993 年 5 月 4 日，黄达在杜克大学图书馆。

On May 4, 1993, Huang Da was in the library of Duke University.

286

287

288

289

图 287 为 1993 年 5 月 6 日，黄达在英格兰银行大楼前，实现了他自童年阅读狄更斯《双城记》时就一直想亲眼看看这所传奇银行的愿望。

英格兰银行成立于 1694 年，英格兰银行大楼位于伦敦市的 Threadneedle（针线）大街，因此它有时候又被人称为“针线大街上的老妇人”或者“老妇人”。

On May 6, 1993, Huang Da was in front of the Bank of England, and realized his childhood wish of seeing the legendary bank when reading Dickens' *A Tale of Two Cities*.

The Bank of England, established in 1694, is located on Threadneedle Street, so it is sometimes called "the Old Lady of Threadneedle Street" or "the Old Lady."

图 288 为 1993 年 5 月 7 日，黄达在马克思墓前。

On May 7, 1993, Huang Da was in front of the tomb of Marx.

图 289 为 1993 年 5 月 8 日，黄达在位于莎士比亚故居的夏洛克铜像前。

On May 8, 1993, Huang Da was in front of the bronze statue of Shylock in the former residence of Shakespeare.

5-8

七赴日本
The Travels to Japan

5-8-1>

1987年9月，黄达率中美经济学教育交流委员会代表团赴美，回国途经日本东京。这是他第一次来到日本。

为期两天的“途经”，黄达走马观花，仅仅留下点滴观感和些许感慨，“来到从19世纪末到20世纪中叶这半个多世纪的敌对国家——关系中华民族生死存亡并从‘九一八’到1945年直接占领中国领土的敌对国家，对于一个从幼年就时时听老师、听青年大哥哥大姐姐讲述国耻并亲身在日本占领的地区生活了八年的人来说，不会没有感想。也许是由于从1945年到1987年，已经过了40多年，也许是由于自己也从幼年、童年、青年走到了耳顺之年，这时并没有心潮澎湃、思绪万千、不能自已；好像有的只是滔滔历史长河，时迁世异，雄霸东方的帝国今安在哉的朦胧感慨。而且中国在不到半个世纪中，从新中国成立到‘文化大革命’，再到改革开放，也处在不以人们意志为转移的不断调整之中，这就更加深了我对于古往今来多少谱写历史的英雄总爱武断历史发展方向的困惑。面对这一切，恐怕只有‘念天地之悠悠’的苍凉心境了。”

此后的十余年间，黄达又先后六次踏上日本的国土，逐渐对这个国家有了更为深入的认识。

1989年3月31日—4月4日，黄达第二次来到日本，参加日本东海大学开学典礼。中国人民大学与日本东海大学的交往始于20世纪80年代中期，当时的东海大学校长、日本国会议员松前达郎，同时还是中国人民大学名誉教授，非常重视发展与中国高校的关系。此次参加开学典礼，除了带去纪念品之外，黄达还赋诗一首并书写成横幅：“日出日落久往还，文教交流最为先；前贤拓路吾侪继，续句添章友谊篇。”三年后，在杜厚文副校长又代表中国人民大学出席该校开学典礼时，黄达专门托他带去亲笔题写的一帧竖挑。

In September 1987, Huang Da led the delegation of Chinese Committee on Economics Education Exchange with the U.S. to the United States, and returned by way of Tokyo, Japan. It was the first time Huang Da went to Japan.

During his two-day stay there, Huang Da had a hasty visit, and got some impressions and sighs. "In this country hostile to China from the end of the 19th century to the mid 20th century, that is, from the September 18 Incident that was of life and death to the Chinese nation to the direct occupation of China's territory in 1945, I, as a man who has been told, by the teachers, young brothers and sisters, the humiliation brought to China by this country, and lived in an area occupied by Japan for eight years, felt something. Perhaps it is because 40 or more years have passed, or I have grown from childhood to youth to my sixtieths, I was not so thrilled or out of control. What I had was a sigh at the past empire that once dominated the East. In less than half a century, China has been in constant adjustments—from its founding, to the Cultural Revolution ,to reform and opening up, whether people wish them or not. The grandiloquence of the heroes in history that history would be developing in the direction they pointed at, puzzles me more. Seeing all this, I feel nothing but the desolation of 'the sky and earth forever last'. "

In the decade or more after that, Huang Da set foot on the land of Japan six times, and had deeper understanding of the country.

During March 31 and April 4, 1989, Huang Da went to Japan for the second time, and he was to attend the opening ceremony of Tokai University. The Renmin University of China and Tokai University started their friendship in the mid 1980s. The then president of Tokai University and member of the National Diet of Japan Matsumae Tatsuro, who was also an honorary professor of the Renmin University of China, set great store by developing friendship with Chinese universities. Besides some souvenirs for the opening ceremony, Huang Da wrote a poem and wrote it on a banner— "In exchanges, cultural and educational exchanges are the foremost. The former worthies pioneered the road and we follow them to continue and deepen our friendship. " Three years later, Vice President Du Houwen presented the opening ceremony of the same university on behalf of the Renmin University of China, and Huang Da asked him to bring his inscription.

290

291

图 290 为 1988 年 10 月上旬，黄达第二次访日的前一年，东海大学校长松前达郎访问中国人民大学，被授予中国人民大学名誉教授称号。左一为松前达郎，左三为黄达。

In early October 1988, the year before the visit to Japan, Matsumae Tatsuro, president of Tokai University visited the Renmin University of China, and was presented the title of honorary professor of the Renmin University of China. The first from the left is Matsumae Tatsuro, and the third from the left is Huang Da.

图 291 为 1989 年 4 月 3 日，黄达在东海大学开学典礼上致辞。

On April 3, 1989, Huang Da delivered a speech at the opening ceremony of Tokai University.

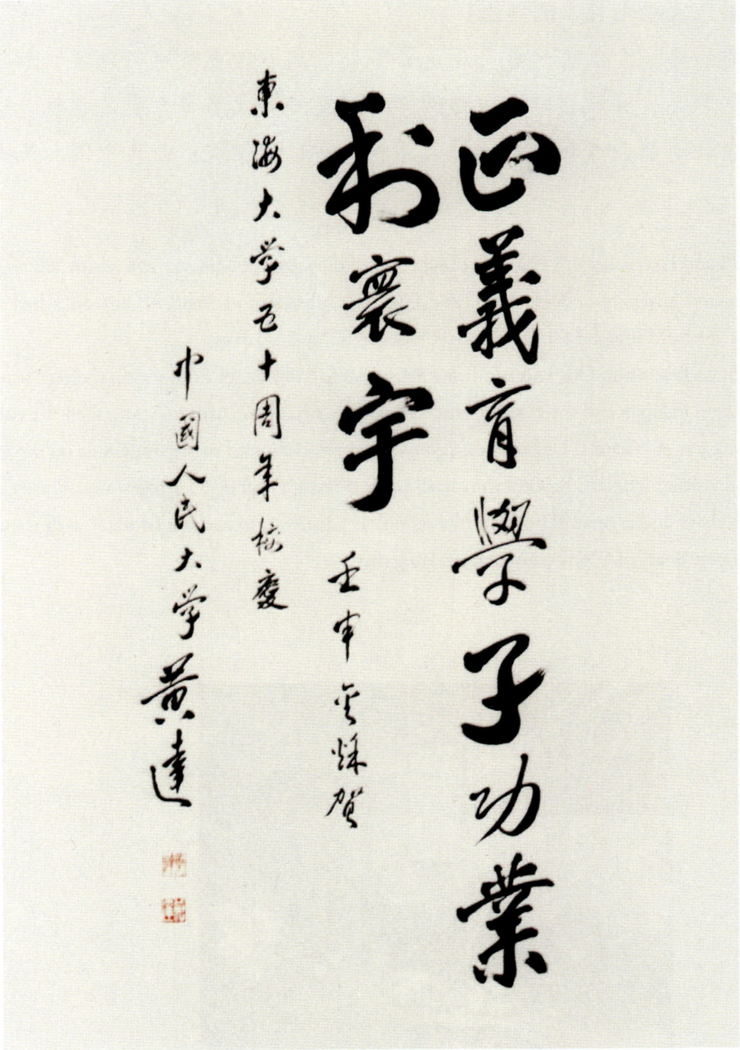

292

图 292 为 1992 年，黄达为当年东海大学开学典礼题写并委托出席典礼的时任中国人民大学副校长杜厚文带去的一帧竖挑：“正义育学子，功业利寰宇”。其中，“正义”和“功业”是该校校训中的关键词。

In 1992, Huang Da inscribed "To Educate the Students with Righteousness, To Benefit the World with Exploits" for Tokai University at its opening ceremony. "Righteousness" and "exploits" are key words in the school motto of the university.

5-8-2>

1990 年 11 月 25 日—12 月 4 日，应日本文部省的邀请，黄达与大连理工大学校长金同稷和四川大学校长林理彬组成中国大学校长访日团，对日本进行了为期十天的访问。这也是黄达第三次踏上日本的国土。

按照国家教委的要求，本次访日主要是考察日本高等教育及科研现状，加强与日本国立大学协会的联系，并就留学生、访问学者的交流事宜与日方交流意见。除了规定日程，黄达此行还有机会顺访日本一桥大学和一所日中学院，并与中国人民大学的留学生进行交流。

During November 25 and December 4, 1990, at the invitation of the Japanese Ministry of Culture, Huang Da, Jin Tongji, president of Dalian University of Technology, and Lin Libin, president of Sichuan University, had a 10-day visit to Japan. It was also the third time for Huang Da to set foot on the land of Japan.

As required by the State Education Commission (now the Chinese Ministry of Education), the visit was mainly to observe higher education in Japan and the status quo of scientific researches in Japan; to strengthen the association with the Japanese Association of National Universities; and to exchange ideas with the Japanese side on the exchange of overseas students and visiting scholars. Beyond the set schedule, Huang Da and the delegation had the chance to visit Hitotsubashi University and a Japan-China middle school in passing; and exchanged ideas with the overseas students of the Renmin University of China who were studying there.

293

图 293 为 1990 年 11 月 27 日，中国大学校长代表团访问日本早稻田大学。左一为黄达。

On November 27, 1990, the delegation of Chinese university presidents visited Waseda University. The first from the left is Huang Da.

294

296

295

297

图 294 为 1990 年 11 月 29 日，中国大学校长代表团访问日本一桥大学。右三为黄达。

On November 29, 1990, the delegation of Chinese university presidents visited Hitotsubashi University. The third from the right is Huang Da.

图 295 为 1990 年 12 月 1 日，中国大学校长代表团参观京都岚山周总理诗碑。从左至右分别为：金同稷、黄达、林理彬。

On December 1, 1990, the delegation of Chinese university presidents visited the stone tables inscribed with the poems of Premier Zhou Enlai in Kyoto. From the left to the right are Jin Tongji, Huang Da and Lin Libin.

图 296 为 1990 年 11 月底，黄达应邀为日本东京大学题字。

At the end of November 1990, Huang Da inscribed for Tokyo University of Japan during a visit to it.

图 297 为 1990 年 12 月 3 日，黄达（右二）在访问一所日中学院期间，与该校师生交流。右一为该校校长。

On December 3, 1990, Huang Da (second from the right) exchanged ideas with the teachers and students of a Japanese-China school. The first from the right is the president of the school.

5-8-3>

1992年6月29日—7月5日，应日本前首相竹下登和众议员原田宪的邀请，黄达第四次赴日，陪同刚刚离任的中国人民大学老校长袁宝华进行了为期六天的访问。

本次访日让黄达有机会接触到日本执政党的高层，以及从事民间交流的知名人士。最让黄达印象深刻的是几位当时被称为自民党“新生代”的大臣。他们年轻有为、敢想敢干，极富创造力和进取心。在日后的报告中，袁宝华校长也提到：“在这次访问中，接触到的日本政府大臣（部长）年龄都在45~55岁之间，年富力强，精力充沛。对比之下，我们的部长级干部年龄偏高，还需进一步年轻化。”

During June 29 and July 5, 1992, at the invitation of former Japanese Premier Noboru Takeshita and member of the House of Representatives Ken Harada, Huang Da went to Japan for the fourth time, and had a 6-day visit to Japan accompanying Yuan Baohua, former president of the Renmin University of China who had just retired.

The visit gave Huang Da an opportunity to contact the senior leadership of the ruling party in Japan and well-known figures engaging in nongovernmental exchanges. The most impressive figures to Huang Da were the "new generation " ministers of the Japanese Liberal Democratic Party. They were young and promising, highly creative and enterprising, and dared to think and act. In the report later, president Yuan Baohua also mentioned, "In the visit, the Japanese government ministers we met are all between 45 and 55 years old. They are young and promising and energetic. By contrast, the ministerial cadres of China are older and younger staff has to be promoted. "

298

图298为1992年6月30日，中方代表团访问日本贸促会。左三为黄达，左四为袁宝华。

On June 30, 1992, the Chinese delegation visited Japan Society for the Promotion of Trade. The third from the left is Huang Da; and the fourth from the left is Yuan Baohua.

299

图 299 为 1992 年 6 月 30 日，中方代表团访问日本自民党总部。从左至右分别为：黄达、袁宝华、原田宪、竹下登。

On June 30, 1992, the Chinese delegation visited the headquarters of the Japanese Liberal Democratic Party. From the left to the right are Huang Da, Yuan Baohua, Ken Harada and Noboru Takeshita.

300

302

301

303

图 300 为 1992 年 7 月 1 日，竹下登宴请中方代表团成员。从左至右分别为：原田宪、袁宝华、竹下登、黄达。

On July 1, 1992, Noboru Takeshita entertained members of the Chinese delegation. From the left to the right are Ken Harada, Yuan Baohua, Noboru Takeshita and Huang Da.

图 301 为 1992 年 7 月 3 日，袁宝华（左二）、黄达（左一）等参观出云大社。

On July 3, 1992, Yuan Baohua (second from the left), Huang Da (first from the left) et al. visited Izumo Taisha.

图 302 为 1992 年 7 月 1 日，中方代表团拜访日本文部大臣。右一为黄达，左二为袁宝华。

On July 1, 1992, the Chinese delegation visited the Japanese Minister of Education. The first from the right is Huang Da; and the second from the left is Yuan Baohua.

图 303 为 1992 年 7 月 3 日，中方代表团访问竹下登老家岛根县饭石郡。左二为黄达，左三为袁宝华。

On July 3, 1992, the Chinese delegation visited the hometown of Noboru Takeshita. The second from the left is Huang Da; and the third from the left is Yuan Baohua.

304

图 304 为 1994 年底，竹下登（右三）回访中国期间，中国人民大学授予其荣誉博士学位。右二为黄达。右四、右六分别为袁宝华、李文海。

At the end of 1994, during his visit to China, Noboru Takeshita (third from the right) was presented the honorary Ph.D. degree by the Renmin University of China. The second from the right is Huang Da. The fourth and sixth from the right are Yuan Baohua and Li Wenhai respectively.

5-8-4>

1993 年 12 月 7—8 日，黄达应日本立命馆大学的邀请，第五次来到日本，与韩国延世大学、菲律宾国立大学、美国夏威夷大学和越南河内工科大学等学校的校长一起出席该校组织的“亚太大学校长论坛”。

之所以接受邀请并经国家教委和外交部审批参与这次论坛，一来因为会议主题为“非战”；二来因为会议邀请函明确把日本在第二次世界大战期间发动的战争定义为“侵略战争”。

在论坛上，黄达并未宣读印发的文稿，而是即席发言。他肯定笃信崇高社会理想，反对侵略战争的主流。同时指出，凭借强权按自己的意志安排全球生活的图谋仍有顽强的表现。

During December 7 and 8, 1993, at the invitation of Ritsumeikan University, Huang Da went to Japan for the fifth time to attend "Asia-Pacific University Presidents Forum " held by the university together with the presidents of Yonsei University, University of the Philippines , University of Hawaii and Vietnam University of Technology, Hanoi.

Huang Da accepted the invitation and was approved by the State Education Commission and the Chinese Ministry of Foreign Affairs because the topic of the forum was "noncombat; " and the letter of invitation to the forum clearly defined the war launched by Japan during WWII as "invasive. "

At the forum, Huang Da did not read the printed subscript, but delivered an impromptu speech. He spoke positively of the mainstream that believed in lofty social ideals and was against invasions. He also pointed out that the plot to arrange global life with power and willingly still existed and was stubborn.

右页图 ⟶

图 305 为 1993 年 12 月 8 日，在日本立命馆大学举办的非正式告别晚宴上，宾主围绕“非战”主题频频发言。黄达（左三）在发言中具体地讲述了他对 50 年前的回忆，并最后落脚在战争不仅是被侵略国国民的灾难，而且对侵略国的国民也是灾难的道理上。宾主皆为之动容。

On December 8, 1993, at the unofficial farewell party held in Ritsumeikan University, the host and the guests expressed their opinions on noncombat topics during the party. Huang Da (third from the left) told his memory 50 years ago, and concluded by saying that war was not only a disaster for the people of the invaded country, but also for those of the invading country. The host and the guests were all touched.

305

5-8-5>

1996 年 10 月 19—24 日，黄达以中国金融学会会长的身份第六次访问日本。一起出访的有东北财经大学校长夏德仁和中国金融学会副秘书长秦池江。

本次访问是黄达应邀出席日本金融学会的秋季大会。按惯例，日本金融学会秋季大会邀请的“特邀代表”均为西方知名学者。此次“破例”邀请中国学者，源自该会副会长清水教授考虑到中国金融问题成为世界性热点的事实。此外，中国人民大学的老朋友、专门讲授《资本论》的日本知名资深教授深町郁弥教授起到了重要作用。

日本金融学会每年有春秋两次大会。春季大会多在东京举办，秋季大会则轮流由日本各地大学承办。本次秋季大会由九州的熊本学园大学承办。大会上，黄达提交了《中国金融改革的回顾与前瞻》一文。同时，由于日本金融学会还希望讲讲中国经济改革的一般情况，所以黄达又准备了《当前中国的经济改革与金融改革》一文。两篇文章均由旅日学人蔡剑波教授译为日文并登载在日本学术期刊上。

During October 19 and 24, 1996, Huang Da, as president of China Society for Finance and Banking, visited Japan for the sixth time. Along with Huang Da were Xia Deren, president of Dongbei University of Finance and Economics, and Qin Chijiang, deputy secretary-general of China Society for Finance and Banking.

Huang Da was to attend the autumn meeting of Japan Society of Monetary Economics at invitation. As usual, the "representatives by special invitation" to the autumn meeting of Japan Society of Monetary Economics were all well-known scholars from the West. That time, given that the issue of China's finance became a hotspot worldwide, professor Shimizu, deputy president of Japan Society of Monetary Economics, expressed the intention to invite Chinese scholars. On the same issue, well-known professor Fukamachi Ikuya, who was specialized in teaching *On Capital*, played a significant role.

Japan Society of Monetary Economics held two meetings each year, the spring meeting and the autumn meeting. The spring meeting was often held in Tokyo, while the autumn meeting was held by the universities around Japan in succession. This year's autumn meeting was sponsored by Kumamoto Gakuen University. Huang Da submitted the article Retrospect and Prospect of China's Financial Reform. Besides, due to the request of Japan Society of Monetary Economics for Huang Da to talk about the general situation of China's economic reform, Huang Da prepared another article The Current Economic and Financial Reform in China. The two articles are both translated into Japanese by Prof. Cai Jianbo who was a visiting scholar to Japan and published on the Japanese academic journal.

306

图 306 为 1985 年夏，本次访日前，黄达（左五）以中国人民大学副校长的身份，在北京接待日本专门讲授《资本论》的知名资深教授深町郁弥（右三）。深町郁弥原是公立九州大学经济学部学部长。退休后，转到私立的熊本学园大学任教。自 1985 年开始，他多次访问中国，1996 年 2 月被中国人民大学经济学院聘为客座教授，为推动中国人民大学与九州大学的合作交流起到了积极作用。

In the summer of 1985, before his visit to Japan, Huang Da (fifth from the left), as vice president of the Renmin University of China, received well-known Japanese professor Fukamachi Ikuya (third from the right), who specifically taught *On Capital*, in Beijing.

Fukamachi Ikuya used to be the dean of the School of Economics of Kyushu University. He taught in Kumamoto Gakuen University after retirement. Since 1985, he visited China many times, and in February 1996, he was hired by the Renmin University of China to be a visiting professor, playing an active role in advancing the cooperation and exchange of the Renmin University of China and Kyushu University.

图 307 为 1996 年 10 月 19 日，黄达一行参加日本金融学会组织的“恳亲会”（自助餐形式的会员聚会）。从左至右分别为：秦池江、黄达、坂本正、夏德仁、蔡剑波。坂本正教授是日本金融学会的负责人之一，具体组织本次秋季大会。

On October 19, 1996, Huang Da and his delegation attended a member get-together in the form of cafeteria. From the left to the right are Qin Chijiang, Huang Da, Professor Sakamoto, Xia Deren and Cai Jianbo. Professor Sakamoto was one of the persons in charge of Japan Society of Monetary Economics and was in charge of organizing this autumn meeting.

307

图 308 为 1996 年 10 月 20 日，黄达在 1996 年度日本金融学会秋季大会上作“特别讲演”。

“特别讲演”是日本金融学会的一项惯例——在每年的秋季大会上邀请一位世界知名的经济学者到会演说。

On October 20, 1996, Huang Da delivered a "Keynote Speech" at the autumn meeting held by Japan Society of Monetary Economics in 1996.

"Keynote Speech" is a routine of Japan Society of Monetary Economics, that is, Japan Society of Monetary Economics invites a world-renowned eonomist to deliver a speech at its autumn meeting each year.

308

309

图 309 为 1996 年 10 月 24 日，黄达在福冈参观游览。

On October 24, 1996, Huang Da visited and travelled in Fukuoka.

310

图 310 为 1996 年 10 月 23 日，黄达一行赴福冈出席由西日本银行国际财团、西日本金融制度研究会、西日本银行株式会社联合举办的“中国金融・经济讲演会”。左三为黄达。

On October 23, 1996, Huang Da and his delegation went to Fukuoka to attend "China Finance-Economy Lecture" that was jointly held by the consortium of Nishi-Nippon City Bank Ltd., the Nishi-Nippon Financial System Council and the Nishi-Nippon City Bank Ltd. The third from the left is Huang Da.

311

图 311 为 1998 年 4 月 16 日，本次访问结束的两年之后，黄达（主席台右一）以中国金融学会会长身份与日本金融学会会长三木谷良一（主席台左一）在北京正式签订学术交流协议。后排左五和左六分别为坂本正、深町郁弥。

On April 16, 1998, two years after the visit, Huang Da (first from the right on the rostrum), as president of China Society for Finance and Banking, officially signed an academic exchange agreement with Ryoichi Mikitani (first from the left on the rostrum), president of Japan Society of Monetary Economics in Beijing. The fifth and the sixth from the left in the back row are Sakamoto and Fukamachi Ikuya.

5-8-6>

1998 年 5 月 26—31 日，黄达应日本三井物产贸易经济研究所所长弘中喜捷的邀请访日，并在该所作题为《在亚洲金融危机中的中国》的讲演。随后顺访熊本学园大学。本次访问是黄达第七次也是最后一次踏上日本的国土。会后，他的演讲稿由三井物产贸易经济研究所译为日文并以《中国に金融危机は起こるが》为题登载在该所《调查研究月报·THE COMPASS》（1998 年第 6 期）上。

During May 26 and 31, 1998, at the invitation of Hironaka, head of Mitsui Trade Economics Institute (now known as Mitsui Global Strategic Studies Institute), Huang Da visited Japan and delivered a speech titled China in the Asian Financial Crisis. Later, he visited Kumamoto Gakuen University in passing. It was the seventh time that Huang Da ever set foot on the land of Japan. After the meeting, the speech made by Huang Da was translated by Mitsui Trade Economics Institute and published in Chugoku Keizai Kenkyu Jippo ·THE COMPASS (Issue 6, 1998) under the title of 中国に金融危机は起こるが.

312

图 312 为 1998 年 2 月 16 日，本次访问日本前，黄达（右一）在中国人民大学接待来访的日本三井物产贸易经济研究所所长弘中喜捷（居中）和曾在该所任职多年的中国访问学者、中国社会科学院沈才彬（左一）。

On February 16, 1998, before the visit to Japan, Huang Da (first from the right) received Hironaka (in the middle), head of Mitsui Trade Economics Institute, and Shen Caibin (first from the left), a Chinese visiting professor who had been working for the institute for years and was from the Chinese Academy of Social Sciences, in the Renmin University of China.

313

图313为1998年5月29日，黄达（右三）与日本熊本学园大学师生进行座谈。

On May 29, 1998, Huang Da (third from the right) had an informal discussion with the students and teachers of Kumamoto Gakuen University.

5-9

南美之行
The Travel to South America

1985 年 10—11 月，受中共中央对外联络部的委托，黄达率领中国国际交流协会经济学家代表团访问古巴并顺访苏里南。

从 20 世纪 60 年代起，在中苏关系紧张的背景下，中古两党“绝交”，关系十分冷淡。到 80 年代中期，两国之间仅维持着国家关系——彼此大使馆维持最低限度的活动。古方实际视中国的改革开放路线为背叛性质的修正主义。当时，不止中国，包括苏联在内的苏东各国均处于“改革”的进程之中，而古巴尽管也讲“改革”，但实际上是极少数坚持最正统的苏联模式的社会主义国家之一。在 1985 年左右，古巴派了一个经济学家代表团到中国访问。当时中国已经走出“文化大革命”时生活用品匮乏的局面，而古巴依然存在典型的物资短缺，对比鲜明。中联部组建中国经济学家访古，属对应性的回访。

黄达一行是当年仅有的两个中国访古代表团的其中之一，访问从 10 月 4 日抵达到 22 日离开，共 19 天。期间，古巴规划的接待日程是沿着卡斯特罗起义的路线参观访问，对中国代表团进行革命的传统教育；以及阐明古巴对于坚持社会主义传统路线的坚定立场和独立于任何指挥棒的态度。之后，代表团取道圭亚那，来到苏里南进行访问。此次南美之行，让黄达较为深入地了解到该地区的独特历史、风土人情和政治经济文化等，极大地开阔了思路和视野，“总的来说，受益终身”。

314

315

图 314 为 1986 年 10 月 3 日，黄达在墨西哥金字塔前。

当时去古巴先要取道美国。但美国封锁古巴，无直达哈瓦那的飞机，还要取道墨西哥。墨西哥城具备一个较早起步的发展中国家的特征，比如有超市、汽车以及整洁的马路等等，整体发展水平远超当时的中国。

On October 3, 1986, Huang Da was in front of a pyramid in Mexico.

One had to go to Cuba by way of America at the time, but America sealed Cuba off, so no flight flew directly to Havana. One had to go to Cuba by way of Mexico. Mexico had the features of a developing country that developed earlier. It had supermarkets, cars and clean roads, etc., and its overall development level was far higher than China in the same period.

图 315 为 1986 年 10 月 5 日，黄达（右二）参观古巴哈瓦那古城堡。

On October 5, 1986, Huang Da (second from the right) visited an ancient castle in Havana.

In October and November, 1985, commissioned by the International Department of the Central Committee of the Communist Party of China, Huang Da led the delegation of economists of China Association for International Understanding to visit Cuba, and then Suriname in passing.

Since the 1960s, against the background of tension between China and the Soviet Union, the Communist Party of China and the Communist Party of Cuba "split up, " and mutual relations were deep in freeze. In the mid 1980s, China and Cuba maintained mutual relations only, and their embassies maintained minimum diplomatic interaction. China's reform and opening up was seen as revisionism, betrayal to its belief. At the time, not only China, but the Soviet Union, the Eastern Europe countries were all in the process of "reforms. " Although Cuba had "reforms, " it was one of the few "socialist " countries sticking to the most proper Soviet model. In about 1985, Cuba designated a delegation of representative economists to visit China. China had got rid of the extreme shortage of daily supplies during the era of the Cultural Revolution, while Cuba was still stuck in a typical shortage of materials, forming a sharp contrast to China. That the International Department of the Central Committee of the Communist Party of China set a delegation of Chinese economists to visit Cuba was a return visit.

Huang Da and his delegation was one of the two Chinese delegations to visit Cuba that year. They reached Cuba on October 4 and left on October 22. During those 19 days, Cuba received them and led them to visit along the route of uprising by Castro, and gave the Chinese delegation traditional revolutionary education; and clearly explained Cuba's firm stance toward sticking to the traditional socialist route and its attitude of keeping independent of any baton. Later, the delegation took way of Guyana, and visited Suriname. The travel to South America enabled Huang Da to understand the local unique history, customs, politics, economy and culture more profoundly; and greatly broadened his horizons. In his words, he was "benefited for life in general. "

316

图 316 为 1986 年 10 月 10 日，黄达（左三）参观菲德尔·卡斯特罗在 1953 年举行起义的蒙卡达兵营。

蒙卡达兵营是由西班牙殖民者在 1859 年建设的，1874 年参与领导古巴独立战争的吉列尔莫·蒙卡达曾被关押于此。古巴独立后，政府决定以蒙卡达命名此兵营以示对他的纪念。1953 年 7 月 26 日，由菲德尔·卡斯特罗带领的 120 名革命分子向蒙卡达兵营发动进攻，以期推翻巴蒂斯塔政权，但最后失败。1967 年，原兵营的一部分被改建成了纪念馆。

On October 10, 1986, Huang Da (third from the left) visited Moncada Barracks where Fidel Castro rose up in 1953.

Moncada Barracks was built in 1859 by the Spanish colonists. Guillermo Moncada, who played a part in leading the Cuban war of independence in 1874, was imprisoned here. After Cuba became independent, the government decided to name the barracks after Moncada to commemorate him. On July 26, 1953, 120 revolutionists led by Fidel Castro attacked Moncada Barracks to overthrow the Batista regime, only to fail. In 1967, part of the original barracks was rebuilt into a memorial hall.

317

图 317 为 1986 年 10 月 15 日，黄达（后排右一）参观古巴奥尔金幼儿园。

On October 15, 1986, Huang Da (first from the right in the back row) visited Holguín Kindergarten in Cuba.

318

图 318 为 1986 年 10 月 23 日，黄达在圭亚那出海口岸。

On October 23, 1986, Huang Da was in a seaport in Guyana.

319

图 319 为 1986 年 10 月 27 日，黄达与援建苏里南首都帕拉马里博体育场的中国工人在一起。这是当年中国援建苏里南的两个项目之一。黄达专程前往探望，援建工人见到家乡同胞非常高兴。

On October 27, 1986, Huang Da was with the Chinese workers who were in Suriname helping Suriname build Paramaribo Stadium. It was one of the two projects launched by China to help build Suriname. Huang Da made a special trip there, and the Chinese workers were all very happy seeing a compatriot.

320

图 320 为 1986 年 10 月 27 日，苏里南总统（左一）会见黄达（右二）一行。左三为中国驻苏里南大使。

On October 27, 1986, Suriname President (first from the left) met Huang Da (second from the right) and his delegation. On the right side of Huang Da is the Chinese ambassador to Suriname.

321

图 321 为 1986 年 10 月 27 日，苏里南总理(左二)会见黄达(右一)一行。

On October 27, 1986, Suriname Premier (second from the left) met Huang Da (first from the right) and his delegation.

图 322 为 1986 年 10 月 28 日，黄达(左二)在苏里南举行的和平周记者招待会上作和平问题报告。

报告中，他大概表达了“凡有助于和平与稳定的事情中国都支持，凡属霸权主义的行径，不论来自何方，以何种形式出现，我们都反对；中国决不依附于任何一个超级大国，也不同任何一方结盟，愿在和平共处五项原则的基础上同世界各国发展友好关系；中国坚决站在第三世界国家一边，伸张正义”等观点。

On October 28, 1986, Huang Da (second from the left) made a report on the issue of peace at Week for Peace Press Conference which was held in Suriname.

He expressed the following viewpoints — "China supports everything good for peace and stability, and objects all hegemonistic acts, no matter who has them or in what form they appear; China will never cling to any superpower, or form an alliance with any side, but it is willing to develop friendship with world countries on the basis of the five principles of peaceful coexistence. China is firmly with the Third World countries, and upholds righteousness."

322

5-10

加拿大之行
The Travel to Canada

1993 年 11 月 4—16 日，黄达等八所中国高校校长（包括两位代理校长）组成的代表团赴加拿大出席“第二届中加大学校长会议”，代表团团长由南开大学校长毋国光担任。后由于中途毋国光离团，团长由黄达代理。

20 世纪 80 年代初，加拿大政府出资设立了中国和加拿大双方大学之间的合作交流项目（简称 CIDA 项目）。中国人民大学与国外大学之间常规的、成规模的交流也始于该项目。1988 年曾经举行过第一届中加大学校长会议。当时，中加双方曾商定要间隔一两年举行第二届会议。后由于 1989 年政治风波的影响，直到 1993 年才重启中加双方校长会议。

大会上，受代表团委派，黄达作为中方代表之一以“校园国际化”为题发言。

在发言之前，照例要有几句承前启后的话。由于加方的发言都说下次开会不要像第二届距离第一届这么久，接着这个话头，黄达讲：“我的英语没有学好，但倒是从小学就开始学的。现在还记得几句：‘Long long ago, there was a king’，‘Many years upon, there was a queen’。希望下次会议的主持人，在开场白中不会讲‘Long long ago, there was a conference ...’”这给与会者留下了深刻印象。

而后于世纪之交，黄达再次碰到当年赴加代表团成员、兰州大学校长李发伸，他端详了黄达一会儿说，“你是 Long long ago 吧？”据李发伸讲，在时隔多年后的第三届中加大学校长会议上，他作为中方代表团团长还在致辞中专门讲到了“Long long ago”的故事。

值得一提的是，黄达发言的英译稿，由于经过曾游学加拿大的徐二明教授以及当时中国人民大学的加拿大学者和留学生反复推敲、润色，颇受与会专家好评。

During November 4 and 16, 1993, a delegation that was made up of eight Chinese university presidents (including two acting presidents), including Huang Da, attended the "Second China-Canada University Presidents Conference " in Canada. Wu Guoguang, president of Nankai University, was the head of the delegation. Wu Guoguang left the delegation halfway, so Huang Da acted as the head of the delegation.

In the early 1980s, the Canadian government initiated an exchange program between Chinese and Canadian universities (shortened as the CIDA program). The large scale of regular exchanges between the Renmin University of China and foreign universities originated from this program. The first China-Canada University Presidents Conference was held in 1988. At the time, China and Canada decided through consultation to hold the second conference one or two years later. But due to the 1989 political incident in China, the China-Canada University Presidents Conference was not resumed till 1993.

The delegation designated Huang Da to be one of the Chinese addressers to address the conference with the topic of "campus internationalization. "

Before the speech, there should be transitional words. Since the Canadian addressers all said that they expected the third conference to be held soon, Huang Da said, "I don't learn English well, but I have been learning it since I was in primary school. I still remember some English, like 'Long long ago, there was a king, 'Many years upon, there was a queen.' I hope that the host of the next conference will not say 'Long long ago, there was a conference...' " It left a deep impression on the attendees.

At the turn of the centuries, Huang Da met Li Fashen, a member of the delegation to Canada that year and the president of Lanzhou University. He watched Huang Da for a while, and asked, "Are you the 'Long long ago'? " According to Li Fashen, he told the story of "Long long ago " at the third China-Canada University Presidents Conference years later as the head of the Chinese delegation.

The English translation of Huang Da's speech, after being weighed and polished by professor Xu Erming who once studied in Canada, the Canadian scholars and students in the Renmin University of China then, was spoken highly of.

323

图 323 为 1993 年 11 月 5 日，在卡尔加里大学出席“第二届中加大学校长会议”的中外大学校长在一起。右一为南开大学校长毋国光、右二为黄达。

On November 5, 1993, the Chinese and foreign university presidents attending the "Second China-Canada University Presidents Conference" in Calgary University were together. The first from the right is Wu Guoguang, president of Nankai University; and the second from the right is Huang Da.

图 324 为 1993 年 11 月 5 日，黄达（右一）与出席“第二届中加大学校长会议”的加方大学校长互换名片。

On November 5, 1993, Huang Da (first from the right) exchanged name cards with the presidents of Canadian universities attending the "Second China-Canada University Presidents Conference."

324

325

图 325 为 1993 年 11 月 5 日，中方代表团参观卡尔加里大学。左七为黄达。

On November 5, 1993, the Chinese delegation visited Calgary University. The seventh from the left is Huang Da.

326

图326为1993年11月7日，“第二届中加大学校长会议”期间，黄达参观当地景点。

On November 7, 1993, during the "Second China-Canada University Presidents Conference," Huang Da visited local scenery spots.

327

图 327 为 1993 年 11 月 10 日，中方代表团访问多伦多大学。前排右一为黄达，左三为北京师范大学方福康，左四为毋国光。后排右四为兰州大学校长李发伸。

On November 10, 1993, the Chinese delegation visited Toronto University. The first from the right in the front row is Huang Da; the third from the left is Fang Fukang from Beijing Normal University; the fourth from the left is Wu Guoguang. The fourth from the right in the back row is Li Fashen, the then president of Lanzhou University.

5-11

澳大利亚 & 香港特区之行
The Travel to Australia and Hong Kong SAR

1994 年 4 月 2—14 日，黄达最后一次以中国人民大学校长的身份出境访问，先后到访澳大利亚和香港特区。

本次访问由两方面的积极努力促成。一是当时在澳大利亚国立大学已接近完成攻读博士学位并确定留在该校任教的宋立刚教授的推动。他是中国人民大学教师，也是“福特项目”中方委员会第一任秘书长。二是澳大利亚国立大学的 Ross Garnaut 和 Peter Drysdale 两位知名教授的推动。Ross Garnaut 曾在 20 世纪 80 年代中期担任澳大利亚驻华大使。王传纶教授曾邀黄达共同接待过他，讨论人民币的开放和汇率问题。90 年代初期，福特基金会聘请他评估“福特项目”，与黄达再次有进一步的交往。本次访问就是他以澳大利亚国立大学经济系主任的身份邀请。而 Peter Drysdale 则是澳大利亚国立大学澳日研究中心负责人，在此之前也与黄达有过多次交往。

本次澳大利亚之行途经墨尔本、堪培拉、悉尼，先后访问了墨尔本大学、澳大利亚国立大学以及外交贸易部、财政部和澳大利亚储备银行等澳大利亚政府和准政府的经济部门。在此期间，黄达与澳大利亚高校深入探讨加强与中国人民大学交流的可行途径，并解决了一些具体问题。同时对澳大利亚的经济社会发展有了较为深入的了解。

而后，借返程途经香港的机会，黄达还访问了香港树仁学院（现已更名为香港树仁大学）、香港城市理工学院（现已更名为香港城市大学）和香港中文大学等院校并看望香港校友。

| 右页图 |⟶

图 328 为 1994 年 4 月 5 日，黄达（左二）与墨尔本大学校长（右一）进行会谈。

On April 5, 1994, Huang Da (second from the left) talked with the president of Melbourne University (first from the right).

During April 2 and 14, 1994, Huang Da visited Australia, and then visited Hong Kong SAR in passing as the president of the Renmin University of China.

They had the visit thanks to the efforts of both sides—Professor Song Ligang, a teacher of the Renmin University of China and the first secretary-general of the Chinese Committee of the Ford Program, who was to complete his Ph.D. program in Australian National University and had decided to stay and become a teacher of the university; renowned professors Ross Garnaut and Peter Drysdale from Australian National University. Ross Garnaut used to be the Australian ambassador to China in the mid 1980s. Professor Wang Chuanlun invited Huang Da to receive him together and talked with him about opening RMB business to foreign banks and the exchange rate. In the early 1990s, the Ford Foundation appointed him to evaluate the Ford Program, and he furthered contacts with Huang Da. Ross Garnaut was the one to invite Huang Da and the delegation to visit Australian National University as the head of its Economics Department. Peter Drysdale was the head of Australia-Japan Research Center at Australian National University, who had many exchanges with Huang Da.

During the trip to Australia, Huang Da and the delegation stopped in Melbourne, Canberra and Sydney, and visited the Melbourne University, the Austrian Department of Foreign Affairs and Trade, the Australian Department of Finance and the Reserve Bank of Australia, among other economic departments of the Australian government. Huang Da held profound discussions with the Australian universities on feasible ways of strengthening exchanges with the Renmin University of China, and solved some specific problems. Meanwhile, he had deep understanding of the economic and social development of Australia.

Taking the chance of stopping in Hong Kong, Huang Da visited Hong Kong Shue Yan College (now known as Hong Kong Shue Yan University), City Polytechnic of Hong Kong (City University of Hong Kong) and the Chinese University of Hong Kong to some alumna in Hong Kong.

328

329

330

图 329 为 1994 年 4 月 6 日，黄达（右一）与澳大利亚国立大学校长（左一）互赠礼物。

On April 6, 1994, Huang Da (first from the right) and the president of Australian National University (first from the left) exchanged gifts.

图 330 为 1994 年 4 月 6 日，黄达（左二）与澳大利亚国立大学 Ross Garnaut 教授（右一）、Peter Drysdale 教授（左一）在一起。

On April 6, 1994, Huang Da (second from the left) was with two professors of Australian National University, namely Ross Garnaut (first from the right) and Peter Drysdale (first from the left).

331

图 331 为 1994 年 4 月 7 日，黄达（最后排右二）参观澳大利亚国立大学中国中心，与中外学生在一起。

On April 7, 1994, Huang Da (second from the right in the back row) visited China Center of Australian National University, and was with some Chinese and foreign students.

图 332 为 1994 年 4 月 8 日，黄达参观堪培拉当地景点。

On April 8, 1994, Huang Da visited places of interests in Canberra.

332

333

图 333 为 1994 年 4 月 10 日，黄达在悉尼歌剧院前。

On April 10, 1994, Huang Da was in front of the Sydney Opera House.

334

图 334 为 1994 年 4 月 10 日，黄达（左一）与宋立刚（右一）在悉尼。

On April 10, 1994, Huang Da (first from the left) and Song Ligang (first from the right) were in Sydney.

图 335 为 1994 年 4 月 13 日，黄达（右一）访问香港树仁学院。与该院领导大律师胡鸿列（左一）和钟期荣（左二）合影。

On April 13, 1994, Huang Da (first from the right) visited Hong Kong Shue Yan College. Group photo with the barrister Hu Honglie (first from the left) and Zhong Qirong (second from the left).

335

图 336 为 1994 年 4 月 14 日，黄达（左二）访问香港城市理工学院，与该校校长郑耀宗（左三）等在一起。

On April 14, 1994, Huang Da (second from the left) visited City University of Hong Kong and was with its president Zheng Yaozong (third from the left), et al.

336

5-12

始终积极参与学术活动
Teaching and Scientific Researches

5-12-1 >

1990年7月15—21日，全国高校物价教学研究会第九次年会在北京市密云县召开，来自全国50多所高校的近90名教授、副教授和青年教师参加了会议。中国社会科学院副院长刘国光、国家物价局局长成致平、中国人民大学副校长黄达、北京商学院院长贺名仑、中国价格学会秘书长王振之到会祝贺并分别作了报告。

During July 15 and 21, 1990, the National Universities Commodity Price Teaching Seminar held its 9th annual meeting in Miyun County, Beijing. Nearly 90 professors, assistant professors and young teachers from over 50 universities around China attended the meeting. Liu Guoguang, vice president of the Chinese Academy of Social Sciences, Cheng Zhiping, head of the State Price Bureau, Huang Da, vice president of the Renmin University of China, He Minglun, president of Beijing College of Commerce, and Wang Zhenzhi, secretary-general of China Society of Price, attended the meeting, expressed their congratulations, and made reports, respectively.

| 右页图 |⟶

图337为1990年7月19日，黄达（左一）在大会上作报告。右一为成致平。

On July 19, 1990, Huang Da (first from the left) made a report at the meeting. The first from the right is Cheng Zhiping.

337

5-12-2>

1990 年 7 月，应国家教委的要求，中国人民大学面向全国分别组织了 1990 年暑期财政学和货币银行学师资讲习班。

黄达在货币银行学师资讲习班上做了《建国以来〈货币银行学〉的足迹》的报告。他系统回顾了新中国成立以来货币银行学的发展历程，并就如何进一步推进货币银行学的建设谈了自己的想法。他特别强调应该编出“中国人，在中国大学的讲台上，为了使中国的学生掌握在中国建设中国特色社会主义的本领而传授货币银行学所需的教材”。

会后，为了较为充分地表达自己对于建设这门学科的想法，黄达在这篇讲稿的基础上加以增补、推演，进而写出《建国以来〈货币银行学〉课程发展的回顾及如何进一步建设》一文，后发表于《中国人民大学学报》1991 年第 1 期，并编入《财经类专业核心课程教学大纲使用参考》（四川人民出版社，1991）。

338

339

图 338 为 1990 年 7 月，中国人民大学 1990 年暑期财政学师资讲习班全体成员在一起。前排左四至左七分别为：袁振宇、陈共、黄达、韩英杰。

In July 1990, all students of the teachers' workshop of Public Finance of the Renmin University of China in the summer vocation of 1990 were together. The fourth to the seventh from the left in the front row are Yuan Zhenyu ,Cheng Gong ,Huang Da and Han Yingjie.

图 339 为 1990 年 7 月，中国人民大学 1990 年暑期货币银行学师资讲习班全体成员合影留念。前排左五至左七分别为：周升业、黄达、韩英杰。

In July 1990, all students of the teachers' workshop of the Economics of Money and Banking of the Renmin University of China in the summer vocation of 1990 were together. The fifth to the seventh from the left in the front row are Zhou Shengye, Huang Da and Han Yingjie.

In July 1990, as required by the State Education Commission, the Renmin University of China organized and opened the workshops of Public Finance and the Economics of Money and Banking during the summer vocation of 1990.

Huang Da made the report of Footprints of the Economics of Money and Banking since new China during the workshop. He made a systematical review of the development of the Economics of Money and Banking since the founding of the People's Republic of China, and expressed his ideas on the ways to advance the construction of the Economics of Money and Banking. Meanwhile, he especially pointed out the necessity to compile "textbooks for the Chinese people to teach the Economics of Money and Banking on the rostrums of Chinese universities to enable the Chinese students to grasp the skills to build socialism with Chinese characteristics in China."

After the workshop, in order to fully express his ideas on building the course, Huang Da added new contents and deductions to the manuscript, and came out with Review of the Development of the Economics of Money and Banking since the Founding of the People's Republic of China and Proposed Ways to Further Build It. The article was later published in the first issue of *Journal of Renmin University of China* in 1991, and was selected into *Reference for Core Courses Syllabi Drafting Seminar* (Sichuan People's Publishing House, 1991).

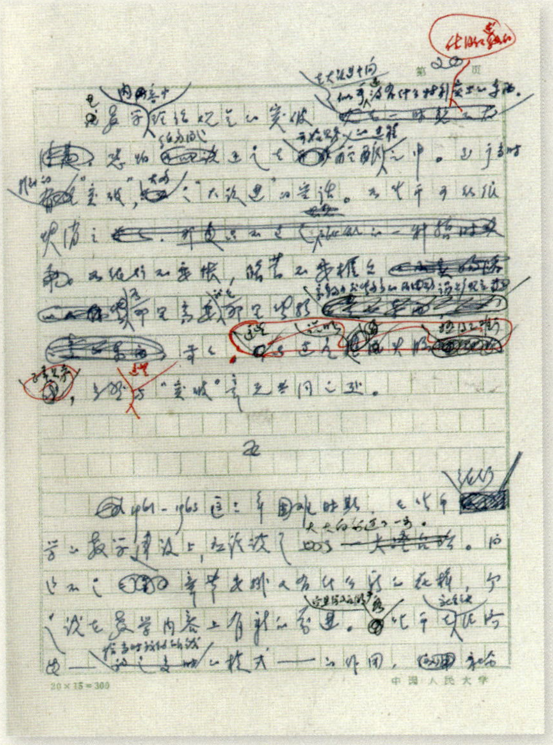

340

图 340 为 1990 年 7 月，《建国以来〈货币银行学〉课程发展的回顾及如何进一步建设》一文的手稿。

This is the manuscript of Review of the Development of the Economics of Money and Banking since the Founding of the People's Republic of China and Proposed Ways to Further Build It in July 1990.

5-12-3>

1990年12月中旬，黄达应邀赴上海参加由中国金融学院组织的理论研讨会，并出席上海证券交易所成立仪式。

In the middle of December 1990, Huang Da participated in the seminar held by China Institute of Finance and Banking in Shanghai and the inauguration of Shanghai Stock Exchange.

341

图341为1990年12月中旬，中国金融学院在上海召开的理论研讨会，黄达（第二排左五）出席会议并于18日参加上海证券交易所挂牌仪式。第一排左二为赵海宽，左五为周正庆，右二至右五分别为杨培新、周道炯、刘光弟和刘鸿儒。

In mid December 1990, China Institute of Finance and Banking held a symposium in Shanghai. Huang Da (the fifth from the left in the second row) attended the symposium and then attended the opening ceremony of Shanghai Stock Exchange on December 18. The second from the left in the first row is Zhao Haikuan; the fifth from the left is Zhou Zhengqing; the second to the fifth from the right are Yang Peixin, Zhou Daojiong, Liu Guangdi and Liu Hongru.

342

图 342 为 1990 年 12 月中旬，黄达（右一）在会议期间与周正庆（左一）交谈。

In mid December 1990, Huang Da (first from the right) was talking with Zhou Zhengqing (first from the left) on the symposium.

5-12-4>

1991 年以来，在经历了 1989 年政治风波引起的短暂压抑之后，各类学术活动开始逐渐多起来。从经济学领域来看，由于“市场经济”的提法还没有被正式承认，大家关注的焦点集中在如何看待商品经济的问题上。尽管当时的气氛并不鼓励市场原则，但以市场化为导向的改革却在持续推进。以物价问题为例，在 1988 年“物价闯关”时未能采取的措施，在此期间却得以逐步实施。可以看出，不管人们主观愿望如何，经济生活本身已成为推动市场化改革的客观力量。

在这样的大背景下，黄达主要思考了两个问题。一是从商品经济本身的要求，从经济改革的整体出发，探讨物价水平变动趋向，也就是后来他概括的“从不完全的价格向接近完全的价格转化的必然性”问题。二是如何认识和运用货币政策的问题。在 1989 年下半年和 1990 年，货币政策的运用相当简单、急躁，以计划经济思路运用市场经济政策工具的特征非常明显，无论是理论界还是实务界对于货币政策的认识均存在明显不足。为此，黄达不仅认真回顾了新中国成立以来学术界在这一问题上的认识演变，而且较为全面地分析了西方有关这方面的理论发展。

在前后一两年的时间里，黄达的几次演讲主要围绕上述问题展开。其中包括 1991 年 6 月 1 日，他在无锡金融学会和高级经济师联谊会上的演讲。演讲稿后经整理为《金融物价政策的一点思考》一文（发表于《江南金融》1991 年第 6 期）。

343

图 343 为 1991 年 5 月 27 日，会议开始前，黄达（居中）与出席本次会议的周骏（左一）和曾康霖（右一）在太湖游船上。

On May 27, 1991, before the sociable started, Huang Da (middle) was on a yacht with Zhou Jun (first from the left) and Zeng Kanglin (first from the right) attending the sociable.

Since 1991, after the temporary depression caused by the 1989 political incident, scholarly activities of different types became active. In the economics sector, the wording of "market economy " was not officially acknowledged, and people focused on how to treat the commodity economy. Although the then atmosphere did not encourage the market-based principles, the marketization-oriented reform kept pushed forward. Take the example of commodity price, the measures that were not taken when "commodity prices crashing through barriers " in 1988 were adopted gradually now. As can be seen, regardless of people's wishes, the economic life in itself had become an objective force that pushed the marketization reform forward.

Against such background, Huang Da mainly thought about two problems: the changing trend of commodity prices according to the requirements of the commodity economy and the overall situation of economic reform, that is, the problem of "the necessity to converse from incomplete prices to nearly complete prices; " and the ways to understand and apply the monetary policy. In the second half of 1989 and 1990, the monetary policy was simple and impatient; had obvious characteristics of applying the tool of the market economic policy with the mindset of the planned economy. The understanding of the monetary policy is significantly insufficient, neither in theory nor in practice. To this end, Huang Da carefully reviewed the course of cognition of the problem by the academic circles since the founding of the People's Republic of China; but also comprehensively analyzed the development of theories in this area in the West.

For one or two years, Huang Da focused on the above problems in his speeches, including the one he gave at the sociable between Wuxi Society for Finance and Banking and senior economists held on June 1, 1991. The manuscript of the speech was later written into Some Thoughts on the Policy on Currency and Commodity Prices and published in issue 6 of *Jiangnan Finance and Banking* in 1991.

344

图 344 为 1991 年 6 月 1 日，出席“无锡金融学会和高级经济师联谊会”的全体与会专家合影留念。前排左四为黄达。

On June 1, 1991, all the attendees of the sociable between Wuxi Society for Finance and Banking and senior economists took a group photo. The fourth from the left in the front row is Huang Da.

5-12-5>

1992 年 8 月 15—23 日，中国金融学会、甘肃金融学会和《金融研究》编辑部在兰州召开“中国货币政策高级研讨会”。

黄达向大会提交了《认真推进宏观分析的理论建设》一文。该文阐述了黄达对于当时财政政策、价格政策和货币政策等问题的认识，并重点讨论了宏观分析的方法论问题。“人们在分析宏观经济问题时，往往用的是微观经济分析方法。孤立地看，很有道理；但放在实际生活中，往往不是那么一回事。在改革开放前就有这样的问题，但关系不大；而当几乎人人谈‘宏观’的时候，不掌握正确的方法，就使许多的讨论劳而无功。但对于这样的矛盾却认识不足。比如，小平同志南方讲话之后，股份制的紧箍咒解除了，论股份制的谈话、文章多了起来。这是好事。在论及股份制的好处时，往往有一条：可以解决资金不足的困扰。大多论据，如用宏观分析的标准衡量，颇失之于就事论事，甚至就是想当然。”

During August 15 and 23, 1992, China Society for Finance and Banking, Gansu Society for Finance and Banking and the editorial office of *Journal of Financial Research* held "Advanced Seminar on China's Monetary Policy " in Lanzhou.

Huang Da submitted paper Push Forward the Development of Theories on Macro Analyses Seriously to the seminar, in which he laid out his understanding of the then financial policy, price policy and monetary policy, and gave priority to discussing the methodology of macro analyses. "People tend to use microeconomic analytical methods to analyze macroeconomic issues. Such analyses seem to be reasonable if seen alone; but are more than often not the case in real life. The problem has been there before the reform and opening up, but it did not matter. When almost all people are talking about 'macro,' in the wrong way, many discussions will go nowhere. However, such contradiction seems to have not been fully realized. For example, after Deng Xiaoping made the remarks during his inspection tour of southern China, the inhibition of the joint stock system was eliminated; and the talks and papers on the joint stock system grew. It is good. Speaking of the advantages of the joint stock system, people usually mention one—it can solve the problem of fund shortage. Most arguments, if measured by the standards on macro analyses, would not be matter-of-fact, but taken for granted."

345

图 345 为 1992 年 8 月 16 日，部分与会专家参观刘家峡水电站。左三至左七分别为：杨希天、刘光弟、马建堂、黄达、赵海宽，右一为张忠山，右三和右四分别为江其务和林继肯。

On August 16, 1992, some attendees were at Liujiaxia Hydroelectric Power Station. The third to the seventh from the left are Yang Xitian, Liu Guangdi, Ma Jiantang, Huang Da and Zhao Haikuan; the first from the right is Zhang Zhongshan; the third and the fourth from the right are Jiang Qiwu and Lin Jiken.

346

图 346 为 1992 年 8 月 17 日，部分与会专家在敦煌参观。左一至左三分别为：刘光弟、林继肯、江其务，右一至右四分别为：杨希天、张忠山、赵海宽和黄达。

On August 17, 1992, some attendees were in Dunhuang. The first to the third from the left are Liu Guangdi, Lin Jiken and Jiang Qiwu. The first to the fourth from the right are Yang Xitian, Zhang Zhongshan, Zhao Haikuan and Huang Da.

5-12-6>

由交通银行、中信实业银行、广东发展银行、深圳发展银行、兴业银行、招商银行、光大银行7家全国性、区域性商业银行联合发起的“社会主义市场经济与商业银行”研讨会，于1993年初在珠海经济特区召开。国务院研究室、国家体改委、中国人民银行、国家外汇管理局的领导以及有关专家学者袁木、刘鸿儒、殷介炎、黄达等应邀参加会议。

会议围绕适应社会主义市场经济需要，积极完善和发展社会主义商业银行这一议题，展开讨论，就如何建立以中央银行为领导，以商业银行为主体，多种金融机构分工协作的金融组织体系，提供了许多富有建设性的意见。

In early 1993, the workshop of "Socialist Market Economy and Commercial Banks " jointly initiated by seven national or regional commercial banks, namely the Bank of Communications, China CITIC Bank, Guangdong Development Bank, Shenzhen Development Bank, Industrial Bank, China Merchants Bank and China Everbright Bank, was held in Zhuhai Special Economic Zone. Leaders of the Research Office of the State Council, the State Commission for Restructuring the Economic System, the People's Bank of China, the State Administration of Foreign Exchange, related experts and scholars Yuan Mu, Liu Hongru, Yin Jieyan and Huang Da attended the workshop on invitation.

Around the topic of adapting to the need of the socialist market economy and actively improving and developing the socialist commercial banks, the attendees had discussions and put forward many instructive suggestions on the ways to build a system of financial organizations where the central bank led; commercial banks were the main body; and multiple financial institutions cooperated based on division of labor.

347

图 347 为 1993 年 1 月 1 日，黄达（前排中间）在“社会主义市场经济与商业银行”研讨会上发言。

On January 1, 1993, Huang Da (middle in the front row) expressed his opinions at the workshop of "Socialist Market Economy and Commercial Banks ".

348

图 348 为 1993 年 1 月 1 日，出席“社会主义市场经济与商业银行”研讨会的全体专家合影留念。前排右三为黄达。

On January 1, 1993, all the attendees of the workshop of "Socialist Market Economy and Commercial Banks" took a group photo. The third from the right in the front row is Huang Da.

5-12-7>

1993 年 7 月 1—3 日，由中国（海南）改革发展研究院、中国留美经济学会和中国经济学会（英国）共同主办的“中国走向市场经济进程中的理论与现实问题国际研讨会”在海口召开。

本次研讨会有以下特点：一是出席会议的代表来自不同的背景及专业领域，大都是在各学科尤其是经济理论、经济改革方面享有盛誉的专家学者。二是这次会议的议题具有相当的深度和难度，涉及的都是中国走向市场经济进程中的紧迫、复杂而又重要的问题。三是这次研讨会气氛热烈，大家畅所欲言，各抒己见，互相争论，大胆发表自己的学术观点，并提出富有建设性的政策建议。

国务委员李铁映向大会作了书面致辞。孙尚清、董辅礽、安志文、高尚全、马凯、童大林、杨启先、周小川、黄达、王珏、萧灼基以及来自中国香港、中国台湾、美国、新加坡等地的著名经济学家，美国福特基金会、美国商会、亚洲开发银行和世界银行的代表，部分中国留英、留美学者等 130 多人出席了会议。

During July 1 and 3, 1993, "International Symposium on the Theoretical and Practical Issues in China's Moving to the Market Economy " was held jointly by China Institute for Reform and Development (CIRD), The Chinese Economists Society and Chinese Economic Association (UK) in Haikou.

The symposium had the following features: First, the representatives attending the symposium were expert scholars with different backgrounds and fields of expertise and highly reputed in economic theories and reforms. Second, the topics of the symposium were in-depth and difficult, and involved the urgent, complicated and important issues in China's moving to the market economy. Third, the symposium was heated; and the attendees were all free and open, expressed their opinions and argued with one another, gave utterance to their views and instructive policy suggestions.

Member of the State Council Li Tieying delivered a written speech. More than 130 people attended the symposium, including Sun Shangqing, Dong Fureng, An Zhiwen, Gao Shangquan, Ma Kai, Tong Dalin, Yang Qixian , Zhou Xiaochuan, Huang Da, Wang Jue and Xiao Zhuoji; famous economists from Hong Kong of China, Taiwan of China, the US and Singapore; representatives of the Ford Foundation, American Chamber of Commerce, Asian Development Bank and World Bank; some Chinese scholars who were studying in the UK or the US.

349

图 349 为 1993 年 7 月 1 日，出席“中国走向市场经济进程中的理论与现实问题国际研讨会”的全体专家合影留念。前排右六为黄达。

On July 1, 1993, all the attendees of the International Symposium on the Theoretical and Practical Issues in China's Moving to the Market Economy took a group photo. The sixth from the right in the front row is Huang Da.

350

图 350 为 1993 年 7 月 1 日，黄达（右一）与于宗先（右二）、高尚全（右三）等与会专家在一起。

On July 1, 1993, Huang Da (first from the right) was with Yu Zongxian (second from the right), Gao Shangquan (third from the right) and other attendees.

351

图 351 为 1993 年 7 月 1 日，黄达（右二）与于宗先（右三）、张维迎（右一）等与会专家在一起。

On July 1, 1993, Huang Da (second from the right) was with Yu Zongxian (third from the right), Zhang Weiying (first from the right) and other attendees.

5 - 12 - 8 >

20 世纪 80 年代中期，当绝大部分留学生滞留国外之际，中国开始强烈意识到人才流失这一早在印度和部分非洲国家就存在的问题。为此，1994 年 5 月 24—26 日，南开大学组织召开“国际大学联合会年会”，专门讨论人才流失问题。

对于人才本来就极少的国家，留学人员不归的负面影响非常大。对于中国是否有着同样的影响？如何估价？黄达在大会发言中从盈亏平衡的角度，综合考虑中国面临的主客观因素，给出了自己的看法。他认为，由于对外开放，环绕人才问题的得失，只会得大于失，而非失大于得。

In the mid 1980s when most Chinese students studying abroad chose to stay abroad, China began to keenly realize the problem of brain drain, a problem that had long been seen in India and some African countries. During May 24 and 26, 1994, Nankai University held "International Association of Universities Annual Meeting" to specifically discuss the problem of brain drain.

For countries with less professional people, it would have great negative impacts if their students studying abroad chose not to come back. Did it have the same impacts on China? How to measure such impacts? Huang Da, from the break-even perspective, took into full consideration the objective and subjective factors faced by China and held, "Given China's opening up policy, China would benefit from brain drain instead of suffering loss."

352

图 352 为 1994 年 5 月 26 日，出席“国际大学联合会年会”的全体专家合影留念。前排左三为会议主持者南开大学校长毋国光，最后排左十为黄达。

On May 26, 1994, all the attendees of the International Association of Universities Annual Meeting took a group photo. The third from the left in the front row is Wu Guoguang, the presider of the meeting and the then president of Nankai University; and the tenth from the left in the last row is Huang Da.

5-12-9>

1994年9月下旬，黄达应邀在山西金融学会研讨会上作了题为《形势·改革·资金一窥》报告。他主要谈到了三个问题：一是形势，特别是难以控制的物价上涨。二是改革，特别是金融改革。他一直不赞同金融改革滞后的提法。金融改革的问题在于微观基础，主要是国有经济。而国有经济的改革绝不是一句私有化所解决得了的——谁来买、谁能买得起中国的国有经济？三是资金供给的松紧度问题。他将此概括为："虽说是偏紧的扩张，但已是扩张，所以不能再扩张。"

In late September 1994, Huang Da made a report titled A Glimpse of the Situation, the Reform and Fund at the workshop held by Shanxi Society for Finance and Banking. In the report, he focused on three major issues: the situation, especially inexorable price rises; the reform, especially the financial reform; and the elasticity of finance. He was never very happy with the suggestion that financial reform in China stagnated. The problem of financial reform was found in the micro foundation, mainly the state-owned sector of the economy. The reform of the state-owned sector of the economy can't be solved only by privatization. Who was to buy and was capable of buying the state-owned sector of the Chinese economy? About the elasticity of finance, he said, "Although it was slightly narrow expansion, it is expansion anyway, so it should not be continued. "

353

图353为1994年9月26日，黄达（主席台居中）在研讨会上发言。

On September 26, 1994, Huang Da (in the middle of the rostrum) delivered a speech at the symposium.

| 右页图 |→

图354为1994年9月23日，黄达在参会途中经过大同，顺便游览云冈石窟。

On September 23, 1994, during the symposium, Huang Da passed Da Tong and visited Yungang Grottos.

354

5-12-10>

1994 年 2 月 5—17 日，黄达应香港中文大学之邀赴港进行校际学术交流。2 月 8 日，他以《中国改革开放以来的通货膨胀问题》为题在该校经济系举行的学术讨论会上发言。当时正值 1994 年通货膨胀率 21.7% 引起普遍关注期间，他在演讲中详细分析了中国通货膨胀的成因与现状，其中的成因分析大体形成了黄达日后分析这一问题的基本框架。

2 月 16 日，回程途经福州期间，黄达应福建金融学会之邀，在福州作了题为《物价与改革》的演讲，演讲内容跟在香港的演讲基本保持一致。

February 5 and 17, 1994, Huang Da was invited to the Chinese University of Hong Kong as a visiting scholar. On February 8, he delivered a speech titled Inflation Issues since China's Reform and Opening Up on a seminar held by the economics department. At the time when inflation rate of 21.7% caused widespread concern in 1994, he analyzed the reason and situation of China's inflation in details. The analysis of the reason generally formed a basic framework for his research on this issue.

On February 16, he arrived at Fuzhou on his way back. Invited by Fujian Society for Finance and Banking, Huang Da gave a speech on Price and Reform which was consistent with his speech in Hong Kong.

355

图 355 为 1994 年 2 月 7 日，访问香港中文大学期间，黄达（前排右三）、王传纶（前排左二）顺访中国银行香港分行。

On February 7, 1994, during the visit to the Chinese University of Hong Kong, Huang Da (third from the right in the front row) and Wang Chuanlun (second from the left in the front row) visited the People's Bank of China Hong Kong branch in passing.

356

图 356 为 1994 年 2 月 16 日，黄达（左二）应邀在福建金融学会作题为《物价与改革》的演讲。左一为时任中国人民银行福建分行行长林敬耀，右一为王传纶。

On February 16, 1994, Huang Da (second from the left) delivered a speech titled Price and Reform at Fujian Society for Finance and Banking. The first from the left was Lin Jingyao, the then head of the People's Bank of China Fujian branch. The first from the right is Wang Chuanlun.

5-12-11>

1996年5月5—8日，中国社会科学院财贸经济研究所、金融研究所等联合举办的“中国财政货币政策协调配合高级研讨会”在广东湛江召开。

黄达向大会提交了《议财政、金融和国有企业资金的宏观配置格局》一文。该文系统考察了当时中国财政、金融实力对比的演变以及与国有企业资金状况、与居民可支配货币收入状况的相互消长关系。同年8月下旬，在国家计委于五台山组织召开的“中国全社会资金配置与宏观调控高级研讨会”上，黄达提交了以该文为基础修改而成的《资金宏观配置格局剖析》一文。

During May 5 and 8, 1996, the Institute of Finance and Trade Economics, and the Institute of Finance and Banking of Chinese Academy of Social Sciences jointly held "Advanced Symposium on the Coordination of China's Fiscal and Monetary Policies " in Zhanjiang, Guangdong.

Huang Da submitted paper On Finance, Banking and the Macro Layout of Funds of the State-owned Enterprises to the symposium. In his paper, Huang Da observed the evolution of the relative strength of finance and banking, and its relationship with the status of the funds of the state-owned enterprises and residents' disposable money income at the time. In late August of the same year, at "Advanced Workshop on the Distribution and Macro Control of Social Capital in China " held by the State Planning Commission (now known as the National Development and Reform Commission) in Mount Wutai, Huang Da submitted paper An Analysis of the Macro Distribution Pattern of Funds, a revision of the above paper.

357

358

图357为1996年5月5日，出席“中国财政货币政策协调配合高级研讨会”的全体专家合影留念。前排左七为黄达。

On May 5, 1996, all the attendees of "Advanced Symposium on the Coordination of China's Fiscal and Monetary Policies" were together. The seventh from the left in the front row is Huang Da.

图358为1996年5月5日，黄达（左三）在“中国财政货币政策协调配合高级研讨会”上发言。

On May 5, 1996, Huang Da (third from the left) delivered a speech at "Advanced Symposium on the Coordination of China's Fiscal and Monetary Policies."

359

图359为1996年8月中旬，出席“中国全社会资金配置与宏观调控高级研讨会”的全体专家合影留念。前排右七为黄达，右八为时任国家计委副主任马凯。

In mid August 1996, all the attendees of "Advanced Workshop on the Distribution and Macro Control of Social Capital in China" were together. The seventh from the right in the front row is Huang Da; and the eighth from the right in the front row is Ma Kai, the then deputy director of the State Planning Commission.

5-12-12 >

1997年4月28日—5月2日，黄达应中国人民银行福建省分行之邀，为该行组织的党政领导学习班作题为《经济形势和金融的改革与发展》的报告。报告中，黄达就经济总体、国有企业、财政、金融、宏观调控等当时的热点问题表达了自己的看法。他强调，正是由于改革的成功推进才使矛盾不断加速暴露，而矛盾的充分暴露也正是矛盾走向本质解决的开端。

During April 28 and May 2, 1997, at the invitation of the People's Bank of China Fujian branch, Huang Da made a report titled "Economic Situation and Financial Reform and Development " for the class organized by such branch for its leading Party and administrative cadres. In the report, Huang Da expressed his views on concurrent hotspots in the general economic situation, state-owned enterprises, finance and banking and macroeconomic control. He highlighted that successful reform exposed conflicts in an accelerated way, which was the beginning of essentially solving the conflicts.

| 右页图 |⟶

图360为1997年4月28日，黄达在中国人民银行福建分行作题为《经济形势和金融的改革与发展》的报告。

On April 28, 1997, Huang Da made a report titled "Economic Situation and Financial Reform and Development" in the People's Bank of China Fujian branch.

360

361

图 361 为 1997 年 4 月 30 日，黄达游览武夷山。

On April 30, 1997, Huang Da was on Mount Wuyi.

362

图 362 为 1997 年 5 月 2 日，黄达为中国人民银行武夷山支行题词：“武夷之胜，贵乎自然；金融之极，亦蕴乎有为无为之间。”

该题词反映了黄达对 20 世纪 90 年代中期繁复的金融实践进行反复思考后的一点醒悟：“分析问题，必须跳出金融、经济与政治视野的局限而求助于哲学。”

On May 2, 1997, Huang Da sent an inscription to the People's Bank of China Mount Wuyi branch—"Mount Wuyi stands out because of its breathtaking natural sceneries; the highest peak of finance lies between action and inaction."

The inscription reflected his awakening after repeatedly thinking about the complex financial practices in the mid 1990s, that is, "To analyze a problem, one must jump out of the box of financial, economic and political horizons and seek help from philosophy."

5 - 12 - 13 >

1997 年 8 月 25—28 日，由中国教育国际交流协会与美国罗得岛大学太平洋盆地资本市场 (PACAP) 研究中心共同主办的“第九届太平洋盆地国家、地区财政金融会议”在上海举行。本次会议主题为“中国金融及资本市场的革新与发展”，与会专家围绕中国和其他亚太国家金融及资本市场发展展开广泛的讨论。

黄达应邀出席并作主题发言。在发言中，除一般介绍中国的金融改革进程和中国国内必须发展资本市场的观点外，他重点剖析了两个问题。一是针对国内外大肆炒作的中国银行体系的不良债权，他指出，中国经济发展自身完全具有消化不良债权的潜力，并非是不可克服的威胁。二是从市场准入角度剖析，中国金融领域的对外开放只应采取积极面对挑战和谨慎渐近相结合的方针。

During August 25 and 28, 1997, China Education Association for International Exchange and Pacific Basin Capital Markets Research Center of University of Rhode Island jointly held "9th Finance and Banking Conference of the Pacific Basin Societies " in Shanghai. On the theme of the conference, namely "Chinese Financial and Capital Market: Renovation and Development, " the experts had wide discussions on the development of the financial and capital market of China and the other Asia-Pacific countries.

Huang Da attended the conference on invitation and delivered a keynote speech. In his speech, Huang Da generally introduced the progresses of financial reform of China and the necessity for the Chinese society to develop the capital market. He focused on analyzing two issues: the bad claim problem of the Chinese banking system which was covered a lot by domestic and foreign media, on which he pointed out that the Chinese economy was totally capable of digesting bad claim, and that bad claim was never an invincible threat; and from the angle of market access, he pointed out that the opening up of the financial sector of China shall adopt and only adopt the principle of combining an active attitude toward challenges and prudent progressiveness.

| 右页图 |⟶

图 363 为 1997 年 8 月 26 日，黄达（左四）与“第九届太平洋盆地国家、地区财政金融会议”优秀论文奖获得者在一起。

On August 26, 1997, Huang Da (fourth from the left) was with winners of the award for excellent papers at the 9th Finance and Banking Conference of the Pacific Basin Societies.

363

5-12-14>

1998年8月20—21日，黄达出席由PECC（太平洋经济合作理事会）金融发展中国委员会主办的“亚洲金融危机与中国内地、香港金融市场发展高级研讨会”，并作题为《中国的金融改革及其前景》的主题演讲。

会后，《中国证券报》（8月22日）、《证券时报》（8月22日）以及香港《大公报》（8月26日）发表消息，均重点指出“提高金融效率”问题。《人民日报·内部参阅》（1998年第37期，总第429期）配以编者评语发表，侧重点与上述三报不同，在于对外：“从国际金融环境这一视角出发，对我国金融改革的现况及前景作了理性分析。”并在行文中添加了一些小标题。

此外，《宏观经济研究》（1998年11月创刊号）以及《走向新时代——纪念中共十一届三中全会20年暨中国人民大学复校20年论文集》（中国人民大学出版社，1998）均收录该文。

During August 20 and 21, 1998, Huang Da attended "Advanced Workshop on the Asian Financial Crisis and the Development of the Financial Market in Mainland China and Hong Kong " held by PECC (Pacific Economic Cooperation Council) China Committee for Financial Development, and made a keynote speech titled China's Financial Reform and Its Prospects.

After the workshop, *China Securities Journal* (August 22), *Securities Times* (August 22) and Hong Kong newspaper *Ta Kung Pao* (August 26) published the news, all with focus on "improving the financial efficiency." *People's Daily for Internal Reference Only* (Issue 37 in 1998, Issue 429 in total) published the news with comments, a different focus—"From the perspective of the international financial environment, it makes a rational analysis of the status quo and prospects of China's financial reform, " and subtitles.

Besides, *Macroeconomics* (the first issue in November 1998) and *To a New Era—Essays to Commemorate the 20th Anniversary of the 3rd Plenary Session of the 11th CPC National Congress and the 20th Anniversary of the Resumption of the Renmin University of China* (China Renmin University Press, 1998) both collected his paper.

| 右页图 |⟶

图364为1998年8月22日，《中国证券报》以《要重视提高金融效率》为题刊发黄达在“亚洲金融危机与中国内地、香港金融市场发展高级研讨会”上的讲话。

On August 22, 1998, *China Securities Journal* published Huang Da's speech at the Advanced Workshop on the Asian Financial Crisis and the Development of the Financial Market in Mainland China and Hong Kong under the title of Attention Has to Be Paid to Improving the Efficiency of Finance.

南宁 福州 长沙 重庆 深圳 济南 杭州 郑州 昆明 呼和浩特 合肥 乌鲁木齐 兰州 南昌 石家庄 哈尔滨同时印刷 国内统一刊号

中国人民银行货币政策委员会委员黄达强调

要重视提高金融效率

本报北京讯（记者**于力**）中国人民银行货币政策委员会委员、中国金融学会会长黄达昨天在京强调指出，目前条件下，发挥和提高金融效率，对于推进金融改革有着与规范金融行为和防范金融风险同等或偏重的意义。可以说，没有金融效率，规范金融行为和防范金融风险，也就没有出发点。

他说，来势凶猛的亚洲金融危机和急速转向需求拉动不足的国内市场格局，使我国金融改革面对的国内外环境都发生了巨大变化，如果在通货膨胀压力很大的背景下，强调规范行为和防范风险的同时，金融效率受到某些抑制，难以避免。但在需求不足的背景下，刺激而不是抑制需求占主导地位时，对发挥和提高金融效率的要求就会突显出来。规范行为和防范风险的同时，多强调一些效率就是必要的。

他同时指出，在需求不足的条件下，起主导作用的是财政政策而不是货币政策，简单的金融扩张扭转不了需求不足以带动经济发展的局面。事实上，用于宏观调控的财政措施罕有不需要通过金融环节的，所以，注重两者相互配合，才有利于改革，有利于提高效益和降低实施调控的成本。

他认为，深化金融改革　，除推进中央银行管理体制、加快国有商业银行的商业化等项改革外，今后还必须推进利率市场化、推广使用金融衍生工具及实现人民币资本项下可兑换等。

黄达还谈到，目前金融改革开放的现实途径是解决“接轨”“溶入”与“自我防卫”的统一。应根据时间的推移、条件的变化时时寻求两者的理想结合点、均衡点。这是从与国际接轨的角度来考虑的，是关系金融改革大局的问题。因此，引进国外资本、开放金融服务市场、开放资本市场、人民币的完全可兑换，以及外汇储备和汇率等具体政策的处理，都必须纳入这个大局的总体框架之中。

国家发展计划委员会权威分析报告指出

应进一步加大投资力度

本报北京讯（记者**刘敏慧**）国家发展计划委员会权威宏观形势分析报告认为，受亚洲金融危机继续动荡，以及长江、松花江流域地区遭受历史上最严重的一次水灾的双重影响，我国既定的扩大投资带动经济增长的作用有可能打折扣。当前，需要全党和全国人民增强信心，防止悲观和急躁情绪，加大投资力

公共投入；其次，加大对技术改造项目的投资力度，特别是要尽快落实技改项目的资金问题，上半年技改项目到位资金仅比去年同期增长 9.5%，增幅回落

折旧政策。50 年代初出台的《合理化促进法》进一步大幅度提高了政府鼓励投资的部门所购置设备的折旧率；

——要适当扩大政府采购范围。此举既可降低生产成本，

成本上升，又可达到减少库存，动市场的目的。

——尽管特大水灾造成了巨大损失，但应充分利用重建家园的契机，乡村住宅适度集中，推进农村城市化进程，确保我国

364

5-12-15>

1999年5月5—11日，黄达赴大连进行学术交流。他准备了一份交流提纲，合并形成《经济与金融·形势与政策·国内与国际·问题与信心》一文。

该文包含了他当时重点思考的一些问题，第一，对1997—1999年春的经济形势，偏于紧张的估价是舆论主流，但不宜反应过度。第二，在扩大内需中，财政政策终于出台，并开始扭转金融无所不能、货币政策无所不能的观念。这是宏观决策观念的一次重大进展。第三，在金融领域，扩大内需是扩张的决策意向，但种种决策又几乎无一不意味着营造紧缩的环境。诸多决策思路没有找到均衡点。第四，金融的生命力在于活，在于效率；必须把搞活金融、提高效率与加强监管、防范风险统一起来。第五，必须清醒地看到，国际环境是实力悬殊的竞争环境，我们是弱者，不能不时时被人家"敲打"，必须时时有自我防卫意识。第六，代替轰轰烈烈的，是指导思想在一点一滴地前进。这应是信心之所在。第七，应该学司马迁。他推崇道家，但对诸子百家也强调"弗能易也""弗能废也""弗能改也"以及"不可不察也"。

During May 5 and 11, 1999, Huang Da went to Dalian for academic exchanges. He prepared an outline for the exchanges, and wrote paper Economy and Finance · Situation and Policies · China and the World · Problems and Confidence.

The paper incorporated some problems he thought with priorities back then. Firstly, it was the mainstream opinion that the economic situation from 1997 to the spring of 1999 was tense, but people should not overreact to it. Secondly, in expanding domestic demands, fiscal policies were finally introduced and began to converse the concept that finance and monetary policy were almighty. It was a major progress of the macro decision-making concept. Thirdly, in the financial sector, expanding domestic demand meant to expand the economy, but the decisions made were creating an environment of economic inflation. Many decisions or ideas did not have a balancing point. Fourthly, the force of finance lies in its vitality and efficiency. Vitalizing finance, improving the efficiency of finance, strengthening supervision and preventing risks must be combined. Fifthly, China had to soberly realize that the international environment was a highly competitive one, and that it was weaker and was "bullied " from time to time. China must always hold this self-defense awareness. Sixthly, the leading ideology did not have to be vigorous, but progressive, which should be the source of confidence. Seventhly, China should learn from Sima Qian, a man who advocated Taoism, but highlighted that schools of various thoughts "can't be replaced," "can't be annulled," "can't be changed" and "have to be observed."

| 右页图 ⟼

图365为1999年5月6日，时任大连市副市长南昌明（居中右一）会见黄达（居中左一）一行。

On May 6, 1999, the then deputy mayor of Dalian Nan Changming (first from the right in the middle) met Huang Da (first from the left in the middle) and the others.

365

366

图 366 为 1999 年 5 月 7 日，黄达（右一）在大连庄河市的农贸市场调研。

On May 7, 1999, Huang Da (first from the right) was researching and studying the farmer's market in Zhuanghe, Dalian.

367

图 367 为 1999 年 5 月 8 日，黄达（右一）与时任大连市副市长、现任辽宁省政协主席夏德仁（左一）在大连金石滩参观。

On May 8, 1999, Huang Da (first from the right) was at Jinshitan Dalian with Xia Deren (first from the left), the then deputy mayor of Dalian and now chairman of the Chinese People's Political Consultative Conference(CPPCC) of Liaoning Province.

5 - 12 - 16 >

1999 年 5 月 28 日，黄达受邀在上海金融学会年会上作了题为《分点精力思考一些基本思路问题》的报告。在黄达看来，金融战线的工作者，日常的学习、工作、调研很忙；教师和科研单位工作者，手头的事情也不少，不太容易静下心来，清理一下基本思路。利用这次机会，他从如何认识世界的政治格局，如何看待市场经济，对于经济过程的货币方面和实体方面如何把握其统一性，如何面对通货膨胀与通货紧缩的转化，安全、规范与效率应否统一等五个方面问题进行了系统思考和讲解。

On May 28, 1999, Huang Da made a report titled Give the Problem of Basic Ways of Thinking a Thought at the annual meeting of Shanghai Society for Finance and Banking on invitation. To Huang Da, those working in the sector of finance were busy with studies, work and researches; teachers and researchers had a lot to do, too, so it was uneasy for them to calm down and straighten the basic way of thinking. Taking the chance, he systematically thought and explained the problems on how to understand the world political pattern, how to treat the market economy, how to grasp the integrity of nominal and real aspects in economic progresses, how to face the conversion of inflation and deflation, and how to combine safety, regularity and efficiency.

368

图 368 为 1999 年 5 月 28 日，黄达（左一）在会议期间专程拜访正在病中休养的复旦大学教授陈观烈（右一）。

On May 28, 1999, Huang Da (first from the left) paid a special visit to Chen Guanlie (first from the right), professor of Fudan University who was resting for illness.

369

图 369 为 1999 年 5 月 29 日，黄达（右一）与出席本次会议的洪葭管（左一）在上海金茂大厦。

On May 29, 1999, Huang Da (first from the right) and Hong Jiaguan (first from the left) were in Jinmao Tower, Shanghai.

5 - 12 - 17 >

1999 年 6 月 12—13 日，国务院发展研究中心宏观经济部、国家发展计划委员会经济研究所、中国社会科学院财贸经济研究所、财政部财政科学研究所、中国金融学会、东北财经大学、辽宁省财政科学研究所在大连联合举办“现阶段财政政策与货币政策的协调与配合高级理论研讨会”。

黄达出席会议并作总结，会后据此形成《冷静思考经济紧缩带来的启示 重新审视我们对待经济、金融问题的思路》一文。文中，他指出，要使走出紧缩的举措得当，应在紧迫之中保持一分从容。只有从容才能学习，才能思考。

During June 12 and 13, 1999, the Macro Economy Research Department of the Development Research Center of the State Council, the Institute of Economics of State Development and Planning Committee, the Institute of Finance and Trade Economics of Chinese Academy of Social Sciences, Institute of Financial Science of the Ministry of Finance, China Society for Finance and Banking, Dongbei University of Finance and Economics and Liaoning Institute of Financial Science jointly held "Advanced Theoretical Symposium on the Coordination and Cooperation of Fiscal and Monetary Policies at the Current Stage " in Dalian.

Huang Da attended the symposium, and summarized it, and wrote article Calmly Think about the Inspirations Brought about by Economic Deflation, Review Our Way of Thinking of Economic and Financial Problems after the symposium. He held it to be necessary to keep calm in emergency in order to take proper deflation measures. Only with calmness can people study and think.

| 右页图 |—>

图 370 为 1999 年 6 月 12 日，出席“现阶段财政政策与货币政策的协调与配合高级理论研讨会”的全体专家合影留念。前排右五为黄达。

On June 12, 1999, all the attendees of the Advanced Theoretical Symposium on the Coordination and Cooperation of Fiscal and Monetary Policies at the Current Stage took a group photo. The fifth from the right in the front row is Huang Da.

370

5-12-18>

1999年7月18—21日，由国际管理学者协会联盟、中国人民大学、国家自然科学基金会管理科学学部、中国工业经济联合会、国家经济贸易委员会经济研究咨询中心、中国固定资产投资建设研究会、中国总会计师协会、中国管理科学研究院、《人民日报》(海外版)、国家外国专家局培训中心、首都企业家俱乐部等联合主办的“99世界管理大会”在北京召开。

黄达向大会提交了《面对经济全球化的中国金融改革》一文。该文重述了《完善中国金融体制的目标和思路》和《中国的金融改革及其前景》等几篇文章的基本观点，并就中国金融体系如何融入国际金融大舞台等问题表达了个人见解。

During July 18 and 21,1999, "1999 World Management Conference" was jointly held in Beijing by International Federation of Scholarly Associations of Management, the Renmin University of China, the Department of Management Science of National Natural Science Foundation of China, China Federation of Industrial Economics, Economic Studies Information Center of State Economic and Trade Commission, China Fixed Assets Investment and Construction Council, China Association of Chief Financial Officers, China Academy of Management Science, *People's Daily* (overseas), Training Center of State Administration of Foreign Expert Affairs and Capital Entrepreneurs Club.

Huang Da submitted article China's Financial Reform Facing Economic Globalization. In the article, he reiterated his basic views in Improve China's Financial System: Targets and Thoughts and China's Financial Reform and Its Prospects, and expressed personal opinions on the ways of the Chinese financial system getting integrated into the world financial stage.

右页图 ⟼

图371为1999年7月18日，“99世界管理大会”会议现场。

On July 18, 1999, the "1999 World Management Conference" was held in Beijing.

国际管理学者协会联盟 99世界管理大会
WORLD MANAGEMENT CONFERENCE '99
IFSAM

371

5 - 12 - 19 >

1999 年 7 月 21—28 日，由西南财经大学举办的“证券市场与扩大内需高级研讨会”在云南召开。期间，黄达一行参观了昆明世博园和香格里拉等。

During July 21 and 28, 1999, "Advanced Symposium on the Securities Market and the Expansion of Domestic Demand " was held in Yunnan by Southwestern University of Finance and Economics. During the period, Huang Da and the other attendees visited Kunming World Expo and Shangri-La.

372

374

373

375

图 372 为 1999 年 7 月 22 日，出席“证券市场与扩大内需高级研讨会”的全体专家在昆明世博园合影留念。

On July 22, 1999, all the attendees of the Advanced Symposium on the Securities Market and the Expansion of Domestic Demand took a group photo at the Kunming World Expo.

图 373 为 1999 年 7 月 25 日，黄达在香格里拉纳帕海游览。

On July 25, 1999, Huang Da was by Napahai wetland, Shangri-La.

图 374 为 1999 年 7 月 24 日，部分与会专家游览位于云南省中甸县东部的碧塔海。从左至右分别为：王国刚、王松奇、黄达、周升业、房郁琴、王广谦和邓乐平。

On July 24, 1999, some attendees toured Bita Sea in eastern Zhongdian County, Yunnan Province. From the left to the right are Wang Guogang, Wang Songqi, Huang Da, Zhou Shengye, Fang Yuqin, Wang Guangqian and Deng Leping.

图 375 为 1999 年 7 月 26 日，黄达参观云南玉峰寺。

On July 26, 1999, Hung Da visited Yufeng Temple in Yunnan.

376

图 376 为 1999 年 7 月 25 日，黄达游览长江第一湾。

On July 25, 1999, Huang Da was at the first gulf of the Yangtze River.

5 - 12 - 20 >

1999 年 8 月 8 日，黄达出席在山西太原召开的“金融制度变迁与风险防范研讨会”。

On August 8, 1999, Huang Da attended the Workshop on the Vicissitudes of Financial System and Risk Prevention in Taiyuan, Shanxi Province.

377

图 377 为 1999 年 8 月 8 日，“金融制度变迁与风险防范研讨会”在太原召开。全体与会专家合影留念。第二排左九为黄达。

On August 8, 1999, the Workshop on the Vicissitudes of the Financial System and Risk Prevention was held in Taiyuan. The attendees took a group photo. The ninth from the left in the second row is Huang Da.

378

图 378 为 1999 年 8 月 11 日，黄达在会议结束返程途中参观黄河壶口瀑布。

On August 11, 1999, Huang Da visited and toured Hukou waterfall on his way back.

5-12-21>

黄达在此期间参加的其他学术交流活动及题词

Other Academic Activities He Participated in and Inscriptions by Huang Da

379

右页图

图 379 为 1991 年 6 月 18—23 日，中国人民银行组织的《银行法》研讨会在广东江门召开。全体与会专家合影留念。前排右七为黄达，右八为研讨会主持人、中国人民银行原副行长尚明。

During June 18 and 23, 1991, the Banking Law symposium held by the People's Bank of China was held in Jiangmen, Guangdong. All the attendees took a group photo. In the front row, the seventh from the right is Huang Da; and the eighth from the right is Shang Ming, the symposium presider and former deputy governor of the People's Bank of China.

图 380 为 1991 年 6 月 18—23 日，《银行法》研讨会后，在中国人民银行广东省分行负责人、中国人民大学校友何伟荣（右一）的陪同下，黄达（右二）参观了孙中山先生诞生地——广东省中山市东南南节区南朗镇的翠亨村。

During June 18 and 23, 1991, after the Banking Law symposium, Huang Da (second from the right) was accompanied by He Weirong (first from the right), the person in charge of the People's Bank of China Guangdong branch and an alumnus of the Renmin University of China to visit Cuiheng Village, Nanlang Town, Nanjie District in southeastern Zhongshan City, Guangdong Province, the birthplace of Sun Yat-sen.

380

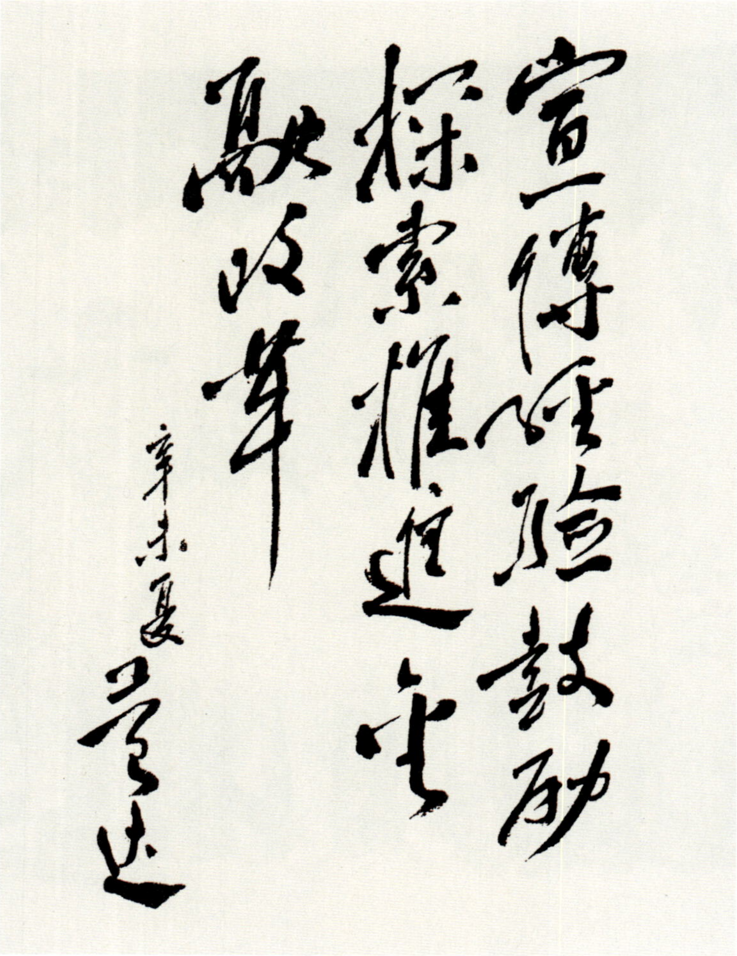

381

图 381 为 1991 年 10 月，应王松奇之邀，黄达为《城市金融报》题词：“宣传经验，鼓励探索，推进金融改革。”

In October 1991, at the invitation of Wang Songqi, Huang Da inscribed "Spread Experience, Encourage Explorations, Push Forward Financial Reform" for newspaper *City Financial.*

382

图 382 为 1992 年 1 月 19 日，黄达（左二）在南京大学经济系讲学。左一为周三多，右一为洪银兴。

On January 19, 1992, Huang Da (second from the left) gave a lecture to the Department of Economics of Nanjing University. The first from the left is Zhou Sanduo and the first from the right is Hong Yinxing.

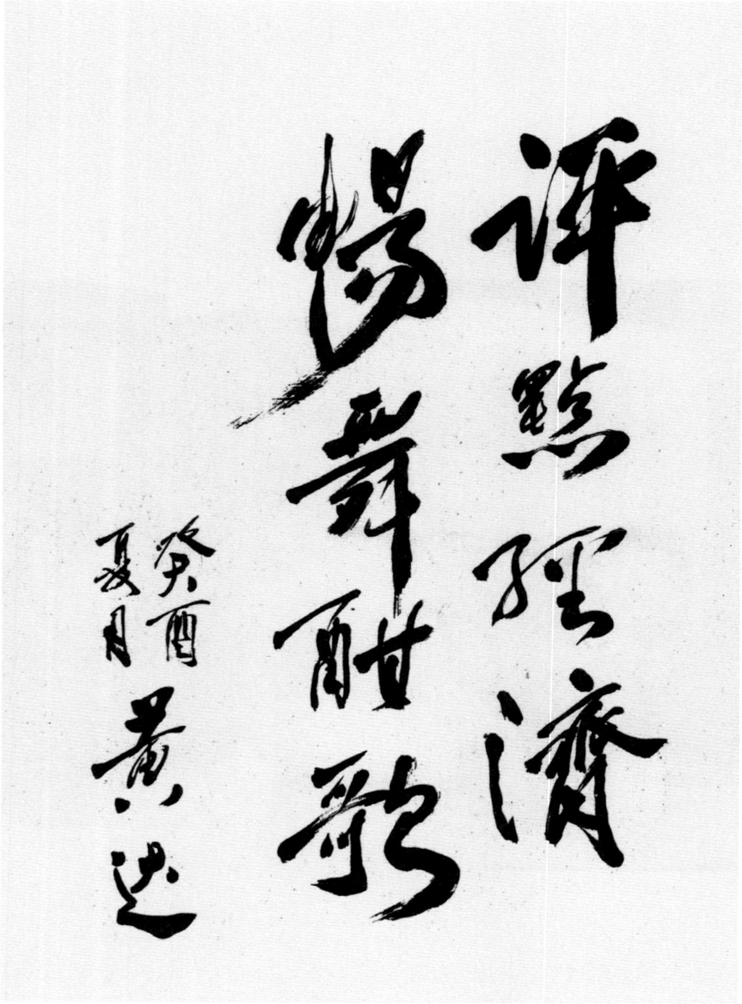

383

图 383 为 1993 年 6 月 21 日，黄达为武汉大学《经济评论》题词："评点经济，畅舞酣歌。"

On June 21, 1993, Huang Da inscribed "Commenting on the economy thoroughly" for *Economic Review* of Wuhan University.

384

图 384 为 1993 年 7 月 28 日，黄达赴内蒙古考察期间，为额尔古纳左旗题词：“保卫绿色，开拓净土；兴林富民，北陲增辉。”

本次内蒙古之行为应中国人民大学财政金融系校友、当时挂职内蒙古呼伦贝尔盟副盟长的李茂生之邀，与时任中国社会科学院党委书记、副院长王忍之一起访问。这是黄达第一次直接感触北部边陲，收获颇丰。期间，多处要求题字，这是其中一幅。

On July 28, 1993, Huang Da inscribed "To protect the environment, reclaim land; to plant trees, make the northern border of China more vigorous" for Erguna.

Huang Da went to Inner Mongolia together with Wang Renzhi, the then secretary of Party Committee and deputy president of Chinese Academy of Social Science at the invitation of Li Maosheng, the alumna of the Department of Finance and Banking of the Renmin University of China and the then temporary deputy head of Hulun Buir, Inner Mongolia. It was the first time for Huang Da to directly feel the northern borderland of China, and he learned a lot. During his visit there, he was invited to give inscriptions. This is one of the inscriptions he gave.

385

图 385 为 1993 年 8 月 24 日，黄达为《光明日报》撰写《关于当前宏观调控的一些想法》一文，手稿保存至今。

文中，黄达对 1993 年 7 月初开始实施的“加强宏观调控”表达了自己最初的想法。日后，经过近三年的调控，中国经济实现了从过热到“软着陆”的转变。在他看来，这次调控尽管还存在一定问题，但总体上还是非常成功的，领导艺术可圈可点。

On August 24, 1993, Huang Da wrote Some Thoughts on the Current Macroeconomic Regulation for *Guangming Daily,* and the manuscript has been kept so far.

In the article, Huang Da expressed his first thoughts on "strengthening macroeconomic control" which had been carried out since early July 1993. After nearly three years of macroeconomic control since then, the Chinese economy realized the conversion from being overheated to "soft landing." Although it had some problems, the macroeconomic control was successful in general, and the leadership was commendable.

386

387

图 386 为 1994 年 10 月 6—9 日，黄达在出席杭州金融学会活动期间，参观绍兴鲁迅纪念馆。

During October 6 and 9, 1994, when attending the activities held by Hangzhou Society for Finance and Banking, Huang Da visited Luxun Memorial Hall in Shaoxing.

图 387 为 1995 年 8 月中旬，黄达在成都出席四川金融学会活动期间，游览黄龙溪。

In mid August 1995, Huang Da toured and visited Huanglong River when attending the activities held by Sichuan Society for Finance and Banking.

388

图 388 为 1995 年 6 月 8 日，黄达（右二）在北京接待著名美籍华人经济学家王念祖（左二）。

On June 8, 1995, Huang Da (second from the right) was with Wang Nianzu (second from the left), a famous American-Chinese economist.

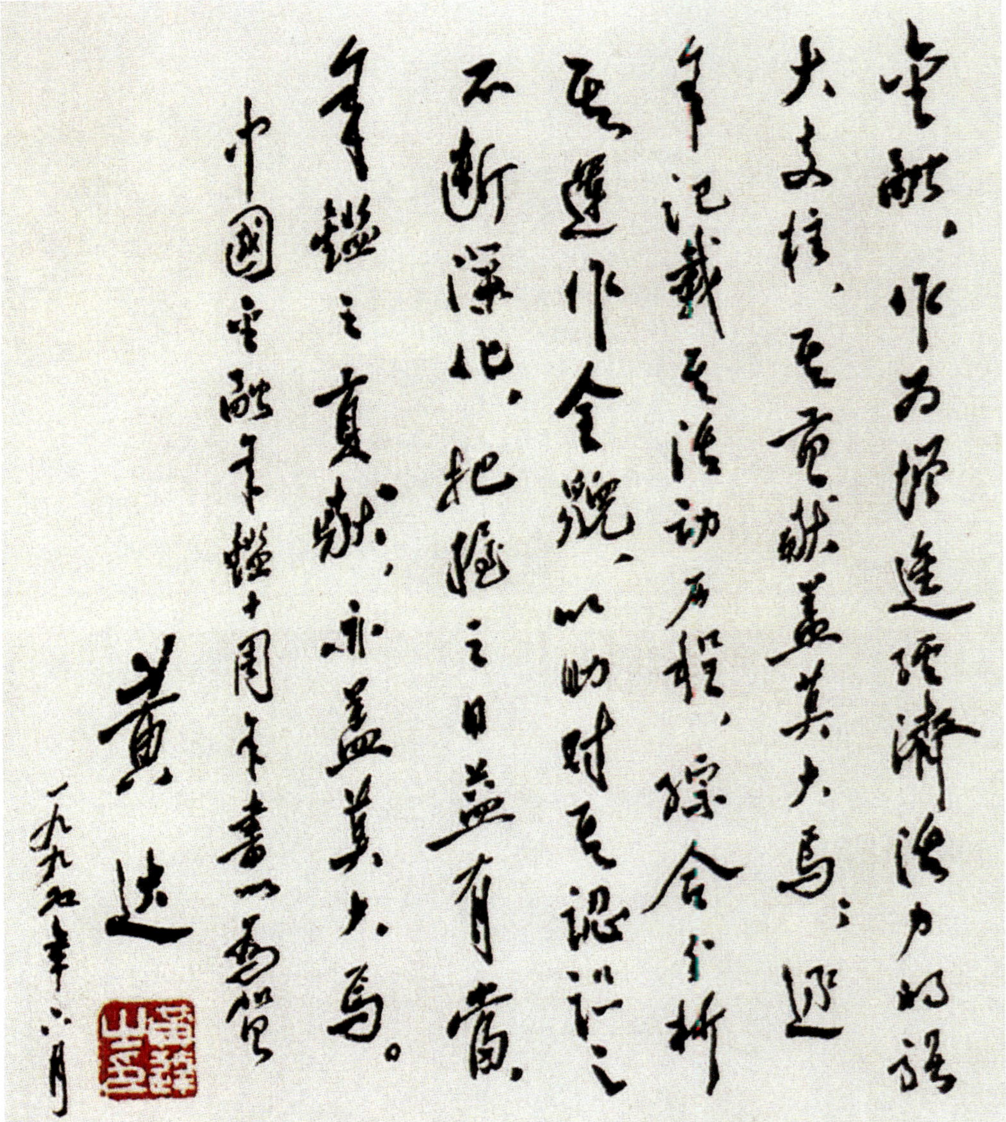

389

图 389 为 1995 年夏，黄达为《中国金融年鉴》十周年题词：“金融，作为增进经济活力的强大支柱，其贡献盖莫大焉；逐年记载其活动历程，综合分析其运作全貌，以助对其认识的不断深化，把握之日益有当，年鉴之贡献，亦盖莫大焉。”这是黄达最为满意的题词之一。

In the summer of 1995, Huang Da sent an inscription to *Almanac of China's Finance and Banking*—"Finance contributes a lot to the economy as a strong force to make the economy more vibrant. Recording the development of finance year by year and making comprehensive analyses of its operation bring people's understanding of it deeper and enable them to have a better command of it. In this aspect, the Almanac has done quite a lot." This is one of Huang Da's favourite inscriptions.

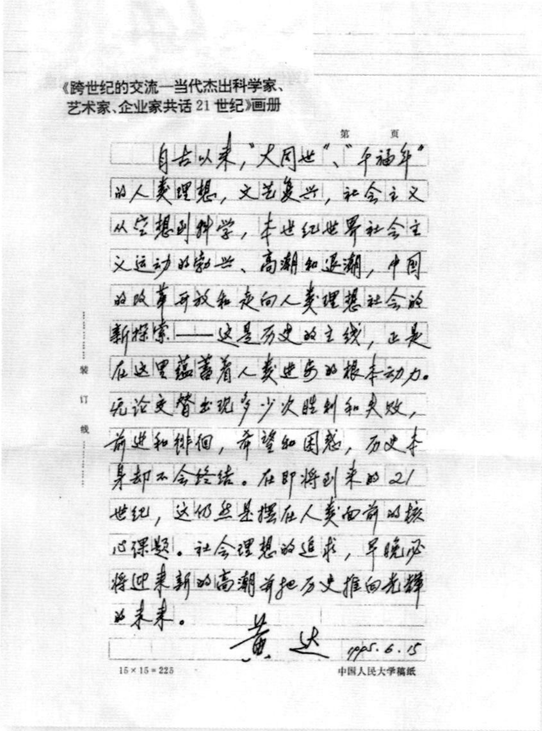

《跨世纪的交流—当代杰出科学家、艺术家、企业家共话 21 世纪》画册

第　页

自古以来，"大同世"、"千福年"的人类理想，文艺复兴，社会主义从空想到科学，本世纪世界社会主义运动的勃兴、高潮和退潮，中国的改革开放和走向人类理想社会的新探索——这是历史的主线，正是在这里蕴蓄着人类进步的根本动力。无论交替出现多少次胜利和失败，前进和徘徊，希望和困惑，历史本身却不会终结。在即将到来的21世纪，这仍然是摆在人类面前的核心课题。社会理想的追求，早晚必将迎来新的高潮并把历史推向光辉的未来。

黄达　1995.6.15

装订线

15×15=225　　中国人民大学稿纸

390

图 390 为 1995 年 6 月 15 日，黄达为《跨世纪的交流 —— 当代杰出科学家、艺术家、企业家共话 21 世纪》画册题词。

On June 15, 1995, Huang Da inscribed for the album of *Cross-century Communication — Outstanding Contemporary Scientists, Artists and Entrepreneurs in the 21st Century.*

391

图391为1997年6月19—21日，“《金融数学、金融工程、金融管理》重大项目研究发展大会暨金融高级人才培养基地揭牌仪式”在山东大学召开。全体与会专家合影留念。前排右五为黄达。

During June 19 and 21, 1997, the "Financial Math, Financial Engineering, Financial Management Major Program Studies Development Conference and the Opening Ceremony of Senior Financial Elite Cultivation Base" was held in Shandong University. The fifth from the right in the front row is Huang Da.

392

图 392 为 1998 年 6 月 20 日，出席“中国保险业：比较与选择”研讨会的全体专家合影留念。前排左四为黄达。

On June 20, 1998, the attendees of the symposium of "China Insurance: Comparison and Selection" took a group photo. The fourth from the left in the front row is Huang Da.

393

图 393 为 1998 年 7 月 20 日，2001 年诺贝尔经济学奖得主约瑟夫·斯蒂格利茨受聘担任中国人民大学名誉教授并发表题为《经济学与中国的经济改革与发展》的演讲。部分与会专家合影留念。左二为王传纶，右一至右四分别为：李文海、高鸿业、斯蒂格利茨和黄达。

On July 20, 1998, Joseph E. Stiglitz, the 2001 Nobel Economics Laureate, was invited by the Renmin University of China to be its honorary professor and delivered a speech of Economics and China's Economic Reform and Development. This is a group photo of some of the attendees. The second from the left is Wang Chuanlun; and the first to the fourth from the right are Li Wenhai, Gao Hongye, Stiglitz and Huang Da.

394

图 394 为 1999 年 10 月 19 日，由中国社科院金融研究中心、浙江大学金融研究中心以及台州市银座城市信用合作社联合举办的“中小金融机构与地方经济发展研讨会”在台州召开。主席台左七为黄达。

On October 19, 1999, Institute of Finance and Banking of the Chinese Academy of Social Sciences, Center of Financial Research of Zhejiang University, and Taizhou Yinzuo Urban Credit Cooperative jointly held "Small and Medium-sized Financial Institutions and Local Economic Development Forum" in Taizhou. The seventh from the left on the rostrum is Huang Da.

395

图 395 为 1999 年 10 月 19 日，黄达（居中）在“中小金融机构与地方经济发展研讨会”上发言。

On October 19, 1999, Huang Da (the middle) addressed "Small and Medium-sized Financial Institutions and Local Economic Development Forum."

396

图 396 为 1999 年 11 月 11 日，应张亦春教授之邀，黄达在厦门大学经济学院作了题为《有关金融一些问题探析》的报告。期间，黄达再游鼓浪屿。

On November 11, 1999, at the invitation of Prof. Zhang Yichun, Huang Da gave a report titled On Some Issues Relating to Finance to the School of Economics, Xiamen University. During his stay there, Huang Da toured and visited Gulangyu once again.

397

398

图 397 为 1999 年 12 月 25 日，由经济科学出版社主办的“经济学界迎接新世纪团拜会”在北京昆仑饭店召开，中国经济学界新老学者近 300 人出席了会议。右一至右三分别为：杜润生、黄达、朱厚泽。

On December 25, 1999, the "Get-together of the Economics World to Welcome the Arrival of the New Century" held by Economic Science Press was held in Beijing Kunlun Hotel, and nearly 300 senior and young scholars in the Chinese economics world went for the get-together. The first to the third from the right are Du Runsheng, Huang Da and Zhu Houze.

图 398 为 1999 年 12 月 25 日，黄达在“经济学界迎接新世纪团拜会”会议现场。

On December 25, 1999, Huang Da was at the "Get-together of the Economics World to Welcome the Arrival of the New Century".

399

400

图399为1999年12月25日，黄达（右一）与朱厚泽（左一）在会场交谈。

On December 25, 1999, Huang Da (first from the right) was talking with Zhu Houze (first from the left).

图400为1999年12月25日，黄达（右一）与出席本次会议的董辅礽（左一）在一起。

On December 25, 1999, Huang Da (first from the right) was with Dong Fureng (first from the left).

5-13

与我们在一起
Be With Us

401

图 401 为 1994 年 5 月 15 日，黄达（第二排右四）与中国人民大学校部机关工作人员春游松山。

On May 15, 1994, Huang Da (fourth from the right in the second row) had a spring hiking to Songshan Mountain with the staff of the university offices of the Renmin University of China.

402

图402为1997年10月25日，黄达（第二排右三）与参加中国人民大学财政金融学院院庆的老师和校友在一起。

On October 25, 1997, Huang Da (third from the right in the second row) was with the teachers and alumni attending the anniversary celebration of the School of Finance, the Renmin University of China.

403

图 403 为 1997 年秋，中国人民大学财政金融学院部分教师合影留念。前排从左至右分别为：周升业、黄达、王传纶、陈共和侯梦蟾；后排从左至右分别为：吴晓球、朱毅峰、朗荣燊、陶湘、安体富、高培勇。

In the autumn of 1997, some teachers of the School of Finance of the Renmin University of China took a group photo. From the left to the right in the front row are Zhou Shengye, Huang Da, Wang Chuanlun, Chen Gong and Hou Mengchan; from the left to the right in the back row are Wu Xiaoqiu, Zhu Yifeng, Lang Rongshen, Tao Xiang, An Tifu and Gao Peiyong.

404

图 404 为 1997 年，黄达在大北照相馆拍摄的个人标准像。

It is a personal picture of Huang Da taken in Dabei Photo Studio in 1997.

405

图 405 为 1998 年 12 月 24 日，黄达（后排左四）与中国人民大学货币银行学专业 97 级学生在图书馆前合影留念。

On December 24, 1998, Huang Da (fourth from the left in the back row) took a picture with the majors of money and banking of Class 1997 of the Renmin University of China.

406

图 406 为 1999 年秋，中国人民大学财政金融学院部分教师与校友在一起。前排从左至右分别为：陈共、黄达、王传纶、周升业和韩英杰；后排从左至右分别为：丁玮夫人、朱毅峰、安体富、丁玮和谭荣华。

In the autumn of 1999, some teachers and alumni of the School of Finance of the Renmin University of China were together. From the left to the right in the front row are Chen Gong, Huang Da, Wang Chuanlun, Zhou Shengye and Han Yingjie; from the left to the right in the back row are the wife of Ding Wei, Zhu Yifeng, An Tifu, Ding Wei and Tan Ronghua.

第六章

Chapter Six

老骥伏枥

新世纪以来

Aiming for the Far-off Future in the 21st Century

“大金融”之争与《金融学》

Debating on Macro-Finance and *Economics of Money and Finance*

什么是金融？什么是金融学科？如何培养金融学人才？

对于一个跟金融打了一辈子交道的人来讲，这些似乎是不应该成为问题的问题，却在新世纪之交让黄达“纠结”了很久。为此，他不得不亲自上阵，正本清源。

20世纪50年代以来，中国金融学界不是完全照搬苏联模式，就是淹没于政治运动的洪流，学术研究处于“闭关修炼”的状态。直到改革开放以后，中国的金融学人才才开始真正走出国门，开始接触、了解西方的金融思想。

这时候大家才发现，已经发展成为显学中的显学的西方现代金融学早已是“面目全非”。它在诺贝尔经济学奖方面“屡有斩获”便可见一斑。1990年诺贝尔经济学奖被授予哈里·马科维茨的资产组合选择理论、威廉·夏普的资本资产定价模型以及默顿·米勒的MM定理。1997年诺贝尔经济学奖被授予迈伦·斯科尔斯和罗伯特·默顿，前者给出了著名的布莱克·斯科尔斯期权定价公式，该公式已为全球创造了一个衍生工具市场；后者进一步削弱了布莱克·斯科尔斯公式所依赖的假设条件，在许多方面对其做了推广。

20世纪90年代中期以来，一方面，大量从国外商学院学成归来的金融学“海归”，“惊奇”地发现他们眼中的金融学与本土学者讲授了近半个世纪的金融学竟然如此不同。另一方面，西方金融学所关注的资本市场发展迅速，而在中国传统定义中的金融学所重点关注的银行却遭遇了前所未有的危机。诸如“抛弃银行”、“传统银行即将没落”等观点甚为流行。

一个紧急、棘手却又无法回避的问题摆在黄达面前——究竟是按照原来兼顾宏观调控、银行和证券的方向走，还是把主攻方向定位到以资本市场为主要研究对象的西方金融学上去，两者是“非此即彼”，还是可以“相互融合”？

从2000年下半年开始，黄达相继走访了西南财经大学、武汉大学、中南财经政法大学、湖南大学、暨南大学以及西安交通大学等几所兄弟大学的金融院系，与学界同仁进行座谈、讲演并先后发表了《金融学学科建设若干问题》（《中央财经大学学报》，2000年第9期）、《由讨论“金融”与“金融学”引出的“方

What is finance? What is financial discipline? And how to train finance personnel?

For a man who spent his whole life in dealing with finance, these questions should be out of question. However, Huang Da considered them for a long time at the turn of the century, and was obliged to tackle the issue thoroughly.

From the 1950s, China's finance either copied the model of the Soviet Union, or drifted along with political movements. So the academic research went no further. The financial talents in China didn't go abroad to contact and understand financial ideology until the launch of reform and opening up.

Not until then did people find that the Western modern finance had already become a notable discipline among distinguished disciplines, a discipline beyond recognition. It had made many achievements to win the Nobel Prize in Economics. In 1990, the Prize went to Harry Markowitz for his theory of portfolio selection, William Sharpe for his capital asset pricing model and Merton Miller for his theorem of Modigliani-Miller. In 1997, it went to Myron Scholes and Robert Merton. The former worked out the Black-Scholes Option Pricing Model, which created a derivatives market for the world. The latter promoted wide application of the Black-Scholes Option Pricing Model in other fields by weakening the limit of assumed conditions on which the Model based.

Since the mid-1990s, a great number of overseas graduates from foreign business universities came back and got surprised that the finance that they had learned abroad was totally different from what local scholars had taught for nearly half a century. On the other hand, western finance focused on the rapid development of capital market, but neglected banking industry, which was the very center that China's traditional finance focused on. For a while, some viewpoints such as "discarding bank " and "traditional bank is declining " were prevalent.

Huang Da had to face this urgent and sticky issue — should we go on the direction of balancing macro-control, banking and security? Or should we shift to the western finance and mainly study capital market? How to treat the two sides, alternation or integration?

Starting from the second half of 2000, Huang Da visited the departments of finance of Southwestern University of Finance and Economics, Wuhan University, Zhongnan University of Economics and Law, Hunan University, Ji'nan University, Xi'an Jiaotong University and other universities, had informal

法论”思考》（《经济评论》，2001 年第 3 期）以及《从银行不被看好谈起》（《金融时报》，2001 年 1 月 13 日；《经济导刊》，2001 年第 2 期）等文章，并编写出版了《金融——词义、学科、形势、方法及其他》（中国金融出版社，2001）一书。新世纪元年，黄达还带着近距离了解美联储对“Finance”用法的任务亲赴美国，与美联储的专家们进行专门沟通。

正是黄达“刨根问底”的这种精神，让他对于“究竟什么是金融？什么又是Finance？”这些问题有了更为清晰的认识。

“金融”一词并非古而有之。在《康熙字典》之前的工具书均没有将“金”与“融”连在一起。究竟连起来的“金融”始于何时，是否直接译自 Finance？并无从考证。在黄达看来，最有可能但同样无法考证的可能是——“金融”来自明治维新时期的日本。而中国最早列入“金融”条目的工具书分别是《辞源》和《辞海》。前者于 1908 年开始编撰，1915 年出版；而后者于 1915 年开始酝酿编撰，1936 年开始刊行。近百年前的两条金融条目说明，在 20 世纪初期之前，至少已经有数十年的使用经历才能够形成较为成形的条目。

较之上述两个词条仅指“通过信用中介机构的货币资金融通”，《辞海》的 20 世纪 60 年代试行本和 1979 年首次公开发行版的释文，给出了一个与今天日常使用的口径基本一致、相对宽泛的“金融”概念：“货币资金的融通。一般指与货币流通与银行信用有关的一切活动，主要通过银行的各种业务来实现。如货币的发行、流通和回笼，存款的吸收和提取，贷款的发放和回收，国内外汇兑的往来，以及资本主义制度下贴现市场和证券市场的活动等，均属于金融的范畴。”

与此相对应，从国外商学院传来的窄口径的“金融”，亦即 Finance，仅限于有价证券及其衍生品市场等资本市场范畴。但是，从 Finance 一词在西方的用法来看，又存在宽口径、窄口径和介于两者之间的口径（或者说中口径）。其中宽口径的 Finance 比宽口径的中文词“金融”含义更为广泛，除了包括后者之外，还包括国家财政、公司理财以及个人货币收支等内容；而介于宽口径、窄口径之间的

discussions with academic colleagues and delivered speeches. Moreover, he issued many articles, such as Several Issues on Financial Discipline Construction (published in Vol. 9, *Journal of Central Finance & Economics* in 2000), Reflection on Discussion of "Finance " and "Financial Discipline " (published in Vol. 3, *Economic Review* in 2001), Starting with Banks being Seen as Underdog (published in *Financial Times* on January 13, 2001, and in Vol. 2, *Economic Herald*, in 2001), and the book *Finance—Definitions, Discipline, Situation, Methods and Others* (published by China Financial Publishing House in 2001). In 2001, Huang Da went to the United States to communicate with experts of Fed about the usage of the word "Finance ".

Through his efforts, Huang Da got a clear understanding about the two Chinese characters " 金融 " and the English word "Finance ".

The word " 金融 " was not a term from ancient time. The two Chinese characters didn't appear together in Chinese reference books in the *Kangxi Dictionary* or earlier dictionaries. When did it come into use? Was it from a direct translation from Finance or not? No textual research could prove that. According to Huang Da, it most probably came from Japan in Meiji Restoration period. The earliest reference books containing this term are *Ci Yuan* and *Ci Hai*. The former was started in 1908 and published in 1915 and the latter was started in 1915 yet published in 1936. It proved that the term had been used for several decades in the early 20th century.

The two books defined the term as "Accommodating monetary capital through credit intermediary organs ". In comparison, the *Ci Hai* gave another interpretation in its trial version in the 1960s and its first public version in 1979. This definition was closer to the concept that we use today, reading: "Accommodation of monetary capital. It usually refers to these activities involving currency circulation and bank credit, which are mainly conducted through banking practices, such as the issuance, circulation and withdrawal of currency, deposit taking and deposit withdrawal, offer and recovery of loans, domestic and foreign remittance of expenditure and income, and discount market and stock market under the capitalism system, all belonging to the category. "

Oppositely, the Finance of graduates from foreign business colleges was in a narrow sense. It was limited to the capital market category, such as securities and derivatives market. However, the word "Finance " is used in wide, narrow and medium ranges in the West. Among them, the wide sense is larger than our definition, including state revenue and expenditure, company management of money matters and individual income

Finance，所指范围有的则与宽口径的中文词“金融”大体相当。

显而易见，就中文“金融”而言，宽窄口径相去甚远。按照黄达的思路，既然两种口径并存是客观事实，难以存此废彼，难以定于一尊，那就必须互相理解、互相尊重彼此不同的用法。

在此基础上，更进一步来看，有金融就要有以金融为对象的金融学，有宽窄口径的金融自然也应该有与宽窄口径相对应的金融学。

宽口径的金融学基本应该包括金融理论的宏观分析层面和微观分析层面。前者是 Monetary Economics，属于宏观经济学的一部分，具体包括货币供求、宏观均衡以及国际宏观政策等内容。而后者为 Financial Economics，大体包括从金融市场、金融机构与金融功能角度的分析层面等。此外，独立于上述两个部分，但是同属宽口径金融学的还包括货币、信用、利率乃至金融本身这些范畴的剖析和论证。

与此不同，部分西方教科书当中的窄口径金融学仅仅关注金融市场，由此延伸出两个有关学科建设当中的“难解之谜”：一是金融领域的宏观分析如何处理；二是金融中介机构的学问如何看待。这两个问题不仅关系到中国金融学科发展的方向，而且事关货币银行学的前途与命运。对于第一个谜题，黄达认为，以宏观金融分析为主的货币银行学是从金融的角度去考量宏观经济运行，而宏观经济学是对整个经济的宏观分析，尽管对于金融有所涉猎，但其钻研深度有限。同时，对于金融的宏观分析与微观分析，相互支撑，互为依托，无法生硬切割。由此可见，金融的宏观分析理应抛开所谓“重复”的羁绊，独立于宏观经济学而存在。对于第二个谜题，在黄达看来，20 世纪 50 年代以来金融市场的长足发展，特别是诺贝尔经济学奖频频光顾，好像已经使金融机构的“光辉”尽失。事实上，有关金融机构的理论研究同样丰富而有深度，只是人们缺少应有的重视而已。

解决了上述问题，也就解决了长期困扰着黄达的金融学科建设问题，也就让黄达阶段性地为所谓金融学找到了一个未来方向——要建设一门以宽口径金融为研究对象，“包罗万象”的金融学，形成“大金融”学科体系。

and expenditures. While the medium sense of Finance has similar meaning with Chinese characters " 金融 ".

Obviously, the wide and narrow senses of the Chinese characters " 金融 "are totally different . So, following Huang's strain of thought, the two senses are in coexistence, and thus we should gain mutual understanding and respect on different usages.

On this basis, the finance needs a discipline, and further, the finance in different senses needs corresponding disciplines.

The financial discipline in a wide range should contain the macro-analysis and micro-analysis levels of financial theory. The former refers to Monetary Economics, a part of macro-economics, including money supply and demand, macroscopic equilibrium, international macro-policies, etc. The latter refers to Financial Economics, mainly containing analysis level of financial market, agency and function. Apart from the former two parts, the wide-range financial discipline also contains dissect and demonstration of currency, credit, money rate and finance itself.

In contrast, some western textbooks are limited to the narrow sense of finance, and only focus on financial market. Hence, there come two puzzles in discipline construction. One is how to deal with the macro-analysis in the financial field. The other is how to treat financial intermediaries. The two issues were not only related to the development direction of China's financial discipline, but also concerned the destiny of the Economics of Money and Banking. For the first puzzle, Huang Da believed that the Economics of Money and Banking centering on macro-analysis on finance was to discuss macroeconomy from the financial angle, while the macroeconomics was to make macro-analysis on the whole economy. It dealt with some issues related to finance, but with a limit depth. In addition, macro analysis and micro-analysis on finance interrelate with each other. Therefore, macro-analysis on finance should be free from repetition and be independent from the macroeconomics. As for the second puzzle, he believed that the financial market had developed greatly since the 1950s. Especially when Nobel Prize was awarded to who made achievements on financial market one after another, it seemed that financial intermediaries lost their glory. Actually, theory research on financial intermediaries was also profound and far-reaching. It just lacked people's necessary attention.

Having clarified those issues, Huang Da found the direction for the construction of the financial discipline, which aimed at covering a lot of contents, studying the wide-range finance, and establishing a "macro-finance " system.

具体而言，该体系至少包括以下三个层次的问题：

第一个层次：宽口径的金融学；

第二个层次：宏观金融分析与微观金融分析；

第三个层次：技术层面与经营管理层面的金融问题。

再回到金融学科建设的实践来看，2000 年 4 月初，在中国人民大学财政金融学院组织的“跨入 21 世纪的金融学科建设研讨会”上，与会学者已经就“21 世纪金融学科必须跨上一个新台阶”达成了共识。更重要的是，本次会议后，黄达受学院委托，决定将《货币银行学（第三版）》升级换代，修订成为“杂货铺”式的《金融学》。英文名定为：*Economics of Money and Finance*。这为那个时期黄达思考金融与金融学科发展方向的历程画上了一个句号，而且真正迈出了构建“大金融”学科体系具有里程碑意义的关键一步。

事实上，新中国成立以来，由老一代中国金融学人牵头，全国金融学界团结一致，共同推动金融学科建设的大事件屡见不鲜。整个中国金融学界更像一个和谐温馨的大家庭，尽管不乏观点之争，但难掩老中青三代每个人内心的那份温情和守护。

20 世纪 60 年代初期，中国人民银行召开的一次会议集中讨论了金融学科教材，特别是《货币银行学》的建设问题。会议由丁冬放副行长主持，参加者皆为当时金融学界骨干。会议倾向于由黄达牵头编写一本中国人自己设计的《货币信用学》，但是由于而后的政治运动，这次教材建设活动被无声无息地搁置起来。而第二次则是在粉碎“四人帮”之后的 1977 年，同样由中国人民银行召集，专门讨论《货币银行学》教材建设问题。讨论过程中，大家一致要求黄达牵头编写一本教材，但由于黄达深知“统编”之难，便明确表明态度：“支持但不参与具体编写”。最终，这项工作落在王克华的肩上，张玉文、周骏、王佩真、荣韫瑶、周升业和陶湘等参与编写，中国财政经济出版社以《社会主义货币信用学》（1981 年 6 月）的题名出版。第三次是上文提到的 1987 年 8 月在复旦大学召开的“中国财经教学

Specifically, the system involves the following three levels:

The first level: wide-range finance;

The second level: macro-analysis and micro-analysis on finance;

The third level: financial issues on technology level and management level.

Back to the practice on the financial discipline construction, consensus was reached that "the financial discipline should step into a new level in the 21st century " at the Seminar on the Development of Financial Discipline Construction in the 21st Century hosted by the School of Finance, the Renmin University of China in early April, 2000. More importantly, after the meeting, the School of Finance, the Renmin University of China entrusted Huang Da to upgrade the *Economics of Money and Banking (the third edition)* into a financial discipline involving many contents. Its English name became *Economics of Money and Finance.* By this, Huang Da finished his consideration about finance and development direction of financial discipline, and set up the milestone for the construction of macro-finance system.

In fact, since the founding of PRC, there have been many events witnessing that the whole financial circle united to promote the construction of the financial discipline under the lead of the old generation financial scholars. China's financial circle is more like a big family. There are different ideas, but there are more tender and support among the old, middle and young generations in this circle.

In the early 1960s, the People's Bank of China held a meeting to discuss the issue on textbook of financial discipline, especially *Economics of Money and Banking.* The meeting was presided over by Vice-governor Ding Dongfang and participants were all core members of the financial circle. The meeting was apt to entrust Huang Da to take the lead in compiling our own book *Money and Credit.* However, it was suspended by political movements. After the downfall of the Gang of Four in 1977, the People's Bank of China held a meeting again to discuss the compilation of *Economics of Money and Banking.* This time, everybody agreed to entrust Huang Da to take the lead in compiling a textbook. But Huang Da fully knew the difficulties on the compilation nationwide, so he expressed his attitude "to support but not join in the compiling work ". At last, the work was entrusted to Wang Kehua, and Zhang Yuwen, Zhou Jun, Wang Peizhen, Rong Yunyao, Zhou Shengye and Tao Xiang joined in writing. In June, 1981, it was published by the China Financial and Economic Publishing House, with the name of *Socialist Money and Credit.* The third

计划国际研讨会”。会上确定了包括货币银行学在内的10门财经类专业核心课程目录。而后黄达中标获得了该课程的编写权，并于1989年开始组织力量编写。其间于1991年7月底至8月初，在长春工商银行的银行管理学校召开“审稿会”。尽管对于教材编写并未能提出重大修订意见，但是本次会议却成为处于金融学界第一线的老一代与新一代金融学人的首次聚会，所谓“群贤毕至、老少咸集”，值得纪念。论及第四次，当属1997年9月由西南财经大学主办的“中国金融学科建设与发展研讨会”，这是最后一次金融学界老人参加最全并且对学科建设进行了激烈讨论、争论的会。会议主题是当时最为引人关注的金融学科定位问题。而后围绕着这一话题，先后召开的2000年4月由中国人民大学财政金融学院在北京组织的“跨入21世纪的金融学科建设研讨会”、2001年8月由中央财经大学在西宁组织的“金融学专业教育教学改革与发展战略研究研讨会”以及2002年由对外经济贸易大学在银川主办的“加入WTO与中国高等金融教育的改革与创新高级研讨会”等系列会议构成了第五次全国金融学界集体推动金融学科建设的活动。

作为《货币银行学》编写的亲历者与见证者，在写完《金融学（第一版）》，也就是《货币银行学（第三版）》之后，黄达本打算“退出江湖”。然而，他的身影似乎并没有消失于“江湖”之中。之后的四五年，他考察了货币银行学在西方走上大学讲坛的开端和演进，并写出《回顾1950年之前“货币银行学”学科的发展（初稿）》一文。又经过一年多，以两张幻灯片概括了《金融学科的演进及前瞻》。面对始于美国的金融海啸，还向他所在的团队提出《金融海啸和G20格局下的货币银行学》等问题。

直到现在，尽管对于“大金融”体系的争论已不再如新世纪初期那样引人关注，但是黄达对于金融学科发展未来之路的探索并未因此而停止……

time was when the International Symposium of China Financial and Economic Teaching Program was held in Fudan University in August, 1987. The meeting decided the contents of 10 core courses on finance, including *Economics of Money and Banking.* And Huang Da gained the right to write the book and started to compile it in 1989. In the end of July and the beginning of August of 1991, the bank management school of the Industrial and Commercial Bank of Changchun opened a meeting to examine and approve manuscripts of the book. Though they didn't provide major revising suggestions, this meeting was the first time for the old and the new generations of financial scholars to get together. It was worthy of remembering. The fourth time was when the Symposium on the Construction and Development of China's Financial Discipline was held by Southwestern University of Finance and Economics in September, 1997. This was the last meeting that gathered the oldest financial scholars and they made a drastic debate on discipline construction. The main topic of the meeting was the position of financial discipline. For this topic, the School of Finance, the Renmin University of China held a Seminar on the Development of Financial Discipline Construction in 21 Century in Beijing in April, 2000, the Central University of Finance and Economics held a Seminar on Finance Professional Education Reform and Development Strategy in Xining in August, 2001, and the University of International Business and Economics held an Advanced Seminar on Joining WTO and the Reform and Innovation of China's Higher Financial Education in Yinchuan in 2002. These meetings combined to form the fifth activity of the national financial circle contributing to promote the financial discipline construction.

As the witness of the textbook compiling of financial discipline, Huang Da planned to resign after the publication of the first edition of *Economics of Money and Finance (*the third edition of *Economics of Money and Banking).* However, he didn't really leave the circle. In the following four and five years, he investigated the beginning and evolution of money and banking in the West campus, and wrote the article A Review on the Disciplinary Development of Money and Banking before 1950 (draft). Over a year later, he summarized the Evolution and Prospect of Finance with two slides. In front of the American financial crises, he proposed to his team such issues as the Economics of Money and Banking under the Financial Crisis and G20 Structure.

Nowadays, although the debate on "macro-finance " system is no longer eye-catching, Huang Da does not stop exploring the future development of financial discipline.

培养在东西方两个文化平台上自由漫步的人才

Training Personnel Who Can Roam Free on Both Cultural Stages in the East and in the West

自1968年瑞典银行增设诺贝尔经济学奖以来，一共有七十余位经济学家获此殊荣。这七十余位经济学大师当中，1999年获奖者、“欧元之父”罗伯特·蒙代尔是其中较为“另类”的一位。

“另类”无关学术，而关乎其之于中国的情怀。

蒙代尔是这个群体当中，能够持续将目光投向中国，能够持续亲身参与中国经济学研究与实践，能够不懈拓宽中西经济学交流桥梁的大师之一。近年来，在中国各类重要的国际研讨会上，我们经常能看到老先生的身影。

事实上，论及西方经济学家的中国情怀，除了蒙代尔，美国斯坦福大学教授、当代金融发展理论奠基人罗纳德·麦金农同样不得不提起。

新世纪以来，在国际社会“胁迫”人民币升值的呼声一浪高过一浪，特别是一些西方经济学者对中国进行无端指责的情况下，蒙代尔与麦金农则“据理力争”，共同呼吁人民币应该选择盯住美元的汇率政策，应该保持相对稳定，避免大幅升值。

2004年5月30日，在中国人民大学主办的“中国人文社会科学论坛”上，黄达、王传纶、吴敬琏、厉以宁等国内学界泰斗，与蒙代尔、斯宾塞、费尔普斯和麦金农等美国经济学家一一展开中外对话。这场中外大师云集的学术盛会，吸引了来自全国的几千观众，人大世纪馆座无虚席、一票难求。

蒙代尔做主旨发言，麦金农则与黄达以“货币国际化的利益、风险与路径——人民币会成为世界第三大货币吗”为题展开对话。中国人民大学财政金融学院院长陈雨露作主持。就论题来看，当年遥不可及的目标，在今天看来似乎已经近在咫尺。2015年12月1日，国际货币基金组织（IMF）宣布，将人民币作为除英镑、欧元、日元和美元之外的第五种货币纳入SDR（特别提款权）货币篮子，2016年10月1日正式生效，人民币成为可以自由使用的货币。五种货币的权重分别为美元41.7%、欧元30.9%、人民币10.92%、日元8.3%、英镑8.1%。另外，从中国人民大学国际货币研究所首创的人民币国际化指数（RII）来看，乐观估计，只要没有重大不利事件发生，未来3~5年人民币很有希望成为继美元和欧元之后的世界第三大货币。此外，令人印象深刻的是，两位教授在会上不约而同地再次呼吁人民币应避免大幅升值，并从不同角度对人民币国际化提出了具有建设性的意见。

Since the Swedbank added the Nobel Prize in Economics in 1968, more than 70 economists in total have won the prize. Among them, Robert Mundell, the Father of the euro, the winner of the 1999 Nobel Prize in Economics, is different from others.

His difference is not in academic term but in his feelings for China.

Mr. Mundell is one of the masters who constantly paid close attention to China, took part in the research and practice on economics and made unremitting efforts to broaden the bridge for economics exchanges between China and the West. In recent years, we have frequently found him in all kinds of important international seminars in China.

When talking about western economists' special feelings for China, besides Mr. Mundell, there is another remarkable professor, Ronald McKinnon, from Stanford University, the founder of modern financial development theory.

Entering the new century, there was a growing call for appreciation of the RMB in the international community. When some western economists made groundless accusations towards China, Mr. Mundell and Mr. McKinnon argued and appealed together that RMB should keep pace with the exchange rate policies of the US dollars, maintaining relatively stable and avoiding skyrocketing.

On May 30, 2004, on the Chinese Forum on Humanities and Social Science hosted by the Renmin University of China, domestic leading authorities such as Huang Da, Wang Chuanlun, Wu Jinglian, Li Yining and American economists including Robert A. Mundell, Michael Spence, Edmund Phelps and Ronald McKinnon got together to make a dialogue. This academic event converged many masters, attracting thousands of audience. All seats were occupied in the stadium of the university.

Mr. Mundell delivered a keynote speech. Huang Da and Mr. McKinnon had a dialogue on the topic of "Benefit, Risk and Path of Currency Internationalization—Will RMB Become the Third World Currency? " The dean of the School of Finance of the Renmin University of China Chen Yulu acted as the host. In terms of the proposition, the unreachable target in those days is now near at hand. On December 1, 2015, the International Monetary Fund (IMF) announced that RMB was included into the currency basket of the Special Drawing Right (SDR) as the fifth currency following pound sterling, euro, Japanese yen and US dollar, which marks the renminbi became a freely usable currency. The SDR inclusion will take effect from October 1, 2016. The weights of the five currencies in the new SDR basket are: US dollar 41.7%, euro 30.9%, renminbi 10.92%, Japanese yen 8.3% and pound sterling 8.1%. In terms of RII, RMB Internationalization Index, which was initiated by the International Monetary Institute of the Renmin University of China, RMB was expected to become the third world

遗憾的是，2014 年 10 月 1 日，麦金农教授不幸辞世。之后他的家人还将他生前的重要著述和藏书共计 1 897 本全部捐给中国人民大学货币研究所。

不难看出，蒙代尔、麦金农与中国、与黄达有着不解的“情缘”。而在这段“情缘”当中，黄达与蒙代尔——两位已是耄耋之年的老人，携手推动中国金融教育事业发展并由此结下深厚友谊的故事，更是被传为佳话。

“1995 年，在中国人民大学做访问学者期间，能够认识黄达教授并结下深厚的友谊，我深感荣幸。特别是能与黄达教授共同冠名‘黄达—蒙代尔经济学奖’及‘黄达—蒙代尔经济学讲座’，我感到非常高兴。未来，真诚地希望黄达教授能永远健康和快乐！”2011 年，蒙代尔在听到黄达获得首届“中国金融学科终身成就奖”后，写下了这段文字。

寥寥数语，我们能够读出埋藏在两位老朋友内心的情感。

从相识于“福特项目”，到携手设立“黄达—蒙代尔经济学讲座”与“黄达—蒙代尔经济学奖”，一路走来，两位老人希望在中国已经逐渐融入世界的大背景下，探索出一条国际化金融学人才培养的新路。那么，在他们眼中究竟什么样的人才能够适应全球范围内金融日新月异的变化，真正成为新金融时代的弄潮儿？

2001 年 10 月 17 日，在中国人民大学中国财政金融政策研究中心主办的“黄达—蒙代尔经济学讲座”的启动仪式上，黄达给出了一个“答案”——“我们最需要的就是在东西方两个文化平台上，可以无障碍地自由往返、自由漫步的人才。”

此后，已经有包括 10 余位诺贝尔经济学奖获得者在内的逾百位专家学者做客“黄达—蒙代尔经济学讲座”，宣讲自己的学术思想和教育理念，为推动中国金融人才培养以及国际学术交流做出了不可估量的贡献。

一年多之后的 2003 年 3 月 19 日，首届“黄达 — 蒙代尔经济学奖”（原称“黄达 — 蒙代尔优秀博士论文奖”）颁奖典礼在中国人民大学举行。该奖项主要奖励国内科研院所的优秀博士论文。截至 2015 年，在已经举行的七次评奖中，先后有来自中国人民大学、北京大学、清华大学、中国社会科学院、财政部财政科学研究所等科研院所的 28 位青年才俊获此荣誉，其中多位获奖者又相继获得全国百篇优秀博士学位论文奖或提名奖。

currency after US dollar and euro in the future 3 or 5 years, unless any major unfavorable event happens. Besides, what was impressive is that the two professors invariably called for the prevention of RMB's substantial appreciation and put forward constructive comments from different aspects on RMB internationalization.

Unfortunately, Prof. McKinnon passed away on October 1, 2014. His families donated the 1,897 books of his collection to International Monetary Institute of the Renmin University of China.

Mr. Mundell, Mr. McKinnon and Huang Da have special emotions for China. Huang Da and Mr. Mundell, two old men at their 80s, worked together to promote the development of China's financial educational industry, which becomes a story on everybody's lips.

"I am honored to meet Professor Huang Da and make friends with him when I was a visiting scholar in the Renmin University of China in 1995. I am very glad to share the title of Mundell-Huang Da Prize " and "Mundell-Huang Da Lectures " with him. Mr. Mundell wrote down these words on hearing that Huang Da won the first China's Annual Financial Discipline Lifetime Achievement Award in 2011.

We could understand their friendship through a few words.

From their first meeting at Ford Program to the establishment of Mundell-Huang Da Lectures and the Mundell-Huang Da Prize, the two old men wished to explore a new way to train finance personnel under the circumstances that China had merged into the world.In future, what kinds of talents are able to adapt to the increasing changes and ride the tides in the new financial age?

On the launching ceremony of the Mundell-Huang Da Lectures which was hosted by the China Financial Policies Study Center of the Renmin University of China on October 17, 2001, Huang Da gave his "answer ": "We need more talents who can roam free in both cultural contexts of China and the West. "

With this guidance, more than a hundred of experts, including over 10 Nobel Prize winners, had come to give lectures, sharing their academic thoughts and education philosophy. The lecture made great contributions to promoting the training of finance personnel and the international academic exchanges.

On March 19, 2003, the first award ceremony of Mundell-Huang Da Prize (originally named Mundell-Huang Da Excellent Doctoral Dissertation Prize) was held in the Renmin University of China . In the seven appraisals up to 2015, 28 young talents from the Renmin University of China, Peking University, Tsinghua University, Chinese Academy of Social Sciences and Institute of Financial Science of the Ministry of Finance won the prize and many of them achieved the National 100 Excellent Doctoral Paper Award or award nomination.

永远奋进在时代的前沿

Always Advancing on the Leading Edge of the Times

从抗日烽火中建校的陕北公学，到挺进敌后开展国防教育的华北联合大学，再到迎接新中国的华北大学，最后到为新中国经济建设而创办并经历风风雨雨而迎来改革开放的中国人民大学，不管时代如何变迁，这所学校始终都在为中华民族的振兴贡献着自己的所有力量。

“在这个漫长的历史进程当中，一定有一种精神在始终鼓舞着中国人民大学不断前进，或者说一定有一种无形的力量自始至终都在推动着中国人民大学的发展”，这样一种模糊的意识始终萦绕在黄达的脑海当中。

直到1992年，在中国人民大学已经走完55个春秋之际，这样的意识才逐渐地清晰起来。当年的11月1日，时任中国人民大学校长的黄达在庆祝中国人民大学建校五十五周年大会的讲话中，将这种意识做了一个精准的概括——“永远奋进在时代的前沿”。

事实上，作为一名“纯粹”的人大人，黄达自己的奋斗历程或许就是践行“永远奋进在时代的前沿”最为生动的范例。

从坎坷的少年时代走出，投身于革命洪流，到偶然间“邂逅”金融，并与金融“相识”、“相爱”，再到虽几经风雨仍对其“不离不弃”，在此期间，黄达始终用一种乐观上进的心态，迎接着人生当中的每一个挑战，直至达到事业和学术的巅峰。

如今，已是耄耋之年的黄达，仍然进行着永不停止的追问与思考，仍然延续着“永远奋进在时代的前沿”的历程。与此同时，对于他本人及其对于金融学科贡献的褒奖也纷至沓来。

2011年6月1日，黄达获得首届“中国金融学科终身成就奖”。他的老朋友、中国证监会首任主席刘鸿儒、中国人民银行行长周小川与教育部副部长郝平共同为黄达颁发了这一代表中国金融学科最高荣誉的奖项，以表彰他在过去的六十多年里为中国金融学科建设做出的突出贡献。马凯副总理为此专门写来贺信：“您是我十分敬重的老师。三十多年来，听您讲学，读您著述，向您请教，与您交流，每感滋味厚重，受益匪浅。您给我的突出印象是，在教学、学术研究和政策咨询中，您始

From Shanbei Public School established during the Anti-Japanese War, to the North China Union University providing national defense education in the enemy-occupied areas, to the North China University, and finally the Renmin University of China founded for the economic construction of PRC, this university was always striving for making contribution to the revitalization of China.

"During this long course of history, there must be a spirit inspiring the Renmin University of China to move on. Or there must be an intangible power to promote the development of the Renmin University of China. " This is a hazy awareness lingering on Huang Da's mind.

The awareness didn't come clear until 1992 when the Renmin University of China was 55 years old. On November 1 that year, the president of the Renmin University of China delivered a speech on the 55th anniversary of the Renmin University of China and summarized that the university was "always advancing on the leading edge of the times ."

Actually, as a "pure" person of the Renmin University of China, Huang Da's own struggle course is a contemporary history that complies with the motto "always advancing on the leading edge of the times ."

After the hard time in his early youth, he pitched into the revolution. He encountered finance by chance, and then he got to know about and fell in love with it. And his life is all about finance even amid ups and downs. Huang Da has always been optimistic about each challenge in his life and has achieved the summit of his career and the academic peak.

Now, in his 80s, Huang Da never stops asking and thinking. He still follows his way of "advancing on the leading edge of the times ." Meanwhile, he has been receiving many awards for his contribution to financial discipline.

On June 1, 2011, Huang Da won the first China's Annual Financial Discipline Lifetime Achievement Award. His old friend Liu Hongru, who was the first president of China Securities Regulatory Commission, Zhou Xiaochuan, the governor of China People's Bank, and Hao Ping, the vice-president of the Ministry of Education, jointly awarded him, which represented the highest honor of China's financial discipline. It was cited for his remarkable contributions during the past 60-odd years. Vice Premier Ma Kai sent him a congratulatory letter: "You are my respectable teacher. During the past 30-odd years, I have attended your lectures, read your books and consulted you on issues. Every time, my communication with you gave me great help. With regard to your teaching, academic research and policy consultation, you always have an independent mind and never follow what others have said. You always start from the actual facts, extracting and expounding economic

终坚守着独立思考精神，从不人云亦云；您总是从中国经济的实际出发提炼和阐述经济理念，而不是拿本本（或马列本本，或西方经济学本本，等等）剪裁中国经济现实；您虽寿高耄耋，但思想从不停滞；您总是深入浅出，决不故弄玄虚。所有这些，都是当下经济学界应当学习和弘扬的。期盼着您为促进金融学、财政学、价格学等经济理论的发展和人才的培养做出更大的贡献！”

在颁奖典礼上，黄达从东西方古圣先贤们关于金融真知的至理名言谈起，回顾了金融学科源远流长的历史。在他看来，对于既需时日而又难以收显赫之功的哲学社会科学领域的学科建设，要表示支持、尊重和奖励之情，也需以国家兴盛为前提。“我20世纪20年代出生，那是积贫积弱的中国。小学老师时时讲国耻、国难，觉得天是灰蒙蒙的，一种耻辱感总是挥之不去。今天的中国，虽然必须应对的紧迫问题接连不断，而且唱衰中国的声音也总是不甘寂寞，但中华振兴，昭如日月，确定无疑。这就使奖励哲学社会科学门类的基础学科建设，已有余力。”他认为，刘鸿儒金融教育基金会为此做出了现实的努力。在他的话语中，我们感受到的除了对于金融学科建设再上台阶的期许，更多看到的是一位中国传统知识分子心中那份浓烈的家国情怀。

为此，中国人民大学张杰教授还专门题写了一首七律，以表达对于先生的崇敬。“从来淡泊是利名，甲子回望路峥嵘。曾挥椽笔突禁囿，更捧琴心荐平衡。学纳东西江海阔，教综南北星斗明。寻常巷陌隐巨擘，耄耋谈笑意纵横。”

2013年11月28日，黄达凭借“财政信贷综合平衡理论”，高票荣获第六届“中国经济理论创新奖”。此前，“农村家庭联产承包责任制理论”“国有企业股份制改革理论”“整体改革理论”“价格双轨制理论”以及“中国经济结构调整理论”五项理论，因为对中国改革与发展产生的重大影响而先后获奖。在黄达看来，要达到富裕社会主义的彼岸，没有现成道路，只能是“摸着石头过河”。经济学界在选择过河路线、在选择起步应该登上哪块、哪几块石头方面，不顾社会政治生活中依然充斥着许许多多的禁忌，激情满怀地议论、讨论、争论、辩论，进而产生的这些

ideology rather than cutting pieces from book (books of either Marxist or western economics) for application in China's economy. You never stick to old ways but advance forward even at your 80s. You always explain profound theories in simple language rather than deliberately mystifying them. All these merits are what we should learn from and carry forward in the economic circle. I am looking forward that you will make greater contributions to promoting the development of economic theories on finance, banking, price and other respects as well as the training of personnel."

On the awarding ceremony, Huang Da made his speech starting from the true sayings of wise men of ancient times in the East and in the West, and reviewed the long history of financial discipline. In his point of view, the construction of disciplines on philosophy and social science field, which are time consuming and hard to make eminent achievements, need more support, respect and prize, and can not be developed well without the premise of national prosperity. "I was born in the 1920s when our country was poor and weak. The teachers in elementary school always talked about national humiliation and national calamity. I felt that the sky was always gray, and the sense of humiliation lingered around us. Today, although China are faced with many urgent issues and there are voices dampening down expectations of China, China will surely develop vigorously. So there is spare strength for rewarding the construction of disciplines on philosophy and social science." He thought the Liu Hongru Endowment for Financial Education had made practical efforts in that respect. In his words, we could read his expectation on further development of financial discipline construction, and moreover, we could feel the strong emotions of a traditional intellectual for his country.

Professor Zhang Jie from the Renmin University of China wrote a poem to express his respect to Huang Da. "Always indifferent to fame and fortune, you have been in the steep and lofty path for over 60 years. You have broken many limits with your pen, and put forward measures with a soul of a musician. You have integrated knowledge of both the East and the West, and taught students with a clear mind. You live like a hermit in an ordinary street, but old age cannot hide your radiating glamour."

On November 28, 2013, Huang Da won the 6th China's Economic Theory Innovation Award owing to his "Introduction of General Equilibrium on Public Finance and Credit". Before that, five theories were awarded for their influences on China's reform and development. They included the "Theory on Household Contract Responsibility System", "Theory on SOEs Shareholding Reform", "Overall Reform Theory", "Theory on Dual Price System" and the "Theory on the Restructuring of China's Economy". Huang Da

理论为改革开放做出了实实在在的贡献。

作为经济学人，黄达知道，自己的武器就是经济学，就是经济理论。然而，当前世界的经济学，显得有点迟钝、有点保守、有点缺乏锐气。当今世界的新发展、新课题，显然无法靠几个计量模型来解决，无法靠简单重复经济学本身那些论证了几百年、几千年的规律、原理去解决，只有在提升指导经济学的基本思想，在寻求哲理、宇宙观、方法论等指导思想层面下足功夫，才能得到根本性解决。

为此，黄达提出要将东方文化精粹作为哲理性的指导思想引入经济学研究，以改造当前以西方文化为基础构建的现代经济学，特别是因其传统思维和认知惯性而滋生的固守和片面。只有这样，才能推动世界经济学跨上一个新的、更有活力、更能指导实际、更能引领实践的高度，进入一个全新的境界。

2014 年 12 月 18 日，黄达获得第三届“吴玉章人文社会科学终身成就奖”。获奖之际，黄达在演讲中首先提到的不是他的学术贡献，而是饱含深情地回顾了奖项冠名人、中国人民大学第一任校长吴玉章先生。“先后有十八年，经常直接聆听吴玉章老人家循循善诱、慈祥平和的教导，一再被这位长者毕生为祖国、为民族、为共产主义理想忠诚奉献的坚定信念和高贵品德所感染，永生难忘。现在，中华民族已经走上振兴富强之路。虽然世界遍布荆棘，前面并非坦途，但中华民族前进的步伐已无可阻挡。这应是最能告慰他老人家在天之灵的。”

或许正是这样难得的历史机遇，才让我们亲身感受到了先后两任中国人民大学老校长对于民族、对于国家、对于共产主义理想的坚定与执着。

四年三获大奖！三个大奖三个“一百万”，黄达采用了相同的方式，将全部三百万奖金捐献给了钟爱一生的中国金融学科。

事实上，这样的做法也完成了黄达长久的心愿——“就我现在的自然状况，已经难以披坚持锐，拔寨摧城。因而，利用这笔奖金支持处于学科建设第一线的同行，或许更可体现我自己致力于推进中国金融学科建设的一贯志向。”

believed that there was no ready-made path to an affluent socialist society, and that we could only feel our way over the stones. The economics community neglected the scruples in social political life, and they discussed, argued and debated with passions. The theories originating from it did make practical contributions to the reform and opening up.

As an economist, Huang Da knows that his weapon is economics and economic theories. However, the economics circle today seems sluggish, conservative and lacking of dashing spirit. Apparently, today's new development and problems cannot be solved either by few econometric models or by repeating economic rules and principles that have been demonstrated for over hundreds or thousands of years. Only by making efforts to upgrade the basic idea of guiding economics and seek philosophy, world view and methodology can we settle these problems in a fundamental way.

For this reason, Huang Da has proposed that we should introduce the essence of the Eastern culture into the study on economics, so as to transform the modern economics which was built on the Western culture. In particular, we should change the single-faceted and rigid concepts resulting from traditional thinking and cognitive inertia. Only in this way can we push world economics to a higher level so that it can vigorously guide practice towards a new realm.

On December 18, 2014, Huang Da won the 3rd Wu Yuzhang Humanities and Social Sciences Lifetime Achievement Award. At the ceremony, he didn't talk about his academic contribution first, but reviewed the achievements of Wu Yuzhang, the first president of the Renmin University of China in his speech. "I listened to his instructions for 18 years. He was amiable and good at teaching. I am deeply impressed by his moral character and his fortitude, loyalty and dedication for the country, the nation and the ideal of communism, and I will never forget that. Today, the Chinese nation is on the way of revitalization. There are thorns and thistles around the world, ups and downs on the road, but our steps are unstoppable. This is the best news that can comfort his spirit."

This is the historic opportunity for us to witness that the two old presidents of the Renmin University of China held such firm confidence in and persistent pursuit for the nation, the country and the ideal of communism.

Three rewards in four years! Each came with a million yuan. Huang Da donated all of the bonus to his be-loved Chinese financial discipline.

Actually, this helped to make his wish come true. "Due to my health, it is hard for me to charge on the front line of finance. So, sending the bonus to support my colleagues on the forefront of the discipline construction might accord more with my consistent ambition on promoting China's finance construction."

6-1

“大金融”学科建设

Financial Discipline Development

6-1-1>

20世纪90年代中期，随着海外学成归国人数的不断增多，Finance或者说“现代金融学”出现了一次引进潮。于是，对于在我国存续了百余年的“金融”这个经济词汇有了不同的解读，对于国内的“金融学科”形成了相当大的冲击。

为此，西南财经大学于1997年9月组织召开“中国金融学科建设与发展研讨会”，专门研讨“金融”学科的“定位”问题。这是最后一次金融教学界老人出席最全并且对学科建设进行了讨论、争论的会议，成为世纪之交以来全国金融教学界共同关心、讨论、推动学科建设的起点。

此后，关于金融概念的诠释众说纷纭，“货币银行学的命运可能将要终结”的观点甚嚣尘上。黄达开始意识到这是一个非常严肃的问题，不能掉以轻心。于是，接下来几年，他将主要精力都集中在了这个问题上。

2000年4月，在中国人民大学财政金融学院组织的“跨入21世纪的金融学科建设研讨会”上，与会专家明确了一个共识：面对21世纪金融学科的建设必须跨上一个新的台阶。会后，学院决定由黄达主持，把20世纪90年代的《货币银行学》升级换代。这就督促他不能不直接面对1997年西南财大那次会议上所提出的而在2000年已经日益明朗了的金融学科定位问题。

407

图407为2000年4月1日，“跨入21世纪的金融学科建设研讨会”在北京召开。部分与会专家合影留念。前排从左至右分别为：马绍孟、黄达和王传纶。

On April 1, 2000, the" Seminar on the Development of Financial Discipline Construction in the 21st Century" was held in Beijing. Some experts took a group photo. From the left to the right in the front row are Ma Shaomeng, Huang Da and Wang Chuanlun.

408

图408为2000年4月1日，“跨入21世纪的金融学科建设研讨会”期间，出席会议的中国人民大学教师在一起。前排从左至右分别为：林岗、马绍孟、黄达、王传纶和安体富。

On April 1, 2000, teachers of the Renmin University of China who attended the" Seminar on the Development of Financial Discipline Construction in the 21st Century" took a group photo. From the left to the right in the front row are Lin Gang, Ma Shaomeng, Huang Da, Wang Chuanlun and An Tifu.

In the mid-1990s, as more and more overseas Chinese chose to return to China after finishing their studies abroad, China saw a tide of introducing from abroad Finance or "Modern Finance. " Therefore, "finance, " the economic term that had existed in China for over a hundred years, was understood in different ways, greatly shocking the "financial discipline " of China.

For this reason, the Southwestern University of Finance and Economics held "Symposium on the Construction and Development of China's Financial Discipline" in September 1997 to focus on studying the "positioning " of "finance. " Being the last seminar attended by the most senior teachers of finance who then had discussions and arguments on developing the financial discipline, it became the starting point of the Chinese financial teachers' paying attention to, discussing about, and pushing forward disciplinary development.

After that, opinions on the concept of finance varied, and the one holding that "the science of monetary banking may be put to an end " was widely speculated. Huang Da began to realize that it was a very serious problem against which people could never let down guard. Therefore, he focused mainly on the problem in the following years.

In April 2000, experts attending the" Seminar on the Development of Financial Discipline Construction in the 21st Century " held by the Finance School of the Renmin University of China reached a consensus: development of the financial discipline facing the 21st century must take a step forward. After the seminar, the Finance School of the Renmin University of China decided to designate Huang Da to preside over the updating of *Economics of Money and Banking* complied during the 1990s. It urged him to confront the problem of the positioning of the financial discipline which was raised at the seminar in Southwestern University of Finance and Economics in 1997 and had become increasingly clear since 2000.

409

图 409 为 2000 年 4 月 1 日，黄达在“跨入 21 世纪的金融学科建设研讨会”上发言。

On April 1, 2000, Huang Da delivered a speech at the" Seminar on the Development of Financial Discipline Construction in the 21st Century."

6-1-2>

2000年4月下旬，黄达带着一些经济学领域的问题赴美访问，其中的问题之一就是近距离了解美联储对Finance的用法。在中国留美金融学会的大力协助下，黄达拜访了美联储前主席沃尔克（Paul Volker）、“第三把手”梅耶（Laurence H. Meyer）、里士满区主席J. Alfred Broaddus, Jr.，世界银行章声曼副行长、中国执董祝宪，国际货币基金组织中国执董魏本华、金琦以及交往多年的老朋友斯坦福大学刘遵义、美联储旧金山区前副主席程杭生、南加利福尼亚大学经济学系郑学成（Harrison Cheng）和萧政、普林斯顿大学邹至庄等。

访问中，他了解到，美联储“只管Money不管Finance”的说法，其含义就是资产价格不是货币政策目标。由于在美联储任职前，曾长期在大学任教，梅耶的说法代表了美联储和美国学界对于Finance的一般理解：从广义上讲，Finance可以表示公共财政、公司财务、个人预算等含义，但是必须有形容词作为前缀；而如果单独用Finance，则指狭义上的资本市场。本次赴美访问，从学术角度收获甚多，这反映在他当年整理出的《访美随记》中。

In late April 2000, Huang Da visited the US with some problems in economics. One of them was to understand the use of the concept of Finance by the US Federal Reserve. With great help from the Chinese Finance Association of America, Huang Da visited Paul Volker, former president of the US Federal Reserve, Laurence H. Meyer, third-in-command of the US Federal Reserve, J. Alfred Broaddus, Jr., chairman of the Federal Reserve Bank of Richmond, Zhang Shengman, deputy governor of the World Bank, Zhu Xian, Chinese executive director of the World Bank, Wei Benhua, Chinese executive director of the International Monetary Fund, Jin Qi, and his old friends Lawrence J. Law from Stanford University, Cheng Hangsheng, former vice chairman of the Federal Reserve Bank of San Francisco, Harrison Cheng and Cheng Hsiao from the Department of Economics of University of Southern California, Gregory Chow from Princeton University, etc.

During the visit, he understood that the US Federal Reserve "cares about Money only, but not Finance, " which meant that asset price was not the goal of its monetary policy. Since Meyer was a university teacher for years before he took the post in the US Federal Reserve, his explanation of Finance represented the general understanding of it by the US Federal Reserve and the US academic circle: In the broad sense, Finance could mean public finance, company finance or personal budget, but must be used with an adjective prefix; if used alone, Finance referred to the capital market in the narrow sense. Huang Da learned a lot from his visit to the US academically, which was reflected in his *Essays on the Visit to the US* he wrote that year.

410

图410为2000年4月24日，黄达（右一）与程杭生（左一）交流。

On April 24, 2000, Huang Da (first from the right) was communicating with Cheng Hangsheng (first from the left).

411

图411为2000年4月24日，黄达（左一）赴斯坦福大学拜访刘遵义（右一）。

On April 24, 2000, Huang Da (first from the left) went to Stanford University to visit Lawrence J. Law (first from the right).

412

413

图 412 为 2000 年 4 月 26 日，黄达（右二）、黄卫平（右一）访问加州大学洛杉矶分校，与蔡洪滨（左二）等在一起。

On April 26, 2000, Huang Da (second from the right) and Huang Weiping (first from the right) visited the University of California, Los Angeles, and were with Cai Hongbin (second from the left) et al.

图 413 为 2000 年 4 月 29 日，黄达（左四）、黄卫平（右三）与留美学生在一起。左一为李波，右二为向松祚。

On April 29, 2000, Huang Da (fourth from the left) and Huang Weiping (third from the right) were with the Chinese students in the US. The first from the left is Li Bo and the second from the right is Xiang Songzuo.

414

415

416

图 414 为 2000 年 4 月 30 日，黄达（左一）在沃尔克（右一）家中讨论当时美国经济金融的热点问题。

On April 30, 2000, Huang Da (first from the left) and Volcker (first from the right) discussed about the then hot economic and financial topics in the US at Volcker's.

图 415 为 2000 年 5 月 2 日，黄达（右一）与美联储里士满区主席 J. Alfred Broaddus, Jr. 进行交谈。

On May 2, 2000, Huang Da (first from the right) talked with J. Alfred Broaddus, Jr., president of the Federal Reserve Bank of Richmond.

图 416 为 2000 年 5 月 2 日，本次访美期间黄达游览美国著名历史名城和旅游胜地威廉斯堡。

On May 2, 2000, Huang Da toured and visited Williamsburg, a famous historical city and a tourist attraction.

417

图 417 为 2000 年 5 月 3 日，黄达（右三）、黄卫平（左三）等拜访美联储第三把手梅耶（左四）。

On May 3, 2000, Huang Da (third from the right) and Huang Weiping (third from the left) visited Laurence Meyer (fourth from the left), the third-in-command of the US Federal Reserve.

6-1-3>

2000年7月，在教育部高教司举办的“‘中央银行学’课程中青年骨干教师培训班”上，黄达做了题为《金融学学科建设若干问题》的演讲。这次演讲是他自己厘清思路的起点。随后，他又走访了西南财经大学、武汉大学、中南财经政法大学、湖南大学和暨南大学等多所兄弟院校，与金融教学同行反复交流切磋。

由于当时引进的诠释“金融”的声音处于强势，几乎所有金融专业都有如何确定方向的困惑。大体有两种意见：一是多年从事金融教育的人士，认为“金融”专业沿着原来的路，即兼顾培养金融宏观分析和微观分析两方面人才的方向走，没有错；二是强调应走国外商学院的路，只培养现代金融管理人才。

通过深入交流和冷静分析，大家对问题的来龙去脉有了清醒的认识，本非真正科学意义的对立却搅浑了一池春水。在切磋之中，黄达也日渐对金融覆盖范围、金融学科体系设计和金融专业办学方向等几个问题有了较为清晰的看法。

In July 2000, the Department of Higher Education of the Ministry of Education held "Young and Middle-aged Teachers Training Class on the Course of Central Bank ", and Huang Da delivered a speech titled Several Issues on Financial Discipline Construction. It was since that speech that Huang Da began to clarify his ideas. Later, he visited Southwestern University of Finance and Economics, Wuhan University, Zhongnan University of Economics and Law, Hunan University and Jinan University to communicate with their teachers of finance.

Because the introduced voices interpreting "Finance(金融) " at the time was popular, almost all financial majors were confused by how to determine the direction. There were basically two opinions: first, those who had been engaged in financial education for years held it to be right for the "financial " majors to follow the past road, that is, to focus on cultivating talented people in both macro and micro financial analyses; while the others highlighted that the road of schools of business should be followed to cultivate only talented people in modern financial management.

Through in-depth communication and composed analyses, they had a clear understanding of the whole problem—confrontation that is not in real scientific meaning just messed it. In the exchanges, Huang Da got clear ideas on the coverage of finance, the system design of the financial discipline and the educational direction of the financial majors.

418

图418为2000年11月14日，黄达（左一）在武汉大学金融系做了题为《当前的金融热点两三题》的演讲。期间，与谭崇台教授（右一）漫步在武大校园。

On November 14, 2000, Huang Da (first from the left) delivered a speech titled On the Current Hot Issues in Finance to the Department of Finance of Wuhan University. He strolled around the campus of Wuhan University with Prof. Tan Chongtai (first from the right) during his visit there.

419

图 419 为 2000 年 11 月 16 日，黄达为中南财经政法大学金融学院师生做题为《当前的金融热点两三题》的演讲。

On November 16, 2000, Huang Da delivered a speech titled On the Current Hot Issues in Finance to the students and teachers of the School of Finance of Zhongnan University of Economics and Law.

图 420 为 2000 年 11 月 17 日，黄达（居中）与中南财经政法大学周骏（左一）、朱新蓉（右一）在一起。

On November 17, 2000, Huang Da (middle) was with Zhou Jun (first from the left) and Zhu Xinrong (first from the right) of Zhongnan University of Economics and Law.

420

421

图421为2000年11月21日，黄达（右六）在湖南大学商学院举办的“金融学科建设发展座谈会”上做了题为《当前经济热点问题刍议》的演讲。

On November 21, 2000, Huang Da (sixth from the right) delivered a speech titled On the Current Hot Issues in Economics at the "Workshop on the Building and Development of the Financial Discipline" held by the School of Business of Hunan University.

422

图 422 为 2000 年 11 月 28 日，黄达在暨南大学经济学院做了题为《从专业方向的选择谈起》的演讲。之后，与暨南大学教师和人大校友合影留念。左四为黄达。

On November 28, 2000, Huang Da delivered a speech titled From the Selection of Majors to the School of Economics of Jinan University. Later, he took a group photo with the teachers of Jinan University and the alumni of the Renmin University of China. The fourth from the left is Huang Da.

6-1-4>

2001年5月，黄达在西安交通大学做了题为《金融、金融学及其学科建设》的演讲。这次演讲是黄达自1997年以来对于“金融”和“金融学科”定位问题进行系统思考的阶段性收尾。基本结论包括两个方面：

第一，通常情况下，由中国文字组成的“金融”与英文的Finance（在多种西文中，这个词是同源的）可一对一地互译，但两者并非恒等。在中国，“金融”概念的形成已有一百多年；在西方，Finance这个词则古老得多。西方日常生活中对Finance这个词的使用范围极广，比中文“金融”概念的外延大得多；用来专指资本市场和微观金融管理的Finance这个概念大约定型于20世纪下半叶，则小于中文“金融”概念的外延。从经济理论视角概括这后一区别：外文Finance，在今天的西方学界和业界的高级管理层，是专指微观金融分析；中文“金融”则指微观金融分析和宏观金融分析两方面。

这里采用微观分析与宏观分析来概括金融学科的两个构成部分。一是金融领域确确实实存在着“宏观”和“微观”两个方面。二是在讨论中常常有“金融学就是微观管理学科”的提法，应予澄清；也即金融学科中还有“宏观管理”这么一大块。三是受到了诺贝尔奖得主默顿·米勒在20世纪末的一次演讲中关于“商学院方法”与“经济系方法”，以及相对应的“微观规范分析”与“宏观规范分析”这组提法的启发。米勒在演讲中本来是用“两种方法和两种分析”来概括现代金融学自身发展的两股潮流。黄达借用他的提法，把“商学院方法”和“微观规范分析”归纳为微观金融分析，用以专指现代金融学；而把“经济系方法”和“宏观规范分析”归纳为宏观金融分析，用以指论证金融领域有关宏观均衡和宏观管理的学问。

第二，中国人自然不能、也不应以自己对中文“金融”词语百余年形成的用法为据，而阻止引进把Finance（其译文不能不是“金融”）用来专指资本市场和微观金融管理的用法。把Finance的这一用法引进中国的人士，则不应认为中国人对中文“金融”的用法有误——百余年形成的概念外延是不能逆转的历史积淀；要求中国人的中文“金融”词语也只应用来专指资本市场和微观金融管理，也难以行得通。事实上，已经形成了两种用法并存的局面。用法不同，不能定于一尊；应相互了解，尊重不同用法。

此后，除了把近几年来有关“金融”和“金融学科”定位问题的相关论述集结成册——《金融——词义、学科、形势、方法及其他》（中国金融出版社，2001）之外，黄达还在不同的场合反复阐述了自己对于此问题的看法。

In May 2001, Huang Da delivered a speech titled Finance, the Science of Finance and Its Disciplinary Development to Xi'an Jiaotong University. It was a phased conclusion of his systematic thinking over the positioning of "Finance " and "the financial discipline " since 1997. His basic conclusion comprised two aspects:

Firstly, under normal conditions, Chinese word " 金融 " and English word "Finance " (in many Western languages, finance is homogenous) corresponded to each other, but were not always identically equal. In China, the concept of "finance" had existed in China for over 100 years; in the West, the word "Finance" was more ancient. The word "Finance" was used widely in daily life in the West, and had much greater denotation than Chinese word " 金 融 . " Finance used to especially refer to the capital market and micro financial management took shape basically in the second half of last century, and had much smaller denotation than Chinese word " 金融 . " The latter difference between the two, if generalized from the angle of economic theories, shall be—foreign word "Finance" especially refers to micro financial analyses to the Western academic circle and senior management of the industry now; while Chinese word " 金融 " refers to both micro and macro financial analyses.

Here, micro and macro analyses were used to generalize the two components of the financial discipline because the field of finance does comprise the "micro " and "macro " aspects; the much-mentioned formulation— "finance is a micro control discipline " — in discussions shall be clarified, that is, there was a big part of "macro control " in the financial discipline; and because Huang Da was inspired by the formulation of "business school method " and "economic department method " in a speech delivered by Merton Miller, Nobel Prize winner at the end of last century, and corresponding formulations of "micro canonical parse " and "macro canonical parse. " Miller used "two methods and two analyses " to generalize the two trends of development of modern finance in itself. By referring to his formulation, Huang Da generalized "business school method " and "micro canonical parse " into micro financial analysis, which referred especially to modern finance; while generalized"economic department method " and "macro canonical parse " into macro financial analysis and used it to refer to the knowledge on demonstrating macroscopic equilibrium and macro management in the field of finance.

Secondly, the Chinese people could not and should not prevent the introduction of the use of Finance (whose Chinese translation had to be " 金融 ") as especially referring to the capital market and micro financial management on the ground of the use of " 金融 " which had been shaped by their use of it for over a century. For those who introduced such use of "Finance " to China, they should never hold the use of Chinese word " 金融 " by the Chinese people to be wrong—the denotation of it in the past over 100 years made the use of " 金 融 " by the Chinese people an irreversible historical accumulation. It was unworkable to use Chinese word " 金融 " to refer only to the capital market and micro financial management. As a matter of fact, the situation in which two uses co-exist has been there. There should be mutual respect between them.

Later, Huang Da collected his essays on finance and financial discipline into *Finance—Definitions, Discipline, Situation, Methods and Others* and had it published by China Financial Publishing House in 2001.

423

图 423 为 2001 年 8 月 17—18 日，由中央财经大学、厦门大学、复旦大学、中国人民大学共同主办的“21 世纪中国金融学专业教育教学改革与发展战略研讨会”在西宁举行。全体与会专家合影留念。前排左九为黄达。

黄达在开幕和总结时的两次发言被收入《财贸经济》（2001 年第 11 期）和《金融学科建设与发展战略研究》（高等教育出版社，2002）。

During August 17 and 18, 2001, the "Strategic Workshop on the Reform and Development of the Education and Teaching of Financial Majors in China in the 21st Century" jointly sponsored by the Central University of Finance and Economics, Xiamen University, Fudan University and the Renmin University of China was held in Xining. All the attendees were together. The ninth from the left in the front row is Huang Da.

The speeches delivered by Huang Da at the opening ceremony and at the conclusion were collected into *Finance & Trade Economics* (Issue 11, 2001) and *Studies on the Strategies for Building and Developing the Financial Discipline* (China Higher Education Press, 2002).

424

图 424 为 2002 年 5 月 20 日，由对外经济贸易大学主办的“加入 WTO 与中国高等金融教育的改革和创新高级研讨会”在银川举行。全体与会专家合影留念。前排左六为黄达。

On May 20, 2002, "Advanced Seminar on Joining WTO and the Reform and Innovation of China's Higher Financial Education" sponsored by the University of International Business and Economics was held in Yinchuan. All the experts attending the seminar were together. The sixth from the left in the front row is Huang Da.

图 425 为 2002 年 5 月 21 日，黄达与部分与会专家同游西夏博物馆。从左至右分别为：张亦春、刘亚、黄达、史燕平、王传纶、郭红玉。

On May 21, 2002, Huang Da visited Xixia Museum with some experts attending the seminar. From the left to the right are Zhang Yichun, Liu Ya, Huang Da, Shi Yanping, Wang Chuanlun and Guo Hongyu.

425

426

图 426 为 2003 年 10 月 17 日，黄达在华中科技大学金融系做有关金融与金融学科的演讲。

On October 17, 2003, Huang Da delivered a speech on finance and the financial discipline to the Department of Finance of Huazhong University of Science and Technology.

6-1-5>

在2001年之后的两年左右时间里，黄达集中精力主持编写《货币银行学》的升级版《金融学》，也即《货币银行学（第三版）》。2003年8月，该教材由中国人民大学出版社出版。英文译名定为*Economics of Money and Finance*。次年5月出版精编版。

《金融学》及其精编版第二版的修订，由与黄达一直合作编写货币银行学和金融学教材的沈伟基主持，2009年出版。《金融学》及其精编版的第三版和第四版，则是由张杰教授接过主持修订的接力棒，并分别于2012年和2017年出版。

During the two years after 2001, Huang Da presided over the writing of *Economics of Money and Finance,* i.e. *Economics of Money and Banking* (3rd Edition). The textbook was published by China Renmin University Press in August 2003. The special edition was published in May 2004.

The revision of second edition of *Economics of Money and Finance* and the special edition was presided over by Shen Weiji who cooperated with Huang Da in writing of the textbook. The revised edition was published in 2009. Professor Zhang Jie presided over the revision of the third and fourth edition of the textbook and the special edition, which was published in 2012 and 2017 respectively.

427

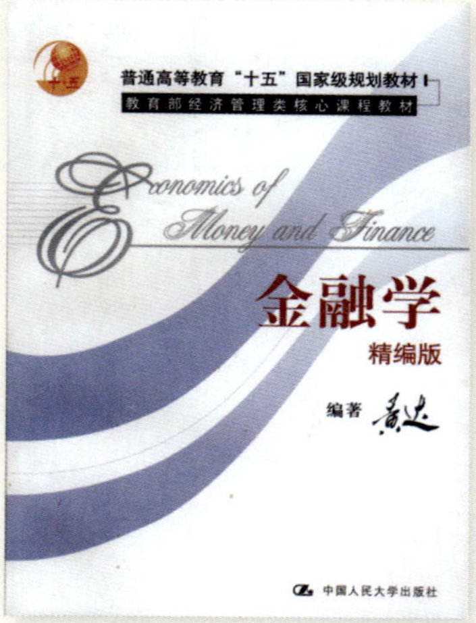

428

图427为《金融学》［《货币银行学（第三版）》］

Economics of Money and Finance(*Economics of Money and Banking*, third edition)

图428为《金融学（精编版）》［《货币银行学（第三版·精编版）》］

Economics of Money and Finance (first special edition; *Economics of Money and Banking*, third special edition)

429

431

433

430

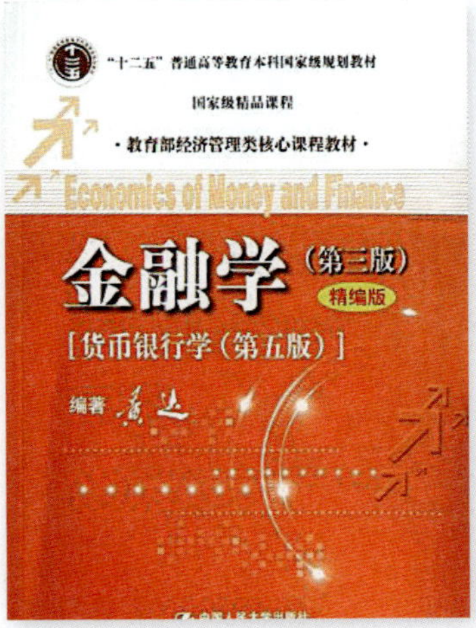

432

434

图 429 为《金融学（第二版）》[《货币银行学（第四版）》]

Economics of Money and Finance (second edition; *Economics of Money and Banking*, fourth edition)

图 430 为《金融学（第二版·精编版）》[《货币银行学（第四版·精编版）》]

Economics of Money and Finance (second special edition; *Economics of Money and Banking*, fourth special edition)

图 431 为《金融学（第三版）》[《货币银行学（第五版）》]

Economics of Money and Finance (third edition; *Economics of Money and Banking*, fifth edition)

图 432 为《金融学（第三版·精编版）》[《货币银行学（第五版·精编版）》]

Economics of Money and Finance (third special edition; *Economics of Money and Banking*, fifth special edition)

图 433 为《金融学（第四版）》[《货币银行学（第六版）》]

Economics of Money and Finance (fourth edition; *Economics of Money and Banking*, sixth edition)

图 434 为《金融学（第四版·精编版）》[《货币银行学（第六版·精编版）》]

Economics of Money and Finance (fourth special edition; *Economics of Money and Banking*, sixth special edition)

| 右页图 ⟼

图 435 为 2008 年 9 月 3 日，黄达为中国人民大学财政金融学院 2006 级金融学专业本科生讲授《货币银行学·导论》。

On September 3, 2008, Huang Da taught the financial majors enrolled by the Finance School of the Renmin University of China in 2006 *Economics of Money and Banking—An Introduction.*

黄达教授《货币银行学·导论》讲座
财政金融学院 2008.9.3
中国人民大學
RENMIN UNIVERSITY OF CHINA

435

6-1-6>

在完成教材的编写之后，年逾八旬的黄达决定“退出江湖”。但是，难以割舍的情感又让他开始了追溯货币银行学起源和发展脉络的征程。随后，在中国人民大学财政金融学院的大力支持下，依据何平、宋玮等教师搜集的有关我国货币银行学、货币学、银行学等148本书籍以及19世纪末到20世纪上半叶国外有关货币银行学的10本重要著述的文献资料，他在2007年底整理出了《回顾1950年之前“货币银行学”学科的发展（初稿）》一文。而后根据自身的经历，黄达又系统总结了1950年之后货币银行学的发展历程。

还不到一百年，货币银行学就经历了三个发展阶段：学科建立；第一次跨越——引进宏观分析，发展宏观金融分析；第二次跨越——引进微观金融分析的精华。与这三个阶段相对应，货币银行学有三个代表性的名字：Money and Banking；Economics of Money and Banking；Economics of Money，Banking，and Financial Markets。

对货币银行学的“来龙”理出了基本脉络，那么，它的“去脉”将走向何方？货币银行学在经历了百年间的两次跨越之后，是否还将实现新的跨越？

2008年9月27日，中国人民大学财政金融学院主办的“纪念改革开放30周年暨中国财政金融体制改革与学科建设”研讨会在三亚举行。会上，黄达提交的《金融学科建设是否面临攀升一步的转折点》一文，对货币银行学和当今堪称显学的“现代金融学”提出了必须提高认识的学术任务，并向大家提供了第一份金融学科发展框架图。

当年10月份，黄达先后在中央财经大学和西南财经大学为本科生讲过两次课。他将之前在三亚会议上提出的框图作了补充修订。不过，对于修订的框图他觉得缺陷明显。依据这张缺陷明显的框图，黄达与陈雨露、张杰、汪昌云几位教授不止一次讨论过……

此时，在国际金融危机的冲击之下，金融学科建设又面临着具有根本性的挑战。在这样的背景下，2009年4月4日，中国人民大学财政金融学院和中国财政金融政策研究中心联合召开了“金融学的演进与结构”学术研讨会。会议就黄达绘出的“金融学科演进历程”框图，讨论了金融学科，特别是现代金融学的演进与结构问题。更为重要的是，会议就金融海啸背景，讨论了如何推进金融学科发展的根本性理论问题。

会后，根据大家提出的意见，黄达又对框图进行了修改，并在此后的多次会议中讲解和征求意见。

After completing the compilation of the book, Huang Da who was over eighty years old then decided to "withdraw." However, it was difficult for him to detach himself from his scholarly studies. So Huang Da began to trace the origin and development of monetary economics and banking. Later, with the help of the Finance School of the Renmin University of China, Huang Da wrote A Review on the Disciplinary Development of Money and Banking before 1950 (Draft) at the end of 2007 based on the 148 books on China's monetary banking, monetary science and banking that were collected by He Ping and Song Wei, and 10 books with important writings on foreign monetary banking from the end of the 19th century to the first half of the 20th century. Later, according to his personal experience, Huang Da reviewed the development of monetary banking after 1950.

In less than 100 years, monetary banking had experienced three development stages: discipline establishment; first leapfrog—the introduction of macro analysis and the development of macro financial analysis; second leapfrog—the introduction of the essence of micro financial analysis. Monetary banking has three representative names in these three stages: Money and Banking; Economics of Money and Banking; and Economics of Money, Banking, and Financial Markets.

Now where would monetary economics and banking develop? Would monetary economics and banking achieve new leapfrogs after the previous two in the century?

On September 27, 2008, the Finance School of the Renmin University of China held a seminar titled "Commemorate the 30th Anniversary of the Reform and Opening Up and the Reform of China's Financial System and Disciplinary Development " in Sanya. At the meeting, Huang Da submitted an article titled Is the Development of the Financial Discipline Faced with a Turning Point to Ascend. In the article, Huang Da raised the academic task to deepen the understanding of monetary economics and banking and "modern finance, " which is a noted school of thought today, and provided the first development framework of the financial discipline to the attendees.

In October 2008, Huang Da gave lectures to the undergraduates of the Central University of Finance and Economics and the Southwestern University of Finance and Economics twice. He supplemented and revised the block diagram, but thought that the revised block diagram to be obviously defective. On this obviously defective block diagram, Huang Da, Chen Yulu, Zhang Jie and Wang Changyun discussed more than once.

At this point, the international financial crisis shocked the world, and raised many fundamental problems on the development of the financial discipline. Against such background, on April 4, 2009, the Finance School of the Renmin University of China and China Financial Policy Research Center jointly held an academic seminar titled "Evolution and Structure of the Science of Finance. " Around the block diagram of "Evolution and Structure of the Science of Finance " drawn by Huang Da, the meeting discussed the evolution and structure of the financial discipline, especially modern finance. More importantly, it discussed the fundamental theoretical issue of pushing forward the development of the financial discipline against the background of financial crisis.

After the meeting, according to the opinions held by the attendees, Huang Da revised the block diagram once more, and explained it and solicited public opinions in many meetings after that.

436

图 436 为 2008 年 9 月 27 日，“纪念改革开放 30 周年暨中国财政金融体制改革与学科建设”研讨会在三亚召开。全体与会专家合影留念。前排左七为黄达。

On September 27, 2008, the seminar titled "Commemorate the 30th Anniversary of the Reform and Opening Up and the Reform of China's Financial System and Disciplinary Development" was held in Sanya. All attendees took a group photo. The seventh from the left in the front row is Huang Da.

图 437 为 2008 年 9 月 27 日，黄达（右一）与刘锡良（左一）、白钦先（左二）在会场交流。

On September 27, 2008, Huang Da (first from the right) exchanged ideas with Liu Xiliang (first from the left) and Bai Qinxian (second from the left) at the conference venue.

437

438

439

图 438 为 2009 年 4 月 4 日，“金融学的演进与结构”学术研讨会在京郊召开。全体与会专家合影留念。前排从左至右分别为：郭庆旺、宋逢明、黄达、李健、陈雨露；后排从左至右分别为：宋科、李芹、汤珂、瞿强、汪昌云、张杰。

On April 4, 2009, the academic seminar of "Evolution and Structure of the Science of Finance" was held in the suburb of Beijing. All attendees took a group photo. From the left to the right in the front row are Guo Qingwang, Song Fengming, Huang Da, Li Jian and Chen Yulu. From the left to the right in the back row are Song Ke, Li Qin, Tang Ke, Qu Qiang, Wang Changyun and Zhang Jie.

图 439 为 2009 年 4 月 17 日，黄达在中国人民大学财政金融学院召开的“结合学院教学发展，学习实践科学发展观，创世界一流财政金融学院”的教职工大会上，讲解“金融学的演进与结构”问题。

On April 17, 2009, at the faculty and staff meeting titled "Study and Thoroughly Implement the Scientific Outlook on Development and Build a World-class School of Finance Based on the Development of Teaching of the School" held by the Finance School of the Renmin University of China, Huang Da explained the evolution and structure of finance.

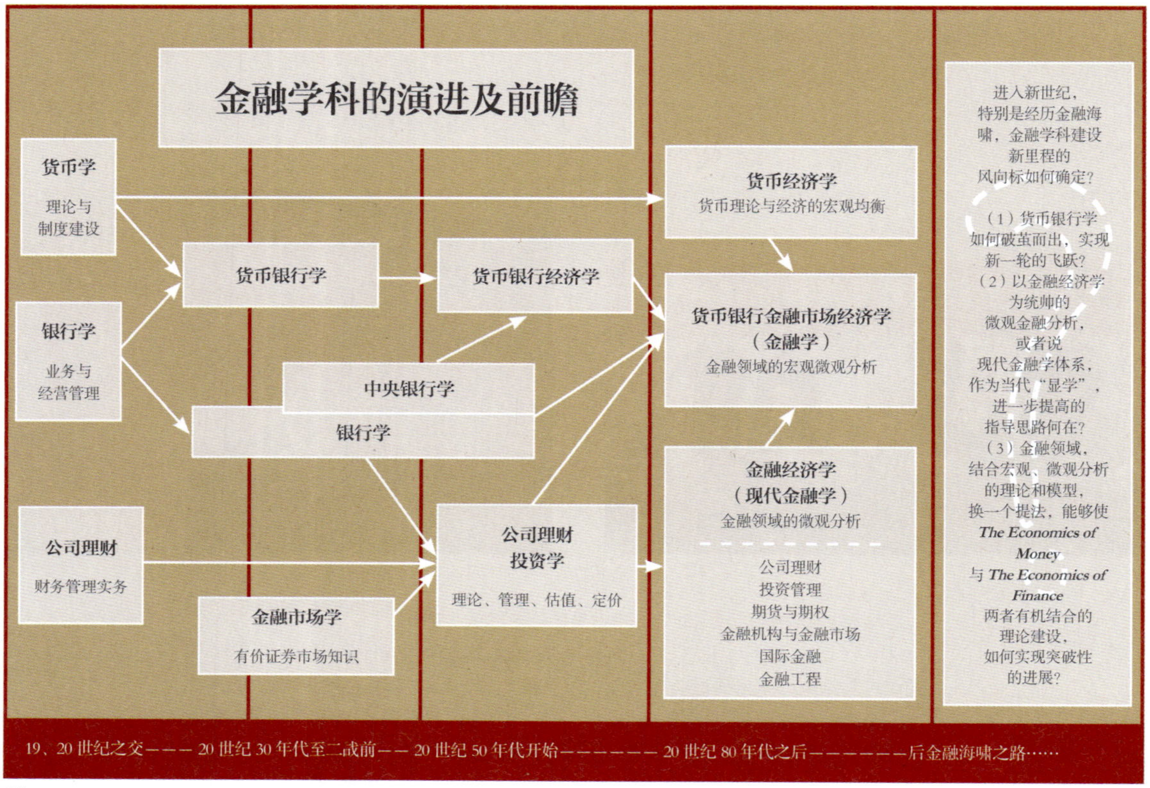

440

图 440 和图 441 为 2009 年 4 月，黄达自己用电脑绘制的"金融学科的演进及前瞻"中英文两张框图。

These are the two block diagrams, in Chinese and in English, respectively, of "Evolution and Prospect of Finance" made by Huang Da on the computer in April 2009.

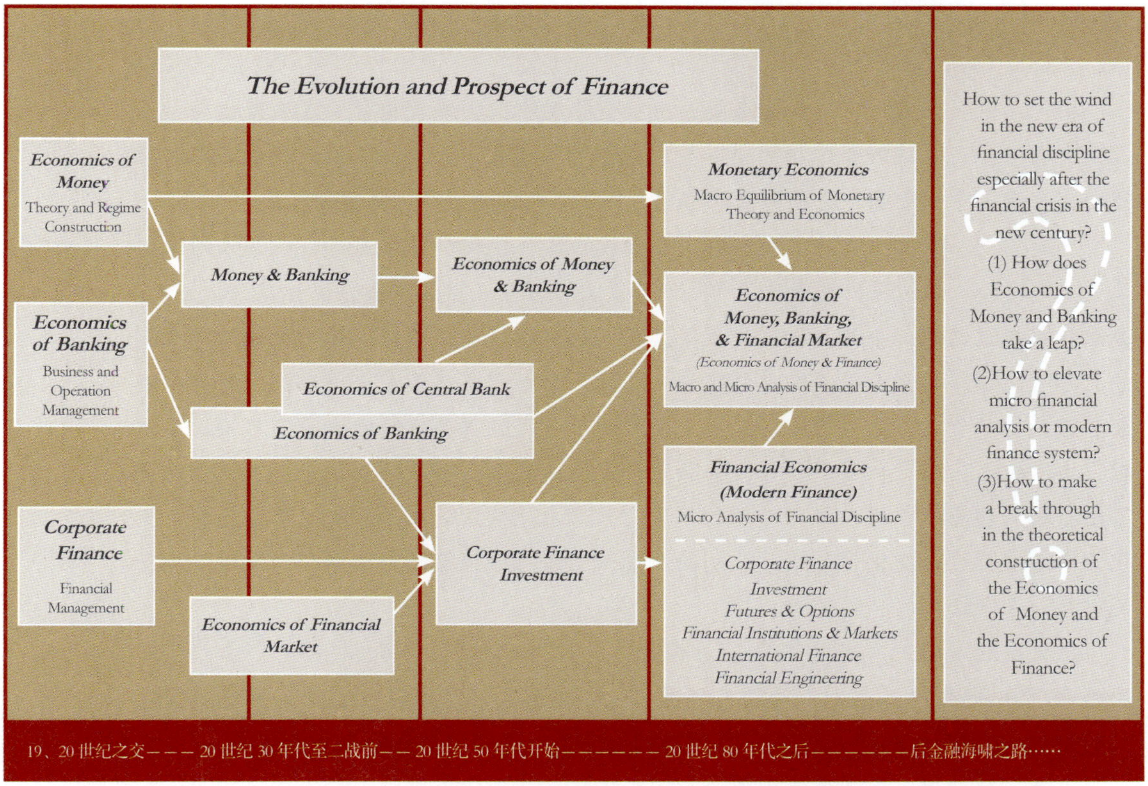
The Evolution and Prospect of Finance
Economics of Money
Theory and Regime Construction
Economics of Banking
Business and Operation Management
Corporate Finance
Financial Management
Money & Banking
Economics of Central Bank
Economics of Banking
Economics of Financial Market
Economics of Money & Banking
Corporate Finance Investment
Monetary Economics
Macro Equilibrium of Monetary Theory and Economics
Economics of Money, Banking, & Financial Market
(Economics of Money & Finance)
Macro and Micro Analysis of Financial Discipline
Financial Economics (Modern Finance)
Micro Analysis of Financial Discipline
Corporate Finance
Investment
Futures & Options
Financial Institutions & Markets
International Finance
Financial Engineering
How to set the wind in the new era of financial discipline especially after the financial crisis in the new century?
(1) How does Economics of Money and Banking take a leap?
(2)How to elevate micro financial analysis or modern finance system?
(3)How to make a break through in the theoretical construction of the Economics of Money and the Economics of Finance?
19、20 世纪之交——— 20 世纪 30 年代至二战前—— 20 世纪 50 年代开始——————— 20 世纪 80 年代之后———————后金融海啸之路……

441

6-2

《黄达书集》

Selected Books of Huang Da

2005年6月2日，“《黄达书集》出版暨推动中国金融理论繁荣发展座谈会”在人民大会堂举行。许毅等学界同仁、吴晓灵等业界代表、于友仁等出版界代表出席座谈会，会议由中国金融学会秘书长、中国人民银行研究局局长唐旭主持。

座谈会上，除了向支持《黄达书集》出版的各个方面和多年支持自己写作的同仁表达感谢之情，黄达还借机表达了自己对于金融基础理论建设的看法。他认为，首先，金融学科建设需要一个开放的思维框架，马克思当年吸收、凝练一切文化精华建立起马克思主义科学体系是最为经典的范例。其次，金融学科建设需要一个批判的思维框架。既应勇于肯定，又应勇于否定；一切取决于是否经得住实践的检验而不论源于何时，出于何人，来自何方。最后，金融学科建设又需要一个从不满足于现有认识，更不把自己的现有认识视为绝对真理的框架。只有永葆持续进取，才能为迅速发展、变化万千的实际生活提供理论服务。总的来看，上述思维框架又可以用“古今中外、含英咀华”来概括。

此次出版发行的《黄达书集》共6卷7册，约400万字，包括黄达从1957年到2003年间出版的11本教材、专著和译著。它们分别是：《资本主义国家的货币流通与信用》，《货币信用学（上册）》，《我国社会主义经济中的货币和货币流通》，《第二次世界大战后资本主义体系中的黄金》，《工农产品比价剪刀差》，《社会主义财政金融问题》，《财政信贷综合平衡导论》，《宏观调控与货币供给》（修订版），《货币银行学》，《金融——词义、学科、形势、方法及其他》及《金融学》。这11本书，不仅记述了黄达教学研究的历程，刻画了金融学科教师群体建设这一学科的轨迹，而且，它们的写作是一个持续50余年连绵不断的过程，在一定程度上也可以作为剖析新中国成立以来我国金融学科教学研究发展脉络以及经验教训的系统资料。

On June 2, 2005, "Publication of *Selected Books of Huang Da* and Symposium on Advancing the Prosperous Development of China's Financial Theories " was held in the Great Hall of the People. Xu Yi and other figures in the academic circle, Wu Xiaoling and other industry representatives, Yu Youren and other representatives of the publishing circle attended the symposium. Tang Xu, secretary-general of China Society for Finance and Banking and director of the Research Bureau of the People's Bank of China, presided over the symposium.

At the symposium, besides expressing his gratitude for all the parties to the publication of *Selected Books of Huang Da* and his colleagues who had supported him to write the books over the years, Huang Da took the chance to express his views on developing fundamental financial theories. In his opinion, firstly, the disciplinary development of finance needed an open framework of thinking—the Marxist scientific system built by Marx by absorbing and condensing the essence of all cultures was the most typical example; secondly, the disciplinary development of finance needed a critical framework of thinking—being courageous to confirm and to deny; all depended on whether they could stand the test of practice instead of who and where they were from. Meanwhile, the disciplinary development of finance needed a framework which was never satisfied with the established understanding or deemed its existing understanding as absolute truth. Only by always forging ahead could finance provide theoretical service for the fast-developing and ever-changing real life.In general, the above framework of thinking can be concluded as to connect ancient and modern, home and abroad, and to study and relish the beauties of literature.

Selected Books of Huang Da comprises 11 textbooks, monographs and translations in six volumes (seven books), and contains about 4 million Chinese characters. The 11 textbooks by Huang Da, published from 1957 to 2003, are *Currency Circulation and Credit in Capitalist Countries,Money and Credit* (Volume 1),*Money and Currency Circulation in China's Socialist Economy,Gold in the Capitalist System after WWII,Scissors Difference Between Prices of Industrial and Agricultural Products,Issues on Socialism Finance,Introduction of General Equilibrium on Public Finance and Credit,Macroeconomic Regulation and Money Supply* (Revised), *Economics of Money and Banking,Finance—Definitions, Discipline, Situation, Methods and Others* and *Economics of Money and Finance.* They record his studies and researches, and depict the development of the finance teachers as a group. As the writing of them lasted over 50 years continuously, they can be used as systematic materials to analyze the development and researches of, the experience in and the lessons drawn from finance teaching since the founding of new China to some extent.

442

图 442 为 2005 年 6 月 2 日，“《黄达书集》出版暨推动中国金融理论繁荣发展座谈会”在人民大会堂举行。从左至右分别为：苏星、于友仁、黄达、吴晓灵、唐双宁、程天权、周延礼。

"Publication of *Selected Books of Huang Da* and Symposium on Advancing the Prosperous Development of China's Financial Theories" was held in the Great Hall of the People. From the left to the right are Su Xing, Yu Youren, Huang Da, Wu Xiaoling, Tang Shuangning, Cheng Tianquan and Zhou Yanli.

443

图 443 为 2005 年，中国金融出版社和中国人民大学出版社联合出版的《黄达书集》。

This is a picture of *Selected Books of Huang Da* jointly published by China Financial Publishing House and China Renmin University Press in 2005.

6-3

“黄达—蒙代尔经济学讲座”&“黄达—蒙代尔经济学奖”
"Mundell-Huang Da Lectures" & "Mundell-Huang Da Prize"

6-3-1>

1995年春季学期，著名经济学家、美国哥伦比亚大学教授罗伯特·蒙代尔到中国人民大学为“福特项目”一年制培训班授课。作为该项目中方委员会主席的黄达接待蒙代尔教授并由此开始了两人二十年的友谊。

当时，蒙代尔教授尽管还没有获得诺贝尔经济学奖，但已经是世界顶级教授。“福特项目”所能支付的薪酬，至多相当于他正常所得的一半。但出于对中国改革发展的特别关切并期望到中国进行零距离的观察，他非常愉快地接受了“福特项目”的聘请。他的优良教学质量和责任心赢得一致的赞扬。当他知道这个连续举办了10年并证明卓有成效的经济学培训班即将宣告终止时，曾多方呼吁，却也未能挽回他作为最后一期讲学教授的命运。

1995年，为了能够更好地延续中美双方的学术交流，蒙代尔教授提出了组建“北京高级经济学院”的设想。他拟出了极为详尽的方案，并请时任中国人民大学校长的李文海教授出具了委托他筹资的函件。随后的若干年，蒙代尔教授为筹资问题四处奔走。但是由于种种困难，这一设想未能实现。

即便如此，蒙代尔教授始终没有放弃推动中美双方的经济学交流的努力。近年来，在国内学术论坛和高校讲坛上，经常能看到他熟悉的身影。

进入新世纪，以中国人民大学中国财政金融政策研究中心为依托，蒙代尔教授与黄达教授再度携手。2001年和2003年，由两位教授冠名的“黄达—蒙代尔经济学讲座”和“黄达—蒙代尔经济学奖”先后在中国人民大学启动。十几年来，这两个平台为推动中国经济学教育和人才培养做出了应有的贡献，得到多方肯定。

In the summer term of 1995, Robert Mundell came to the Renmin University of China to give lectures to the one-year training class of the "Ford Program. " As the Chinese Chairman of the program, Huang Da received Prof. Mundell, and thus started the friendship with him that lasted for twenty years.

At the time, Prof. Mundell had not won the Nobel Prize, but had already become a top professor in the world. His remuneration from the "Ford Program " was at most half of his normal income. However, for the special attention to China's reform and opening up and his expectation to observe China without distance, he happily accepted the invitation of the "Ford Program. " His great teaching and sense of responsibility were spoken highly of. Getting to know that the economics training class—which had been running for 10 years in a roll and turned out to be very productive—was to be ended, he appealed much for it, but still failed to change his fate as its last professor.

In 1995, in order to better continue the scholarly exchanges between China and the US, Prof. Mundell proposed to establish "Beijing Advanced School of Economics. " He developed a very detailed plan, and invited Prof. Li Wenhai, the then president of the Renmin University of China, to issue a letter of authorization in which he was entrusted with raising funds. In the years that followed, he was busy with raising funds. Due to difficulties, his proposal was not realized.

Even though, Prof. Mundell had never abandoned the efforts to push forward the exchanges on economics between China and the US. He is frequently seen in domestic scholarly forums and lectures for university students.

Into the new century, Prof. Mundell and Prof. Huang Da cooperated once again because of China Financial Policy Research Center of the Renmin University of China. In 2001, and then 2003, the "Mundell-Huang Da Lectures " & "Mundell-Huang Da Prize " named after them were launched in the Renmin University of China in succession. For over ten years, the two platforms have contributed to China's economics education and talent cultivation, and are spoken highly of.

444

图 444 为 1995 年 5 月 15 日，蒙代尔教授被授予中国人民大学名誉教授称号。主席台从左至右分别为宋立刚、高鸿业、蒙代尔夫人、蒙代尔、黄达、郑杭生和杜厚文。

On May 15, 1995, Prof. Mundell was granted the title of honorary professor of the Renmin University of China. From the left to the right on the rostrum are Song Ligang, Gao Hongye, Mrs. Mundell, Mundell, Huang Da, Zheng Hangsheng and Du Houwen.

445

图 445 为 1996 年 9 月 21 日，黄达（左一）赴美访问期间拜访蒙代尔教授（右一）。

On September 21, 1996, Huang Da (first from the left) visited Prof. Mundell (first from the right) during his visit to the US.

6-3-2>

2001 年 10 月 17 日，由中国人民大学中国财政金融政策研究中心创设的“黄达—蒙代尔经济学讲座”在中国人民大学正式启动。

“黄达—蒙代尔经济学讲座”分为国外著名经济学家讲座、杰出华人学者讲座、经济政策领导人高层讲座、财税高管讲座、金融高管讲座以及财金名家讲座六大系列，旨在推动中国经济学前沿理论与政策研究。

自讲座创设以来，包括约瑟夫·斯蒂格利茨、迈克尔·斯宾塞、罗伯特·希勒和埃德蒙·费尔普斯等诺贝尔经济学奖得主在内的数十位经济学家和政策领导人登上讲坛。

为了能够让更多人了解到大师们的学术思想，中国人民大学中国财政金融政策研究中心将重要嘉宾的演讲集结整理并配以相关领域国内经济学家的点评，先后编辑出版了中文版《黄达—蒙代尔讲座》第一辑和第二辑，以及英文版《黄达—蒙代尔讲座》。

On October 17, 2001, "Mundell-Huang Da Lectures " created by China Financial Policy Research Center of the Renmin University of China was officially launched in the Renmin University of China.

"Mundell-Huang Da Lectures " comprise six series—lectures by foreign famous economists, lectures by outstanding Chinese scholars, advanced seminars of leaders on economic policies, lectures by fiscal and taxation executives, lectures by financial executives and lectures by famous economists—and aim to push forward the studies of forefront economic theories and policies.

Since the creation of the lectures, dozens of economists and policy leaders have mounted the rostrum to give lectures, including Nobel Prize winners Joseph E. Stiglitz, Michael Spence, Robert J. Shiller and Edmund S. Phelps.

China Financial Policy Research Center of the Renmin University of China edited and published two volumes of *Mundell-Huang Da Lectures (Chinese edition)* and *Mundell-Huang Da Lectures (English edition)* which collect the speeches given by important guests, along with comments by domestic economists in related fields, allowing more people to understand the masters' scholarly ideas.

446

图 446 为中国人民大学出版社分别于 2003 年和 2008 年出版发行的《黄达—蒙代尔讲座》第一辑和第二辑，以及由新加坡世界科技出版公司（World Scientific Publishing Co. Pte Ltd.）于 2013 年出版的 *Realizing Rational Exuberance: An Appreciation of the Mundell-Huang Da Lectures*。

This picture records the first and second volumes of *Mundell-Huang Da Lectures* published by China Renmin University Press in 2003 and 2008, respectively; and *Realizing Rational Exuberance: An Appreciation of the Mundell-Huang Da Lectures* published by World Scientific Publishing Co. Pte Ltd. in 2013.

447

图 447 为 2001 年 10 月 17 日，黄达（左一）在“黄达—蒙代尔经济学讲座”启动仪式上讲话。此次讲话中，他提出了“要培养能够在东西方两个文化平台上自由漫步的人才”的目标。目前，这个思路已经成为中国人民大学人才培养目标的一个重要内容。

On October 17, 2001, Huang Da (first from the left) addressed the opening ceremony of "Mundell-Huang Da Lectures."

In his speech, he put forward the target of "training personnel who can roam free on both cultural stages in the east and in the west". His idea has become an important content of the goals of talent cultivation of the Renmin University of China.

图 448 为 2003 年 2 月 23 日，罗伯特•希勒做客“黄达—蒙代尔经济学讲座”，作了题为“行为金融学的崛起”的演讲。期间，希勒（左一）与黄达（右一）、王传纶（右二）等进行交流。

On February 23, 2003, Robert J. Shiller was invited to be a guest of "Mundell-Huang Da Lectures" and gave the lecture of "Rise of Behavioral Finance." During his visit, Shiller (first from the left) exchanged thoughts with Huang Da (first from the right) and Wang Chuanlun (second from the right).

448

6-3-3>

由中国人民大学中国财政金融政策研究中心于2002年创设的“黄达—蒙代尔经济学奖”，是面向博士学位论文进行评选的学术奖项。在过去的七次评选当中，先后有28位青年才俊荣膺该奖，其中多位获奖者又相继获得全国百篇优秀博士学位论文奖或提名奖。

第一届获奖者：北京大学卜永祥（导师：秦宛顺）、西南财经大学尹龙（导师：谢平）、中国人民大学张晓朴（导师：袁卫）以及厦门大学袁星侯（导师：张馨）。

第二届获奖者：北京大学郑志刚（导师：张维迎）、祝丹涛（导师：王梦奎）、张晏（导师：邹恒甫），中国社会科学院研究生院曾诗鸿（导师：余永定）和中南财经政法大学廖楚晖（导师：杨灿明）。

第三届获奖者：中国人民大学周晴（导师：陈雨露）、南京大学卞志村（导师：范从来）、中国人民大学贾俊雪（导师：郭庆旺）、财政部财政科学研究所冯俏彬（导师：贾康）、上海交通大学朱云（导师：吴冲锋）以及南京大学付文林（导师：沈坤荣）。

第四届获奖者：清华大学钱震杰（导师：白重恩）、上海财经大学张阳（导师：胡怡建）、复旦大学姚斌（导师：姜波克）、中国人民大学黄隽（导师：胡乃武）、中国人民大学高晓红（导师：张杰）。

第五届获奖者：中国人民大学赵文哲（导师：卢荻）、中国人民银行研究生部张怀清（导师：谢平）、复旦大学范子英（导师：张军）。

第六届获奖者：复旦大学刘瑞明（导师：石磊）、上海财经大学孙楚仁（导师：田国强）、中国人民大学马勇（导师：陈雨露）。

第七届获奖者：北京大学茅锐（导师：姚洋）、中国人民大学鞠晓生（导师：卢荻）。

第八届获奖者：中国人民大学李黎力（导师：贾根良）、中国人民大学罗煜（导师：贝多广）、湖南大学胡荣尚（导师：张强）。

China Financial Policy Research Center of the Renmin University of China set the "Mundell-Huang Da Prize " in 2002, an academic prize for excellent PhD theses. In the past seven selections, 28 young talented people have won it, of which several won the prize for National Top 100 Excellent PhD Theses or the nomination to it in succession.

The 1st winners of the "Mundell-Huang Da Prize: " Bu Yongxiang from Peking University (tutored by Qin Wanshun), Yin Long from Southwestern University of Finance and Economics (tutored by Xie Ping), Zhang Xiaopu from the Renmin University of China (tutored by Yuan Wei), and Yuan Xinghou from Xiamen University (tutored by Zhang Xin).

The 2nd winners of the "Mundell-Huang Da Prize: " Zheng Zhigang from Peking University (tutored by Zhang Weiying), Zhu Dantao from Peking University (tutored by Wang Mengkui), Zhang Yan from Peking University (tutored by Zou Hengfu), Zeng Shihong from the Graduate School of Chinese Academy of Social Sciences (tutored by Yu Yongding), and Liao Chuhui from Zhongnan University of Economics and Law (tutored by Yang Canming).

The 3rd winners of the "Mundell-Huang Da Prize: " Zhou Qing from the Renmin University of China (tutored by Chen Yulu), Bian Zhicun from Nanjing University (tutored by Fan Conglai), Jia Junxue from the Renmin University of China (tutored by Guo Qingwang), Feng Qiaobin from the Research Institute for Fiscal Science of the Ministry of Finance, P.R. China (tutored by Jia Kang), Zhu Yun from Shanghai Jiao Tong University (tutored by Wu Chongfeng) and Fu Wenlin from Nanjing University (tutored by Shen Kunrong).

The 4th winners of the "Mundell-Huang Da Prize: " Qian Zhenjie from Tsinghua University (tutored by Bai Chongen), Zhang Yang from Shanghai University of Finance and Economics (tutored by Hu Yijian), Yao Bin from Fudan University (tutored by Jiang Boke), Huang Juan from the Renmin University of China (tutored by Hu Naiwu), and Gao Xiaohong from the Renmin University of China (tutored by Zhang Jie).

The 5th winners of the "Mundell-Huang Da Prize: " Zhao Wenzhe from the Renmin University of China (tutored by Lu Di), Zhang Huaiqing from the Graduate School of the People's Bank of China (tutored by Xie Ping), and Fan Ziying from Fudan University (tutored by Zhang Jun).

The 6th winners of the "Mundell-Huang Da Prize: " Liu Ruiming from Fudan University (tutored by Shi Lei), Sun Churen from Shanghai University of Finance and Economics (tutored by Tian Guoqiang), and Ma Yong from the Renmin University of China (tutored by Chen Yulu).

The 7th winners of the "Mundell-Huang Da Prize: " Mao Rui from Peking University (tutored by Yao Yang) and Ju Xiaosheng from the Renmin University of China (tutored by Lu Di).

The 8th winners of the "Mundell-Huang Da Prize:" Li Lili from Renmin University of China (tutored by Jia Genliang), Luo Yu form Renmin University of China (tutored by Bei Duoguang) and Hu Rongshang from Hunan University (tutored by Zhang Qiang).

449

图449为2003年3月19日，第一届“黄达—蒙代尔经济学奖”颁奖典礼暨学术演讲在中国人民大学举行。黄达（左二）与蒙代尔（右二）共同为获奖者颁奖。

On March 19, 2003, the 1st "Mundell-Huang Da Prize" Presentation Ceremony and scholarly speech was held in the Renmin University of China. Huang Da (second from the left) and Mundell (second from the right) awarded the prize to the prize-winners together.

450

451

图 450 为 2003 年 3 月 19 日，黄达在颁奖典礼上发表演讲。

On March 19, 2003, Huang Da addressed the awarding ceremony.

图 451 为 2003 年 3 月 19 日，蒙代尔在颁奖典礼上发表演讲。

On March 19, 2003, Mundell addressed the awarding ceremony.

452

453

图 452 为 2005 年 11 月 11 日，第二届“黄达—蒙代尔经济学奖”颁奖典礼在中国人民大学举行。全体获奖学生、导师与颁奖嘉宾合影留念。前排从左至右分别为：周升业、陈共、黄达、蒙代尔、程天权、王传纶、袁卫和郭庆旺。

On November 11, 2005, the 2nd "Mundell-Huang Da Prize" Presentation Ceremony was held in the Renmin University of China. All the students winning the prize, their tutors and the awarding special guests took a group photo. From the left to the right in the front row are Zhou Shengye, Chen Gong, Huang Da, Mundell, Cheng Tianquan, Wang Chuanlun, Yuan Wei and Guo Qingwang.

图 453 为 2007 年 9 月 10 日，第三届“黄达—蒙代尔经济学奖”颁奖典礼暨诺贝尔经济学奖得主学术演讲在中国人民大学举行。部分获奖导师与颁奖嘉宾合影留念。从左至右分别为：王传纶、陈雨露、黄达、郭庆旺、纪宝成、贾康、蒙代尔和沈坤荣。

On September 10, 2007, the 3rd "Mundell-Huang Da Prize" Presentation Ceremony and Nobel Prize Winner Scholarly Speech was held in the Renmin University of China. Some award-winning tutors of prize-winners and the awarding special guests took a group photo. From the left to the right are Wang Chuanlun, Chen Yulu, Huang Da, Guo Qingwang, Ji Baocheng, Jia Kang, Mundell and Shen Kunrong.

454

455

456

图 454 为 2009 年 10 月 15 日，第四届“黄达—蒙代尔经济学奖”颁奖典礼暨学术演讲在中国人民大学举行。全体获奖学生、导师与颁奖嘉宾合影留念。前排从左至右分别为：郭庆旺、王传纶、蒙代尔、程天权、黄达和王松奇。

On October 15, 2009, the 4th "Mundell-Huang Da Prize" Presentation Ceremony and Scholarly Speech was held in the Renmin University of China. All the students winning the prize, their tutors and the awarding special guests were together. From the left to the right in the front row are Guo Qingwang, Wang Chuanlun, Mundell, Cheng Tianquan, Huang Da, and Wang Songqi.

图 455 为 2009 年 10 月 15 日，黄达（右一）与蒙代尔（左一）在会前亲切交谈。

On October 15, 2009, Huang Da (first from the right) and Mundell (first from the left) had a cordial talk before the ceremony.

图 456 为 2009 年 10 月 15 日，黄达（右二）、程天权（右三）共同为第四届获奖者颁奖。

On October 15, 2009, Huang Da (second from the right) and Cheng Tianquan (third from the right) awarded the prize to the fourth prize-winners together.

457

图457为2012年6月16日，第五届"黄达—蒙代尔经济学奖"颁奖典礼暨《人民币国际化报告2012》发布会在中国人民大学举行。全体获奖学生、导师与颁奖嘉宾合影留念。前排从左至右分别为：陈雨露、蒙代尔、黄达、陈共和杨慧林。

On June 16, 2012, the 5th "Mundell-Huang Da Prize" Presentation Ceremony and Press Conference of *Annual Report on the Internationalization of Reminbi,2012* was held in the Renmin University of China. All the students winning the prize, their tutors and the awarding special guests were together. From the left to the right in the front row are Chen Yulu, Mundell, Huang Da, Chen Gong and Yang Huilin.

图458为2012年6月16日，黄达（右一）、蒙代尔（左二）与陈雨露（左一）共同为第五届获奖者颁奖。

On June 16, 2012, Huang Da (first from the right), Mundell (second from the left) and Chen Yulu (first from the left) awarded the prize to the fifth prize-winners together.

458

459

图 459 为 2014 年 10 月 18 日，第六届“黄达—蒙代尔经济学奖”颁奖仪式暨“2014 年中国财政金融青年学者论坛”在中国人民大学举行。部分获奖学生、导师与颁奖嘉宾合影留念。前排从左至右分别为：郭庆旺、王利明、黄达和谢平。

On October 18, 2014, the 6th "Mundell-Huang Da Prize" Presentation Ceremony and "2014 China Young Scholars Forum on Finance" was held in the Renmin University of China. Some students winning the prize, their tutors and the awarding special guests were together. From the left to the right in the front row are Guo Qingwang, Wang Liming, Huang Da and Xie Ping.

460

图460为2015年11月1日，第七届“黄达—蒙代尔经济学奖”颁奖典礼暨“经济转型与财政金融理论创新”学术研讨会在中国人民大学举行。全体获奖学生、导师与颁奖嘉宾合影留念。从左至右分别为：郭庆旺、鞠晓生、靳诺、茅锐、黄达、姚洋、王利明。

On November 1, 2015, the 7th "Mundell-Huang Da Prize" Presentation Ceremony and Symposium of Economic Transformation and Innovation of Financial Theory was held in the Renmin University of China. All the students winning the prize, their tutors and the awarding special guests were together. From the left to the right are Guo Qingwang, Ju Xiaosheng, Jin Nuo, Mao Rui, Huang Da, Yao Yang and Wang Liming.

461

图461为2017年10月14日，第八届“黄达—蒙代尔经济学奖”颁奖典礼暨“现代经济与金融研究中的历史维度”学术研讨会在中国人民大学举行。部分获奖学生、导师与颁奖嘉宾合影留念。前排从左至右分别为：贾根良、庄毓敏、刘伟、黄达、刘元春、贝多广。

On October 14, 2017, the 8th "Mundell-Huang Da Prize" Presentation Ceremony and Symposium of Historical Dimension in Modern Economic and Financial Research was held in Renmin University of China. Some students winning the prize, their tutors and the awarding special guests took a group photo. From the left to the right in the front row are Jia Genliang, Zhuang Yumin, Liu Wei, Huang Da, Liu Yuanchun and Bei Duoguang.

6-4

耄耋之年，依然为中国经济金融学科发展而忙碌

Concern about the Development of China's Economic and Financial Discipline in his Venerable Age

6-4-1>

1999年以来，教育部按照“一流”和“唯一”的标准，在全国66所高校相继设立了151个人文社科类重点研究基地。所谓“一流”，就是要求建立的重点研究基地在确定的研究领域应该在全国是一流的，或者至少在全国高校同一研究领域是一流的，并经过若干年的建设有望在全国同一研究领域达到一流。所谓“唯一”，就是说在同一领域、同一研究方向上只设一个重点研究基地，要求建立的重点研究基地切实成为该研究领域的中心，在繁荣和发展我国人文社会科学中明显地居于领先地位。

经过评选，中国人民大学申报的中国财政金融政策研究中心，跨财政与金融两个学科领域，符合教育部“一流”和“唯一”的标准，被评为重点基地。此间，西南财经大学申报成立中国金融研究中心，黄达被教育部指定为评审组组长，赴西南财经大学组织评审。

Since 1999, following the standard of being "first-class " and "exclusive, " the Chinese Ministry of Education has built 151 key research bases of humanities and social sciences in succession in 66 universities across China. The so-called "first-class " means that the key research bases established must be first-class in China in specific research fields, or at least be first-class in the same research fields among the Chinese universities and are expected to become first-class in the same research fields in China after years of construction. The so-called "exclusive " means that there should be one key research base only in the same field and the same research direction, and that the key research base established shall become the center of such research field, and lead in prospering and developing humanities and social sciences in China.

Upon selection, China Financial Policy Research Center of the Renmin University of China covers both public finance and finance, and conforms to the requirement of the Ministry of Education of being "first-class " and "exclusive, " it was therefore selected as a key research base. During the period, the Southwestern University of Finance and Economics applied for establishing Institute of Chinese Finance Studies. Huang Da was designated by the Ministry of Education to be the head of the evaluation group, and went to Southwestern University of Finance and Economics to organize an evaluation of such application.

| 右页图 |⟶

图462为2000年8月2日，黄达（居中）出席西南财经大学中国金融研究中心专家论证会，与著名经济学家、西南财经大学老校长刘诗白（左一），时任西南财经大学校长王裕国（右一）在一起。

On August 2, 2000, Huang Da (middle) attended the feasibility meeting held by the Institute of Chinese Finance Studies of Southwestern University of Finance and Economics. He was with Liu Shibai (first from the left), a famous economist and former president of the Southwestern University of Finance and Economics, and Wang Yuguo (first from the right), the then president of the Southwestern University of Finance and Economics.

462

463

图 463 为 2000 年 12 月 20 日，中国人民大学中国财政金融政策研究中心学术委员会成立大会暨首届学术委员会会议在中国人民大学召开。全体与会专家合影留念。从左至右分别为：贺耀敏、安体富、储敏伟、陈共、王传纶、米建国、中心名誉主任黄达、谢平、袁卫、周升业、刘锡良、王广谦、陈雨露、宋逢明、郭庆旺、吴晓球。

On December 20, 2000, the inauguration meeting and the first academic meeting of China Financial Policy Research Center of the Renmin University of China was held in the Renmin University of China. Huang Da served as its honorary director. From the left to the right are He Yaomin, An Tifu, Chu Minwei, Chen Gong, Wang Chuanlun, Mi Jianguo, Huang Da, Xie Ping, Yuan Wei, Zhou Shengye, Liu Xiliang, Wang Guangqian, Chen Yulu, Song Fengming, Guo Qingwang and Wu Xiaoqiu.

464

图 464 为 2001 年 11 月 21 日，教育部在海南博鳌组织召开经济学基地主任会。全体与会专家合影留念。前排左五为黄达。

On November 21, 2001, the Economics Base Directors Meeting was held in Boao, Hainan. All the attendees took a group photo. The fifth from the left is Huang Da.

6-4-2>

2001年5月19日，首届中国人文社会科学论坛在中国人民大学举行。论坛围绕“二十一世纪中国人文社会科学发展展望”“二十一世纪金融危机问题”“二十一世纪国际政治关系”“二十一世纪的人口、资源环境与可持续发展”等主题展开深入的讨论。时任中共中央政治局委员、中国社会科学院院长李铁映在题为《人文社会科学要站在时代的最前列》的主题报告中提到，在二十一世纪争夺科学的制高点，除了信息科学、生物科学领域外，人文社会科学将是最重要的领域，强调任何轻视人文社会科学、忽视理论的倾向，都是错误的、有害的。

此后，中国人文社会科学论坛持续关注人文社科领域的重大问题，每年举办一次。截至2016年，该论坛已经连续举办十六届，成为中国人文社科领域交流思想、研讨学术、关注社会的重要平台。

值得一提的是，2004年5月30日，第四届“中国人文社会科学论坛”由中国人民大学财政金融学院和中国财政金融政策研究中心联合承办。罗伯特·蒙代尔、帕德玛·德赛、埃德蒙·费尔普斯、迈克尔·斯宾塞、罗纳德·麦金农、贾格迪什·巴格沃蒂、石弘光、吴敬琏、厉以宁、韦钰、黄达、王传纶、龙永图等学界重量级大师共聚一堂，一起探讨“未来之路：全球经济与金融体系中的中国”。该论坛被媒体誉为当年继博鳌论坛之后又一次大师云集的盛会。

会上，黄达就“全球经济发展中的人民币：国有化的利益、风险与路径”问题与金融发展理论的奠基人、美国斯坦福大学教授罗纳德·麦金农展开对话。他以《人民币的风云际会》为题对人民币国际化等相关问题进行了系统性分析，指出人民币国际化是条非常宽阔却绝非平坦的路，需要在摩擦中妥协，在摩擦中协调，在摩擦中寻求合作；并论证，“升值”必将是人民币在一个长期阶段的走势。会后，他的演讲稿被《经济研究》和《国际金融研究》等刊物刊登，《新华文摘》全文转载。

右页图 ⟶

图465为2001年5月19日，黄达（前排左二）与出席首届“中国人文社会科学论坛”的部分专家在一起。

On May 19, 2001, Huang Da (second from the left in the front row) was with some attendees of the first "China Humanities and Social Sciences Forum."

On May 19, 2001, the 1st China Humanities and Social Sciences Forum was held in the Renmin University of China. At the forum, in-depth discussions were held on "Development Prospect of Humanities and Social Sciences in the 21st Century, " "Financial Crises in the 21st Century, " "International Political Relations in the 21st Century, " and "Population, Resources and the Environment and Sustainable Development in the 21st Century. " Li Tieying, the then member of the Political Bureau of the Central Committee of the Communist Party of China and president of Chinese Academy of Social Sciences, mentioned in his report Humanities and Social Sciences Must Take the Lead that humanities and social sciences would become the most important fields, except information science and bioscience, in the struggle for the dominant position of sciences in the 21st century; and that any tendency ignoring humanities and social sciences and theories was wrong and harmful.

Since then, China Humanities and Social Sciences Forum has been paying attention to major issues in the field of humanities and social sciences, and held annually. As of 2016, the forum has been held 16 times, and become an important platform for exchanging ideas, discussing scholarly thoughts and concerning about the society in the field of humanities and social sciences in China.

It is worth mentioning that, on May 30, 2004, the fourth "China Humanities and Social Sciences Forum " was held jointly by the Finance School and China Financial Policy Research Center of the Renmin University of China. Robert Mundell, Padma Desai, Edmund Phelps, Michael Spence, Ronald I.McKinnon, Jagdish Bhagwati, Shi Hongguang, Wu Jinglian, Li Yining, Wei Yu, Huang Da, Wang Chuanlun and Long Yongtu all attended the forum and had discussions on "Road in the Future: China in the Global Economic and Financial System. "

At the forum, Huang Da had a dialogue with Ronald I. McKinnon, founder of finance evolution theories and professor from Stanford University, on "RMB in Global Economic Development: Interests, Risks and Path of Nationalization. " On the topic of RMB Rides the Crest to Fortune, he made a systematical analysis of RMB internationalization and related issues, and pointed out that renminbi internationalization was a wide, but never flat road, so it needed conciliations and coordination in conflicts. He also demonstrated that "appreciation " would inevitably be the trend of renminbi in the long run. After the meeting, his speech was published by *Economic Research Journal* and *Studies of International Finance,* and fully reprinted by *Xinhua Digest*.

465

466

图 466 为 2004 年 5 月 30 日，第四届“中国人文社会科学论坛”在中国人民大学世纪馆隆重开幕。

On May 30, 2004, the 4th "China Humanities and Social Sciences Forum" was held in the Century Hall of the Renmin University of China.

图 467 为 2004 年 5 月 30 日，“全球经济发展中的人民币：国有化的利益、风险与路径”对话单元的主讲人黄达（右一）、麦金农（右二）与主持人陈雨露（左一）合影留念。

On May 30, 2004, Huang Da (first from the right) and Ronald I. McKinnon (second from the right), keynote speakers in the dialogue on "RMB in Global Economic Development: Interests, Risks and Path of Nationalization," took a group photo with presider Chen Yulu (first from the left).

467

图 468 为 2004 年 5 月 30 日，出席第四届“中国人文社会科学论坛”的部分中方专家在会场交谈。从左至右分别为：王传纶、高尚全、龙永图、吴敬琏、厉以宁、黄达。

On May 30, 2004, some Chinese experts attending the 4th "China Humanities and Social Sciences Forum" talked at the conference venue. From the left to the right are Wang Chuanlun, Gao Shangquan, Long Yongtu, Wu Jinglian, Li Yining and Huang Da.

468

6-4-3>

自 1997 年起，由中国人民大学金融与证券研究所 (FSI) 首倡、国内外著名金融机构联合主办的全国性资本市场年会——中国资本市场论坛已成功举办了二十二届。

二十二年来，论坛持续关注着中国金融改革深化及资本市场发展进程中具有重大理论和实践意义的问题，国内外一流研究机构的著名学者以及金融界的资深专家多次与会演讲。其中，黄达是除论坛发起人吴晓球之外唯一一位参加了全部二十二届论坛的专家。

目前，该论坛已经成为业内高度关注的年度资本市场峰会，在此基础上完成的《中国资本市场研究报告》(系列)引起了国内外学术界和有关部门的高度重视和热烈反响。

China Capital Market Forum, a national capital market annual meeting advocated by the Finance and Securities Institute of the Renmin University of China and jointly held by famous financial institutions both at home and abroad, had been held successfully for 22 times since 1997.

Over the 22 years, it has been paying attention to major issues of theoretical and practical significance in the deepening of China's financial reform and the development of the Chinese capital market. Famous scholars and senior experts in the financial circle from first-class Chinese and foreign research institutes attend the forum many times, and except Wu Xiaoqiu,the initiator of the forum, Huang Da is the only expert always attending China Capital Market Forum.

So far, the forum has become an annual summit on the capital market which attracts great attention from the industry. *Annual Research Report on China Capital Market* (Series) completed based on such forum attracts great attention from, and has caused great sensation in the Chinese and foreign academic circles and related departments.

469

图 469 为 2002 年 1 月 19 日，黄达在第六届中国资本市场论坛上发言。

On January 19, 2002, Huang Da addressed the 6th China Capital Market Forum.

470

图 470 为 2002 年 1 月 19 日，以“中国金融大趋势 —— 开放与国际化·银证合作”为主题的第六届中国资本市场论坛在北京召开。黄达（前排左五）出席会议并在主席台就座。

On January 19, 2002, the 6th China Capital Market Forum themed with "General Financial Trend in China: Openness and Internationalization · Cooperation between Banks and Security Companies" was held in Beijing. Huang Da (fifth from the left in the front row) attended the meeting and was seated on the rostrum.

471

图 471 为 2004 年 1 月 10 日，第八届中国资本市场论坛在中国人民大学举行。本次论坛主题为“中国资本市场股权分裂与流动性变革——全流通之路”。

黄达出席论坛并发言。他借用但丁《神曲》的一句话——“这就是炼狱之门”来诠释“全流通之路”。《神曲》为人们的灵魂安排了三个去处：地狱、炼狱、天堂。罪恶深重的灵魂自当下地狱。炼狱则是有罪孽的善人应该经过的地方——在这里，善人要洗净自己的罪孽，以便升入天堂。至于天堂，那是善而又善的人才有资格直接去的胜境。就资本市场而言，中国已经经过了 20 世纪 80 年代末发展股份经济、建立证券交易中心的“下地狱”之路，现在需要将在地狱中演化出来的流通股和不流通股这两个精灵推入炼狱之门。为此，即使是要面对国有资产流失和得罪股民的责难，也要以“李逵三板斧”的勇气闯入炼狱之门。他的这个发言颇受媒体关注。

On January 10, 2004, the 8th China Capital Market Forum themed with "Stock Equity Split up and Liquidity Reform of China's Capital Market—the Road of Full Circulation" was held in the Renmin University of China.

Huang Da attended and addressed the forum. He borrowed "purgatory" from *The Divine Comedy* by Dante Alighieri to interpret "the road of full circulation." *The Divine Comedy* set three destinations for human souls—hell, purgatory and heaven. The guiltiest souls shall go to hell; good men with sins shall go to purgatory, because they will clean their sins so as to go to heaven. Heaven is for those who are kind and good. As for the capital market, China had passed the road "to go to hell" in the late 1980s when it developed the shareholding economy and established stock exchanges. Now it needed to push the two spirits—tradable shares and non-tradable shares evolved from hell—to purgatory. Therefore, it had to break into purgatory with great courage even if that meant the loss of state-owned assets or blame from the shareholders. His speech attracted much attention from the media.

图 472 为 2008 年 1 月 12 日，第十二届中国资本市场论坛在中国人民大学举行。本次论坛的主题为“全球视野下的中国资本市场”。黄达（右一）与时任中国证监会主席尚福林（左一）在会场上交谈。

On January 12, 2008, the 12th China Capital Market Forum themed with "China's Capital Market from the Global Perspective" was held in the Renmin University of China. Huang Da (first from the right) talked with Shang Fulin (first from the left), the then chairman of China Securities Regulatory Commission.

472

473

图 473 为 2017 年 1 月 7 日，第二十一届（2017 年度）中国资本市场论坛在北京举行。本次论坛主题为“中国金融监管改革”。部分与会嘉宾在贵宾室合影留念。右七为黄达。右六与左三分别为中国人民大学校长刘伟、副校长吴晓球。

On January 7, 2017, the 21st China Capital Market Forum was held in Beijing themed with "Reform of China's Financial Regulation". Some of the participants took a group photo in the VIP room. The seventh from the right is Huang Da. The sixth from the right and the third from the left are Liu Wei and Wu Xiaoqiu, president and vice president of Renmin University of China respectively.

6-4-4>

2003年2月25日，由中国人民大学财政金融学院、北京大学中国经济研究中心和梁晶工作室主办，中国人民大学信托与基金研究所承办的“中国金融：走向理性繁荣”研讨会在中国人民大学举行。诺贝尔经济学奖得主、著名经济学家罗伯特·希勒发表主题演讲，吴敬琏、林毅夫、谢平担任评论人。会议由陈雨露主持。

黄达在会议总结时提到，大家一般从两个视角来观察希勒教授的主张。一是看到他的主张好像是以理想主义的笔触描绘着对社会公平、公正的追求。吴敬琏教授关注他的“金融民主化”属于这样的视角。二是关注他设计的六个新的金融工具能否一一实现，要求怎样的条件，等等；当然也会有人认为难以实现。对此，他认为，这两个视角会集中于这样一点，那就是它体现着一种对人类社会前景充满乐观的期望，并认为可以有途径、有办法实现这种期望的信心和理念。这是极其可贵的理念，是人类社会进步的精神支柱。泛泛地说，以这样的理念修身齐家治国平天下，当无往而不胜。具体到我们关注的问题，用这样的理念建设金融学，研究金融学，无疑会使金融学在社会科学诸学科中取得更加光彩夺目的成就。

On February 25, 2003, "China's Finance: To Rational Prosperity "—sponsored by the Finance School of the Renmin University of China, China Center for Economic Research at Peking University and Liangjing Publishing House, and undertaken by the Trust and Fund Institute of the Renmin University of China—was held in the Renmin University of China. Robert J. Shiller, winner of Nobel Prize for Economics and famous economist, delivered a keynote speech. Wu Jinglian, Justin Yifu Lin and Xie Ping served as commentators. The seminar was presided over by Chen Yulu.

When summarizing the seminar, Huang Da mentioned that people observed the views of Prof. Shiller from two perspectives—some said that his ideas seemed to be depicting the pursuit of social justice and fairness with idealism; and others focused on whether his six new financial tools could be realized one by one, what the conditions were, etc. From the former perspective, Prof. Wu Jinglian was concerned about his "financial democracy. " Of course, there were also people who held that his six new financial tools could be hardly realized. Huang Da believed that the two perspectives would be centralized in one point, that is, the optimistic expectation for the prospects of human society, and the belief and idea that such expectation could be realized in some way. The idea was extremely precious, and was the breath of life for the progress of the human society. Speaking in generalities, the idea helped rule the kingdom and pacify the country. When it came to the problems we were concerned about, using such idea to develop and study the science of finance would undoubtedly enable the disciplines of social sciences to make more glorious achievements.

474

图474为2003年2月25日，黄达（居中）在“中国金融：走向理性繁荣”研讨会期间，与罗伯特·希勒（右一）、李剑阁（左一）等交谈。

On February 25, 2003, Huang Da (middle) talked with Robert Shiller (first from the right) and Li Jiange (first from the left) at the workshop of "China's Finance:To Rational Prosperity".

475

图475为2003年2月25日，黄达在“中国金融：走向理性繁荣”研讨会上进行会议总结。从左至右分别为：黄达、林毅夫、刘振亚、罗伯特·希勒、吴敬琏、谢平、陈雨露。

On February 25, 2003, Huang Da made a summary at the workshop of "China's Finance: To Rational Prosperity." From the left to the right are Huang Da, Justin Yifu Lin, Liu Zhenya, Robert Shiller, Wu Jinglian, Xie Ping and Chen Yulu.

6-4-5>

2002年1月11日，黄达赴南京大学讲学。他在题为《充实自我——谈金融人才成长之路》的演讲中强调，金融人才的培养需要从三方面入手：一是融会东西——关注东西方两个文化平台的链接；二是必要的“容忍”——排除概念带来的干扰；三是重视对自己思维的打造。

On January 11, 2002, Huang Da lectured in Nanjing University. In his speech titled Self-fulfillment—On the Growth of Financial Talent, he stressed that efforts had to be done in three aspects in order to cultivate financial talent—to blend the East with the West, that is, to pay attention to connecting the Western and the Eastern cultural platforms; to "tolerate, " that is, to eliminate the obstruction of concepts; and to set great store by rebuilding one's way of thinking.

| 右页图 |⟶

图476为2002年1月13日，黄达（左一）在结束南京大学讲学后，与胡乃武（左二）、南京大学裴平教授等赴无锡参观游览。

On January 13, 2002, after lecturing in Nanjing University, Huang Da (first from the left) visited and toured Wuxi with Hu Naiwu (second from the left) and Prof. Pei Ping from Nanjing University.

476

6-4-6>

2004年3月26日，教育部“新世纪高等教育教学改革工程”项目研究结项会在杭州召开。

会议结束后，部分与会专家同游千岛湖。期间，有感于股市的不可抗拒的诱惑力，黄达与同游诸公戏联七言打油诗一首：一路炒来一路割，割来割去奈我何；纵然割得皮包骨，明天还得再去割！其中前两句是黄达起的头，第三句为宋逢明教授所拟，第四句大家一直没有想好。2008年在三亚开会，大家又提起这首戏作，但仍然想不好第四句。后来，突然想到这样一句：“天塌地陷志不挪”，但似嫌过于“严肃”，格调不符。

On March 26, 2004, the conclusion meeting of the studies on the Ministry of Education's project "Teaching Reform of Higher Education in the New Century" was held in Hangzhou.

After the meeting, Huang Da toured Qiandao Lake with some attendees. During the tour, Huang Da made a seven-character ragged verse. Huang Da started the first two lines, while Prof. Song Fengming contributed the third line. As for the fourth line, it was not well thought. When having a meeting in Sanya in 2008, the ragged verse was mentioned again, but the fourth line was still in the balance. Later, they had the fourth line but disliked it for it was too "serious" and did not match the style of the whole verse.

477

图477为2004年3月27日，教育部“新世纪高等教育教学改革工程”项目研究结项会结束后，黄达游览孙权故里——杭州近郊富阳市境内的龙门古镇。

On March 27, 2004, after the conclusion meeting of the studies on the Ministry of Education's project "Teaching Reform of Higher Education in the New Century," Huang Da toured the hometown of Sun Quan—Longmen Ancient Town in Fuyang City in the suburbs of Hangzhou.

478

图 478 为 2004 年 3 月 26 日，“新世纪高等教育教学改革工程”项目研究结项会期间，同游千岛湖的各位专家合影留念。从左至右分别为：陈雨露、李玉书、王广谦、马君璐、宋逢明、白钦先、黄达、张亦春、刘锡良、刘红忠、朱新蓉。

On March 26, 2004, during the conclusion meeting of the studies on the Ministry of Education's project "Teaching Reform of Higher Education in the New Century, "experts touring Qiandao Lake took a group photo. From the left to the right are Chen Yulu, Li Yushu, Wang Guangqian, Ma Junlu, Song Fengming, Bai Qinxian, Huang Da, Zhang Yichun, Liu Xiliang, Liu Hongzhong and Zhu Xinrong.

6-4-7>

2004年6月19—20日，由东北财经大学金融学院主办的“中国金融学教育与金融科学发展的历史回顾和经验总结会”在大连举行。

会上，黄达提交了《教学中应该做到却不容易做到的两三点》一文。文中，黄达根据自己五十四年的从教经验，总结了跟上最新科学成就、教活而别教死以及跳出自己的“井底”三条经验。

他强调，从事金融教学，只盯住金融学这一小块天地，无疑是井底之蛙。在具体的教学当中，第一步，要跳出货币银行学，进入经济学及其各个领域，并且要注意在教学中引导学生。第二步，要跳出经济学，进入经济与政治、经济与社会相互作用的更为宽广的领域。

During June 19 and 20, 2004, "Review and Experience Summing-up Meeting of the Development of Financial Education and Science in China " sponsored by the School of Finance of Dongbei University of Finance and Economics was held in Dalian.

Huang Da submitted article titled A Few Things That Should Be Done, but Are Uneasy to Be Done in Teaching. In the article, with his experience in teaching in the past 54 years, Huang Da summed up three pieces of experience of keeping up with the latest scientific achievements, teaching flexibly instead of stiffly, and jumping out of "the shaft bottom. "

According to him, one who was engaged in teaching finance, but focused on finance only would undoubtedly be a frog at the bottom of a well. In order not to be a frog at the bottom of a well, one had to jump out of monetary banking and into economics and other fields, and pay attention to guiding students in teaching; and then jump out of economics and into broader fields where the economy interacts with politics and the society.

右页图 ⟼

图479为2004年6月19日，黄达（右一）在“中国金融学教育与金融科学发展的历史回顾和经验总结会”上发言。右二、右三分别为王传纶和林继肯。

On June 19, 2004, Huang Da (first from the right) made a speech at the "Review and Experience Summing-up Meeting of the Development of Financial Education and Science in China". The second and the third from the right are Wang Chuanlun and Lin Jiken, respectively.

479

6-4-8>

2003 年 12 月，教育部哲学社会科学重大课题攻关项目“全球经济调整中的中国经济增长与宏观调控体系研究”获批设立。黄达担任该项目首席专家，课题组成员包括陈共、陈雨露、吴晓球、杨瑞龙、郭庆旺和张杰。该项目由中国人民大学财政金融政策研究中心组织实施，张杰担任总协调人——实际实施并完成项目写作的负责人。

该项目旨在讨论全球经济调整背景下中国经济增长面临的新机遇和新挑战以及国家的应对方略和政策取向；在国家的宏观经济政策取向中，集中关注面对经济全球化和全球经济调整的新的宏观经济格局及国家建立适应新形势宏观调控体系的要求，以及财政政策与货币政策的有效组合应该作怎样的新诠释等问题。

经过三年多的系统研究，该课题最终形成两项标志性成果。一是《全球经济调整中的中国经济增长与宏观调控体系研究》（七卷本，中国人民大学出版社，2007）；二是《全球经济调整中的中国经济增长与宏观调控体系研究——新时期国家经济调节的基本取向与财政金融政策的有效组合》（经济科学出版社，2009）。

In December 2003, a major project of the Ministry of Education in humanities and social sciences—Studies on China's Economic Growth and Macroeconomic Control System in Global Economic Readjustments—was approved. Huang Da served as the chief expert of the project research team. Members of the project research team included Chen Gong, Chen Yulu, Wu Xiaoqiu, Yang Ruilong, Guo Qingwang and Zhang Jie. The project was carried out under the organization of China Financial Policy Research Center of the Renmin University of China. Zhang Jie served as the general coordinator—the person in charge of actual project implementation and project writing.

The project aimed at discussing the new opportunities and challenges faced by China's economy and China's countermeasures and policy orientation against the background of global economic readjustments. While studying China's macroeconomic policy orientation, the project focused on the new macroeconomic pattern facing economic globalization and global economic readjustments, the national requirements on building a macroeconomic control system adapting to the new situation, and the new interpretation of effective combinations of fiscal and monetary policies.

The project saw two significant achievements: *Studies on China's Economic Growth and Macroeconomic Control System in Global Economic Readjustments* (a 7-volume book, published by China Renmin University Press in 2007) and *Studies on China's Economic Growth and Macroeconomic Control System in Global Economic Readjustments—Basic Orientation of National Economic Adjustments and Effective Combination of It with Fiscal and Financial Policies in the New Period* (published by Economic Science Press in 2009).

480

图 480 为 2007 年 12 月，“全球经济调整中的中国经济增长与宏观调控体系研究”项目 2007 年度例会在北京召开。部分与会专家在一起交谈。从左至右分别为：黄达、赵锡军、杨瑞龙、张杰、郭庆旺。

In December, 2007, the 2007 annual regular meeting of the project of Studies on China's Economic Growth and Macroeconomic Control System in Global Economic Readjustments was held in Beijing. Some experts attending the meeting had a talk during the meeting. From the left to the right are Huang Da, Zhao Xijun, Yang Ruilong, Zhang Jie and Guo Qingwang.

481

图 481 为 2006 年 7 月 13 日，“全球经济调整中的中国经济增长与宏观调控体系研究”项目 2006 年度例会暨最终成果审定会在大连召开。全体与会专家合影留念。前排从左至右分别为：王传纶、黄达、陈共、周升业。

On July 13, 2006, the 2006 annual regular conference and the final achievements finalization conference of the project of Studies on China's Economic Growth and Macroeconomic Control System in Global Economic Readjustments was held in Dalian. All the attending experts took a group photo. From the left to the right in the front row are Wang Chuanlun, Huang Da, Chen Gong and Zhou Shengye.

6-4-9>

在此期间参加的其他学术交流活动

Other Academic Activities He Participated in

482

图482为2000年10月26—27日，“2000年中国金融国际论坛：全球化与金融风险管理”在中国人民大学举行。会议结束后，黄达（前排左二）、陈雨露（前排左一）与全体工作人员和学生志愿者合影留念。

During October 26 and 27, 2000, "2000 International Forum on China Finance: Globalization and Financial Risk Management" was held in the Renmin University of China. After the forum, Huang Da (second from the left in the front row), Chen Yulu (first from the the left in the front row) and all the meeting staff and student volunteers took a group photo.

483

图 483 为 2000 年 12 月 8 日，中国外汇交易中心主办的"'十五'发展规划专家顾问组"会议在上海召开。全体与会专家合影留念。前排左一至左四分别为：宋逢明、王国刚、黄达、李晓西。

On December 8, 2000, the meeting of "Expert Advisory Group for Development and Planning during the '10th Five-year Plan' Period" was held by China Foreign Exchange Trade System in Shanghai. All the attendees took a group photo. The first to the fourth from the left in the front row are Song Fengming, Wang Guogang, Huang Da and Li Xiaoxi.

484

图 484 为 2000 年 12 月 23 日，“首都经济学界新年联谊会”期间，黄达（右一）与著名经济学家高鸿业（左一）一起交谈。

On December 23, 2000, Huang Da (first from the right) and Gao Hongye (first from the left) talked with each other at "New Year Sociable of the Capital Economic Circle."

485

图 485 为 2001 年 6 月，著名经济学家、信息经济学和激励理论的奠基人之一让 · 雅克 · 拉丰（Jean-Jacques Laffont）教授，为中国人民大学师生做了题为《互联网的互联与定价》的演讲。讲座开始前，拉丰教授（左四）与中国人民大学领导和教师合影留念。左二为黄达。

In June 2001, Jean-Jacques Laffont, famous economist and one of the founders of information economics and motivation theory, gave the students and teachers of the Renmin University of China a lecture on Interconnection and Pricing of the Internet. Before the lecture, Prof. Laffont (fourth from the left) took a group photo with the leaders and teachers of the Renmin University of China. The second from the left is Huang Da.

486

图 486 为 2001 年 7 月 6 日，西南财经大学项目评审会期间，黄达（后排左五）等游览位于四川省成都市大邑县境内的西岭雪山。

On July 6, 2001, Huang Da (fifth from the left in the back row) toured and visited Xiling Snow Mountain in Dayi County, Chengdu, Sichuan Province, when attending the project evaluation meeting held by Southwestern University of Finance and Economics.

487

图 487 为 2001 年 9 月 15 日，西南财经大学主办的“中国风险投资与资本市场高级研讨会”在贵州黄果树宾馆召开。黄达（前排左三）出席会议并发言。

On September 15, 2001, "Advanced Workshop on China's Venture Capital and Capital Market" sponsored by Southwestern University of Finance and Economics was held in Huangguoshu Hotel, Guizhou. Huang Da (third from the left in the front row) attended the workshop and delivered a speech.

488

图 488 为 2003 年 3 月 5 日，黄达（后排左六）在“教育部新世纪教改工程金融学专业教材审定会议”期间，与部分与会专家赴海边游览。

On March 5, 2003, Huang Da and some attendees to the "Ministry of Education Finalization Meeting of Textbooks on Engineering Finance in the Teaching Reform in the New Century" toured by the sea.

489

图 489 为 2003 年 3 月 2 日，“教育部新世纪教改工程金融学专业教材审定会议”在海南三亚召开。全体与会专家合影留念。最后排左五为黄达。

On March 2, 2003, "Ministry of Education Finalization Meeting of Textbooks on Engineering Finance in the Teaching Reform in the New Century" was held in Sanya, Hainan. All attendees took a group photo. Fifth from the left in the back row is Huang Da.

490

图 490 为 2003 年 9 月 20 日，由西南财经大学主办的“第三届中国金融论坛”在四川成都举行。全体与会专家合影留念。第一排左六为黄达。

On September 20, 2003, "The 3rd China Finance Forum" sponsored by Southwestern University of Finance and Economics was held in Chengdu, Sichuan. All the attendees to the forum took a group photo. The sixth from the left in the first row is Huang Da.

491

图 491 为 2003 年 9 月 20 日，“第三届中国金融论坛”期间，黄达与部分与会专家在一起。左二至左七分别为：李扬、陈耀先、吴晓灵、黄达、王裕国、谢平。

On September 20, 2003, during "The 3rd China Finance Forum," Huang Da was with some attendees. From the second to the seventh from the left are Li Yang, Chen Yaoxian, Wu Xiaoling, Huang Da, Wang Yuguo and Xie Ping.

492

图 492 为 2003 年 12 月 21 日，黄达（左一）在经济科学出版社主办的“经济学界新年团拜会”上，与许毅（右一）在一起。

在思路、观点上，他们两位好像有不小的差异。但在改革开放后的二十多年里，他们却一直合作得很好。

On December 21, 2003, Huang Da (first from the left) was with Xu Yi (first from the right) at the "New Year Get-together of the Economics Circle" held by Economic Science Press.

They seemed to have quite different ways of thinking and ideas. But in the over 20 years after China adopted the reform and opening-up policy, they worked with each other very well.

493

图 493 为 2004 年 6 月 9 日，黄达（左四）赴新疆财经学院讲学，与该校教师在一起。

On June 9, 2004, Huang Da (fourth from the left) lectured in Xinjiang College of Finance and Economics (now known as Xinjiang University of Finance and Economics), and was with some of its teachers.

494

图 494 为 2009 年 9 月 26 日，黄达（右三）出席"中国与变革中的世界经济——儒家文化与金融危机治理"国际研讨会并讲话。

本次会议由中国人民大学财政金融学院、中国财政金融政策研究中心与留欧经济学会联合主办。

On September 26, 2009, Huang Da (third from the right) attended and addressed international symposium "China and the Changing Landscape of the World Economy: Confucianism and Financial Crisis Management."

The symposium was jointly sponsored by the Finance School of the Renmin University of China, China Financial Policy Research Center of the Renmin University of China, and CEA Europe.

495

图 495 为 2010 年 6 月 9—10 日，黄达出席在上海召开的教育部社会科学委员会经济学学部第二届年会。期间，与部分与会专家同游世博园。从左至右分别为：王广谦、王裕国、李晓西、吴树青、黄达、薛敬孝、朱光华、洪银兴、袁卫、史晋川。

During June 9 and 10, 2010, Huang Da attended the 2nd annual conference of the Department of Economics, Social Sciences Committee of the Ministry of Education, held in Shanghai. He was in the Expo Garden with some attendees. From the left to the right are Wang Guangqian, Wang Yuguo, Li Xiaoxi, Wu Shuqing, Huang Da, Xue Jingxiao, Zhu Guanghua, Hong Yinxing, Yuan Wei and Shi Jinchuan.

6-5

财金“四老”
Four Venerable Masters of the School of Finance of RUC

6-5-1>

王传纶（1922—2012）、黄达（1925—　）、陈共（1927—　）和周升业（1928—2015），均生于20世纪20年代并在1950年左右进入中国人民大学，此后共事一生，未曾离开。

在这里，他们相互鼓励，相互提携，彼此间结下了真挚而深厚的友谊；

在这里，他们精研学问，教书育人，共同守护着他们一手创建的中国人民大学财政与金融学科；

在这里，他们学以致用，资政启民，不遗余力地推动着新中国财政金融改革与发展。

我们无法统计有多少人听着他们的课，读着他们的书，走进了财政金融的大门。也不知从何时起，他们开始被大家亲切地称为财金“四老”……

Wang Chuanlun (1922—2012), Huang Da (1925—　), Chen Gong (1927—　) and Zhou Shengye (1928—2015), were born in the 1920s and entered the Renmin University of China around 1950 and had never left.

Here, they encourage and support each other, and forge a profound friendship;

Here, they conduct research and education, and protect the financial discipline of the Renmin University of China;

Here, they apply knowledge and serve the government, and spare no effort to promote China's financial reform and development.

Many people stepped into financial disciplines under their instruction. At some point, they are known as "four venerable masters" of the School of Finance ...

496

图496为1999年7月22日，黄达（右一）与周升业（左一）在昆明世博园合影留念。

On July 22, 1999, Huang Da (first from the right) took a group photo with Zhou Shengye (first from the left) in Kunming World Expo Garden.

497

图497为2005年4月9日，黄达（左一）与周升业（右一）在北京植物园合影留念。

On April 9, 2005, Huang Da (first from the left) took a group photo with Zhou Shengye (first from the right) in Beijing Botanical Garden.

498

499

图 498 为 2002 年 4 月，黄达（左一）与王传纶（右一）出席“我国金融政策回顾与展望——祝贺王传纶教授八十华诞学术研讨会”。

In April 2002, Huang Da (first from the left) and Wang Chuanlun (first from the right) attended "China's Financial Policy: Retrospect and Respect—Seminar in Commemoration of the 80th Anniversary of Professor Wang Chuanlun."

图 499 为 2007 年 4 月 23 日，黄达（右一）与王传纶（左一）在北京万春园交谈。

On April 23, 2007, Huang Da (first from the right) was talking with Wang Chuanlun (first from the left) in Wanchun Garden in Beijing.

500

501

图 500 为 2004 年夏，黄达（右一）与王传纶（左一）出席《金融学大辞典》提纲讨论会期间，在北戴河中国人民银行培训中心合影留念。

In the summer of 2004, Huang Da (first from the right) and Wang Chuanlun (first from the left) attended the seminar on the outline of *The Great Dictionary of Finance*. There they took a group photo in the training center of the People's Bank of China in Beidaihe.

图 501 为 2007 年 9 月 10 日，第三届“黄达—蒙代尔经济学奖”颁奖典礼开始前，黄达（右一）与王传纶（左一）在中国人民大学逸夫会议中心贵宾室交谈。

On September 10, 2007, before the 3rd "Mundell-Huang Da Prize" presentation ceremony, Huang Da (first from the right) was talking with Wang Chuanlun (first from the left) in the VIP room of Yifu Conference Center of the Renmin University of China.

502

503

504

图 502 为 2002 年 11 月 1 日，黄达（右二）、王传纶（右一）、陈共（左二）和周升业（左一）“四老”共同出席中国人民大学财政金融学院举办的校庆 65 周年联谊会。

On November 1, 2002, Huang Da (second from the right), Wang Chuanlun (first from the right), Chen Gong (second from the left) and Zhou Shengye (first from the left) attended the sociable held by the School of Finance of the Renmin University of China to celebrate its 65th anniversary.

图 503 为 2005 年 9 月 12 日，黄达（左二）、王传纶（右二）、陈共（左一）和周升业（右一）“四老”共同荣获首批“中国人民大学荣誉教授”称号。

On September 12, 2005, Huang Da (second from the left), Wang Chuanlun (second from the right), Chen Gong (first from the left) and Zhou Shengye (first from the right) were the first to win the title of "Emeritus Professor of the Renmin University of China."

图 504 为 2007 年 12 月 9 日，黄达（右二）、王传纶（左二）、陈共（右一）和周升业（左一）“四老”在北京顺义春晖园。

On December 9, 2007, Huang Da (second from the right), Wang Chuanlun (second from the left), Chen Gong (first from the right) and Zhou Shengye (first from the left) were in Chunhui Garden, Shunyi District, Beijing.

505

506

507

图 505 为 2008 年 5 月 10 日，黄达（左二）、王传纶（右二）、陈共（右一）和周升业（左一）“四老”在河北廊坊参加中国人民大学财政金融学院组织的老教授活动。

On May 10, 2008, Huang Da (second from the left), Wang Chuanlun (second from the right), Chen Gong (first from the right) and Zhou Shengye (first from the left) attended the activities held for the senior professors of the School of Finance of the Renmin University of China in Langfang, Hebei.

图 506 为 2007 年 4 月 23 日，中国人民大学财政金融学院为老教授祝寿。前排从左至右分别为：周升业、黄达、王传纶、陈共、安体富。

On April 23, 2007, the School of Finance of the Renmin University of China expressed birthday good wishes to its senior professors. From the left to the right in the front row are Zhou Shengye, Huang Da, Wang Chuanlun, Chen Gong and An Tifu.

图 507 为 2008 年 10 月 25 日，黄达（第二排右二）、王传纶（第二排左二）、陈共（第二排右一）和周升业（第二排左一）“四老”出席“中国人民大学财政金融学院 78 级校友入学三十周年师生座谈会”，与返校校友在一起。

On October 25, 2008, Huang Da (second from the right in the second row), Wang Chuanlun (second from the left in the second row), Chen Gong (first from the right in the second row) and Zhou Shengye (first from the left in the second row) attended "Symposium of the Teachers and Students on the 30th Anniversary of the Alumni and Alumna of Class 1978 of the School of Finance of the Renmin University of China," and were together with the alumni and alumna.

6-5-2>

2005年，财金“四老”共同获得首批“中国人民大学荣誉教授”称号，而后又先后被评聘为一级教授或荣誉一级教授。

In 2005, the four masters were the first to win the title of Emeritus Professor of the Renmin University of China, and were honored as first-class professors or emeritus first-class professors respectively.

508

图508为2005年9月12日，黄达等33位老教授荣获首批“中国人民大学荣誉教授”称号。全体与会老教授与校领导合影留念。前排从左至右分别为：程天权、彭明、高铭暄、钟契夫、王传纶、高放、黄达、宋涛、戴逸、甘惜分、卫兴华、方汉奇、许崇德、纪宝成。第二排从左至右分别为：庄福龄、王作富、许征帆、陈共、蓝鸿文、王思治、刘佩弦、周诚、孙国华、黄顺基、李占祥、周升业、胡钧。后排从左至右分别为：马俊杰、冯惠玲、袁卫、林岗、陈雨露。

On September 12, 2005, Huang Da and another 32 senior professors were presented with the title of "Emeritus Professor of the Renmin University of China." All the attending senior professors took a group photo with leaders of the Renmin University of China. From the left to the right in the front row are Cheng Tianquan, Peng Ming, Gao Mingxuan, Zhong Qifu, Wang Chuanlun, Gao Fang, Huang Da, Song Tao, Dai Yi, Gan Xifen, Wei Xinghua, Fang Hanqi, Xu Chongde, Ji Baocheng; from the left to the right in the second row are Zhuang Fuling, Wang Zuofu, Xu Zhengfan, Chen Gong, Lan Hongwen, Wang Sizhi, Liu Peixian, Zhou Cheng, Sun Guohua, Huang Shunji, Li Zhanxiang, Zhou Shengye and Hu Jun; and from the left to the right in the back row are Ma Junjie, Feng Huiling, Yuan Wei, Lin Gang and Chen Yulu.

509

图 509 为 2009 年 5 月 20 日，“中国人民大学首批一级教授聘任仪式暨首批荣誉一级教授称号授予仪式”隆重举行，黄达等 14 位教授获聘一级教授。全体与会一级教授与校领导合影留念。从左至右分别为：程天权、刘大椿、曾宪义、胡乃武、吴易风、李文海、戴逸、黄达、陈先达、方立天、周新城、张立文、郑杭生、纪宝成。

On May 20, 2009, "First First-class Professors of the Renmin University of China Appointment Ceremony and Presentation Ceremony of the Title of Emeritus First-class Professor" was held. Huang Da and another 13 professors were presented with the title of First-class Professor. All the attending first-class professors took a group photo with leaders of the Renmin University of China. From the left to the right are Cheng Tianquan, Liu Dachun, Zeng Xianyi, Hu Naiwu, Wu Yifeng, Li Wenhai, Dai Yi, Huang Da, Chen Xianda, Fang Litian, Zhou Xincheng, Zhang Liwen, Zheng Hangsheng and Ji Baocheng.

6-6

与我们在一起
Be with Us

6-6-1>

与中国人民大学校领导在一起
Be with Leaders of the Renmin University of China

510

图 510 为 2005 年 6 月 7 日，黄达（左一）赴袁宝华（右一）老校长家中拜见并呈送刚刚出版的《黄达书集》。

On June 7, 2005, Huang Da (first from the left) went to visit Yuan Baohua (first from the right) at the latter's home and presented the latter with *Selected Books of Huang Da*.

511

图 511 为 2011 年 2 月 9 日，黄达与中国人民大学部分退休校领导在一起。前排从左至右分别为：郑杭生、李文海、黄达、马绍孟、沈云锁。后排从左至右分别为：周建明、郑英良、杨德福、杜厚文、张建明。

On February 9, 2011, Huang Da was with some retired leaders of the Renmin University of China. From the left to the right in the front row are Zheng Hangsheng, Li Wenhai, Huang Da, Ma Shaomeng and Shen Yunsuo; and from the left to the right in the back row are Zhou Jianming, Zheng Yingliang, Yang Defu, Du Houwen and Zhang Jianming.

512

图 512 为 2014 年 1 月 21 日，中国人民大学举办新老领导干部新春座谈会。全体与会校领导合影留念。前排从左至右分别为：周新城、郑杭生、程天权、黄达、马绍孟、李震中、郝彦桐。后排从左至右分别为：徐志宏、周建明、马俊杰、靳诺、李昭公、沈云锁、陈雨露、袁卫、王利明、陈一兵、杨慧林、查显友。

On January 21, 2014, Huang Da attended "New Year Symposium of the Old and New Leading Cadres of the Renmin University of China." From the left to the right in the front row are Zhou Xincheng, Zheng Hangsheng, Cheng Tianquan, Huang Da, Ma Shaomeng, Li Zhenzhong, and Hao Yantong; and from the left to the right in the back row are Xu Zhihong, Zhou Jianming, Ma Junjie, Jin Nuo, Li Zhaogong, Shen Yunsuo, Chen Yulu, Yuan Wei, Wang Liming, Chen Yibing, Yang Huilin and Zha Xianyou.

513

图 513 为 2013 年 5 月 14 日，中国人民大学党委书记靳诺（左二）与时任校长陈雨露（左一）赴家中看望黄达（右一）。

On May 14, 2013, Jin Nuo (second from the left), secretary of the Party Committee of the Renmin University of China, and Chen Yulu (first from the left), president of the Renmin University of China, visited Huang Da (first from the right) at the latter's home.

514

图 514 为 2016 年 1 月 22 日，中国人民大学党委书记靳诺（右一）与校长刘伟（左一）赴家中看望黄达（左二）。

On January 22, 2016, Jin Nuo (first from the right), secretary of the Party Committee of the Renmin University of China, and Liu Wei (first from the left), president of the Renmin University of China, visited Huang Da (second from the left) at the latter's home.

515

图 515 和图 516 为 2012 年 5 月 24 日，中国人民大学七十五周年校庆之际，黄达为学校组织的校庆义卖活动捐献泥塑“我们热爱天安门”并题写捐献说明。

这是 20 世纪 60 年代 70 年代之交，以无锡惠山泥人手法注释儿歌“我们热爱天安门”的一件代表性作品。大约在 1970 年，黄达从江西余江县“五七干校”回京探亲途中，在无锡惠山脚下的泥人店铺购得此件泥塑。从那时起，一直摆在书架上，陪伴黄达四十多年。

These are the pictures of "We Love Tian'anmen," a clay sculpture donated by Huang Da on May 24, 2012 to the bazaar held by the Renmin University of China to celebrate its 75th anniversary, and explanations on the donation.

It was at the turn of the 1960s and 1970s that children's song "We Love Tian'anmen" annotated by the technique of Huishan clay sculpture became a representative piece of work. It was about 1970 when Huang Da passed the clay sculpture in a clay sculpture store at the foot of Mount Hui, Wuxi, on his way back from the "May 7th School for Cadres" in Yujiang County, Jiangxi Province, that Huang Da bought it. Since then, it had been on the bookshelf of Huang Da and accompanying him for over 40 years.

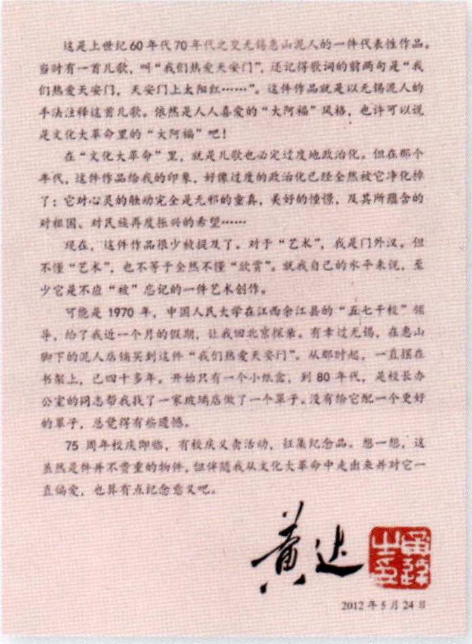

这是上世纪60年代70年代之交无锡惠山泥人的一件代表性作品。当时有一首儿歌，叫“我们热爱天安门”，还记得歌词的前两句是“我们热爱天安门，天安门上太阳红……”。这件作品就是以无锡泥人的手法注释这首儿歌。依然是人人喜爱的“大阿福”风格，也许可以说是文化大革命里的“大阿福”吧！

在“文化大革命”里，就是儿歌也必定过度地政治化。但在那个年代，这件作品给我的印象，好像过度的政治化已经全然被它净化掉了：它对心灵的触动完全是无邪的童真，美好的憧憬，及其所蕴含的对祖国、对民族再度振兴的希望……

现在，这件作品很少被提及了。对于“艺术”，我是门外汉。但不懂“艺术”，也不等于全然不懂“欣赏”。就我自己的水平来说，至少它是不应“被”忘记的一件艺术创作。

可能是 1970 年，中国人民大学在江西余江县的“五七干校”领导，给了我近一个月的假期，让我回北京探亲。有幸过无锡，在惠山脚下的泥人店铺买到这件“我们热爱天安门”。从那时起，一直摆在书架上，已四十多年。开始只有一个小纸盒，到 80 年代，是校长办公室的同志帮我找了一家玻璃店做了一个罩子。没有给它配一个更好的罩子，总觉得有些遗憾。

75 周年校庆即临，有校庆义卖活动，征集纪念品。想一想，这虽然是件并不贵重的物件，但伴随我从文化大革命中走出来并对它一直偏爱，也算有点纪念意义吧。

黄达

2012 年 5 月 24 日

516

6-6-2>

与中国人民大学财政金融学院教师在一起

Be with Faculty of School of Finance of the Renmin University of China

517

图 517 为 1999 年 10 月 27 日，中国人民大学财政金融学院货币金融系秋游颐和园。全体教师合影留念。从左至右分别为：何平、沈伟基、周升业、黄达、庄毓敏、尹继红、庞红、涂永红、李世银。

On October 27, 1999, faculty of the Department of Money and Finance of the School of Finance, the Renmin University of China, had an autumn outing in the Summer Palace. All the teachers took a group photo. From the left to the right are He Ping,Shen Weiji, Zhou Shengye, Huang Da , Zhuang Yumin, Yin Jihong, Pang Hong, Tu Yonghong and Li Shiyin.

518

519

图 518 为 2001 年 12 月 19 日，中国人民大学财政金融学院货币金融系进行期末总结聚会活动。全体教师合影留念。前排从左至右分别为：关伟、赵锡军、沈伟基、朱毅峰、黄达、周升业、吴晓球。后排从左至右分别为：涂永红、李世银、瞿强、尹继红、季冬生、李向科、林清泉、向东、类承曜、龚明华、庄毓敏、庞红。

On December 19, 2001, after the summing-up get-together at the end of the term, teachers of the Department of Money and Finance of the School of Finance, the Renmin University of China, took a group photo at the restaurant. From the left to the right in the front row are Guan Wei, Zhao Xijun, Shen Weiji, Zhu Yifeng, Huang Da, Zhou Shengye and Wu Xiaoqiu; and from the left to the right in the back row are Tu Yonghong, Li Shiyin, Qu Qiang, Yin Jihong, Ji Dongsheng, Li Xiangke, Lin Qingquan, Xiang Dong, Lei Chengyao, Gong Minghua, Zhuang Yumin and Pang Hong.

图 519 为 2002 年 12 月 25 日，中国人民大学财政金融学院货币金融系在数码大厦进行期末总结聚会活动。全体教师合影留念。前排从左至右分别为：尹继红、宋玮、庄毓敏、庞红、涂永红、向东。第二排从左至右分别为：陈雨露、朱毅峰、黄达、吴晓球、沈伟基、赵锡军。后排从左至右分别为：瞿强、类承曜、李世银、林清泉、何平、龚明华、季冬生、李向科。

On December 25, 2002, after the summing-up get-together at the end of the term, teachers of the Department of Money and Finance of the School of Finance, the Renmin University of China, took a group photo at the restaurant on the top floor of the building of Digital Beijing. From the left to the right in the front row are Yin Jihong, Song Wei, Zhuang Yumin, Pang Hong, Tu Yonghong and Xiang Dong; from the left to the right in the second row are Chen Yulu, Zhu Yifeng, Huang Da, Wu Xiaoqiu, Shen Weiji and Zhao Xijun; and from the left to the right in the back row are Qu Qiang, Lei Chengyao, Li Shiyin, Lin Qingquan, He Ping, Gong Minghua, Ji Dongsheng and Li Xiangke.

520

图 520 为 2003 年 11 月 28 日，中国人民大学财政金融学院货币金融系集体组织游览居庸关长城。全体教师合影留念。前排从左至右分别为：季冬生、尹继红、向东、涂永红、李凤云、宋宝玲、庄毓敏、庞红。后排从左至右分别为：李向科、张杰、李世银、黄达、陈雨露、何平、吴晓球、周炜、类承曜。

On November 28, 2003, the Department of Money and Finance of the School of Finance of the Renmin University of China organized a group visit to Juyongguan Great Wall. All the teachers took a group photo. From the left to the right in the front row are Ji Dongsheng, Yin Jihong, Xiang Dong, Tu Yonghong, Li Fengyun, Song Baoling, Zhuang Yumin and Pang Hong; and from the left to the right in the back row are Li Xiangke, Zhang Jie, Li Shiyin, Huang Da, Chen Yulu, He Ping, Wu Xiaoqiu, Zhou Wei and Lei Chengyao.

| 右页图 ⟼

图 521 为 2003 年 11 月 28 日，黄达漫步在居庸关长城。

On November 28, 2003, Huang Da strolled around Juyongguan Great Wall.

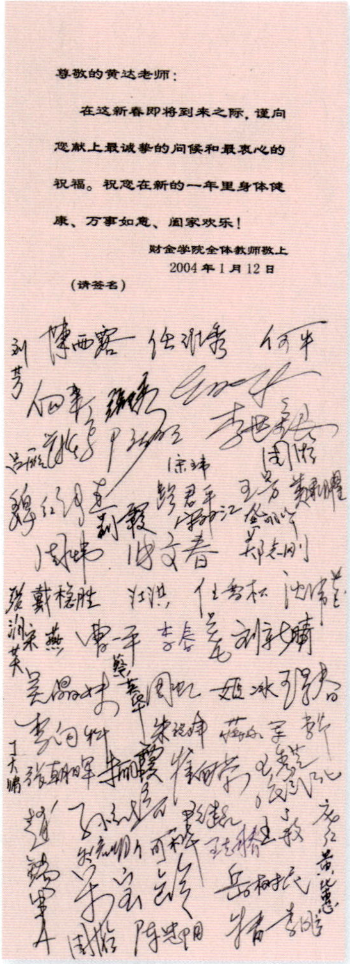

尊敬的黄达老师：

在这新春即将到来之际，谨向您献上最诚挚的问候和最衷心的祝福。祝您在新的一年里身体健康、万事如意、阖家欢乐！

财金学院全体教师敬上
2004年1月12日

（请签名）

522

图522为2004年1月12日，中国人民大学财政金融学院为黄达精心制作的全体教师签名贺卡。

This is a delicately-made greeting card with the signatures of all the teachers of the School of Finance of the Renmin University of China on January 12, 2004,

523

图 523 为 2004 年 11 月 6 日，中国人民大学货币金融系与应用金融系教师同游慕田峪长城。最后排左一为黄达。

On November 6, 2004, teachers of the Department of Money and Finance and the Department of Applied Finance of the Renmin University of China toured and visited Mutianyu Great Wall and took a group photo. The first from the left in the back row is Huang Da.

524

图 524 为 2005 年 4 月 9 日，黄达与中国人民大学货币金融系与应用金融系教师在北京植物园游览。中间为黄达。

On April 9, 2005, Huang Da and some teachers of the Department of Money and Finance and the Department of Applied Finance of the Renmin University of China were in Beijing Botanical Garden. Huang Da is in the middle.

525

图 525 为 2006 年 11 月 3 日，黄达与中国人民大学货币金融系部分女教师在北京雁栖湖。从左至右分别为：涂永红、庄毓敏、黄达、尹继红、王芳。

On November 3, 2006, Huang Da was by Yanxi Lake with some women teachers of the Department of Money and Finance of the Renmin University of China. From the left to the right are Tu Yonghong, Zhuang Yumin, Huang Da, Yin Jihong and Wang Fang.

526

图 526 为 2007 年 4 月 29 日，中国人民大学货币金融系赴西安调研。全体教师合影留念。前排从左至右分别为：张成思、庄毓敏、尹继红、王芳、李芹、涂永红、庞红、季冬生、李向科。后排从左至右分别为：宋宝玲、赵锡军、朱毅峰、陈雨露、黄达、林清泉、李世银、何平、张杰、沈伟基。

On April 29, 2007, the Department of Money and Finance of the Renmin University of China went to Xi'an, Shaanxi, for investigation and research. From the left to the right in the front row are Zhang Chengsi, Zhuang Yumin, Yin Jihong, Wang Fang, Li Qin, Tu Yonghong, Pang Hong, Ji Dongsheng and Li Xiangke; and from the left to the right in the back row are Song Baoling, Zhao Xijun, Zhu Yifeng, Chen Yulu, Huang Da, Lin Qingquan, Li Shiyin, He Ping, Zhang Jie, and Shen Weiji.

527

528

图 527 为 2008 年 9 月 13 日，中国人民大学货币金融系秋游北京龙庆峡。全体教师合影留念。前排从左至右分别为：季冬生、何平、张杰、吴晓球、庄毓敏、黄达、沈伟基、朱毅峰、庞红、宋玮、尹继红。后排从左至右分别为：李向科、林清泉、赵锡军、陈雨露、孙红培、涂永红。

On September 13, 2008, teachers of the Department of Money and Finance of the Renmin University of China took a group photo at Longqing Gorge, Beijing. From the left to the right in the front row are Ji Dongsheng, He Ping, Zhang Jie, Wu Xiaoqiu, Zhuang Yumin, Huang Da, Shen Weiji, Zhu Yifeng, Pang Hong, Song Wei and Yin Jihong; and from the left to the right in the back row are Li Xiangke, Lin Qingquan, Zhao Xijun, Chen Yulu, Sun Hongpei and Tu Yonghong.

图 528 为 2015 年 3 月 25 日，中国人民大学货币金融系全体教师在工作例会后合影留念。前排从左至右分别为：张杰、林清泉、李世银、黄达、何平、庞红、赵锡军。后排从左至右分别为：涂永红、尹继红、钱宗鑫、李向科、刚建华、张成思、宋玮、马勇、季冬生、尹继红、何青、罗煜。

On March 25, 2015, teachers of the Department of Money and Finance of the Renmin University of China took a group photo. From the left to the right in the front row are Zhang Jie, Lin Qingquan, Li Shiyin, Huang Da, He Ping, Pang Hong, Zhao Xijun; and from the left to the right in the back row are Tu Yonghong, Yin Jihong, Qian Zongxin, Li Xiangke, Gang Jianhua, Zhang Chengsi, Song Wei, Ma Yong, Ji Dongsheng, Yin Jihong, He Qing and Luo Yu.

图 529 为 2009 年 4 月 18 日，中国人民大学财政金融学院全体教师合影。前排从左至右分别为：庄毓敏、张杰、郭庆旺、安体富、陈共、黄达、王传纶、周升业、陈雨露、王宏伟、庞红、黄文彬。

On April 18, 2009, teachers of the School of Finance of the Renmin University of China took a group photo. From the left to the right in the front row are Zhuang Yumin, Zhang Jie, Guo Qingwang, An Tifu, Chen Gong, Huang Da, Wang Chuanlun, Zhou Shengye, Chen Yulu, Wang Hongwei, Pang Hong and Huang Wenbin.

529

6-6-3 >

与中国人民大学财政金融学院校友和学生在一起

Be with Alumni and Students of School of Finance of the Renmin University of China

530

图 530 为 2001 年 6 月，黄达（左五）与中国人民大学财政金融学院 2001 届毕业生在一起。

In June 2001, Huang Da (fifth from the left) was with the graduates of 2001 of the School of Finance of the Renmin University of China.

531

图 531 为 2008 年 10 月 25 日，黄达出席中国人民大学财政金融学院 78 级校友联谊会，与返校校友合影留念。

On October 25, 2008, Huang Da attended the sociable of the alumni and alumna of Class 1978 of the School of Finance of the Renmin University of China, and took a group photo with the returned alumni and alumna.

图 532 为 2009 年 10 月 24 日，黄达（右三）出席中国人民大学财政金融学院 79 级校友联谊会，与返校校友亲切交谈。右一为周升业。

On October 24, 2009, Huang Da (third from the right) attended the sociable of the alumni and alumna of Class 1979 of the School of Finance of the Renmin University of China, and talked cordially with the returned alumni and alumna. The first from the right is Zhou Shengye.

532

6-6-4>

七十、八十和九十大寿

The 70th, 80th and 90th Birthday

533

534

图 533 为 1995 年 2 月 22 日，中国人民大学校领导为黄达庆贺七十大寿。前排从左至右分别为：杨德福、马绍孟、黄达、李文海、力康泰。后排左二至左八分别为：杜厚文、郝彦桐、牛继生、李昭公、沈云锁、郑英良、张慧。

On February 22, 1995, leaders of the Renmin University of China celebrated the 70th birthday of Huang Da. From the left to the right in the front row are Yang Defu, Ma Shaomeng, Huang Da, Li Wenhai and Li Kangtai; and the second to the eighth from the left in the back row are Du Houwen, Hao Yantong, Niu Jisheng, Li Zhaogong, Shen Yunsuo, Zheng Yingliang and Zhang Hui.

图 534 为 1995 年 2 月 22 日，弟子为黄达庆贺七十大寿。前排从左至右分别为：袁振宇、黄达、王松奇。后排从左至右分别为：沈伟基、王广谦、李焰、陈雨露、吴晓球。

On February 22, 1995, the students held a celebration for the 70th birthday of Huang Da. From the left to the right in the front row are Yuan Zhenyu, Huang Da and Wang Songqi; and from the left to the right in the back row are Shen Weiji, Wang Guangqian, Li Yan, Chen Yulu and Wu Xiaoqiu.

535

图 535 为 1995 年 2 月 22 日，黄达切生日蛋糕。

On February 22, 1995, Huang Da was cutting the birthday cake.

536

图 536 为 2005 年 2 月 22 日，中国人民大学为黄达八十大寿赠送的寿礼。

This is the birthday gift sent on February 22, 2005 by the Renmin University of China to Huang Da for the latter's 80th birthday.

537

538

图 537 为 2005 年 2 月 22 日，为黄达庆贺八十大寿来的弟子们较多，这是他与部分弟子的合影。前排从左至右分别为：左毓秀、李晓西、张洪涛、黄达、宋逢明、王松奇、欧明刚。后排从左至右分别为：张杰、李鹰、邓乐平、洪琦、王广谦、李健、沈伟基、李扬、王国刚、夏斌、贝多广、吴晓球、刘成。

On February 22, 2005, many students came to celebrate the 80th birthday of Huang Da. This is a group photo of Huang Da with some of his students. From the left to the right in the front row are Zuo Yuxiu, Li Xiaoxi, Zhang Hongtao, Huang Da, Song Fengming, Wang Songqi and Ou Minggang; and from the left to the right in the back row are Zhang Jie, Li Ying, Deng Leping, Hong Qi, Wang Guangqian, Li Jian, Shen Weiji, Li Yang, Wang Guogang, Xia Bin, Bei Duoguang, Wu Xiaoqiu and Liu Cheng.

图 538 为 2005 年 2 月 26 日，中国人民大学财政金融学院为黄达庆贺八十大寿。全体教师合影留念。前排从左至右分别为：安体富、王传纶、黄达、陈共、周升业。后排从左至右分别为：吴帆、庞红、赵锡军、谭荣华、陈雨露、孙红培、何平、宋宝玲、郭庆旺、李芹、瞿强。

On February 26, 2005, the School of Finance of the Renmin University of China celebrated the 80th birthday of Huang Da. From the left to the right in the front row are An Tifu, Wang Chuanlun, Huang Da, Chen Gong and Zhou Shengye; and from the left to the right in the back row are Wu Fan, Pang Hong, Zhao Xijun, Tan Ronghua, Chen Yulu, Sun Hongpei, He Ping, Song Baoling, Guo Qingwang, Li Qin and Qu Qiang.

539

图 539 为 2015 年 2 月 21 日，弟子为黄达庆贺九十大寿。前排从左至右分别为：刘玮、向东、吴晓灵、刘曼红、李焰、李健。第二排从左至右分别为：张洪涛、吴炯、黄达、沈伟基。后排从左至右分别为：韩文秀、张杰、王广谦、周慕冰、王松奇、袁振宇、李扬、高培勇、陈雨露。

On February 21, 2015, the students held a celebration for the 90th birthday of Huang Da. From the left to the right in the front row are Liu Wei, Xiang Dong, Wu Xiaoling, Liu Manhong, Li Yan and Li Jian; from the left to the right in the second row are Zhang Hongtao, Wu Jiong, Huang Da and Shen Weiji; and from the left to the right in the back row are Han Wenxiu, Zhang Jie, Wang Guangqian, Zhou Mubing, Wang Songqi, Yuan Zhenyu, Li Yang, Gao Peiyong and Chen Yulu.

540

图 540 为 2015 年 2 月 22 日，中国人民大学为黄达九十大寿赠送的寿礼。

This is the birthday gift sent on February 22, 2015 by the Renmin University of China to Huang Da for the latter's 90th birthday.

6-7

与老年伴侣在一起

Be with His Companion

541

图 541 为 2012 年 10 月 19 日，黄达与老年伴侣吴炯在张家口大境门前留影。

1946 年暮春开始，在张家口华北联合大学，黄达与吴炯是法政学院的同学——黄达在财经系，吴炯在政法系。但学院的共同活动甚多，而且宿舍极近，同在“东山坡”。吴炯的年龄比黄达小，但吴炯是抗战时期进入革命根据地的，“革命资格”老，而黄达则是刚刚进入根据地的“非党群众”。在那时的黄达眼里，吴炯无可置疑是“大师姐”。但无论如何，那一阶段，他们在华北联合大学，共同度过了难忘的青春岁月。

On October 19, 2012, Huang Da and his companion Wu Jiong took a photo in front of the Dajingmen Pass, Zhangjiakou.

Since late spring 1946, in North China Union University, Huang Da and Wu Jiong were schoolmates of the School of Law and Politics —Huang Da was in the Department of Finance and Wu Jiong was in the Department of Law and Politics. However, the two schools held many activities together, and their students' dorms were really close. Wu Jiong was younger than Huang Da, but she went to the revolutionary base during the Anti-Japanese War, so she was more "revolutionary." Huang Da was a "non-Party member civilian" who just went to the revolutionary base. In the eyes of Huang Da, Wu Jiong was his "senior scholarly sister." No matter what, they spent unforgettable years of youth in North China Union University.

542

图 542 为 1946 年 6 月，在张家口华北联合大学大礼堂举行的校学生会第一次选举上，吴炯当选为校学生会执委。站在椅子上接受竞选提名的就是吴炯，站着介绍吴炯的是孙超，后排就座的为陈英茨、刘兢生，前排为周平、济民等。这是由我国一级演员陈强拍摄的珍贵照片。

In June 1946, at the first election of candidates for the students' union of North China Union University, Wu Jiong was elected as an executive of the students' union. The one standing on the chair for nomination is Wu Jiong, and the man standing there introducing Wu Jiong is Sun Chao. The two sitting in the back row are Chen Yingci and Liu Jingsheng; and the two sitting in the front row are Zhou Ping and Ji Min. This is a picture taken by Chen Qiang, a first-grade actor of China.

6-8

陕公、联大、华大旧址行

Visiting the Former Site of Shanbei Public School, North China Union University and North China University

新世纪以来，黄达以专程探访，或以出席学校组织的典礼、会议的方式，先后来到陕北公学旧址，以及曾经学习、工作和生活过的华北联合大学和华北大学旧址，重温当年难忘的青春岁月。

Since the new century, Huang Da came to visit the former site of Shanbei Public School, North China Union University and North China University to relive the unforgettable days.

543

图 543 为 2000 年，陕公联大校友会会长凌云（右二）率队出席陕北公学碑亭揭幕仪式。吴炯（左二）作为华北联合大学的代表出席此次活动，黄达遗憾未能出席。修建陕北公学碑亭是当年陕公联大校友的重要活动之一。

In 2000, Ling Yun (second from the right), President of the Alumni Association of Shanbei Public School and North China Union University, attended the inauguration ceremony of the monument of Shanbei Public School. Wu Jiong (second from the left) attended the ceremony representing North China Union University. Huang Da did not attend. Establishing the monument of Shanbei Public School was one of the major activities of the alumni of Shanbei Public School and North China Union University.

544

545

图 544 为 2012 年 11 月 1 日，黄达在“陕北公学旧址和中国人民大学培训基地揭牌仪式”上讲话。他用几个“是不是”来诠释陕北公学的精神：是不是对时代脉搏的敏锐体察和把握？是不是激情迸发地响应时代的召唤？是不是为时代的使命而全身心地奉献青春年华和毕生精力？是不是永远在时代大潮的前沿搏击、奋进，或者说永远做时代的弄潮儿？

On November 1, 2012, Huang Da addressed the inauguration ceremony of the former site of Shanbei Public School and the Training Base of the Renmin University of China. In his speech, Huang Da used a few questions to interpreted the spirit of Shanbei Public School —Was it a sensitive observation and grasp of the pulse of the times? Was it a passionate response to the call of the times? Was it the devotion of youth and life energy to the mission of the times? Was it always in the forefront of the tide of the times?

图 545 为 2012 年 11 月 1 日，黄达在陕北公学和华北联合大学校友会所立的纪念碑亭留影。

On November 1, 2012, Huang Da took a photo in front of the monument set by the Alumni Association of Shanbei Public School and North China Union University.

图 546 为 2012 年 10 月，黄达为“陕北公学展览馆”题写馆名。

In October 2012, Huang Da inscribed for "Shanbei Public School Exhibition Hall."

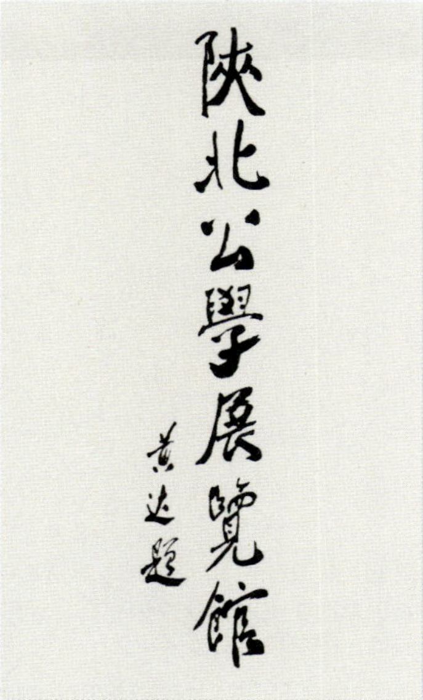

546

547

图 547 为 2012 年 10 月 20 日，黄达（左六）重回张家口，参观华北联合大学旧址（图中校名有误）。

On October 20, 2012, Huang Da (sixth from the left) returned to Zhangjiakou to visit the former site of North China Union University (the name of the university in the picture is erroneous).

548

图 548 为 2013 年 8 月 25 日，黄达（左一）出席在河北省正定县召开的“弘扬华北大学光荣传统”群众路线教育实践主题活动座谈会，与吴炯（左二）、卫兴华（右二）、陈共（右一）在一起。会上，黄达回顾了那段激情燃烧的岁月和华北大学对兴办新中国高等教育的探索历程。在 1948 年秋，华北大学正是在全国即将解放和一个崭新中国即将建立的时代召唤下成立的，并在自己存在的短短一年半时间内向全国各地输送了两万余名为新中国组建新社会所需要的最有活力的骨干。他强调，这正是我们必须铭记和弘扬的传统。

On August 25, 2013, Huang Da (first from the left) attended the symposium on the thematic activities held to put the mass line education into practice—titled "Carry Forward the Glorious Tradition of North China University"—held in Zhengding County, Hebei Province. He was with Wu Jiong (second from the left), Wei Xinghua (second from the right) and Chen Gong (first from the right).

At the symposium, Huang Da reviewed the years of passion and the explorations made by North China University on initiating higher education in new China. In the autumn of 1948, North China University was established on the eve of national liberation of China and the birth of a brand-new China. In a short period of less than one year and a half, it transferred more than 20,000 talented people of the greatest vitality to across China for the purpose of building a new Chinese society. He held it to be a tradition that must be kept in mind and carried forward.

图 549 为 2013 年 8 月，黄达为“华北大学展览馆”题字。

In August 2013, Huang Da inscribed for "North China University Exhibition Hall."

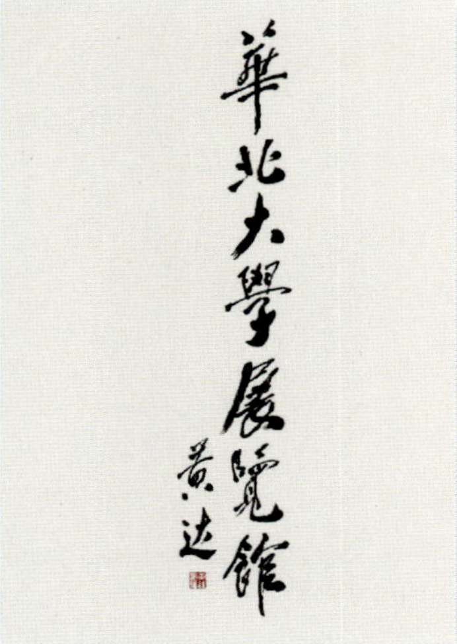

549

6-9

“三项大奖”
Three Great Awards

2011 年，首届“中国金融学科终身成就奖”；
2013 年，第六届“中国经济理论创新奖”；
2014 年，第三届“吴玉章人文社会科学终身成就奖”。
耄耋之年，黄达—— 一个与金融学科相伴一生的教书先生，获得了应有的肯定和褒奖。

In 2011, the first "China's Annual Financial Discipline Lifetime Achievement Award ".
In 2013, the sixth "China's Economic Theory Innovation Award ".
In 2014, the third "Wu Yuzhang Humanities and Social Sciences Lifetime Achievement Award ".
In his later years, Huang Da, a financial discipline lifetime teacher received recognition and praise.

550

图 550 为中国金融学科终身成就奖。

China's Annual Financial Discipline Lifetime Achievement Award

551

552

图 551 为中国经济理论创新奖。

China's Economic Theory Innovation Award

图 552 为吴玉章人文社会科学终身成就奖。

Wu Yuzhang Humanities and Social Sciences Lifetime Achievement Award

6-9-1>

中国金融学科终身成就奖

China's Annual Financial Discipline Lifetime Achievement Award

6-9-1-1>

“中国金融学科终身成就奖”由刘鸿儒金融教育基金会设立，目的在于表彰优秀金融学科带头人在金融学科建设中的突出贡献，推动高校、科研机构开展金融研究和金融教育，促进中国金融学科建设发展，为中国金融改革、创新和发展培养优秀人才。奖项采取“集中评审、按年颁奖”的方式，每年奖励1~3位在中国金融学科建设方面做出卓越贡献，长期从事金融学科教学与科研工作的优秀学者。

2011年6月1日，黄达获得首届中国金融学科终身成就奖。

在颁奖典礼上，黄达把自己近五六年来探讨国内外金融学科建设轨迹和自己形成的一些看法跟大家进行了分享。他指出，东方、西方的古圣先贤都有蕴含着金融真知的至理名言。我国先秦、汉初诸子有关货币金融的见解透彻、精辟，至今依然熠熠生辉。西方伴随着现代经济的萌生，逐步形成了服务于现代经济的经济学。19世纪，马克思的《资本论》面世，其中金融理论占有极其重要的地位，许多论点，其历史的穿透力令人折服。

19世纪后半叶，货币论、银行论从经济学中独立出来——货币银行学成为走进大学讲堂的一门重要课程。也就是在进入20世纪之后，我国游学于西方的学子，把引进金融学科作为传播先进文明的重点，做了大量工作；他们结合中国实际的研究，则反映着中国学人在世界金融学科建设史上所做出的努力。

第二次世界大战和解放战争打断了金融学科的引进过程；而新中国的建立，则改变了引进的方向，即全面引进自苏联和戛然关闭了引进自西方的门户。对于这段历史，似乎有一种任凭岁月磨灭记忆的趋势。但建立计划经济，必然有为之服务的金融理论和实务，而在计划经济中的金融学科事实上不能不包含有金融学科的基本原理。

在闭关锁国的背景下，中国人对于金融学科建设也有着自己独立的贡献。如指导新中国成立之初制止极端恶性通货膨胀的经济思想；如发展了以“财政、信贷、物资三平”论断所表述的宏观均衡理论；如在全国建立通存通汇制度的实务理论；等等。这对于全国金融队伍在改革开放后吸收西方金融学科建设的成果，是一个不能忽视的基础。

改革开放重新打开了从西方引进的大门。在改革开放之初的20世纪80年代，我们引进的主要是20世纪上半叶西方金融学科建设的发展成果，即宏观经济分析被引入货币银行学。至于对西方在20世纪50年代之后快速发展起来的现代金融学的引进，则主要开始于改革开放后出国的学子归来后的90年代中期。今天，西方金融学科全面发展的内容我们已经可以及时把握。

总的来说，一百多年以来，我们的金融学科建设不论如何曲折萦回，基本属于“引进”型。其间，间或有自己创新的亮点，但影响极难越出国境。当今，中国元素在国际经济、国际金融的舞台上已然有着越来越难以忽视的权重。在这样的背景下，中国的金融学科建设也必将为世界金融学科的建设做出自己的贡献。

日后，他的讲话稿被《百年中国金融学说思想史》收录为该书的序文之一。

"China's Annual Financial Discipline Lifetime Achievement Award, " established by Liu Hongru Financial Education Foundation, aims at commending excellent pace-setters in the development of the financial discipline for their outstanding contribution; pushing universities and scientific research institutes forward in financial researches and financial education; promoting the development of the financial discipline in China; and cultivating more talented people for China's financial reform, innovations and development. "China's Annual Financial Discipline Lifetime Achievement Award " is issued annually through centralized evaluation and election. Each year, one to three excellent scholars who make outstanding contribution to the development of the financial discipline and have been engaged in finance teaching and researches would be selected and given the award.

On June 1, 2011, Huang Da was the first to win "China's Annual Financial Discipline Lifetime Achievement Award. "

At the ceremony, Huang Da shared with people his views on the development orbits of the financial discipline in China and abroad in the recent five or six years, and some of his own views. He pointed out that the finest men of past centuries in the East and the West all had wise sayings that contained true knowledge of finance. The sages in the Pre-Qin Dynasty and the early Han Dynasty had thorough, clear and penetrating opinions on monetary finance, which are shining even today. With the emergence of modern economy, economics serving modern economy had gradually taken shape. In the 19th century, Marx's *on Capital* came out and the financial theories in the book held an extremely important position. Many views in the book were convincingly penetrating in history.

In the second half of the 19th century, money and banking got separated from economics, and monetary banking became an important course for university students. It is also in the 20th century that Chinese students who were furthering their studies in the West made the introduction of the financial discipline the priority of spreading advanced civilization, and did a lot of work. Their studies based on China's reality reflected the efforts made by the Chinese scholars for the development of the financial discipline in the world.

The Second World War and the war of the liberation of China interrupted the introduction of the financial discipline; while the founding of new China changed the introduction direction, that is, to introduce it from the Soviet Union and abruptly shut down the door of introducing it from the West. That period seems to have worn away in history. However, to build the planned economy, there must be financial theories and practices to serve it. The financial discipline in the planned economy cannot but contain the basic principles of the financial discipline.

Against the background of seclusion, the Chinese people had their unique contribution to developing the financial discipline, like the economic thought that helped stop the hyperinflation in the early days after the founding of new China; developing the macroequilibrium theory represented by "the balance of finance, credit and material; " putting forward the theory of building a system where deposits and remittances are processed at any bank across Mainland China, etc. These theories became a basis that could not be ignored by China's financial experts and scholars in absorbing the achievements of Western financial discipline after the reform and opening up.

The reform and opening up reopened the door of introduction from the West. In the 1980s in the early days of the reform and opening up, China mainly introduced the development achievements of the financial discipline in the West in the first half of the 20th century, that is, the introduction of macroeconomic analysis in monetary economics and banking. For modern finance which developed fast in the West after the 1950s, it was introduced in the mid 1990s by the returned Chinese students from abroad after China adopted the reform and opening up policy. Today, we can grasp information on the overall development of the financial discipline in the West in a prompt way.

All in all, he believed that, for more than a century, the development of the financial discipline in China was mainly and basically the "introduction "type, during which there were innovations, but its influence was within China. Now Chinese elements have had weighting that is increasingly hard to ignore in the international stage of economics and finance. Against such background, the development of the financial discipline in China would surely make its own contribution to the development of the financial discipline in the world.

His speech was later collected by *China's Financial Theory and Thoughts in the Past Century* as one of its forewords.

553

图553为2011年6月1日，首届"中国金融学科终身成就奖"颁奖典礼暨中国金融学科发展论坛在中国人民大学举行。获奖者黄达与主席台就座嘉宾合影留念。从左至右分别为：周慕冰、吴晓灵、袁卫、郝平、刘鸿儒、黄达、周小川、纪宝成、李扬、张志平。

On June 1, 2011, the 1st "China's Annual Financial Discipline Lifetime Achievement Award" Presentation Ceremony and China's Financial Discipline Development Forum was held in the Renmin University of China. Award-winner Huang Da took a group photo with other experts on the rostrum. From the left to the right are Zhou Mubing, Wu Xiaoling, Yuan Wei, Hao Ping, Liu Hongru, Huang Da, Zhou Xiaochuan, Ji Baocheng, Li Yang and Zhang Zhiping.

554

555

图 554 为 2011 年 6 月 1 日，中国人民银行行长周小川（右一）为黄达（左一）颁发获奖证书。

On June 1, 2011, Zhou Xiaochuan (first from the right), governor of the People's Bank of China, presented the certificate of award to Huang Da (first from the left).

图 555 为 2011 年 6 月 1 日，教育部副部长郝平（左一）为黄达（右一）颁发奖牌。

On June 1, 2011, Hao Ping (first from the left), vice minister of the Ministry of Education, presented a medal to Huang Da (first from the right).

6-9-1-2>

2011年12月30日，王传纶教授成为第二位荣膺该奖的经济学家。在颁奖典礼上，黄达虽然专门到场祝贺并准备了发言稿，但最终并未发言。在这篇发言稿中，黄达提到了对于王传纶教授的两点评价。一是有真学问或真有学问！得奖，实至名归！“我与王传纶教授是近60年的同僚，但我与你们一样，也把他视为老师——是真心实意不断向之求教的老师。”“我敬重王老的学问比较早，这也许与我的‘白专’类型有关。具体讲点事实：第一，西方对马克思生产价格存在矛盾（数学上无解）的讨论是他在20世纪60年代初写了一份材料，介绍给我的。第二，增值税在法国刚刚实施，我就看到他写的材料；资金流量，好像也是他最早介绍到我们国内的。”二是在政治的风风雨雨中一贯的和平心态——积极的和平心态。“根基，应该是对‘善’、对‘真知’、对‘正义’、对我们的‘民族’、对人类的‘美好理想’这些积极面，出于内心的真挚而持久不移的信念。在‘文化大革命’中，在‘革命群众’监管之下，意外地有一夜与他同处一室，他对我有一番忠告：‘不要把人生看成只不过是粉墨舞台；不要过分看穿、看透……’用意是鼓励我要积极面对人生，不要消沉下去。在那种气氛中，肯于忠告一个重点监管对象，使我历久铭记在心。”

遗憾的是，次年9月13日，王传纶教授因病于当天下午3时许不幸去世。

为深切缅怀王传纶教授光辉的一生，追思他对中国财政金融高等教育事业、对中国人民大学财政金融学院的发展所做出的杰出贡献，中国人民大学财政金融学院于2014年4月24日组织召开《王传纶经济文论》《学术泰斗王传纶》出版座谈会。会上，除了坚持三年前在王传纶教授获奖时提到的两点评价外，黄达还专门谈到王传纶教授的社会发展理念。“作为一个终身研究社会、研究经济的学人，对生活信念的直接支撑，应该在于他内心的社会发展理念。在他的《计划经济的想法，曾是很有吸引力的》一文里，透露了在学习市场理论的同时，计划经济理念也进入他逐渐形成的社会发展理论体系之中；在英国留学，他关注了当时的国际共产主义运动并对西方理论界剖析计划经济的论证有所了解。但他毅然回国，说明他对民族的责任感和进一步投身于实践自己社会发展理念的勇气。坦率地说，回到新中国，他并非生活在坦途之中，而能一直以积极进取的平和心态处之，说明他有着自己不为种种冲击而动摇的社会发展理念。这是极其坚韧的理念，否则，不可能把平和的心态持之以恒。作为经济学学人，形成并坚持自己独立的社会发展理念，恐怕这更是我们应该学习之处。”

此后，洪葭管、周骏、林继肯、曾康霖、周升业、张亦春、王永明、杨培新、赵海宽、俞天一、王佩真、吴念鲁等著名经济金融学家先后获得这项代表中国金融学科最高荣誉的奖项。

On December 30, 2011, Prof. Wang Chuanlun was the second to win this award. On the award ceremony, Huang Da expressed his two observations of Prof. Wang Chuanlun in his speech that he did not deliver. First, Prof. Wang was truly learned and deserved the award. "Prof. Wang and I are colleagues for nearly 60 years. But like you, I see him as a teacher, one from whom I truly am asking for advice. " "I respected his scholarship earlier, which may be related to my being a 'white-expert'. Specifically, I got to know the discussion in the West about the contradictions in Marxist production price (mathematically unsolved) because of some material he wrote in the early 1960s and introduced to me. When value-added tax was first implemented in France, I saw the materials he wrote; and capital flow seemed to have been first introduced into China by him. Secondly, Prof. Wang had been calm in the turbulence of politics and held a positive and peaceful mind. "Foundation shall be a truly sincere—from the bottom of one's heart—and lasting belief in the positive aspects like 'kindness,''real knowledge,' 'righteousness,' this 'nation,' and human beings' 'beautiful ideals.' In the Cultural Revolution, under the supervision of the 'revolutionary mass,' we spent a night together, which neither of us had expected. That night, he told me not to see life just as a stage; and not to get too crystal-minded or see all things through... He encouraged me to face life positively instead of passively. In that situation, he truly touched me because he gave sincere advice to me, one who was under key supervision. "

Regretfully, Prof. Wang passed away at 3:00p.m. on September 13 in the following year.

To deeply cherish the memory of the glorious life of Prof. Wang and recollect his outstanding contribution to the higher education of finance in China and to the development of the Finance School of the Renmin University of China, on April 24, 2014, School of Finance held a seminar on the publication of *Selected Works of Wang Chuanlun on Economics* and *Magnate Scholar Wang Chuanlun.* At the conference, Huang Da especially mentioned Professor Wang Chuanlun's concept of social development. "As a scholar who was engaged in studying the society and economics for his whole life, his faith in life was directly backed by his concept of social development, a concept he held inside. In article The Thought of the Planned Economy Was Very Attractive, he revealed that the concept of the planned economy was penetrating into his system of theories on social development while he was learning market theories; and that he paid attention to the then international communist movement and somewhat understood the argumentation, by the Western theorists, on the planned economy when furthering his studies in the UK. However, he was determined to come back to China, demonstrating his sense of responsibility for the nation and his courage to further practice his concept of social development. Frankly speaking, his life was full of trials and hardships after he returned to new China, yet he was always able to face it with a positive and peaceful mind, indicating that he would never waive his concept of social development for the shocks he once suffered. He was really determined about the concept, or it is impossible for him to always be peaceful and calm. As a scholar in economics, he developed and stuck to his unique concept on social development, and that probably is what we should learn more from him. "

Later, famous economists and financial experts Hong Jiaguan, Zhou Jun, Lin Jiken, Zeng Kanglin, Zhou Shengye, Zhang Yichun, Wang Yongming, Yang Peixin, Zhao Haikuan, Yu Tianyi, Wang Peizhen and Wu Nianlu won the prize in succession.

556

图 556 为 2011 年 12 月 30 日，2011 年"中国金融学科终身成就奖"颁奖典礼暨中国金融学科发展论坛在中国人民大学举行。获奖者王传纶教授与主席台就座专家合影留念。从左至右分别为：曹凤岐、苏宁、王广谦、黄达、李扬、王传纶、刘鸿儒、郭树清、陈雨露、张志平、贝多广。

On December 30, 2011, 2011 "China's Annual Financial Discipline Lifetime Achievement Award" Presentation Ceremony and China's Financial Discipline Development Forum was held in the Renmin University of China. Prof. Wang Chuanlun, the award-winner, took a group photo with other experts on the rostrum. From the left to the right are Cao Fengqi, Su Ning, Wang Guangqian, Huang Da, Li Yang, Wang Chuanlun, Liu Hongru, Guo Shuqing, Chen Yulu, Zhang Zhiping and Bei Duoguang.

557

图 557 为 2014 年 4 月 24 日，《王传纶经济文论》《学术泰斗王传纶》出版座谈会在中国人民大学召开。全体与会专家在会议结束后合影留念。前排左七为黄达，左八为王传纶教授夫人路奇。

On April 24, 2014, a seminar on the publication of *Selected Works of Wang Chuanlun on Economics* and *Magnate Scholar Wang Chuanlun* was held in the Renmin University of China. All the attendees took a group photo after the seminar. The seventh from the left in the front row is Huang Da, and the eighth from the left in the front row is Lu Qi, the wife of Prof. Wang.

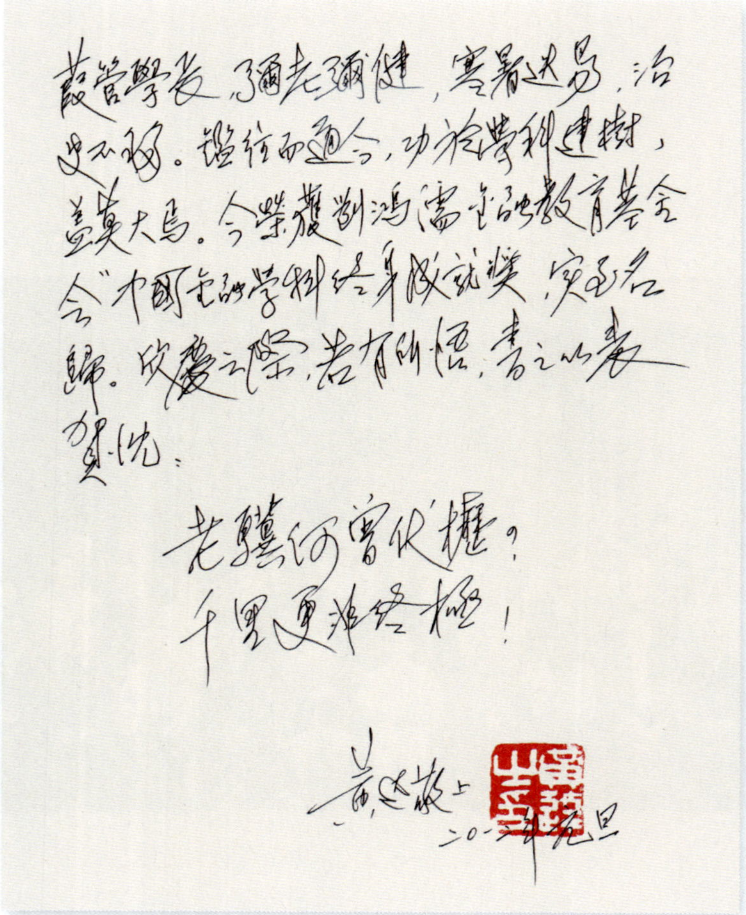

葭管學長，彌老彌健，寒暑迭易，治史不移。鑒古而通今，功於學科建樹，蓋莫大焉。今榮獲劉鴻儒金融教育基金會“中國金融學科終身成就獎”，實至名歸。欣慶之際，若有所悟，書之以表賀忱：

老驥何曾伏櫪？
千里更非終極！

黃達敬上
二〇一二年元旦

558

图 558 为 2012 年元旦，黄达为洪葭管获得“中国金融学科终身成就奖”撰写贺信：“葭管学长，弥老弥健，寒暑迭易，治史不移。鉴古而通今，功于学科建树，盖莫大焉。今荣获刘鸿儒金融教育基金会‘中国金融学科终身成就奖’，实至名归。欣庆之际，若有所悟，书之以表贺忱：老骥何曾伏枥？千里更非终极！”

On the New Year's Day of 2012, Huang Da wrote a letter of congratulations to Hong Jiaguan to congratulate the latter for winning "China's Annual Financial Discipline Lifetime Achievement Award." In the letter, he wrote that Hong Jiaguan deserved the honor for his actual achievements; commended the latter for being persistent in scholarly studies, for being erudite and informed, and for contributing a lot to the discipline; and expressed his happiness hearing the news. He spoke highly of Prof. Hong Jiaguan's pursuit of science in the letter.

559

图 559 为 2012 年 4 月 21 日，2012 年度“中国金融学科终身成就奖”颁奖典礼在中南财经政法大学举行，周骏获此殊荣。黄达专程到会祝贺。主席台左四至左六分别为：周骏、黄达、刘鸿儒。

On April 21, 2012, 2012 "China's Annual Financial Discipline Lifetime Achievement Award" Presentation Ceremony was held in Southwestern University of Finance and Economics. Zhou Jun won the award, and Huang Da attended the ceremony to congratulate him. From the fourth to the sixth from the left on the rostrum are Zhou Jun, Huang Da and Liu Hongru.

图 560 为 2007 年秋，黄达曾为祝贺周骏教授八十华诞题写贺词：“风流儒雅，吾侪翘楚；立论立说，后学景仰！”

20 世纪 50 年代初，周骏教授曾在中国人民大学货币流通与信用教研室学习。当时与其在该教研室共同学习生活的有黄达、肖清、刘绍之和周升业四人。故此，贺词以上述四人共同署名。

本次周骏教授获奖之际，黄达请善于书法的张杰教授重书以为贺。

In the autumn of 2007, Huang Da inscribed congratulations—"Distinguished and gentile, you are topping your generation; with theories and books, you are admired and respected by the young scholars"—to Prof. Zhou Jun for the latter's 80th birthday.

In the early 1950s, Prof. Zhou Jun studied in the teaching office of Money Circulation and Credit of the Renmin University of China. Along with him in the same teaching office were Huang Da, Xiao Qing, Liu Shaozhi and Zhou Shengye. Therefore, Huang Da signed the names of them four in the above congratulations.

When Prof. Zhou Jun was presented with "China's Annual Financial Discipline Lifetime Achievement Award," Huang Da asked Prof. Zhang Jie who was good at calligraphy to rewrite the congratulations.

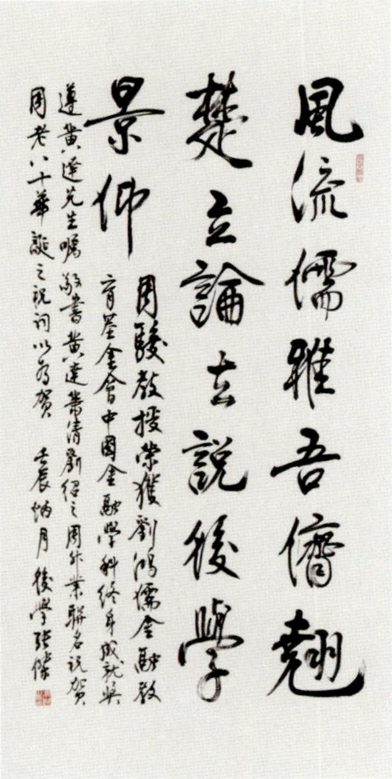

560

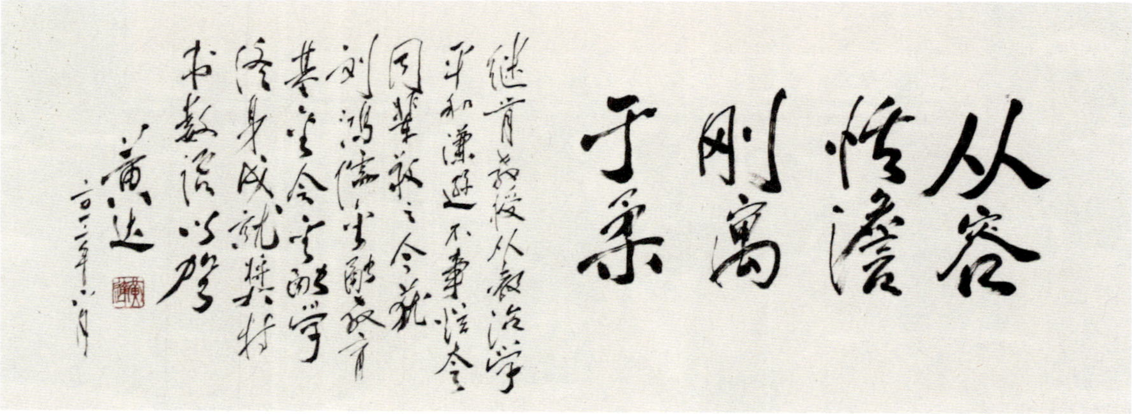

561

图 561 为 2012 年 6 月 9 日，黄达为林继肯教授获得“中国金融学科终身成就奖”题写贺词：“从容恬淡，刚寓于柔。继肯教授，从教治学，平和谦逊，不事炫夸，同辈敬之。今获刘鸿儒金融教育基金会中国金融学科终身成就奖，特书数语以贺。”

On June 9, 2012, Huang Da wrote congratulations to Prof. Lin Jiken to congratulate the latter for winning "China's Annual Financial Discipline Lifetime Achievement Award," and commended the latter for being always calm and indifferent to fame and gain, gentle while tough, and that Prof. Lin Jiken was always humble in teaching and scientific researches, never ostentatious, so was respected by his colleagues.

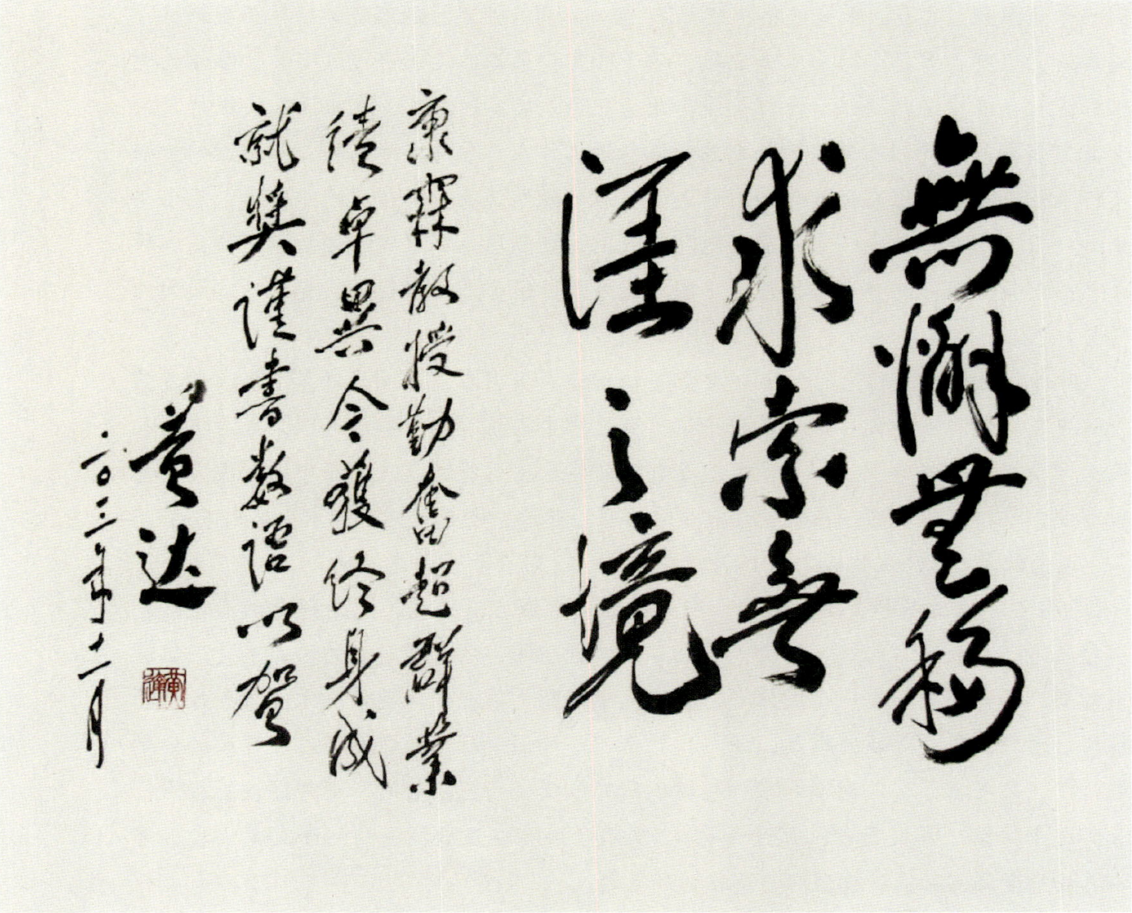

562

图 562 为 2012 年 11 月，黄达为曾康霖教授获得“中国金融学科终身成就奖”题写贺词：“无懈无移，求索无涯之境。康霖教授勤奋超群，业绩卓异，今获终身成就奖，仅书数语以贺。”

In November 2012, Huang Da wrote congratulations to Prof. Zeng Kanglin to congratulate the latter for winning "China's Annual Financial Discipline Lifetime Achievement Award." In the congratulations, he commended the latter for being persistent in the pursuit for knowledge.

6-9-1-3>

2013 年 6 月 1 日，2013 年度“中国金融学科终身成就奖”颁奖典礼暨中国金融学科发展论坛在中国人民大学举行。周升业教授获此殊荣。

在颁奖典礼上，黄达与大家分享了他与周升业教授在一个教研室、一个系，讲授同一专业课程，共事六十有一年的经历。“第一，周升业教授的经济学经过正规训练，与那时的教师大多是半路出家来比较，底子扎实；第二，几乎讲授过有关金融学的大部分课程，其中包括《银行会计》等，兼通理论、实务；第三，在中国人民银行总行和北京市分行的计划等部门曾长期作为银行的工作人员参与实际工作，对中国的金融实际及业务操作有零距离的体验，非大多数教师之所能及。”“在我的印象中，几十年来如一日，周升业教授一直是静静地、默默地、勤勤恳恳不事宣扬地教学、研究、联系兄弟院校、联系业务部门，作为中国人民大学金融专业的台柱子，受到方方面面的赞誉。”

此外，他重点提到了周升业与侯梦蟾于 1963 年 8 月在《光明日报》上发表的《信贷收支差额问题》一文。该文最先论证出有关货币与信贷的最本质道理，成为中国人民大学金融专业在学术上得到国家决策部门研究人士首肯的起点；而中国人民大学金融专业，包括黄达在内，在宏观金融方面的理论建设，也是从这个基点生发出来的。

遗憾的是，周升业教授于 2015 年 1 月 20 日 11 时在北京因病逝世。

“周老师性情温和，望之也温，即之也温。大家曾有公论，周老师是谦逊之师，温厚之师，对我个人而言，体会更深切。读博士期间，周老师对我的培养不是列出读书计划，而是安排一个一个的课题，在实践中研究。第一个课题是关于储蓄和投资的转化，老师不仅指导我定课题，还帮我联系业务部门。后来的课题‘对外开放的金融运行’，又安排了其他同学和我一起讨论研究。提交研究报告时，老师连我的标点符号都逐个修改。耳提面命，莫过于此。”从弟子洪崎在日后撰写的纪念文章中我们可以真切感受到周升业教授温润与慈祥的师者之风。

右页图 →

图 563 为 2013 年 6 月 1 日，2013 年度“中国金融学科终身成就奖”颁奖典礼暨中国金融学科发展论坛在中国人民大学举行。获奖者周升业教授与部分与会专家合影留念。前排从左至右分别为：李扬、吴晓灵、易纲、黄达、刘鸿儒、周升业、吴念鲁、曹凤岐、陈雨露。

On June 1, 2013, "China's Annual Financial Discipline Lifetime Achievement Award" Presentation Ceremony and China's Financial Discipline Development Forum was held in the Renmin University of China. Award-winner Zhou Shengye took a group photo with some experts attending the ceremony. From the left to the right in the front row are Li Yang, Wu Xiaoling, Yi Gang, Huang Da, Liu Hongru, Zhou Shengye, Wu Nianlu, Cao Fengqi and Chen Yulu.

On June 1, 2013, "China's Annual Financial Discipline Lifetime Achievement Award " Presentation Ceremony and China's Financial Discipline Development Forum was held in the Renmin University of China. Prof. Zhou Shengye won the award.

At the ceremony, Huang Da shared with the attendees his experience of working in the same teaching office and the same department, teaching courses of the same major with Prof. Zhou Shengye, and working with the latter for 61 years. "Firstly, Prof. Zhou received regular trainings on economics, and has solid deposits relative to most of the concurrent teachers who studied economics halfway; secondly, Prof. Zhou has taught the majority of the courses on finance, including Bank Accounting, and knows both theories and practices well; thirdly, he worked for the planning department of the head office of the People's Bank of China and Beijing Branch of the People's Bank of China for long, and has personal experience in China's financial reality and business operation, which can't be matched by most teachers. " "As far as I remember, Prof. Zhou Shengye has been down-to-earth and diligent in teaching and doing scientific studies, contacting brother universities and business departments for years. As the pillar of the major of finance in the Renmin University of China, he is spoken highly of by all. "

He especially mentioned article On the Balance of Receipts and Payments of Credit Funds published by Zhou Shengye and Hou Mengchan in *Guangming Daily* in August 1962. In the article, the authors first demonstrated the most essential truth about money and credit, making the article the starting point where the scholarly achievements of the finance major of the Renmin University of China were acknowledged by researchers of the national decision-making departments. The theoretical development of the finance major of the Renmin University of China, including that of Huang Da, all grew up from this point.

Unfortunately, Prof. Zhou passed away in Beijing at 11:00 a.m. on January 20, 2015.

"Prof. Zhou was mild in disposition. While I was in the PhD program, instead of making a book list, Prof. Zhou assigned research projects for me to study in the practice. The first project was about transformation of savings and investment. He not only provided me guidance on research, but also connected me with the practice sectors. In the project on the opening up of financial operations, he arranged opportunities for discussions with other students. He even corrected the punctuation in my research reports every time." One can feel the warmth and kindness as a teacher in this excerpt from one of the articles by his student Hong Qi.

563

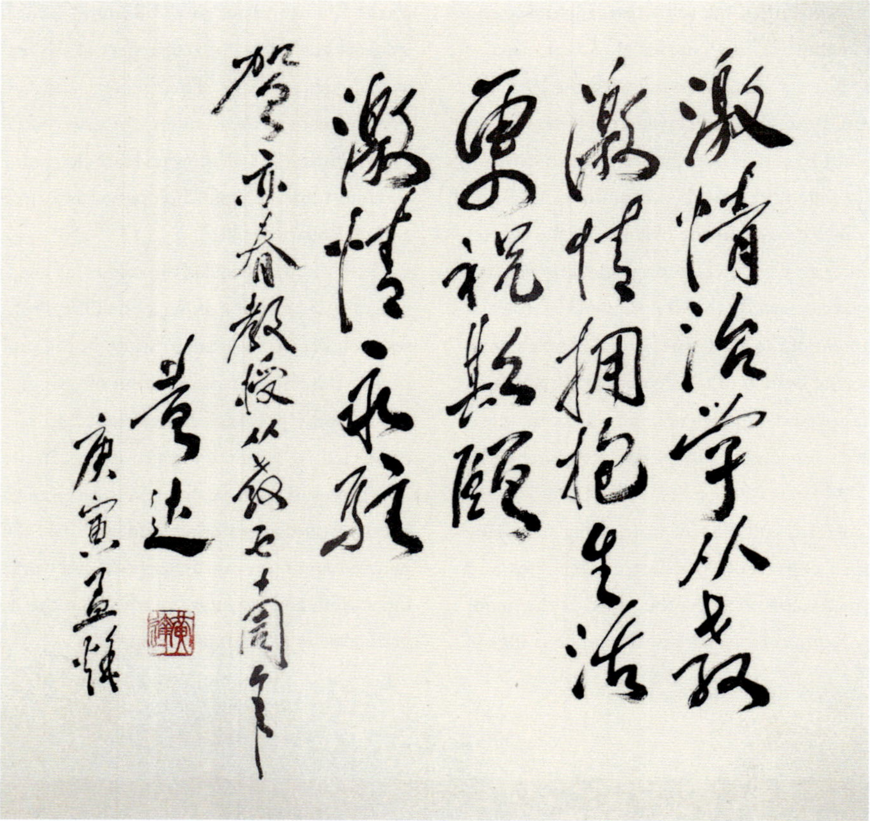

564

图 564 为 2010 年 8 月 17 日，黄达为张亦春教授从教五十周年题写贺词：“激情治学从教，激情拥抱生活；更祝期颐，激情永驻。”张亦春教授于 2013 年 6 月 15 日获得“中国金融学科终身成就奖”。

On August 17, 2010, Huang Da inscribed "Passion for scientific studies, passion for teaching, and passion for embracing life. Wish you longevity and passion forever" for Prof. Zhang Yichun for the latter's 50th anniversary of being a teacher. Prof. Zhang Yichun won "China's Annual Financial Discipline Lifetime Achievement Award" on June 15, 2013.

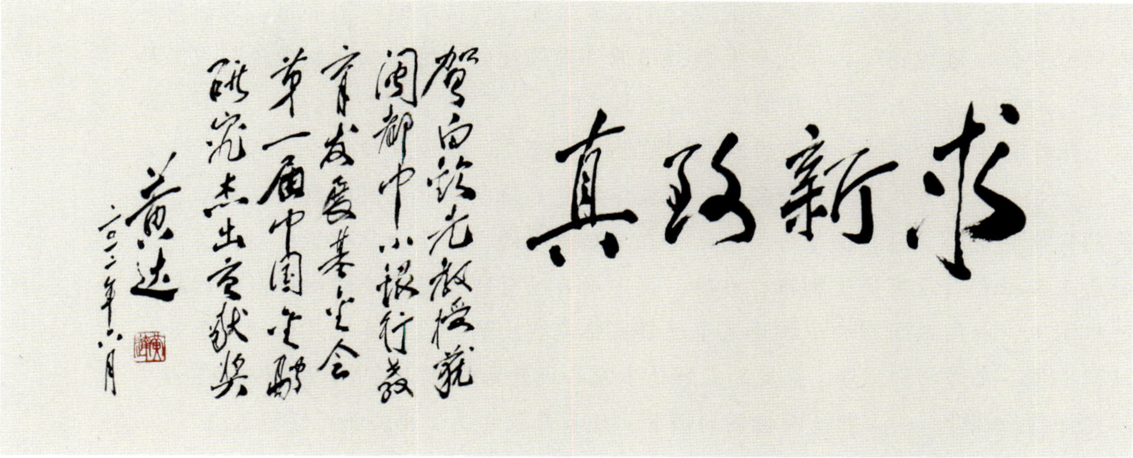

565

图 565 为 2012 年 6 月 6 日，黄达为白钦先教授获得第一届中国金融研究杰出贡献奖题词“求新致真。贺白钦先教授获闽都中小银行教育发展基金会第一届中国金融研究杰出贡献奖”。

此外，黄达本人也获得由该基金会颁发的第一届“中国金融研究杰出贡献荣誉奖”。

On June 6, 2012, Huang Da inscribed "For new and for truth, and congratulations to Prof. Bai Qinxian for winning China Financial Studies Outstanding Contribution Award issued by Fujian Education Development Foundation for Small and Medium Banks" for Prof. Bai Qinxian, the first China Financial Studies Outstanding Contribution Award winner.

Huang Da won "China Financial Studies Outstanding Contribution Honorary Award" issued by the same foundation, too.

6-9-2>

中国经济理论创新奖

China's Economic Theory Innovation Award

2013年11月28日，“中国经济学家年度论坛暨中国经济理论创新奖（2013）颁奖典礼”在武汉大学举行，黄达的“财政信贷综合平衡理论”以高票获得本年度“中国经济理论创新奖”。该奖项奖励给在中国经济理论研究方面做出重大原始创新性成果的主要贡献人。此前，杜润生及中国农村发展研究组的“农村家庭联产承包责任制理论”，厉以宁的“国有企业股份制改革理论”，吴敬琏、周小川、郭树清等人的“整体改革理论”，华生研究组、田源、张维迎的“价格双轨制理论”以及马建堂、周叔莲、江小涓的“中国经济结构调整理论”等曾先后获得该奖。

在颁奖典礼上，黄达将“财政信贷综合平衡理论”的成就归功于他所在的中国人民大学财政金融学院教学研究团队的集体智慧。他指出，当时的财政信贷综合平衡问题研究是与“通货膨胀”问题结合在一起探索的。关于通货膨胀问题，首先是社会主义社会有没有通货膨胀。当时，说中国有通货膨胀是禁忌。但是，黄达从经济机制上，以学术研究的形式论述了通货膨胀事实上的存在。其次是推动改革开放过程中允不允许物价上涨。主流的见解是不能给调升物价开口子。黄达明确地论述：不允许物价调升——当然是有控制的调升，改革开放的具体措施就无法推进。

整体上讲，物价或者说通货膨胀，归根到底是社会商品服务的供给和货币供给的对比关系。“财政信贷综合平衡理论”就是建立货币进入经济生活的基本模型；厘清财政渠道和银行渠道两者之间不可分割的联系；给出基本的、一以贯之的分析方法；并明确对货币供给的控制必须建立在财政与信贷综合平衡的基础之上。

“财政信贷综合平衡理论”产生在改革开放初期，也就是在计划经济机制占主导地位的背景下形成的，而且延续的是我国自己在20世纪50年代独创的“三平”理论。但是，它的理论基础则是在19世纪20世纪之交发展起来的现代货币银行学的有关原理，因而对于分析今天的金融形势依然有用。

On November 28, 2013, "Chinese Economists Annual Forum and China's Economic Theory Innovation Award (2013) Presentation Ceremony" was held in Wuhan University, and Huang Da won "China's Economic Theory Innovation Award" of the year with his "Introduction of General Equilibrium on Public Fiance and Credit."

The award is presented to major contributors with significant, original and innovative achievements in studies on China's economic theories. Before Huang Da, "the theory on household contract responsibility system " held by Du Runsheng and China Rural Area Development Study Group; "the theory on SOEs shareholding reform " held by Li Yining; "the overall reform theory " held by Wu Jinglian, Zhou Xiaochuan and Guo Shuqing; "the theory on dual price system " held by Hua Sheng Study Group, Tian Yuan and Zhang Weiying; and "theory on the restructuring of China's economy " held by Ma Jiantang, Zhou Shulian and Jiang Xiaojuan won the award in succession.

At the award presentation ceremony, Huang Da attributed the achievement of "Introduction of General Equilibrium on Public Fiance and Credit" to the teaching research team of the School of Finance, the Renmin University of China. He pointed out that studies on the overall balance of money and credit were carried out along with "inflation. " As for inflation, the primary question would be whether there was inflation in a socialist society. Of course, it was a taboo to say that China had inflation then. Nevertheless, from the perspective of economic mechanism, Huang Da demonstrated the actual existence of inflation through scholarly studies. The second question relating to inflation would be whether commodity price rise was intolerable in the process of advancing the reform and opening up. The mainstream opinion at the time was to never cut an opening for raising commodity price. On that, Huang Da clearly demonstrated that it would be impossible to carry out specific measures of reform and opening up if commodity price rise were intolerable, which of course was controlled commodity price rise.

Huang Da explained that, on the whole, commodity price or inflation was the contrast relationship between the supply of social commodity service and that of money in the final analysis. "Introduction of General Equilibrium on Public Fiance and Credit" was building the basic model of money entering into the economic life; rationalizing the inextricable relationship between monetary and banking channels; providing a basic and general analytical method; and clarifying that the control of monetary supply must be based on the overall balance of money and credit.

"Introduction of General Equilibrium on Public Fiance and Credit" was put forward in the early days of the reform and opening up, that is, against the background that the planned economic mechanism was in the dominant position; and continued the "three balances " theory (that is, to ensure the balance of financial revenue and expenditure, the balance of credit receipts and payments, and the balance of material supply and demand) China created originally in the 1950s. But it was developed on the basis of related principles on modern monetary and banking that grew at the turn of the 19th and 20th centuries. So it is still of great use to analyzing today's financial situation.

566

图 566 为 2013 年 11 月 28 日，“中国经济学家年度论坛暨中国经济理论创新奖（2013）颁奖典礼”在武汉大学举行。奖项组委会名誉主席吴敬琏（前排左一）、武汉大学校长李晓红（前排左三）、泰康人寿董事长陈东升（前排左四）分别为黄达（前排左二）颁发奖励证书、奖牌和奖金。

On November 28, 2013, "Chinese Economists Annual Forum and China's Economic Theory Innovation Award (2013) Presentation Ceremony" was held in Wuhan University. Wu Jinglian (first from the left in the front row), honorary chairman of the organization committee, Li Xiaohong (third from the left in the front row), president of Wuhan University, and Chen Dongsheng (fourth from the left in the front row), chairman of the Board of Taikang Life Insurance, presented the certificate, medal and prize, respectively, to Huang Da (second from the left in the front row).

567

568

图 567 为 2013 年 11 月 28 日，吴敬琏（左二）为黄达（右一）颁发奖励证书。

On November 28, 2013, Wu Jinglian (second from the left) presented the certificate to Huang Da (first from the right).

图 568 为 2013 年 11 月 28 日，黄达在颁奖典礼上讲话。

On November 28, 2013, Huang Da delivered a speech at the award presentation ceremony.

6-9-3>

吴玉章人文社会科学终身成就奖

Wu Yuzhang Humanities and Social Sciences Lifetime Achievement Award

为纪念中国人民大学第一任校长吴玉章先生，中国人民大学于1983年决定设立吴玉章奖金。吴玉章奖金是面向全国的人文社会科学奖，主要用于奖励国内有重大影响的优秀人文社会科学论著，旨在促进我国人文社会科学的发展和繁荣。吴玉章奖金的基金来源为：中国人民大学从学校基金中拨给专款；编辑出版吴玉章著作的稿费；吴玉章学生、中国人民大学校友、社会知名人士和学者的捐赠款；有关企业、社会组织与学术、教育团体的捐赠款。

目前，基金设有吴玉章人文社会科学终身成就奖、吴玉章人文社会科学优秀成果奖、吴玉章优秀教学奖、吴玉章优秀科研奖以及吴玉章奖学金等奖项。

其中，“吴玉章人文社会科学终身成就奖”于2012年首次设立。该奖项是为表彰在人文科学、社会科学领域做出卓越贡献的学者而设立的专门奖项，每年表彰2~3位卓有成就的学者。

2014年12月18日，黄达与著名伦理学家罗国杰、著名教育学家顾明远共同获得“第三届吴玉章人文社会科学终身成就奖”。

在颁奖典礼上，黄达深情回顾了他有幸能近距离接受吴玉章老校长教诲的过程。他说，“在头脑里构成的形象，他一定是刚毅、果敢、严肃、深沉，望之多少令人生畏的老革命。但有幸近距离接触，其间还有幸与吴老过过一次党的支部生活，却感到他老人家实际是使人非常愿意在他的膝前倾听其教诲的慈祥长者。”“吴老生前的十几年，一心一意要把中国人民大学办好。但他的思路，他的意图，并非总能贯彻。……现在可以告慰吴老在天之灵的是，他担任第一任校长的这所大学，在学术建树、人才汇集、校园建设、办学规模、国内外声望等各个方面均有了极大的成就。他老人家可以期望这所大学必将有更加辉煌的前程。”

此外，黄达还从两个方面谈到了自己从事六十多年的金融学科。第一，当前金融学有了大跨步的发展，成了显学里的显学。特别是学科向管理、量化的细分方向的下渗，成绩斐然。不过，相对来说，向基础原理、向综合方向的提炼，却有越来越薄弱的趋向。从马克思之前的古典经济学到马克思对经济的研究，都投入很大的气力探讨基本范畴、基本规律，并且在溯本求源的过程之中，总是伴随着哲理的思考。哲理指导，关系学科发展的大局，关系后劲，必须认真关注，不能掉以轻心。第二，要注意克服长期以来对中华文化传统的轻视、忽视倾向，认真重视对中华文化精粹的再认识并引入学科的基本建设之中。

In memory of its first president Wu Yuzhang, the Renmin University of China decided to set up the Wu Yuzhang Prize in 1983. The Wu Yuzhang Prize, being a humanities and social sciences award facing the whole country, is mainly used to award excellent works on humanities and social sciences in China, and aims to promote the development and prosperity of humanities and social sciences in China. Funds for the Wu Yuzhang Prize comprise dedicated allocation from its university funds by the Renmin University of China; contribution fees for compiling and publishing the books written by Wu Yuzhang; donations from Wu Yuzhang's students, the alumni and alumna of the Renmin University of China, social celebrities and scholars; and donations from related enterprises, social organizations and scholarly and educational groups.

So far, the Wu Yuzhang Foundation has Wu Yuzhang Humanities and Social Sciences Lifetime Achievement Award, Wu Yuzhang Humanities and Social Sciences Excellent Achievement Award, Wu Yuzhang Excellent Teaching Award, Wu Yuzhang Excellent Scientific Research Award and Wu Yuzhang Scholarship.

"Wu Yuzhang Humanities and Social Sciences Lifetime Achievement Award " was first established in 2012. It is a special award for scholars with outstanding contribution to humanities and human sciences. It is presented to two or three successful scholars each year.

On December 18, 2014, Huang Da, famous ethicist Luo Guojie and famous educator Gu Mingyuan won the "3rd Wu Yuzhang Humanities and Social Sciences Lifetime Achievement Award " together.

At the presentation ceremony, Huang Da reviewed his experience of being keenly taught by President Wu Yuzhang. He said, "I had thought him to be an old revolutionary, tough, resolute, sober, concealing and somewhat formidable person, but in close contacts with him and a lucky Party branch activity, I actually found him to be a very kind man who made people willing to get close to and listen to lectures from." "He was doing his best to run the university, but his thoughts and intentions were not always implemented thoroughly... Now what's comforting to the defunct is that this university, where he served as the first president, has made great achievements in scholarly studies, talent cultivation and gathering, campus construction, size and reputation both at home and abroad. The university can be counted on now, because it will surely have a more glorious future. "

Besides, Huang Da talked about the financial discipline, which he had been engaged in for more than sixty years. Firstly, the financial discipline had made achievements by leaps and bounds, and become the famous school of the famous schools. In particular, the refinement of it in management and quantification had seen striking achievements. But relatively, it tended to be weaker and weaker in the refining of basic theories and the comprehensive direction. From classic economics before Marx to Marx's studies on the economy, it devoted a lot to discussing the basic categories and rules and, in the process of going back to the origins, was accompanied by philosophical thinking. Philosophical guidance was important to the overall development of the discipline and the development momentum, so due attention must be paid. Secondly, attention had to be paid to overcoming the tendency of despising, even ignoring the cultural traditions of China, and the re-understanding of the cultural essence of the Chinese nation and the introduction of it into basic disciplinary development must be highlighted.

569

图 569 为 2001 年 9 月 10 日，黄达出席“‘吴玉章校长和学生们在一起’青铜群雕揭幕仪式”。从左至右分别为：张腾霄、凌云、郝建秀、李东冶、黄达、程天权。

On September 10, 2001, Huang Da attended " 'President Wu Yuzhang with the Students' Group Bronze Sculpture Unrevealing Ceremony." From the left to the right are Zhang Tengxiao, Ling Yun, Hao Jianxiu, Li Dongye, Huang Da and Cheng Tianquan.

570

图 570 为位于中国人民大学科研楼前的“吴玉章校长和学生们在一起”青铜群雕。

This is the "President Wu Yuzhang with the Students" Group Bronze Sculpture in front of Science Building of the Renmin University of China.

571

图 571 为 2002 年 7 月 8 日，第四届吴玉章基金委员会工作会议在中国人民大学召开。全体与会专家合影留念。本届委员会的名誉主任为李鹏和宋平，主任委员为袁宝华（前排左七）。黄达（前排左四）担任副主任委员。

On July 8, 2002, the 4th Wu Yuzhang Foundation Committee work conference was held in the Renmin University of China. Li Peng and Song Ping were the honorary chairmen; Yuan Baohua (seventh from the left in the front row) was the chairman; and Huang Da (fourth from the left in the front row) was the vice-chairman of the 4th Wu Yuzhang Foundation Committee.

572

图 572 为 2008 年 12 月 22 日，黄达出席“纪念中国人民大学首任校长吴玉章诞辰 130 周年座谈会”并讲话。

On December 22, 2008, Huang Da attended and addressed "Seminar on the Commemoration of the 130th Anniversary of the Birth of Wu Yuzhang, the First President of the Renmin University of China."

573

图 573 为 2014 年 12 月 18 日，“第三届吴玉章人文社会科学终身成就奖颁奖典礼”在中国人民大学隆重举行。获奖者黄达与主席台就座嘉宾合影留念。从左至右分别为：靳诺、李扬、马凯、黄达、李卫红、李培林、陈雨露。

On December 18, 2014, the "3rd Wu Yuzhang Humanities and Social Sciences Lifetime Achievement Award Presentation Ceremony" was held in the Renmin University of China. Prof. Huang Da, the award-winner, took a group photo with the other distinguished guests on the rostrum. From the left to the right are Jin Nuo, Li Yang, Ma Kai, Huang Da, Li Weihong, Li Peilin and Chen Yulu.

574

575

图 574 为 2014 年 12 月 18 日，黄达在“第三届吴玉章人文社会科学终身成就奖颁奖典礼”上讲话。

On December 18, 2014, Huang Da addressed the "3rd Wu Yuzhang Humanities and Social Sciences Lifetime Achievement Award Presentation Ceremony."

图 575 为 2014 年 12 月 18 日，第六届吴玉章基金委员会主任委员、国务院副总理马凯（左二）为黄达（右二）颁发奖杯。

On December 18, 2014, Ma Kai (second from the left), chairman of the 6th Wu Yuzhang Foundation Committee and vice-premier of the State Council, presented the cup to Huang Da (second from the right).

6-10

整理上交个人档案

Collate and Submit Personal Records

从 2002 年开始，黄达开始整理个人档案，并逐项提交至中国人民大学档案馆。截至目前，黄达已经提交的个人档案包括以下几类：一是个人履历活动档案。国务院任命书等文件；全国人民代表大会、国务院办公厅、部委等单位聘请文件；学位委员会、哲学社会科学规划组、社科院、教委等关于学术性审议组织的聘请文件；兼职教授、顾问等聘请文件；学校各种聘书；学会、协会聘书及其他聘书；奖励证书、奖杯、奖牌；荣誉证书、纪念证书、纪念牌；国际名人；个人笔记本；《黄氏族谱》；照片及约两千幅照片编成的《电子相册》；等等。二是教学档案。七本教科书与专著的文稿；讲稿（第一部分为 1950 年至“文化大革命”前，第二部分为“文化大革命”之后）；等等。三是有关科研档案。文章、书籍的目录及部分底稿（“文化大革命”以前）；改革开放初几个重点研究课题的手稿及相关资料；1978—2004 年文稿；文稿拾遗（有关资料整理、读书笔记、统计资料、建立计算公式等手稿，发表文稿的复印件和少数发表文章的杂志，为编辑《黄达文集》而选出的 1985 年以后的文稿，《社会主义财政金融问题》出版前的油印稿，以及一套教学参考资料）；卡片四匣（20 世纪 50 年代，读《资本论》摘抄卡片和按学科体系的国别分类的剪报卡片；20 世纪 50 年代，按中国经济建设分类的剪报卡片；20 世纪 70 年代中期之后，读中国史书和典籍的摘抄卡片；改革开放初期，剪报卡片）；等等。四是有关行政档案。任副校长、校长期间的几个专题（办学方向，归属问题，从“两院”到国家行政学院，所谓“一派掌权”，与部门合作建院，中国人民大学“放弃”马克思主义的公案以及“福特项目”始末）；在中国人民大学财政系和校部工作期间的非专题文档及其他。

576

图 576 为 2015 年 10 月 20 日，在中国人民大学档案馆拍摄到的黄达个人档案。据档案管理员介绍，黄达的档案几乎是学校档案馆最为完整、全面和系统的个人档案。

This picture was taken on October 20, 2015, which records the personal records of Huang Da in the Archives Center of the Renmin University of China. According to the archivist, these records are almost the most complete and systematic personal records in the university archives.

Since 2002, Huang Da has started collating his personal records, and submitted them to the Archives Center of the Renmin University of China in succession. So far, he has submitted the following types of personal records: firstly, personal history records—including State Council appointments; invitations of the National People's Congress, the General Office and departments of the State Council; invitations of the Academic Degrees Committee under the State Council, Philosophy and Social Sciences Planning Group, the Chinese Academy of Social Sciences, commissions of education and other scholarly deliberation organizations; letters of appointment as professor and consultant; letters of appointment to him from other universities and schools; letters of appointment by societies and associations, and other letters of appointment; awards, certificates and cups; certificates of honor, commemorative certificates and souvenir metals; international figures; personal notebooks, *Clan Pedigree of the Huang Family;* Pictures and an e-album made of about 2,000 pictures, etc. Secondly, teaching records—including the manuscripts of seven textbooks and monographs; lectures (the first half was from 1950 to the eve of the Cultural Revolution, and the second half was after the Cultural Revolution), etc. Thirdly, records on his researches—including contents of his articles and books and some manuscripts (before the Cultural Revolution); manuscripts and related materials on a few key research projects he did in the early days of the reform and opening up; his manuscripts during 1978 and 2004; gleaning of past manuscripts (related data collation, reading notes, statistics, manuscripts on setting up calculating formulas, duplicates of his published manuscripts and a few magazines publishing his articles, manuscripts since 1985 that were selected for the purpose of editing *Essays of Huang Da,* mimeographed manuscripts of *Issues on Socialism Finance,* and a set of teaching references); four cases of cards (cards with reading notes on *On Capital* and cards of newspaper clippings by classes of countries of disciplinary systems in the 1950s; cards of newspaper clippings by China's economic development in the 1950s; reading notes on China's history books and classic books since the mid 1970s; newspaper clippings in the early days of reform and opening up, etc.). Fourthly, administrative records—including records on the themes when Huang Da served as the vice president and president of the Renmin University of China (educational direction; jurisdiction; from the "Two Schools " to National School of Administration; the so-called "one school in power "; interdepartmental cooperation; details on the complicated case of "abandoning " Marxism by the Renmin University of China and the "Ford Program "); non-thematic files when working in the Finance Department and administrative department of the Renmin University of China, among others.

| 右页图 ⟼

图 577 为 2002 年 1 月 17 日，黄达在中国人民大学档案馆查找已经上交的几份 20 世纪 50 年代初期自己手写的教学资料。从左至右分别为：李芹、黄达、吴静研、吴帆。

On January 17, 2002, Huang Da discovered, in the Archives Center of the Renmin University of China, some teaching materials written in the early 1950s and submitted to the Renmin University of China by him. From the left to the right are Li Qin, Huang Da, Wu Jingyan and Wu Fan.

577

6-11

笔耕不辍——《忆旧纪年》
Keep on Writing—*Chronological Records in Memory*

生于 1925 年，到现在黄达已逾九十二周岁。由于年事这个不可抗拒的原因，他已不能系统、全面、持续不断地思考中国金融学科的问题，但是六十多年寒暑无间地忙碌于教学与研究之间，又让他难以优游岁月，彻底摆脱笔耕生涯。于是，他不求系统、不求繁简深浅一致，开始像古人的笔记、随录那样写一些生平经历。由于内容基本是按年月顺序忆旧，因此他将其命名为《忆旧纪年》，后于 2017 年由中国金融出版社编辑出版。

Born in 1925, Huang Da is over 92 years old. Because of the inevitable aging, he can no longer conduct comprehensive, systematic and consecutive thinking of China's financial disciplines, but due to over 60 years of engagement in the field, he cannot cut the links with money and banking and finance. Therefore, he began to record his experiences like the notes by the ancients. The events were recorded chronically, so he named it *Chronological Records in Memory*, published by China Financial Publishing House in 2017.

578

579

图 578 为 2014 年 10 月 5 日，黄达在北京太申祥和山庄国际敬老院的居室内使用电脑查阅资料。

On October 5, 2014, Huang Da used a computer to search materials in his room in Beijing Taishen Xianghe Villa International Home for the Old-aged.

图 579 为 2015 年 1 月 28 日，黄达在北京世纪城家中写作。

On January 28, 2015, Huang Da wrote at home in Beijing Century Hall.

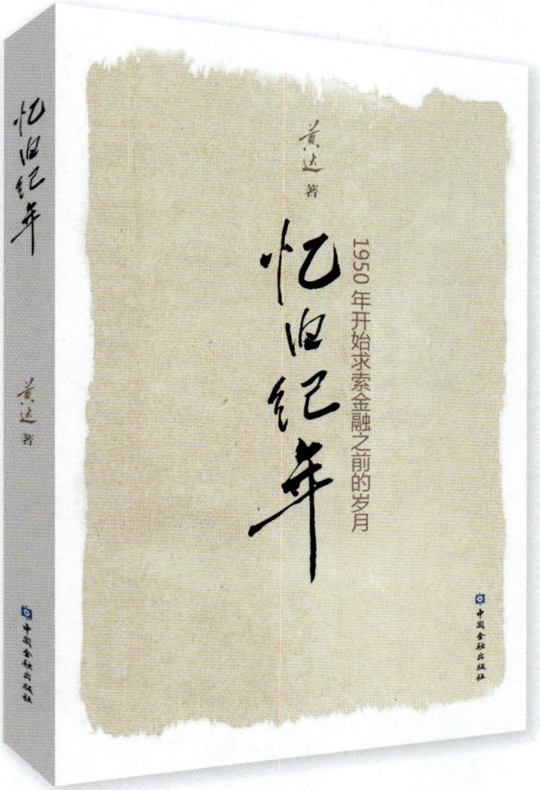

580

图 580 为《忆旧纪年》（中国金融出版社，2017）。本书是黄达教授亲笔撰写的回忆录，讲述了他从记事开始，到 1950 年，整个童年、少年、青年时期的求学、探索社会、走上革命道路、参加新中国建设的完整经历和心路历程。既有对自己成长经历的详细记述，对家人、亲情无限的思念，也有对时代、社会环境的洞察和分析。语言精炼，文字平朴，感情真挚，直指心底，震撼心灵。

This is *Chronological Records in Memory* (published by China Financial Publishing House in 2017) This is a memoir wrote by Huang Da recording his experience and mental history of pursuing studies, exploring society, taking the road to revolution and participating in the construction of New China through his childhood, teenage and youth. It encompasses detailed description of his growth experience, thoughts of family and affection, as well as insight and analysis on the times and society. It features concise language and plain text with sincere and soul-shocking feelings.

黄达著述、获奖全记录

The Full Record of Huang Da's Writings and Awards

黄达著述全记录

The Full Record of Huang Da's Writings

论文

1952

《新中国货币制度的建立》

1953

《关于苏联货币制度的几个问题》

《教学与研究》，1953 年第 5 期

1955

《社会主义经济中货币的本质与职能》

《教学与研究》，1955 年第 3 期

《经济建设初期农村中的货币流通》

1957

《人民币是具有内在价值的货币商品的符号》

《经济研究》，1957 年第 4 期

《资本主义国家的货币流通与信用·编者的话》

中国人民大学出版社 1957 年版

1958

《农村金融工作的大跃进丰富了马克思列宁主义的信用理论》

《金融研究》，1958 年第 4 期

《关于向共产主义过渡的条件》

1959

《货币信用学（上册）·编者的话》

中国人民大学出版社 1959 年版

《货币的本质》

《人民币的价值基础》

《教学与研究》，1959 年第 11 期

1962

《银行信贷原则和货币流通》

《经济研究》，1962 年第 9 期

1963—1964

《评介〈社会主义的银行工作〉》

《如何看待价格》

《关于流动资金和银行基金问题》

《红旗》杂志举办的双周座谈会上的发言提纲

1965

《学习中提出不少问题——关于人民公社》

《第二次世界大战后资本主义体系中的黄金·译者前言》

《第二次世界大战后资本主义体系中的黄金》（[СССР·1952] Ф·И·МИХАЛЕВСКИЙ ЗОЛОТО В СИСТЕМЕ КАПИТАЛИЗМА ПОСЛЕ ВТОРОЙ МИРОВОЙ ВОЙНЫ），中国财政经济出版社 1965 年版

1972

《旧中国工农产品价格剪刀差》

《农产品成本与价格论文集》，中国社会科学出版社 1983 年版

1978—1979

《机关软，企业软？》

《我国社会主义经济发展现阶段货币存在的客观必然性》

《社会主义财政金融问题·第一章》，中国人民大学出版社 1981 年版

《货币与价格》

《社会主义财政金融问题·第三章》，中国人民大学出版社 1981 年版

《就财政金融管理谈谈研究思想必须不断拓宽和深化》

无锡市“计划和市场讨论会”稿件，后以《试论物价的若干

问题》为题发表于《中国社会科学》1980 年第 6 期

《积累增长速度和物价水平》

《财贸经济》，1980 年第 1 期，因排印错误于第 4 期全文重发

《关于目前“货币过多”的几个问题》

《金融研究动态》（中国人民银行总行金融研究所内部刊物），总第 66 期（1980 年 1 月 22 日）

《谈谈当前的通货膨胀问题》

《金融研究动态》（中国人民银行总行金融研究所内部刊物），1980 年第 71 期（总第 87 期）

《利用外资同国家财政的关系》

《对外信用关系》

《财政研究资料》（财政部内部刊物），1979 年第 61 期

1980

《谈长期规划与财力保证问题》

1980 年 4 月在国家计划委员会召开的“长期规划座谈会”上的发言稿

《社会主义也有通货膨胀》

1980 年初在国务院财贸小组召集的讨论会上的发言提纲

《通货膨胀不是我们可以采用的政策》

《经济学动态》，1980 年第 8 期

《黄达同志 11.28 下午发言》

1980 年 11 月在中国金融学会与社科院财贸经济所共同召开的小型“银行作用理论座谈会”上的发言记录稿

《关于货币流通的问题》

《金融研究》（内部刊物），1981 年第 2 期

《关于货币流通的几个问题》

《上海金融研究》（中国人民银行上海分行金融研究所内部刊物），1981 年第 2 期

1981

《社会主义财政金融问题·说明》

《社会主义财政金融问题》，中国人民大学出版社 1981 年版

《为体改委物价座谈会准备的提纲》

《什么是信用膨胀，它是怎样引起的？》

《经济研究》，1981 年第 11 期

《信用膨胀与综合平衡》

《综合平衡与货币流通》

《经济理论与经济管理》，1981 年第 5 期

《财政收支与信贷收支相互配合中的接合部问题》

《财贸经济》，1981 年第 4 期

《论银行聚集资金数量的客观界限》

《安徽金融研究》（内部刊物），1981 年第 4 期

《对当前资金问题的一些看法》

《财政研究》，1982 年第 [illegible] 期

1982

《关于稳定物价方针的一两点看法》

1982 年 2 月于中国价格学会在昆明召开的理论讨论会上的发言稿

《办好财经专业的几个问题》

《对几年来如何估价建设资金供应问题的评介》

《经济学文摘》，1982 年第 7 期

《对于资金运动和经济增长的关系如何进行总量分析》

1982 年 8 月在中国政治经济学社会主义部分研究会第二届年会上的发言稿

《关于我国经济建设的资金问题》

《广东金融研究》（内部刊物），1983 年第 1 期

《中国财政信贷综合平衡和通货物价控制问题》

《中国经济发展战略问题研究》，上海人民出版社 1984 年版

1983

《〈资本论〉和社会主义财政金融理论建设》

《〈资本论〉与社会主义经济》，人民出版社 1983 年版

《认真学习〈资本论〉推进金融理论建设》

《财贸工作研究》，1983 年第 3 期

《关于货币流通范围的问题》

《山西金融研究》（内部刊物），1983 年第 3 期

1984

《财政信贷综合平衡·作者的话》

《财政信贷综合平衡》，中国金融出版社 1984 年版

《关于加强财政信贷综合平衡的意见》

1984 年 2 月国务院经济研究中心以该题目作为“国务院经济研究中心材料［1984］”发文

《物价方针与财政信贷综合平衡》

《价格理论与实践》，1984 年第 2 期

《解放思想和金融教材》

1984 年 5 月底 6 月初在中国金融学会全国代表会议上的发言稿

《所有权和经营权的相互关系问题》

1984 年夏在吉林市全国国家与企业关系理论讨论会上的发言稿

《银行管理体制应与经济体制改革和金融中心建设相适应》

《经济信息报》；《长江日报》以《发展横向金融联系，建立金融中心》为标题发表，1984 年 11 月 8 日

《新形势下的新课题需要我们去探索——学习十二届三中全会〈关于经济体制改革的决定〉笔记》

《经济理论与经济管理》，1985 年第 1 期

《坚决地、不拖延地把价格改革付诸实施》

《价格理论与实践》，1985 年第 3 期

1985

《财经、管理教育进一步大发展的同时必须抓紧解决提高教学质量问题》

1985 年元月教育部于广州召开大学财经、管理教育座谈会的发言稿

《关于控制货币供给量问题的探讨》

《财贸经济》，1985 年第 1 期

《价格改革和货币供给》

《经济理论与经济管理》，1985 年第 6 期

《价格理论与实践》，1985 年第 6 期

1986

《流动资金的供给与宏观控制》

1986 年 1 月全国经济工作会议的发言手稿

《我们的经济改革之路》

1986 年 10 月 21 日在古巴哈瓦那大学的讲演稿

1987

《商品经济与货币流通》

《红旗》，1987 年第 19 期

《马克思主义的经济学要学好 非马克思主义的经济学也要研究》

1987 年 8 月 25 日在世界银行“中国大学发展第二个项目”于复旦大学召开的“财经教育计划研讨会”上的发言稿

1988

《工农产品比价剪刀差·出版时的几点说明》

《工农产品比价剪刀差——从鸦片战争前后到新中国建国之际的史的考察》，中国社会科学出版社 1990 年版

《现代经济生活中的货币》

《吉林财贸学院学报》，1989 年第 4 期

《谈物价与货币供求问题》

《安徽金融研究》，1988 年第 7 期

《应如何看当前的通货膨胀》

1988 年 6 月 26 日为参加国务院发展研究中心某小型会议所准备的书面意见摘要

《金融学》

《中国大百科全书——经济学》1988 年 8 月版的“金融学”词条

《关于中国的改革——简单的介绍》
1988 年 11 月访问匈牙利、波兰准备的文稿

《大河岸边卖水——在波兰讲物价》
1988 年秋出访波兰的讲演手稿

《需要的是长期韧战》
《价格理论与实践》，1989 年第 2 期

1989

《治理通货膨胀中需要思考的几个问题》
《财贸经济》，1989 年第 6 期

1990

《〈货币供求问题研究系列专著〉总序》
《货币供求问题研究系列专著》，中国人民大学出版社 1990—1993 年版

1991

《建国以来〈货币银行学〉课程发展的回顾及如何进一步建设》
《中国人民大学学报》，1991 年第 1 期

《金融》
《中国大百科全书·财政税收金融物价卷》，中国大百科全书出版社 1993 年版

《金融物价政策的一点思考》
《江南金融》，1991 年第 6 期

《财政金融的改革与国家管理经济效率的提高》
《中国行政管理》，1991 年第 12 期

《长期宏观决策必须考虑的一个必然趋势——从不完全的工资、成本、价格向比较接近完全的工资、成本、价格的转化》
《财贸经济》，1991 年第 4 期

1992

《认真推进宏观分析的理论建设》
《金融研究》，1992 年第 10 期
《改革、增长、货币政策》，中国金融出版社 1992 年版

《需要能指导社会主义市场经济建设的经济学》
《经济导刊》，1993 年第 1 期

1993

《积极稳妥地推进学科改革与建设》
《中国教育报》，1993 年 3 月 16 日

《中国证券发展中的规范化和宏观调控问题》
《财贸经济》，1993 年第 9 期
《中国证券百科全书——序》，中国经济管理出版社 1993 年版

《宏观经济观念辨析》
《我的市场经济观》，江苏人民出版社 1994 年版

《宏观调控与货币供给》
《中国社会科学》，1993 年第 5 期
《中国金融》，1993 年第 12 期
《改革、增长、宏观调控》，中国金融出版社 1993 年版

《靠市场经济体制开辟上海与全国联系的新模式》
上海《经济预测》，1993 年第 4 期

《关于当前宏观经济问题的一些思考》
1993 年夏在欧美同学会组织的“美国黄兴基金会第三次讲演”文稿

《一个具体建议——用“货币供给”的概念代替“货币发行”的概念》
1993 年 7 月 20 日给中央办公厅的建议

《关于当前宏观调控的一些想法》
《光明日报》，1993 年 8 月 24 日

《为中共中央征询〈关于建立社会主义市场经济体制若干问题的决定〉稿的意见所准备的提纲》
1993 年 10 月 12 日征询经济学者意见会议的提纲

1994

《改革、发展、稳定——学习建设有中国特色的社会主义理论的体会》

《教学与研究》，1994 年第 3 期
《学习与思考》，首都师范大学出版社 1994 年版

《应明确向经济生活中供给货币是人民银行的一个基本职能》

1994 年 2 月对中国人民银行条法司《中国人民银行法（草稿）》所提意见中的一则

《财税金融体制改革漫议》

《财贸经济》，1994 年第 8 期
《改革·增长·商业银行》，中国金融出版社 1995 年版

《形势、改革、资金一窥》

《山西金融》，1994 年第 11 期

1995

《中国改革开放以来的通货膨胀问题》

《财贸经济》，1995 年第 6 期
《50 位专家献策治理通货膨胀》，中国金融出版社 1995 年版
《中国改革开放二十年（宏观体制改革卷）》，中国文献出版社 1998 年版

《“九五”期间必须扭转国家财政收入占 GDP 的比重不断下降的局面》

第八届人大二次全体会议议案稿，并于北京分组会上直接交给总理，新华社以之为据发表了通稿

《对于人文社会科学建设应给予必要的重视》

第八届第三次全体大会讨论政府工作报告的发言底稿

《高等财经教育学科建设和教学改革的若干问题》

以《高等财经教育学科建设和教学改革》为题发表于《教学与教材研究》，1995 年第 4 期
《教学改革与当代科学技术发展》，高等教育出版社 1995 年版

《第二届两岸金融学术研讨会迎宾晚宴祝酒词》

1995 年 7 月 31 日第二届两岸金融学术研讨会迎宾晚宴的祝酒词

《金融改革和两个银行法》

《人民日报》，1995 年 10 月 19 日

《中国的渐进改革和宏观经济政策》

为参加 UNIVERSITE D'AUVERGNE CERDI（国际发展研究中心）主办的“中国经济国际研讨会”（1995 年 11 月 30 日—12 月 2 日）而作

《议财政、金融和国有企业资金的宏观配置格局》

《经济研究》，1995 年第 12 期
《中国经济丛书·财政货币政策协调论》，中国财政经济出版社 1997 年版

《资金宏观配置格局剖析》

《研究与建议》（国家计委政策研究室内部刊物），1996 年第 37 期（总第 225 期）

1996

《宏观调控与货币供给（第一版）·作者的几点说明》

《宏观调控与货币供给（第一版）》，中国人民大学出版社 1996 年版

《〈中国：迈向现代金融体制〉国际研讨会欢迎词》

1996 年 8 月 23 日在北京召开的国际研讨会上的欢迎词

《中国金融改革的回顾与前瞻》

日本金融学会《金融经济研究》，1997 年第 13、14 期

《当前中国的经济改革与金融改革》

日本熊本学园大学附属海外事情研究所《海外事情研究》，1997 年第 25 卷第 1 号（通卷第 49 号）

《货币供给的宏观分析方法》

《城市金融论坛》，1996 年第 8 期

1997

《经济形势和国有经济》

全国人民代表大会八届五次大会北京组发言稿

《对经济金融领域一些问题的看法》

《中国金融》，1997 年第 4 期

《经济形势和金融的改革与发展》

1997 年 4 月 28 日在中国人民银行福建省分行组织的党政领导学习班上的讲演稿

《就财政金融管理谈谈研究思想必须不断拓宽和深化》

1997年7月20日在复旦大学《现代国际经济管理》高级研讨班上的讲演稿，载于《世界经济文汇·1998特刊——世界管理论坛》

《改革开放中走向市场机制的中国金融事业》

《中国金融》，1997年第10期

《乐观的前瞻》

《财贸经济》，1997年第11期

《最重要的是学科内容的建设》

《金融时报》1997年10月26日择要发表

《中国金融学科建设与人才培养》，西南财经大学出版社1998年版

《与会随想》

1997年11月在中国人民银行研究生部的讲课稿（部分）

《努力理解〈价格法〉的深刻内涵》

《价格理论与实践》，1997年第12期

《能否多视角地观察和思考》

1997年12月3日在中国人民银行深圳分行的讲演稿

1998

《要学会用好实施宏观调控的货币政策——访著名财政金融专家黄达教授》

《前线》，1998年第2期

《金融》

《中华金融词库》概述条，中国金融出版社1998年版

《在亚洲金融危机中的中国》

以《中国に金融危机は起こるが》为题刊于三井物产贸易经济研究所《调查研究月报·THE COMPASS》（日语），1998年第6期

《完善中国金融体制的目标和思路》

《奔向2020》，中国物价出版社1998年版

《不能总是绷紧一根弦》

《国际金融研究》，1998年第6期

《中国的金融改革及其前景》

《人民日报·内部参阅》1998年第37期（总第429期），1998年9月23日

《宏观经济研究》1998年11月创刊号

《走向新时代——纪念中共十一届三中全会20年暨中国人民大学复校20年论文集》，中国人民大学出版社1998年版

《当前经济金融形势同我们的学习》

1998年9月22日对中国人民大学财政金融学院博士生的讲课提纲

《正确的理论指导，信念增强的保证》

《经济研究》，1998年第11期

CHINA FINANCIAL QUARTERLY, Spring Issue, 1999 摘要刊登（伦敦出版）

1999

《经济与金融·形势与政策·国内与国际·问题与信心》

《金融——词义、学科、形势、方法及其他》，中国金融出版社2001年版

《分点精力思考一些基本思路问题》

1999年5月28日在上海金融学会年会上的讲演稿

《冷静思考经济紧缩带来的启示，重新审视我们对待经济、金融问题的思路》

《财贸经济》，1999年第8期

《中国社会科学文摘》，2000年第2期

《中国通货紧缩1998—2000》，北京大学出版社2000年版

《转轨时期财政货币政策的协调与配合》，经济管理出版社2000年版

《面对经济全球化的中国金融改革》

《中国行政管理》，1999年第11期

《证券时报》，1999年7月24日

《通货紧缩及一些相关问题的联想》

《就名词术语讲点学习方法问题》

《金融理论与政策（提纲）》

《宏观调控与货币供给·修订版说明》

《宏观调控与货币供给（修订版）》，中国人民大学出版社 1999 年版

《货币政策》

《宏观调控与货币供给（修订版）》，中国人民大学出版社 1999 年版

2000

《处于这样极富挑战的时代是幸福的》

《金融时报》，2000 年 1 月 29 日

《实事求是谈》

《北京高等教育丛书·中国人民大学专家学者治学经验谈》，2000 年

《金融形势和金融改革》

2000 年 4 月 30 日在中国留美金融学会和中国留美金融协会讲演的提要

《访美随记》

2000 年 4 月 22 日—5 月 8 日访美期间将有关学术、专业的记录整理成本文

《中国金融学会第六次代表大会开幕词》

《金融学学科建设若干问题》

《中央财经大学学报》，2000 年第 9 期

《CUPA 高等学校文科学报文摘》，2001 年 1 月

《需要资金，更需要营造吸引资金和发挥资金效益的环境》

全文刊于《2000·中国西部论坛·论文》

以《资金，更需要环境》为题摘刊于《开放导报》，2000 年第 11 期

《中国金融学学科建设的若干问题》

《光华经世集·第二辑》，西南财经大学出版社 2004 年版

《第六届两岸金融学术研讨会上的致词》

《当前的金融热点问题引起的一些思考》

2000年11月2日在中国人民大学研究生会组织的讲演会《当前金融热点问题》上的讲演稿

《够不上方法论的“方法论”——由“金融”与“金融学”引起的》

以《由讨论金融与金融学引出的“方法论”思考》为题刊于武汉大学《经济评论》，2001 年第 3 期

《当前的金融热点两三题》

《中南财经大学学报》，2001 年第 1 期

《当前经济热点问题侧议》

2000 年 11 月 21 日在湖南大学商学院的讲演稿

《从专业方向的选择谈起》

2000 年 11 月 28 日在暨南大学经济学院的讲演稿

《从银行不被看好谈起》

《金融时报》理论周刊，2001 年 1 月 13 日

《经济导刊》，2001 年第 2 期

2001

《金融学学科体系》

《百花斗艳——金融中介机构体系建设的必然前景》

2001 年 3 月 24 日在“创新与发展——第一届中国信托业发展论坛”上的发言稿

《金融》

为《中华金融词库》改写的词条

《金融、金融学及其学科建设》

《当代经济科学》，2001 年第 4 期

《金融与金融中介》

2001 年 6 月 1 日在华夏银行干部培训班上的讲演提纲

《21 世纪初中国面临的重大金融理论和对策问题》

2001 年 7 月 14 日在中国社会科学院学术委员会经济学座谈讨论“21 世纪初（2001—2020）中国面临的重大理论和对策问题”的提纲

《金融理论面临的挑战》

2001 年 8 月 27 日在中国人民大学金融系与财政金融政策研究中心为中国工商银行开设的分行行长理论培训班的讲演稿

《西宁会议的两次讲话》

《财贸经济》，2001 年第 11 期
《金融学科建设与发展战略研究》，高等教育出版社 2002 年版

《在“黄达—蒙代尔经济学讲座”启动仪式上的发言》
《黄达—蒙代尔讲座·第一辑》，中国人民大学出版社 2003 年版

2002

《充实自我——谈金融人才成长之路》
2002 年 1 月 11 日访南京大学的讲演稿

《经济形势座谈会发言备要》
国务院组织的“经济形势座谈会”上的发言备要

2003

《“走向理性繁荣”研讨会的总结发言》

《点评约瑟夫·E·斯蒂格利茨〈转型与发展〉的讲演》
《黄达—蒙代尔讲座·第一辑》，中国人民大学出版社 2003 年版

《中国与东亚金融合作前景论坛的总结发言》
9 月 23 日在金融街论坛——“中国与东亚：金融合作的前景”上的总结发言稿

《〈蒙代尔经济学文集〉的启迪》
《中国金融》，2003 年第 21 期

《虚拟资本》
《金融学》，中国人民大学出版社 2003 年版

2004

《这就是炼狱之门》
《中国资本市场：股权分裂与流动性变革·附录二》，中国人民大学出版社 2004 年版

《中国人民大学金融学科教师建设〈货币银行学〉—〈金融学〉的轨迹》

《人民币的风云际会：挑战与机遇》
《经济研究》，2004 年第 7 期
《新华文摘》，2004 年第 19 期
以《论人民币完全可兑换及其经济地位》为题发表于《国际金融研究》，2004 年第 7 期

《教学中应该做到却不容易做到的两三点》
向 2004 年 6 月 19—20 日“中国金融学教育与金融科学发展的历史回顾和经验总结会”提交的文章

《金融学·导论——从〈货币银行学〉到〈金融学〉》
2003 年 8 月《金融学》出书后，数次以《金融学·导论》为题介绍该书

《编书领悟数则》
2004 年 11 月 3 日为财政金融学院博士生讲授前沿课程的幻灯片整理

2005

《足迹——〈黄达书集〉说明》
《黄达书集》，中国金融出版社和中国人民大学出版社 2005 年版

《陈云经济思想——经济思想库的宝贵财富》
2005 年 5 月 21 日在“纪念陈云同志百年诞辰——陈云经济思想研讨会”上的发言稿

《古今中外，含英咀华——金融基础理论建设之路》
2005 年 5 月在“《黄达书集》出版暨推动金融理论繁荣发展座谈会”上的发言稿

《培养思考能力》
2005 年 7 月 16 日在由中国人民大学出版社和中国人民大学财政金融学院承办的 2005 年暑期金融专业一线骨干教师高级研讨班上的讲课稿

《是不是可以这样思考》
2005 年 11 月 16 日对中国人民大学财政金融学院博士生的讲课稿

2006

《要有志气把自己的实践作理论升华》
2006 年 3 月 15 日在中国人民大学财政金融学院承接国家开发银行项目的成果《开发性金融论纲》首发仪式上的发言稿

2007

《就金融学（货币银行学）这门课程同大家交换几点意见》

于 2007 年 7 月 16 日在教育部委托中国人民大学财政金融学院和中国人民大学出版社组织的金融骨干教师高级研修班上的讲课稿

《金融杂说》

2007 年 8 月在中国人民大学财政金融学院举办全国优秀大学生夏令营的讲课稿

《点评麦金农讲演——人民币会成为世界第三大货币吗？》

《黄达—蒙代尔讲座·第二辑》，中国人民大学出版社 2008 年版

2008

《回顾 1950 年之前“货币银行学”学科的发展（初稿）》

《货币金融评论》，2008 年第 2、3 期，总第 91 期

《松柏长青学人风范》

《经济研究》，2008 年第 9 期

《建言数则》

2008 年 7 月 18 日在中国人民大学汉青研究院夏令营的讲课稿

《讲在课程的开头——〈货币银行学〉百年》

2008—2009 学年秋季学期开学为财政金融学院本科 2006 级学生所作“货币银行学·导论”的讲座

《金融学科建设是否面临攀升一步的转折点》

为 2008 年 9 月 27 日在三亚举办的“纪念改革开放 30 周年暨中国财政金融体制改革与学科建设研讨会”提供的稿件

2009

《关于金融学科演进的几点认识》

《中国金融》，2009 年第 4 期

《金融学科的演进及前瞻》

2009 年 4 月 17 日在中国人民大学财政金融学院召开的“结合学院教学发展，学习落实科学发展观，创世界一流财政金融学院”的教职工大会上的发言稿

《在金融海啸中思考金融学科的演进及前瞻》

《中国金融》，2010 年第 19、20 期合刊

《金融海啸和 G20 格局下的货币银行学（节略）》

《金融》

《中国大百科全书（第二版）》的金融词条

2010

《学习西方现代经济学与我们的悠久文化传统》

2010 年 6 月 23 日在“中国人民大学实施中美经济学教育交流项目 25 周年纪念大会”上以原中美经济学教育交流委员会主席身份发言的文稿

《结缘货币银行学六十年》

《与货币银行学结缘六十年》，中国金融出版社 2010 年版

《金融学科建设应坚持包容四海与中国化的统一——访中国金融学会名誉会长黄达》

《中国金融》，2011 年第 10 期

2011

《国越富，本币对外越升值，对内的购买力越贬值》

《在中国金融学科终身成就奖授奖仪式上的发言》

《百年中国金融学说思想史》，中国金融出版社 2011 年版

《老生常谈几则》

2011 年暑期在教育部组织的金融学青年骨干教师高级研修班上的讲课稿

《通货膨胀与物价目标》

《货币金融评论》，2011 年第 9 期

《金融评论》，2011 年第 5 期

《新华文摘》，2012 年第 5 期

2012

《新世纪十年拾零》

2012年4月7日开始对进入新世纪10年“思想碎片”的整理

《在世界金融学科的发展中作出具有中国神韵的贡献——周骏教授荣获“终身成就奖”的贺词》

《“人民币国际化报告2012发布会”上的发言》

《金融学（第三版）·主编的话》

《金融学（第三版）》，中国人民大学出版社2012年版

《购房贷款》

《金融学（第三版）》，中国人民大学出版社2012年版

《现代社会之前的信用》

《金融学（第三版）》，中国人民大学出版社2012年版

2013—2014

《贺周升业教授荣获刘鸿儒金融教育基金会“中国金融学科终身成就奖”》

《就“百部史学名著研读计划”想到的》

《关于金融学教学必须讲出的基本观点》

《中国经济理论创新奖：在财政信贷综合平衡理论颁奖仪式上的发言》

《金融博览》，2014年第1期

《西南财经大学“中国金融学说”研讨会上的发言提纲》

《纪念王传纶教授的两点感言》

2014年4月24日在“《王传纶经济文论》和《学术泰斗王传纶》出版座谈会”上的发言稿

教材与著作

（一）教材

1951—1952

1951/1952学年在专修科所讲《货币流通与信用》的考题（抽签口试的考题）及其答案手稿

1957

《资本主义国家的货币流通与信用》

作者之一并主编，中国人民大学出版社1957年版

1959

《货币信用学（上册）》

作者之一并主编，中国人民大学出版社1959年版

1981

《社会主义财政金融问题》

作者之一并主编，中国人民大学出版社1981年版

1992—2000

《货币银行学》

作者之一并主编，四川人民出版社1992年版

《货币银行学（修订版）》

中国人民大学出版社1999年版

《货币银行学大纲》

四川人民出版社1990年第一版&1992年第二版

1997—1999

《宏观调控与货币供给》

中国人民大学出版社1997年版

《宏观调控与货币供给（修订版）》

中国人民大学出版社1999年版

《〈宏观调控与货币供给〉大纲》
1993 年秋季学期开始对硕士生教学使用，未公开出版

2003 —

《金融学》［《货币银行学》（第三版）］
作者之一并主编，中国人民大学出版社 2003 年版

《金融学（精编版）》［《货币银行学（第三版·精编版）》］
中国人民大学出版社 2004 年版

《金融学（第二版）》［《货币银行学（第四版）》］
作者之一并主编，中国人民大学出版社 2009 年版

《金融学（第二版·精编版）》［《货币银行学》（第四版·精编版）》］
中国人民大学出版社 2009 年版

《金融学（第三版）》［《货币银行学（第五版）》］
作者之一并主编，中国人民大学出版社 2012 年版

《金融学（第三版·精编版）》［《货币银行学（第五版·精编版）》］
中国人民大学出版社 2014 年版

（二）专著

1964

《我国社会主义经济中的货币与货币流通》
中国财政经济出版社 1964 年版

1984

《财政信贷综合平衡导论》
中国金融出版社 1984 年版

1990

《工农产品比价剪刀差》
中国社会科学出版社 1990 年版

2010

《与货币银行学结缘六十年》
中国金融出版社 2010 年版

（三）文集、书集

1988

《黄达选集》（1952—1985 年）
山西人民出版社 1988 年版

1999

《黄达文集》
中国人民大学出版社 1999 年版

2001

《金融——词义、学科、形势、方法及其他》
中国金融出版社 2001 年版

2005

《黄达文集（续）》
中国人民大学出版社 2005 年版

《黄达书集》
中国金融出版社、中国人民大学出版社 2005 年版

2007

《黄达自选集》
中国人民大学出版社 2007 年版

2010

《黄达经济文选》
中国时代经济出版社 2010 年版

《黄达文集（再续）》
中国人民大学出版社 2010 年版

2014

《黄达文集（三续）》
中国人民大学出版社 2014 年版

（四）主编类书

1990

《中国金融百科全书》
主编：黄达、刘鸿儒、张肖，经济管理出版社 1990 年版

1993

《中国证券百科全书》
主编：黄达、项怀诚、郭振乾，经济管理出版社 1993 年版

1998

《中华金融词库》
主编：戴相龙、黄达，中国金融出版社 1998 年版

科研项目

1990

国家“七五”哲学社会科学重点课题《货币供求量问题研究》
成果：《货币供求问题研究系列专著》，中国人民大学出版社 1990—1993 年版

1993

国家教委博士项目《社会主义市场经济制度下储蓄向投资转换机制的重构》
成果：《中国经济增长中的外部储蓄机制研究》，1998 年 5 月

1995

国家哲学社会科学基金《关于我国部门经济研究现状与发展趋势调查》
成果：1995 年 6 月，国家哲学社会科学基金印刷版报告

1996

国家哲学社会科学基金《社会资金宏观配置格局的研究》
成果：《中国资金宏观配置问题研究》，中国金融出版社 2001 年版

1997

国家社会科学基金重大项目《邓小平关于社会主义市场经济的理论与深化国有企业改革的总体研究》，由经贸委（马建堂）和中国人民大学（黄达、林岗）共同主持
成果：《世纪之交的国有企业改革研究》，经济科学出版社 2000 年版

2003

教育部哲学社会科学重大课题攻关项目《全球经济调整中的中国经济增长与宏观调控体系研究》
成果：《全球经济调整中的中国经济增长和财政货币政策组合》，中国人民大学出版社 2007 年版；《全球经济调整中的中国经济增长与宏观调控体系研究——新时期国家经济调节的基本取向与财政金融政策的有效组合》，经济科学出版社 2009 年版

译文

20 世纪 60 年代初

《第二次世界大战后资本主义体系中的黄金》
（作者: 弗·米哈列夫斯基 Ф·ИМИХАЛЕВСКИЙ），

黄达负责统校和定稿，中国财政经济出版社 1965 年版

20 世纪 70 年代末 80 年代初

《资金流量核算入门（1952—1970 年）》

作者：Bank of England，黄达译，王传纶校，中国人民大学财政系，1981 年 4 月油印

20 世纪 70 年代末 80 年代初

《货币银行学》

作者：莱・威・钱得勒（L. V. Chandler）、斯・姆・哥尔特菲尔特（S. M. Goldfeld），中国人民大学财政教研室与金融教研室译，黄达译第 16、17 章，王传纶总校订，中国财政经济出版社 1981 年版

约 1981

《对于工资“加 100%”指数化的开放经济的管理》

作者：Franco Modigliani、Tommaso Padoa-Schioppa 等，黄达译，王传纶校，中国人民大学财政教研室与金融教研室，1982 年油印

约 1982

《欧洲市场的信用创造：可供选择的理论和控制的含义》

作者：亚历山大・K. 斯沃博达（Alexander K. Swoboda），黄达译，王翔飞校，中国人民大学财政金融系作为《〈财政与金融〉教学参考资料〈增刊〉》，于 1982—1983 学年或稍晚一些油印

行政工作文稿

1953

《我们是如何制订本学期科学研究工作计划的》

《教学与研究》，1953 年第 1 期

《检查研究工作计划执行情况推动了我们的科学工作》

《教学与研究》，1953 年第 2 期

1965

《校内工作情况向下乡同志的汇报（一九六五年六月）》

1978

《中国人民大学复校后在财政系教工第一次全体会上的讲话》

《中国人民大学复校后在财政系第一次迎新会上的讲话：对学习作点说明，提点希望和要求》

1987

《坚持四项基本原则，坚持改革、开放、搞活》

1988

《在校务委员会上的汇报》

《评议校级领导班子的自我总结》

1989

《团结、依靠、提高——在全体教职工大会上动员学习的讲话》

1990

《1989—1990 学年第二学期的工作要点》

1991

《坚持方向、稳定规模、调整结构、深化改革、改善条件、提高质量——布置 1991 年秋季学期工作》

《宣布中国人民大学校长任免通知时的“表态”讲话》

1992

《有关改革的讲话（提纲）》

《永远奋进在时代前沿——在庆祝中国人民大学建校五十五周年大会上的讲话》

1992 年 11 月 1 日，并非由黄达亲笔起草的文稿，标题“永远奋进在时代前沿”由黄达所加

1993

《积极稳妥推进学科改革和建设》

《中国教育报》，1993 年 3 月 16 日

1994

《人民大学领导班子换届时的卸任讲话》

1996

《对袁宝华同志兼任中国人民大学校长的几点追忆》

2005.10 — 2006.5

《任副校长、校长期间几个重要事件的专题整理》

黄达获奖全记录
The Full Record of Huang Da's Awards

作品获奖

《谈谈我们的物价方针兼及通货膨胀问题》
《中国社会科学》，1980 年第 6 期
1998 第一届“薛暮桥价格研究奖”

《社会主义财政金融问题》
作者之一并主编，中国人民大学出版社 1981 年版
1988.1 全国高等学校优秀教材奖
1989.12 中国财政学会全国优秀理论研究成果荣誉奖
1987.11 北京市哲学社会科学和政策研究优秀成果一等奖

《财政信贷综合平衡导论》
中国金融出版社 1984 年版
1986 孙冶方经济科学 1986 年度著作奖
1989 中国人民银行推荐为全国高校金融类教材
1995.12 全国高等学校人文社会科学研究优秀成果一等奖
2013.11.28 中国金融理论创新奖

《货币银行学》
作者之一并主编，四川人民出版社 1992 年版
1994.12 北京市第三届哲学社会科学优秀成果一等奖
1995.12 中华人民共和国国家教育委员会高等学校优秀教材一等奖
1997.10 1997 年国家级教学成果奖一等奖

《货币银行学（修订版）》
中国人民大学出版社 1999 年版
2002 教育部 2002 年全国普通高等学校优秀教材一等奖

《冷静思考经济紧缩带来的启示，重新审视我们对待经济、金融问题的思路》
《财贸经济》，1999 年第 8 期

《中国社会科学文摘》，2000 年第 2 期
《中国通货紧缩 1998—2000》，北京大学出版社 2000 年版
《转轨时期财政货币政策的协调与配合》，经济管理出版社 2000 年版

1999 财贸经济研究所、《财贸经济》编辑部 1999 年度优秀论文二等奖

《金融学（第三版）》［《货币银行学（第五版）》］
作者之一并主编，中国人民大学出版社 2012 年版

2013 中国（广州）国际金融交易・博览会 2013 首届金融图书“金羊奖”

《与货币银行学结缘六十年》（新写专文与专题性文集结合）
中国金融出版社 2010 年版

2010 中华读书报年度图书之“100 佳”

《中华金融词库》
主编：戴相龙、黄达，中国金融出版社 1998 年版

2003 第三届国家图书奖二等奖（新闻出版总署）

个人获奖

2011.6.1 首届“中国金融学科终身成就奖”

2012.6.20 首届“中国金融研究杰出贡献荣誉奖”

2014.12.18 第三届吴玉章人文社会科学终身成就奖

结语

Epilogue

从 2011 年提出动议，到今天出版，已六年有余。

在此期间，中国人民大学财政金融学院、校史研究室、档案馆和出版社，以及黄达先生家人、朋友、同事和学生等各个方面为本书的编辑出版提供了大力支持。

需要感谢的人很多却又难以一一尽数。或许当您翻阅此书时，看到的一张张熟悉笑脸和一个个闪亮的名字，就是我们应该感谢的人！当然，最应该感谢的还应当是黄达先生本人，没有他几十年如一日，细心专注地收集照片、整理文稿，此书很难如期与大家见面。

行将收笔之际，亦是遗憾丛生之时。有限的图片、贫瘠的文字显然无法勾勒出我们心中的先生之风，也许唯有在大家口口相传之中，才能使之变得更为真实、清晰。

既然无法一一捕捉那精彩而闪亮的历史瞬间，无法真正体悟那份浓烈的家国情怀所裹挟着的金融挚爱，无法切身感受那种淡泊、从容而大度的先生风骨，那就不要勉强“思其力之所不及，忧其智之所不能”。

可能，最好的结语就是祝愿老先生健康长寿，一如既往地继续把他在与金融学结伴中所积累的感悟书写下来……

It has been over six years since the beginning of preparation for the publication of this book in 2011.

It won support from many circles including the School of Finance of the Renmin University of China, Research Office of the University History, the Archives Center, the Publishing House, and families, friends, colleagues and students of Huang Da.

There are countless people to be grateful to. When you are reading this book and see a smiling face or a shining name, that may be the person we are thankful to. Of course, we should be most grateful to Huang Da himself. This book will not go public without his scrupulous collecting photos and sorting out manuscripts for decades.

Pale words couldn't outline Huang Da's demeanor in our mind. Maybe the tales orally handed down could make a clearer and more real figure of him.

Now that it is hard to seize his brilliant historical moments, hard to understand his strong emotions for the country and his passion for finance, and hard to sense his moral characters of seeking no fame and wealth, it is better not to pursue the things out of reach or worry about the things beyond awareness.

Perhaps, the best concluding remark would be the wishes for him to be healthy and keep writing about his understanding of finance.

图书在版编目（CIP）数据

黄达传略 / 宋科编著 .— 北京：中国人民大学出版社，2017.3
ISBN 978-7-300-22933-1

Ⅰ. ①黄… Ⅱ. ①宋… Ⅲ. ①黄达—传记 Ⅳ. ① K825.34

中国版本图书馆 CIP 数据核字 (2016) 第 113892 号

黄达传略

宋 科 编著

Huang Da Zhuanlüe

出版发行	中国人民大学出版社		
社 址	北京中关村大街 31 号	邮政编码	100080
电 话	010—62511242（总编室）		010—62511770（质管部）
	010—82501766（邮购部）		010—62514148（门市部）
	010—62515195（发行公司）		010—62515275（盗版举报）
网 址	http://www.crup.com.cn		
	http://www.ttrnet.com（人大教研网）		
经 销	新华书店		
印 刷	北京瑞禾彩色印刷有限公司		
规 格	210 mm × 265 mm 16 开本	版 次	2017 年 3 月第 1 版
印 张	43 插页 2	印 次	2018 年 1 月第 2 次印刷
字 数	620 000	定 价	368.00 元